Errol Trzebinski: born June 24th 1936 at midnight (mid-summer night), Gloucester, England. Uneducated mainly at Wimborne Convent, Dorset. Flew to Kenya for a holiday in 1952 while waiting to qualify for entry to Middlesex Hospital for nursing training, but married at eighteen instead and settled in Kenya. Her Polish husband is an architect – they have three children.

Twelve years of her life in Africa were spent on part of Karen Blixen's old coffee farm at 'Ngong', as it was known locally. (After Karen Blixen left Kenya in 1931 the local population referred to this area eight miles from Nairobi as 'Karen', which is what it is called today.) Errol Trzebinski has been living in Mombasa for a number of years. When in Nairobi she worked in advertising and became the Assistant Advertising Manager for E.A. Newspapers (Nation Series) Ltd., mainly owned by the Aga Khan. She wrote the cookery column in the *Sunday Nation* for two-and-a-half years and has written eight cookery books.

Silence Will Speak provided one of three main sources for the film *Out of Africa*, starring Meryl Streep and Robert Redford.

ERROL TRZEBINSKI

Silence Will Speak

A study of the life of Denys Finch Hatton
and his relationship with Karen Blixen

GRAFTON BOOKS

A Division of the Collins Publishing Group

LONDON GLASGOW
TORONTO SYDNEY AUCKLAND

Grafton Books
A Division of the Collins Publishing Group
8 Grafton Street, London W1X 3LA

Published by Grafton Books 1985

First published in Great Britain by
William Heinemann Ltd 1977

Copyright © Errol Trzebinski 1977

ISBN 0-586-06696-9

Printed and bound in Great Britain by
Cox & Wyman Ltd, Reading

Set in Times

For Essex,
For Daphne and Diana,
And for Anne and Michael.

Contents

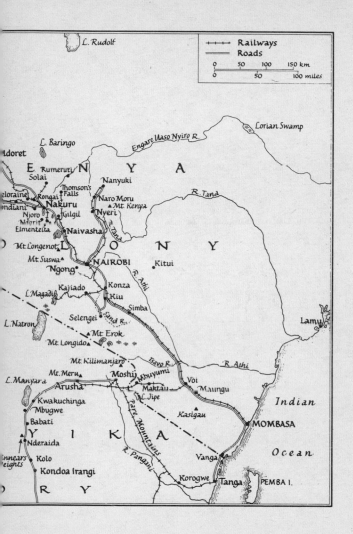

Railways
Roads

0   50   100   150 km
0   50   100 miles

L. Rudolf

Lorian Swamp

Engare Uaso Nyiro R.

L. Baringo

Kdoret

E   N   Y   A

Rumeruti
Solai
Thomson's
Falls   Nanyuki

leloraine
Rongai   Naro Moru
Nakuru   ▲Mt. Kenya
Njoro   Gilgil   Nyeri
ondiani   Naivasha
Ndoru
Elmenteita

R. Tana

Mt. Longenot▲   L   O   N   Y

Mt. Susua▲
Ngong   NAIROBI   Kitui

Kajiado   Konza
L. Magadi▲   Kiu
                              Simba
L. Natron   Selengei   Sand R.

Lamu

Mt. Erok▲
Mt. Longido▲

R. Athi

Mt. Kilimanjaro▲   Tsavo R.   R. Athi

Mt. Meru▲   Moshi   Mbuyumi   Voi
L. Manyara   Arusha   Maktau   Maungu
                         L. Jipe

Kwakuchinga   Kasigau   Indian
Mbugwe
Babati   MOMBASA

Y   I   K   A   Ocean

Nderaida

innears   Kolo   Vanga
eights   Kondoa Irangi
                        Korogwe
O   R   Y   Tanga   PEMBA I.

List of Illustrations

Author's Note

Time and again I have been asked what gave me the idea to write a biography of Denys Finch Hatton. Lately, my response has been that of surprise. Surprise – because I am no longer able to understand why someone has not done it before. But the notion began in 1965 while I was rooting about in a Nairobi auction room looking for bargains. A silver hipflask caught my eye, lying as it was on top of a box of bric-à-brac. Larger than average, it had not seen polish for years but it appealed to me. I picked it up and turned it over in my hand. It bore an inscription which I cannot recall and the name of Denys Finch Hatton. As I put it back the friend who was with me remarked, 'I suppose Karen Blixen gave him that – he was her lover,' and as I did not respond to this he added by way of explanation, '*Out of Africa* and all that.' Though I had read the book on coming to Kenya in 1952 Denys Finch Hatton's name meant nothing to me. Perhaps at that time I had been too busy identifying through the author my own discovery of Africa and was too young to understand then that, as so often in life, that which is left unsaid is of greater importance than that which is said. Later that afternoon my friend offered to telephone the auctioneers and put in a bid for the lot containing the silver flask, if I would like it. I was enthusiastic but pointed out that I did not want the rest of the junk, which he accordingly agreed to keep. Later I learned that the bid had been successful though I never saw the hipflask again. Though this uncharacteristic act seemed ignoble at the time, it also roused my curiosity.

There is little doubt that had the flask been given to me as promised the matter would have rested there. Subsequently, however, I got hold of *Out of Africa* again and in re-reading it became acutely aware of Denys Finch Hatton's presence in Karen Blixen's life. I could not fathom why this had escaped me earlier. I wanted to know more of what she left unexplained, for this appeared to me now to be the vital key to their relationship. Automatically I began to scan every index for either of their names in books relevant to the time they lived in Africa. Five years ago when I made up my mind that I wanted to write something more adventurous than cookery books, I began my search systematically, but the idea was still a dream and I thought quite beyond my reach. A friend who knew of my growing obsession (for that is what it became) then sent me this note: 'Sir Robert Bruce Lockhart kept quite remarkable diaries – the first volume of which has recently been published, and on the 16th of October 1934 he wrote: "Lunched at Huntingdons. Sat next Baroness Blixen (Isak Dinesen) the author of *Seven Gothic Tales* and Ruby Lindsay (Peto that was). The Baroness is a peculiar looking woman – very white and thin with large dark eyes. Very intense. Longs to go back to Kenya where she spent the best years of her life and where she had a love affair with Denys Finch-Hatton [sic] the big game hunter. She loved the natives and if she goes back will probably write in Africa."' This communication served as recognition of the seriousness of my intention and marked a decisive step at a time when I was still floundering with my own impudence at the idea of attempting a biography – let alone that of someone who left nothing tangible for posterity. *Seven Gothic Tales* had been published a month before Karen Blixen lunched with Sir Robert Bruce Lockhart. *Out of Africa* may have been written but was not published for another three years. Therefore, I reasoned, only one person could have communicated this information – Karen Blixen herself – yet she made no attempt to qualify Finch Hatton's status in *Out of Africa*. I now set about my task in real earnest. Many of the books written on that period were recollections of pioneer experiences or hunting expeditions and did not contain indices. One grasps at straws. One takes the chaos of material and tries to give this some sort of order – that which is trivial therefore, in the life of an elusive man, assumes far greater importance – for there is so little available. So far as I knew there were no personal writings to draw from for his opinions, philosophy, etc; how could one calculate how he felt (he was so private that he asked those to whom he wrote to destroy his letters) – indeed it would have been outrageously presumptuous to do so. Rose Cartwright then told me that Denys had once given her a book, a gift from a client whose name she could not recall, who had written and published an account of their safari together. The book had been long since misplaced. She could only remember that it was bound in red leather and seemed to be a tribute to Denys. There was only one thing to do. Thanks to the kindness of my friends Joe and Sheila Murumbi I was able to work in their vast Africana library. I started at one end of the alphabet, taking each book off the shelf which covered 1910–31 in Kenya. After one week when I had almost given up hope and began to believe that the book was a myth, I found it: *African Adventures* by Frederick B. Patterson. As I worked I made a chronology of Denys Finch Hatton's life. I was as intrigued by his evanescence as by the adoration of those who knew him personally. To those who were still alive he seemed as bright as if he had still been living. They all revered him; unquestionably his impact on their lives was one that brought a richness, a bloom, which had he not existed they would have missed significantly. Gradually through talking to his friends and relatives I began to comprehend the quality of his charm – it lacked veneer and all sense of sham. The guilelessness, the wit, the crisp value of understatement began to crystallize with each new interview. Yet curiously, every person prefaced each conversation or letter with 'I'm afraid I cannot tell you much about Denys' – after a while (this was discouraging to begin with) I accepted this for it had become very obvious that if not secretive he was essentially reserved about his personal life and very modest. Gradually the scraps of information, dates, incidents and interviews dovetailed with published material. Strangely, the work, though time-consuming, has never been arduous or dull – perhaps its fascination reflects the intrinsic character of the man himself. My task was made much more difficult by the unsullied impression he left behind – always love, admiration and regret for his foreshortened life. If the result makes him seem too good to be true, it is because I have been unable to pick holes; for those who knew him have conveyed only his goodness, gentleness, honesty and open-mindedness. My final concern is the hope that I have not destroyed the ephemerality of the man, for while I have attempted to define some of his spirit it has never been my intention to hold him captive by the printed word.

Acknowledgements

But for the kindness and co-operation of the people listed here I could not have written this book. I am indebted to them all in one way or another. Not only have many of them given their time unstintingly by delving into their storehouse of memory in personal recollection of Denys Finch Hatton and Karen Blixen, they have checked transcriptions and have extended hospitality to me and helped in other ways too. Despite many protestations of fear that, as individuals, they could contribute little, each fragment of their information has somehow uncannily fitted together to form a whole. I offer my gratitude and thanks to them all – not forgetting those not mentioned by name, my sister and my brother-in-law and my long suffering friends who have supported me with their encouragement and enthusiasm during the research and writing of this book: Mr Ulf Aschan, Mr Owen Barton, Mr Peter Beard for granting me access to Kamante; Mrs 'Ginger' Birkbeck, Mr Wilfrid Blunt, Mrs Essex Brooke, my father F. B. Jones whose early aviation experience in England, Mesopotamia and Kenya has been valuable; Mrs Mavis Buxton, Lord Caccia, Miss Juanita Carberry, Mrs Rose Cartwright, Sir Ferdinand Cavendish-Bentinck, Mrs Arthur Cole, Lady Eleanor Cole, Lady Diana Cooper, Mr Mervyn Cowie, Lady Felicity Cory-Wright, Major D. H. Dempster, Mr and Mrs Thomas Dinesen, Mr and Mrs Donovan Maule, Mr Sid Downey, Mr Tony Dyer, Mr John Eames at whose insistence I wrote my first column which he published, Mr Jens Elers, Major 'Gerry' Edwards, the late Miss Margaret Elkington, Mrs

Leda Farrant, Mr and Mrs David Fielden, Mr Tibor Gaal for the safari on which I observed the hunting of elephant; Mr Kamante Gatura, Sir John Gielgud, the late Mr and Mrs Nigel Grahame, Dr J. R. Gregory, Mr Jamie Hamilton, Mrs Gay Harper for reasons too numerous to mention; Dr A. J. Hayter for showing me the workings of the British Museum Reading Room, thus saving me valuable time; Major 'Jacko' Heath, Lady Betty Holcroft, Mrs 'Cockie' Hoogterp, the late Mr Julian Huxley, Mr Mohammed Juma, Mr Mohammed Juma Kimojino, Countess Lindi Kalnoky, Mr Donald Ker, Mrs Anne Keys, Mr Roy Lane, Sir Alan Lascelles, Mrs Moira Lynd, Lady Katharine Loyd, Mrs Ingrid Lindstrom, Father Denys Lucas, Mrs Betty Leslie-Melville, Dr Duncan MacDonald, Mrs Beryl Markham, Sir Charles Markham, Mr Douglas Matthews, Mr Michael Meyer, Mrs Norma Mohr, Mr Ivan Moffat, Mr Nicholas Mosley, Mr and Mrs Joseph Murumbi who generously put their Africana library in Nairobi at my disposal; Mrs Sallie O'Donnell for the unlimited use of her house whenever I have worked in England; Mrs Richard Percival and the late Mr Richard Percival, Mr and Mrs Alfredo Pelizzoli for the opportunity to experience a memorable professional safari; Mr Viggo Petersen, Mr and Mrs Charles Pick, Mr Will Powys, Mrs F. Rawson-Shaw, Mr Mervyn Ray, Mrs Dylis Rhodes, Miss Janice Robertson, Mr Edward Rodwell, Mr Jonathan Roosevelt who, without knowing me, took the trouble to ascertain that Denys Finch Hatton's letters to Kermit Roosevelt had been preserved in the Roosevelt family papers and in so doing helped me to gain access to them; Mrs Doris Rose for most generous hospitality at a crucial moment in the life of the book; Mrs Joan Rowe, Mrs Gilbert Russell, Mrs 'Day' Ryce, Mr Mansoor Satchu, Mr and Mrs Flemming Schoidt, Princess Lili Schönburg, Miss Pamela Scott, Mr Anthony

Seth-Smith, Sir Dermot Sheridan, Mr and Mrs K. H. Skott, Mrs Viveke Stjernsward, Lady Daphne Straight, Mr Patrick Strong, Miss Clara Svendsen for taking me personally round Rungsted; Mrs Kit Taylor for her meticulous eye for detail and her patience in checking certain sections of the MS; Miss Judith Thurman, Mrs Althea Tebbutt whose conviction that throwing me in at the deep-end would make me swim has proved a valuable lesson in life; Mrs Madeleine Trench, the late Lady Diana Tiarks, Mr K. B. Tindall, Mr A. Visram, Mrs Jeanne Waller, Miss Anne Williams, Sir Osmond Williams who, like so many busy people, always found extra time to unearth family data for me; Mrs Freda Wilson, The Earl of Winchilsea and Nottingham without whose signature I could not have gained access to family papers, diaries and letters; Sir Anthony Wagner, Mr J. H. Wreford Smith, Miss Joan Waddington and Miss D. C. M. Young.

Finally, I would like to thank my editor, Roland Gant, whose patience with a new author reflects that of Job and whose guidance has been invaluable. Last but by no means least I should like to thank my children, Bruce, Tonio and Gabriela, for displaying the sweet tolerance of their youth towards me over the last five years, and my husband Sbish, for his comprehension of my commitment which has amounted sometimes to living in a 'ménage à trois' with my subject! I know this has not always been easy. Without their combined love and understanding the book would never have reached completion.

The author and publisher, wish to place on record their gratitude to the following organizations who have granted access to published and unpublished works or records or have provided facilities for working 'in situ' during the research of this book: The Aero Club of East Africa, Nairobi; Brasenose College Library, Oxford; The British

Council Library, Mombasa; The British Library, Reference Division, London; The British Museum, Department of Egyptology, London; Bromley Public Libraries – Chislehurst Branch; The Ministry of Defence, Army Records Centre, Middlesex; The East African Professional Hunters Association, Nairobi; The East African Standard Ltd. (Archives Section), Nairobi; Eton College Library, Windsor; The Kenya National Archives, Nairobi; The Library of Congress, Washington D.C. (Roosevelt Family Papers); The London Gazette; Muthaiga Country Club, Nairobi; The Nairobi City Council Library (Africana and Archives Sections), Nairobi; Northampton County Records, Delapre Abbey (Winchilsea and Nottingham Family Papers), Northamptonshire; The Rungstedlund Foundation, Denmark; Westminster Central Reference Library, London.

Thanks are also given to all those publishing houses who have allowed the author to use extracts from Copyright works: Messrs Edward Arnold Ltd, for permission to quote from *Kenya Days* by Aline Buxton; George Allen and Unwin (Publishers) Ltd, London 1927, for permission to quote from *Memories* by Julian Huxley; Associated Book Publishers Ltd, for permission to quote from *Lady Muriel* by Wilfrid Blunt; The Bodley Head, for permission to quote from *Out of Africa* by Karen Blixen, *Seven Gothic Tales, Last Tales* and *Winter Tales* by Isak Dinesen, *Isak Dinesen and Karen Blixen: the Mask and the Reality* by Donald Hannah, and *The New Elizabethans* by E. B. Osborne; Boni and Liveright for permission to quote from *The Traveller and Other Poems* by Iris Tree; Jonathan Cape for permission to quote from *Carrington: Letters and Extracts from her Diaries* chosen and edited with an introduction by David Garnett; Cassell & Co. Ltd, for permission to quote from *African Hunter* by Bror von Blixen-Finecke; Chapman & Hall Ltd, for permission to quote from *Ronald Knox* by Evelyn Waugh; Chatto and Windus for permission to quote from *White Man's Country* and *Forks and Hope – An African Notebook* by Elspeth Huxley and *The Gayety of Vision* by Robert Langbaum; W. H. Collingridge for permission to quote from *Eastern Africa and Rhodesia* compiled and edited by Allister Macmillan; East African Publishing House for permission to quote from *Dhows at Mombasa* by John Jewel; E. P. Dutton & Co Inc for permission to quote from *Sport and Travel in East Africa 1928–30* compiled from H.R.H. The Prince of Wales Diaries by Patrick Chalmers; The Press and Information Department of the Royal Danish Ministry of Foreign Affairs for permission to quote from *Mottoes of My Life – A Speech before the Academy of Arts and Letters in America in 1959* by Karen Blixen, arranged by Bent Rying and Askel Danielson; Faber and Faber Ltd, for permission to quote from *Kenya's Opportunity* by Lord Altrincham; Victor Gollancz Ltd, for permission to quote from *Ellen Terry's Memoirs* by Edith Craig and Christopher St John; Dr J. R. Gregory for permission to quote from his publication *Under the Sun*; Grant Richards Ltd, for permission to quote from *Black Laughter* by Llewelyn Powys; Gyldendal for permission to quote from *My Sister, Isak Dinesen* by Thomas Dinesen, V.C., *Out of Africa* by Karen Blixen; *Seven Gothic Tales, Winter Tales* and *Shadows on the Grass* by Isak Dinesen; George C. Harrap & Co Ltd, for permission to quote from *West With the Night* by Beryl Markham, published in 1943 and now out of print; Messrs Harper and Row Publishers Inc, for permission to quote from *Memories* by Julian Huxley; the Hogarth Press Ltd and the author's Literary Estate for permission to quote from *A Room of One's Own* by Virginia Woolf last reprinted in 1974, paperback by Penguin, reissued by Triad/Panther April 1977; Messrs Holt Rinehart and

Winston Inc, for permission to quote from *Julian Grenfell: His Life and the Times of His Death* by Nicholas Mosley; Macdonald and Janes, for permission to quote from *Battle for the Bundu* by Charles Miller; Macmillan Ltd, for permission to quote from *Kenya Chronicles* by Lord Cranworth; Eyre Methuen Ltd, for permission to quote from *The Rainbow Picnic* (1974) by Daphne Fielding; Michael Joseph Ltd, for permission to quote from *My Sister, Isak Dinesen* by Thomas Dinesen, V.C., and *Ehrengard* by Isak Dinesen; John Murray for permission to quote from *War in the Garden of Eden* by Kermit Roosevelt; Oxford University Press for permission to quote from *Early Islamic Architecture of the East African Coast* by P. S. Garlake (1966) and *History of East Africa* (1963: paperback 1968) edited by Roland Oliver and Gervase Mathew; A. D. Peters and Co Ltd, for permission to quote from *Ronald Knox* by Evelyn Waugh and *Hunter's Tales* and *Hunter's Tracks* by J. A. Hunter; G. P. Putnam's Sons for permission to quote from *African Adventures* by Frederick B. Patterson; Random House Inc, for permission to quote from *Out of Africa* by Karen Blixen, *Seven Gothic Tales* and *Winter Tales* by Isak Dinesen, *Isak Dinesen: the Mask and the Reality* by Donald Hannah and *Titania* by Parmenia Migel; Charles Scribner's Sons for permission to quote from *War in the Garden of Eden* by Kermit Roosevelt; The University of Chicago Press for permission to quote from *Anecdotes of Destiny* and *Essays* by Isak Dinesen; Weidenfeld and Nicolson Ltd, for permission to quote from *Julian Grenfell: His Life and the Times of His Death* by Nicholas Mosley.

'Let me have silence, and I will speak, and let come on me what may.'

Job XIII v. 13

'Hear then: Where the story-teller is loyal, eternally and unswervingly loyal to the story, there, in the end, silence will speak. Where the story has been betrayed silence is but emptiness. But we, the faithful when we have spoken our last word, will hear the voice of silence.'

Last Tales – 'The Blank Page' – Isak Dinesen

Prologue
New Year's Day 1928

It was dawn. The sun had not yet risen upon Eastern Africa on the first day of 1928. Three figures, silhouetted gently by the light from an old hurricane lamp, busied themselves with the preparations for a journey. The stars brightly pinpointing the still-dark sky were on the point of withdrawal. One figure, distinguishable from the others by his great height, lifted a basket to a squatting form, in the rear of the boxbody vehicle, then handed him a heavy rifle of the calibre lethal to elephant and rhino.

As the two men settled themselves in the car, the woman joined them, bidding farewell to an unseen inmate of the house, in a low, hushed voice.

The air was cold. The breath of the travellers was revealed in small opaque gusts as the earth gradually leaned towards the sun that morning. No one spoke much. The start of the engine as they moved off seemed to tear into the peace of the dawn, which had an almost subterranean quality about it – being unwritten upon as yet and untrod by man.

They intended to waylay a hunting party which had left for safari the previous day bound for a destination some sixty miles west of Nairobi across very wild and rough country. One of the three protagonists had lent a rifle to a member of the shooting party but had neglected to mention a tricky mechanism of the gun, by which the hair trigger might be put for safety out of action. It was a dangerous oversight which had disturbed the donor greatly and was uncharacteristic for he was, as a rule, meticulously careful in such matters and was known for his keen attention to detail. The implications had troubled him a good deal and had become intrusive, rather spoiling the beauty of the previous night as he and the woman had sat late under the new moon, gazing at the unusual sight of the planets Jupiter and Venus clustered together almost as if to herald the start of a new year in the heavens themselves. The remedy, they concluded after some discussion, was to try and reach the safari convoy on its journey to Narok, lest some unhappy incident befall the hunting group. In an attempt to cut them off, they decided to risk an unknown road to overtake the heavily laden lorries, whose pedestrian pace – governed by the old route, a badly rutted road – would be slower than their own. Now their only fear was uncertainty whether this new road had been completed. But if it did not go as far as Narok the friend would have to take his chance with the unfamiliar rifle.

Now, as the fragile light cleared their field of vision, unveiling the Ngong Hills and the Masai plains beyond, their spirits rose with the sun. They took pleasure in the freshness of the air, the currents of chilliness against their faces, savouring the smell of the tough little leleshwa bushes, the pungent drift of African sage and the acrid aroma of newly burned grass – the result of a custom followed by the nomadic Masai, who burned off the grazing land in patches to propagate fresh fodder for their humped and unfettered herds.

After they had driven about twenty miles and the lights of the vehicle were scarcely needed any longer, the travellers became aware of a strong smell of decay which intensified as they progressed. A few yards from the road an unidentifiable mass sprawled among the scrub. The driver slowed and pulled into the edge of the truck, curious, intending to investigate. The African sitting in the back of the truck reached forward to the woman and lightly touched her shoulder extending his other hand to point out what he had spotted, with his inherent native instinct, more swiftly than she. Before them lay an obscenely prostrate bull giraffe which was responsible for the stench and, on top of the square-blotched mass of skin, crouched a lioness absorbed in feeding off the carcass.

Disturbed by the car, the lioness now looked up from her vile feast. 'Perhaps,' thought the woman, 'this is the thief which has terrorized the squatters on the farm over the last few months.' Her people had come to her with many sad tales of goats and calves being taken by a marauding lion and, although they were some twenty miles from the farm border, that distance meant little to a hungry lion on the prowl. The same thought occurred simultaneously, and the tall man, who was used to dealing with the such situations, took his gun automatically from his servant and asked the woman in a low urgent voice:

'Shall I shoot her, Tania?'

She nodded, holding her breath. It is not uncommon for women to enjoy hunting the cat family. Only the great felines seem to rouse this atavistic, predatory instinct which may have lain dormant for a thousand years within the female nature. In some women this trait may seem non-existent, perhaps it has been concealed by layers of civilization. But woman is by instinct predatory, the claw hidden by the velvet glove is suddenly revealed in the matter of lion hunting. At the moment of destruction, an intense but surprising excitement appears to justify all action and the feeling is powerful enough to obliterate all twinges of conscience or pity.

Tania felt that it was time to put an end to the life of the thief. She and Denys were so attuned to each other that it had been unnecessary for him to query whether the lioness should or should not be slain. The question had been one of deference to Tania. *Who* shall shoot the lioness? You or I?

In such relationships the words themselves were superfluous, and this query had barely been mouthed before the assent was silently given. There was a unity in the action, a strength. However, Tania, appreciated the courtesy of his enquiry for Denys still looked upon that vast, uninhabited stretch beyond her coffee farm in the shadow of the Ngong Hills as her personal and private hunting ground. His deference meant that, even after all the years they had shared, she was not taken entirely for granted. She had sensed in this gesture a courtliness imbued with tenderness.

Denys slipped noiselessly from the car, backing slightly to take aim. The lioness slunk at once behind the body of the giraffe. Half crouching he now skirted the decaying heap to get within range. Seconds later the echo of the shot ricocheted across the valley. Tania did not see the lioness fall. She and Kanuthia, the Kikuyu who worked for Denys, clambered out of the truck to investigate. By the time they reached the immobile body of the lioness, a black pool seeped beyond the edges of her skin, staining the earth darkly.

'We can't skin her,' said Denys, 'or we'll never get to Narok in time and not being sure of this damned road . . .' He hesitated and took his bearings.

'Look, remember that tree; Angalia miti Kanuthia – sisi ta rudi (we will come back),' he added in Swahili for the benefit of his servant.

'We'll come back later – if it's still light. My God the stench – we can't miss that!' They hurried back to the truck and drove off. Denys accelerated purposefully, going much faster than usual over the rough surface, making up for lost time. Every minute was precious. As they drove they discussed the death of the giraffe. It had obviously been killed two or three days ago though there had been no time to establish the cause of its death. As it was forbidden by the Game Department to shoot giraffe it had been rather a puzzling scene. It seemed unlikely that a lion paw could fell such a tall creature, though Denys had experienced rare incidents when this had happened. In fact he had photographed one on the Patterson safari the year before. That particular animal had survived the attack but had been left with a strangely twisted neck – a cripple. Far-fetched as it may seem a lion is capable of bringing a giraffe to its knees by breaking its stately neck. 'If we get back by daylight, we'll skin it and . . .' Even as Denys spoke the road began to dwindle, and after a few hundred more yards they came upon a heap of labourers' tools lying in the middle of the road. They halted. They looked despondently at the landscape and at the abandoned picks and shovels and, with a hopeless shrug, reluctantly agreed that they would have to leave the fate of Denys's friend in the lap of the Gods.

They turned upon their tracks and retraced their way over the hills and plains, now at a leisurely pace signifying their feeling of defeat. Denys was a determined man who did not take failure easily; it disturbed the effortless air with which he generally achieved all his aims. As they drove back to the macabre scene of the giraffe and lioness they speculated on her identity. If she had been the thief, Tania reasoned, then the heart shot had been well placed.

By now the sun was up, bathing and gilding the land of burnt, dry, pottery colours in a benison of light, so that as they approached the spot (the track was slightly lower than the carcass) it picked out the colours of the mottled skin and, as they drew close, threw the new and unmistakable, majestic figure of a male lion into relief. He stood straight up and over the corpse and behind him the sky was all aflame. Tania gasped in awe of the splendour and murmured gently to Denys, 'Lion passant or.'

As swiftly as the first decision to kill had been taken Denys whispered, 'You shoot this time.' But Tania hesitated. She did not like using his gun, which was too heavy and too long for her. But she had not brought her own. If she took the shot, she thought to herself, would she not be completing the fifth act of a classic Greek tragedy – if the lion must die, then surely the weapon of death should be of the highest calibre. For in a way, she believed the slaying of the male lion by her now was in a sense a declaration of love in which complicity was the keynote. Denys had slain the lioness and now she must, as his counterpart, fulfil her role in response by taking the life of its mate. Her shot now represented the sealing of a pact, a tacit covenant between them. In that moment when she discharged her deathly declaration they would be complete. And in the moment of possession, a unity. Since she had met Denys, Tania had 'put away' her gun, seldom shooting except for the pot, but lion hunting had always been irresistible. And so accepting this weakness, which was her strength, she climbed down from the truck quietly and walked with stealth through the dew-heavy grass. It was long and bathed the barrel of the gun, wetting her hands as she slowly crept closer to the lion until she was as near as she dared go. She crouched on the ground getting Denys's rifle into position against her knee and took aim.

The lion stood out against the gold sky; a blue imperial facsimile as if plucked from the Danish royal coat of arms. A bit of his mane lifted in the wind. A perfect target and a perfect gift for the King of Denmark; Tania thought 'If I get him, I shall present him to the King,' and as she promised the lion's destiny to herself, she slowly squeezed the trigger.

As he died, a second echo sounded in the peaceful hills that morning. It seemed to Tania as she watched that the lion was first thrown upwards by the impact, straight up into the air before falling to sink into a lifeless slump. True to her intention she had shot him through the heart. He was hers. His queen, the lioness, the *femme fatale* of the tragedy belonged to Denys. Possession was complete. On closer inspection he was a particularly fine specimen and black maned – king fit for a king. The lioness lay on her back, a haughty smile still upon her mouth; the poor stiff petrified giraffe whose graceful lope had once adorned the mirages of midday, lay gouged out, disembowelled, awkward and ungainly in its rancid exposure. The tell-tale stain of death slowly seeped from beneath the lion. Unlike the first pool of blood, the colour now showed scarlet in the clear morning light. They gazed at the three lifeless bodies which seemed in that instant to accentuate or even promise their own immortality. Tania was still aglow and slightly breathless with the sheer plenipotence of her shot.

'Come on, Kanuthia – we'd better get on and skin them,' remarked Denys. 'It's going to take hours,' he added as he reached for the hunting knife attached to his belt.

While the men set about the flaying of the lions, Tania lit a cigarette. Settling herself on a smooth patch of grass upwind, she watched Denys lovingly. She had seen him so often thus – completely absorbed in whatever task he was undertaking. Skinning is a delicate craft; the art of freeing the flaccid skin had been taught him over the years by his trackers. Watching him now, paring away, his hat as usual pushed absent-mindedly towards the back of his head, the skinning seemed a simple enough, unbloody process. Whatever Denys did it always seemed to be with such ease; there was no sign of exertion as

Tania watched the tawny pelts gradually falling in supple folds across each carcass.

'Are you not reminded of what old Uncle Charles Bulpett used to say?' Tania asked, not waiting for a reply. 'He said, the person who can take delight in a sweet tune without wanting to learn it, in a beautiful woman without wanting to possess her . . .' Denys lifted his head slightly from his task on the word 'possess', joining in with the completion of the quotation which they now chanted in unison . . . 'or in a magnificent head of game without wanting to shoot it, has not got a human heart!' Denys concentrated again on the lion while Tania gazed out into the great blue distance which formed the backdrop for the minute shapes of three giraffe, appearing to float across the plain.

She thought of their many discussions on the question of hunting. They had agreed often enough that hunting is ever a love affair – the hunter being in love with and seduced by the game. They had compared, likened the art in spirit to that of the literary masterpiece *The Diary of the Seducer* written by the Danish author Søren Kierkegaard. The hunter will declare his love of animals in face of strong evidence to the contrary. During the hours of pursuit, time, space, danger and distance mean nothing to him. He is seduced by his quarry in its own time. Ultimate success bestows self-congratulation. In the end his sense of achievement is paramount.

'I can collect the skin from Rowland Ward when we are in London,' Tania commented. She was planning to go to Europe the following year, after the Prince of Wales had finished his safari with Denys. The men's knives were now blunted and it seemed a good time for a break.

Tania asked Kanuthia to fetch the 'kikapu' – a basket fashioned from closely woven and bleached palm fronds, which held their picnic. As it was new year's day she had brought almonds and raisins and a bottle of claret which Denys particularly liked. She unwrapped the wineglasses carefully and handed the bottle to Denys to open. As they sipped their wine, they admired the sparseness of fat on the pink-fleshed bodies of the lions, the linear curve of each exposed muscle, and agreed that they were just as noble in their nakedness as they should be, lithe to the bone, majestic to the core. Tania started to form a poem in her mind. Denys was a good listener – to her as important as his eloquence and wit. He possessed a secret ability to transform the most banal jaunt into an event. An ordinary outing acquired a patina and richness lending a dimension which was difficult to explain. He lived much by the ear. Often, at the farm when they were settling down by the fire after dinner, he would say to her teasingly and with that unaccountably amused expression, 'Have you got a story for me?' As though (yet it was not true), he had been waiting only for this moment when she would sit at his feet like Scheherazade. In the firelight her brown eyes were boldly dark and her pupils dilated, lustrous from the drops of belladonna which worked its magic for her as it had for the Venetian women of the sixteenth century.

The art of listening to a narrative, they agreed, had long been lost in Europe, but with them it was a treasured reciprocity. His inborn gift for music heightened his sensibility to sound. Many cannot sit and listen to a recital, but Denys, schooled from birth to the world of music, never fidgeted. He seemed to give himself up to resonance, in music or in the meaning of a word. Tania's deep voice with its Nordic lilt was a remarkably powerful facet of her personality. It intrigued the listener as she hinted enigmatically at some strange turn, yet to be defined, in one of the fantastic tales she had composed for him.

Denys lit a cigarette and lay back, tilting his hat to shield his eyes from the glare of the late morning sun. As Tania shaped the poem in her mind, a shadow hastened over the ground towards them. She looked up. High above, the vultures were anticipating their feast below. The shadow grew as it came nearer, then it crossed her feet and suddenly swooped away, circumscribing the bizarre little group. She turned the words over in her mind, selecting them carefully and, as though the image of swooping flight had somehow released the order of her words, she spoke the poem out aloud, slowly at first and then with gathering confidence:

> 'The eagle's shadow runs across the plain
> Towards the distant, nameless air blue mountains,
> But the shadows of the round young Zebra
> Sit close between their delicate hooves all day
>   where they stand immovable.
> And wait for evening, wait to stretch out, blue,
> Upon a plain, painted brick-red, by sunset,
> And wander to the water hole.'

Although the sun was now fully risen, the highland air, distilled through six thousand feet of mountain and earth, was like a fine, rare, wine – heady – so intoxicating that for as long as Tania lived she was never to forget that morning. Many years later she recalled the moment. 'My heart was as light as if I had been flying it, up there on a string, as you fly a kite.[1] In two of her books she records the scene with utmost clarity, 'I knew then, without reflecting, that I was up at a great height, upon the roof of the world, a small figure in the tremendous retort of earth and air, yet at one with it.'[2]

What she did not realize, until time and distance

combined with tragedy had lent that morning perspective, was that she was upon the roof and height of her own life, which was never to be quite the same again. Denys Finch Hatton, who had been responsible for many changes in her life since their meeting nine years before, was to leaven it yet again; but there was to be a variation, a departure from their former pattern of existence which, in many ways, was to ensure their immortality. It was not a premeditated path they trod, as they left with their trophies on the sunny, first day of 1928. And, since that date, much of their tale has lain undetected beneath an outer covering of shimmering prose. Tania, better known as the Danish author, Karen Blixen or Isak Dinesen, included this episode in 'The Dreamers', one of her *Seven Gothic Tales*, but shifted the setting to suit her mood:

After this first night we were always together. I have never been able to get anything out of the orthodox love affairs of my country, which begin in the drawing room with banalities, flatteries and giggles and go through touches of hands and feet to finish up in what is generally held to be a climax in the bed. This love affair of mine in Rome, which began in bed, helped on by wine and much noisy music and which grew into a kind of courtship and friendship hitherto unknown to me, was the only one that I have ever liked. After a while I often took her out with me for the whole day, or for a whole day and night. I bought a small carriage and horse with which we went about in Rome and in the *campagna* [sic], as far as Frascati and Nemi. We supped in the little inns, and in the early morning we often stopped on the road and let the horse graze on the roadside, while we ourselves sat on the ground, drank a bottle of fresh, sour, red wine, ate raisins and nuts and almonds and looked up at the many birds of prey which circled over the great plain and whose shadows upon the short grass, would run alongside our carriage.[3]

The unfinished aspect of the story, which stamps almost all of Isak Dinesen's mysterious and kaleidoscopic tales, was fully intended to reflect her implicit belief that the telling of a story is a divine art and that by remaining unswervingly loyal to it, ultimately silence – whatever is left unsaid – will speak for itself. This tantalizing skill which has become synonymous with her gift for storytelling, was in a sense her personal insurance against mortality. A mouthpiece for this philosophy of Tania's which runs through her fable 'The Blank Page' from *Last Tales* is an old hag, a teller of tales, whose words are based on this premise: 'We,' she says at last, 'the old women who tell stories, we know the story of the blank page, but we are somewhat averse to telling it, for it might well, among the uninitiated, weaken our own credit.[4]

There is a twofold attempt in this biography of Denys Finch Hatton. Firstly the aim is to cast a little more light on this elusive man whom Karen Blixen so deeply loved but about whom she has remained singularly reticent. Secondly it aims to elucidate and complete the palimpsest of her life by showing that even through the circumstances of his tragic death he was to serve posthumously as one of the most forceful catalysts in her development as a writer.

For there is hope of a tree, if it be cut down, that it will sprout again, and that the tender branch thereof will not cease.

Job XIV, 7

1

1887 – The Roots of Childhood

The Honourable Denys George Finch Hatton was born at 22 Prince of Wales Terrace, London, on 24 April 1887. He was the third and last child of Henry Stormont, 13th Earl of Winchilsea and 8th Earl of Nottingham, but the place of his birth was not his family home and his father's inheritance of the title was to a great extent unexpected. Although he came from a long line of aristocrats, noble soldiers, seafarers, politicians and scholarly predecessors who served and lavishly entertained the Kings and Queens of England, his father was not directly in the line of inheritance and Denys's birthplace was a temporary dwelling. The story starts three months before his birth, at the beginning of 1887, forty-one years before that new year's day in Africa.

The Honourable Henry Stormont Finch Hatton and his younger brother Harold had first been out to Australia as speculators in the latter half of the 1870s. They had prospected for gold, acquired substantial tracts of land on which to raise cattle and purchased majority shares in a mining company. Their ventures had not been as remunerative as either had hoped. Henry returned to England on a permanent basis in 1885 and Harold's final departure the following year from Queensland left their business interests in the hands of working partners. By 1887 the financial status of their companies had deteriorated to such an extent that both brothers suspected they were being swindled. Convinced that Henry must personally investigate the matter before the situation became irretrievable, they anxiously awaited confirmation of these fears – which arrived in the form of a cable from Queensland in the second week of January 1887. Arrangements were subsequently put in hand for his voyage out, and since his wife, Nan, was expecting their third child in the spring, Henry arranged for her to move into their newly leased London house, 22 Prince of Wales Terrace, to await this event which would now take place in his absence. Henry Finch Hatton was thirty-five years of age, but his tendency to ail (bordering on hypochondria) gave the impression that he was older. This weakness was concealed from the world by a stern and imposing façade, and because of his unyielding nature the sentimental attachment he felt for his family and home, Haverholme Priory, was slightly surprising. It was a gloomy Victorian Gothic pile, damp and cold, but he had been brought up with his brothers and sister within its grey walls of Grantham stone. If the priory looked bleak to an outsider, it epitomized security to the Finch Hattons through sheer familiarity; they regarded the place with indulgent affection – the natural result of happy childhood memories which in their turn form a parental legacy for future generations: the reassuring feeling of continuity. Henry knew every corner of the estate and hoped that his own children would come to know it in the same way. From the first signs of spring, when the new leaves of Evedon woods blurred green against the vast Lincolnshire skies, to the days of black stark branches, cutting into the leaden stretches of winter cloud.

His father, George William Finch Hatton, 10th Earl of Winchilsea and 5th Earl of Nottingham, had succeeded to the peerages in 1826. He married three times, and after his first wife's* death had attempted to improve Haverholme by having it largely rebuilt in 1835. Yet it

* Georgina Charlotte, daughter of the Duke of Montrose.

never was anything but dismal and still retained vestiges of the medieval monastic structure, which had first risen from the ground when its estate was a marshy, three-hundred-acre island on what is now the Old River Slea, near Sleaford in Lincolnshire. Haverholme had not always been their family home. George William had been born at Kirby Hall, Northamptonshire, the family seat for more than three hundred years. It had once been considered 'one of the finest flowers of the Renaissance', though now it hardly bore a trace of its Elizabethan glory. Originally it had belonged to their most illustrious ancestor Sir Christopher Hatton,[1] who danced his way into the favour of Queen Elizabeth I so successfully that those first steps, which brought him the role of bodyguard, ultimately gained him the Chancellorship of England. It was said of him 'His station was great but his humility was greater, giving an easy access to all addresses. He was so just that his sentence was law to the subject, and so wise, that his opinion was an oracle to the Queen.' His friendship was highly esteemed by Sir Francis Drake, who upon reaching the Straits of Magellan changed the name of his ship *Pelican* to the *Golden Hind* 'in honour of his friend and patron Sir Christopher Hatton whose crest it was.' This was the vessel in which Drake returned to Plymouth after his world voyage in 1580. Nevertheless he died in debt to Gloriana over Kirby Hall – and remained a bachelor, it was rumoured, out of loyalty to his Queen. Though described in *The Beauties of England* as 'unaccountably neglected . . . and fast going to ruin and decay' Kirby Hall had still been fit for habitation in 1791 when George William was born there. He served in the Northamptonshire Yeomanry during his first marriage and lived at Haverholme, while Kirby was occupied by a cousin, George Finch, 9th Earl of Winchilsea and 4th Earl of Nottingham. When this cousin died without issue in 1826, George William, Denys's paternal grandfather, inherited. Involved by now in politics, the financial upkeep of Kirby would have imposed such a burden on his resources that he remained at Haverholme. His only son, George James, then a year old, became Kirby's next inhabitant twenty years later. George William gained political fame when he presided at a very large and influential meeting held at Pennenden Heath, Kent, on 10 October 1828 at which 'strongly worded resolutions in favour of protestant principles were carried'. In the House of Lords he violently opposed almost every liberal measure which was brought forward. He was particularly noted as being almost the only English nobleman who was willing to identify himself with the Orange party in Ireland, and he was accustomed to denounce, in frantic terms, Daniel O'Connell, Maynooth and the system of education carried out in that college.[2] His intemperate language apparently prevented him from becoming a leader in Evangelical politics. In 1829 he excelled himself in wilfulness by writing a letter which provoked a duel with the Duke of Wellington when the Catholic Relief Bill 'roused his most vehement hostility'. Lord Winchilsea, in a letter to the Secretary of King's College London, wrote that the Duke 'under the cloak of some coloured show of zeal for the protestant religion, carried on an insideous design for the infringement of our liberties and the introduction of popery into every department of the State'. The Duke replied with a challenge. The meeting took place in Battersea Fields on 21 March 1829, the Duke being attended by Sir Henry Hardinge, and his opponent by Edward Boscawen, Viscount Falmouth. The Duke fired and missed, whereupon Winchilsea fired in the air and then apologized for the language of his letter. He was a very frequent speaker in the Lords, and strenuously opposed the Reform Bill and other Whig measures. He was gazetted Lieutenant-Colonel commandant of the East Kent regiment of Yeomanry in 1830, named a deputy-lieutenant for the County of Lincoln in 1831 and created a D.C.L. of Oxford in 1834.[3] In 1835 George's wife died at Haverholme and was buried in the family grave at Ewerby Church bordering the estate. By now it had become apparent that her son, George James, had inherited his father's impulsiveness in the alarming form of a gambling streak. Headstrong and every bit as impatient as his sire, he had but one year to go before coming of age, and as Viscount Maidstone would inherit everything for there were no other heirs.

Two years later, George married again; Emily Georgina Bagot was only six years older than his own son. Now, as if to ingratiate himself with his heir, he allowed him to move to Kirby Hall – a dire mistake of judgement which he came to regret. The Earl's second marriage was childless and lasted eleven years and, judging by the bleak epitaph which she wrote for herself at Haverholme, Emily's life with her older husband was a joyless decade. Unable to adjust to his loud rather domineering ways, the chill of the old priory seems to have crept into her heart. When she died in the midsummer of 1848 she took her place beside her predecessor at Ewerby. Behind the fine old screenwork, inside the church, a marble slab reflects her sadly defeated nature:

> When the knell for the dying soundeth for me,
> And my corpse coldly lying,
>   'neath the green tree,
> When the turf strangers are heaving,
> Cover my breast,
> Come not to gaze on me weeping,
> I am at rest,
> All my life, coldly and sadly
> The days have gone by,

I who dreamed wildly and madly,
Am happy to die,
Long since my heart hath been breaking,
Its pain is past,
A time has been set to its aching,
Peace comes at last.

In less than a year, Lord Winchilsea, who was now fifty-seven, took a third bride. Fanny, the eldest daughter of Edward Rice of Dane Court, Kent, was only twenty when she married him in October 1949. A great niece of Jane Austen, she brought sunshine and laughter to Haverholme Priory. Her merriment and sense of fun is demonstrated by the wit with which she nicknamed one of her nine brothers who, as an admiral, had run his ship aground under baffling circumstances: she promptly christened him 'Ground Rice'. An epithet which adhered to him as stubbornly as the cereal itself might stick to the pudding dish containing it. Fanny, Denys Finch Hatton's paternal grandmother, was a great raconteur with a generous nature, quickened by the environs and demands of growing up amidst a large, albeit wealthy, family. In what appears to be a final headstrong bid to change destiny by producing an alternative heir to his eldest son, Lord Winchilsea's wife bore him four children: Murray in 1851, Henry in 1852, a daughter Evelyn, then finally Harold Heneage Finch Hatton in 1856. He became Denys Finch Hatton's favourite uncle.

Three years later Winchilsea died, leaving Fanny to bring up the children alone. The young Finch Hatton's gambling half brother now became titular head of the family. He married twice but there were no children and neither lady seemed able to exert any influence over his disastrous inclinations. As Henry and his brothers and sister grew up, Kirby became a sorry sight. The lead was stripped from the roof of the fine house, most of the valuable paintings and statues disappeared to pay his debts. It was said that he could not resist betting on anything – even woodlice.

Fanny's children grew up at Haverholme, the boys attended Eton, and Evelyn was educated at home. All four children were musical and joined in the concerts held on winter evenings, Henry played the violin, Evelyn the piano and Harold the cello, while Murray's musical taste developed into a passion for bell ringing. Of Fanny's three sons, Murray and Harold inherited their father's recklessness, while Henry developed into a melancholy being, not unlike one of his forebears, aptly dubbed 'Don Dismal'.[4] He had no interest in politics, unlike Murray, who looked so juvenile that when he stood for Parliament the down on his cheek caused a heckler to jibe, 'Does your mother know you're out?' Without a moment's hesitation Murray quipped, 'Yes, and tomorrow she'll know I'm in!' In 1875 Murray gained his seat as the Tory M.P. of the Holland or Spalding Division of Lincolnshire, but his chief interest lay in the future of arable farming.

Harold, for some reason, did not graduate from Balliol. He showed the quickness of his fiery temper when once a firm took his name in vain. He stormed into their offices and smashed their furniture to pieces with his own hands. Harold, who appeared as time went on to have no intention of marrying, seemed destined to fulfil the role of Finch Hatton bachelor in his generation. It became apparent too as the years went by, that their half-brother's wife was unlikely to produce an heir, and that Murray would eventually succeed to the Earldoms. Perhaps this was the greatest factor influencing Henry and Harold's shared decision to explore pioneering investments in Australia. They went out, ranched cattle, prospected for gold in the Nebo fields of Queensland, eventually discovering substantial deposits of copper at Mackay, Mt

Britton. Eagerly they bought shares and staked claims but it became clear that the working expenses, high cost of shipping, the price of machinery and above all the defective system of communication from the coast rendered the venture less financially rewarding than they had hoped. In 1881 Henry returned to England filled with Victorian pessimism for the project. Harold's faith in Australia's future however was staunch and later his valuable practical experiences were set down and formed the basis of his ideas in his book *Advance Australia.*

Murray, meanwhile, had married a selfish, dark-haired belle, Edith Harcourt, whom he had met while climbing in the Grampians. Vain and extremely proud of her eighteen-inch waist, she managed, after the birth of her first child, to preserve its wasplike dimensions through grim lacing. Though Murray would have preferred an heir first, he loved his daughter Muriel deeply, unconventionally teaching her Latin and shorthand and encouraging her enjoyment of all the boyish pastimes he had enjoyed himself at Haverholme.

After Henry returned from Australia he fell in love with Anne Codrington, a daughter of Admiral of the Fleet, Sir Henry Codrington of Doddington, whose estate was not far from Haverholme and was famed for its shoot. Little is known of her upbringing and background and both her parents were dead when she married Henry. Her grandfather, Sir Edward Codrington, the British Admiral who was in command of the *Orion* at Trafalgar, was mainly responsible for the destruction of the Turkish fleet off Navarino.

From her portraits and photographs, Anne or 'Nan' as she was always called by her family and close friends, looks as though she might possess northern Italian blood though nothing supports this physical hint of heritage. Her unusual beauty was enhanced by wavy, almost crinkly, copper gold hair, which when unbound fell to her waist. High cheek-bones and dark eyes which seem to burn with intelligence emphasize the possibility of foreign predecessors. Though her expression is seriously composed a sense of fun always plays about her lips as if privately enjoying a situation on another plane. Mysteriously persuasive, she was also by reputation witty, well read, fluent in French and Italian. Her creative energy was mainly applied to her musical abilities though she was a competent water-colour painter and later studied the Hatton papers with the intention of writing the history of the Finch Hatton family. Her grandchildren recall that 'the whole household revolved round her' yet she retained an independence in spite of her loving and unselfish nature.

Two of Nan's closest friends were Mrs Patrick Campbell and Ellen Terry, with whom she maintained a lifelong friendship. Miss Terry describes Nan's attributes in her own memoirs and modelled her interpretation of one of Shakespeare's heroines on her:

At Leeds we produced *Much Ado About Nothing*. I never played Beatrice as well again. When I begun to 'take soundings' from life for my conception of her, I found in my friend Anne Codrington (now Lady Winchilsea) what I wanted. There was before me a Beatrice – as fine a lady as ever lived, a great hearted woman, beautiful, accomplished, merry, tender. When Nan Codrington came into a room it was as if the sun came out. She was the daughter of an admiral and always tried to make her room look as much like a cabin as she could. An 'excellent musician' as Benedick hints Beatrice was, Nan composed the little song that I sang at the Lyceum in *The Cup* and very good it was too.[5]

Nan had travelled frequently to Florence as part of her education, and her visits nurtured a love of Italian opera – she possessed a fine soprano voice, enjoyed composing and played the piano with skill. Her standard of accomplishment was of such high order, that when Joseph Joachim, the Hungarian violinist and composer, came to London, Nan played in trios with him. Joachim's enthusiasm for Grieg's work transferred itself to her and she used her considerable influence to promote the Norwegian's work in London society. Her fascination for Norway, its people and customs drew her back to the country year after year. When her children were old enough to enjoy travel they spent their annual holidays with her in Norway. Keenly interested in photography, her studious approach to this hobby made her one of the pioneers of portrait photography. She loved the countryside and animals, particularly small wild creatures. One of her favourite pets was a jerboa, which perched on her shoulder, content to remain there while she walked about the house. Her unconventional nature, fostered by exposure to the world of the theatre, attracted Henry strongly, compensating perhaps for his own rather conservative attitudes.

Their first child, a daughter born in Melbourne, was such a disappointment – because they were sure Nan would have a son first – that they had not even chosen a name for her by the time she was christened. It was the child's godparents, after some discussion with the priest, who chose 'Gladys Margaret' – names which she never liked and cared for even less when she learned how she had acquired them. She always preferred her nickname 'Topsy' by which she was known to the family all her life. This incident when she was born curiously foreshadows the span of her existence. It reflects Nan and Henry's sub-conscious attitude towards their only daughter to a degree which was almost prophetic. Topsy's life was dominated by a string of unhappy events. Her childhood photographs, taken by her mother, depict a fragile, solemn-eyed girl gazing wistfully at humanity. But her fragility was deceptive. She also possessed reserves of great courage from which she would draw eventually when enforced loneliness might have embittered a less sweetly serene but determined nature.

Henry and Nan returned to England to live at Haverholme when their second child was expected in 1885. That spring the nurseries were bustling with activity again – Edith produced a son and heir – Viscount Maidstone – and then on 28th May Nan's first son arrived. He was christened Guy Montagu George, but his parents nicknamed him 'Toby' – a name which endured until he became 'Maisie' on inheriting the title of Viscount Maidstone.

When Nan was seven months' pregnant with their third child, Henry left England for Queensland to deal with the serious implications arising from the problems of their interests in Australia. The family had chosen him to deal with the matter because of his tact and efficiency. When he departed from Victoria Station on 9 March 1887 he and his wife would not meet again for almost two years. On 10 May, as he arrived in Melbourne, he received a cable from Nan, despatched sixteen days before from London, informing him of the birth of their second son. His diary entry on that date reflects his happiness at this news: 'Hoorah! At last! Cable from Nan – Sunday. Denys, Sovereigns – no words to express relief and delight. Of course its wrong,' he adds fondly. 'Emerald was to mean Denys, but I suppose its all right. At any rate "Sovereigns" means all's well.' Henry Finch Hatton then ringed Denys's date of the birth, 'April 24th Sunday', under a dismal entry which read 'Curse these coasters and the purple on them. The time goes painfully slow'. He kept his journal regularly and it often mirrored his melancholy nature. Then Henry set off 'to the rocks', which meant the mines.

2

1887–1900 – Childhood at Haverholme

While Nan was receiving congratulatory visits on the birth of Denys, London was a gay city preoccupied with the business of setting up the banners and bunting, parades, balls and champagne parties celebrating Her Most Gracious Majesty Queen Victoria's Golden Jubilee celebrations. At 22 Prince of Wales Terrace, the maids, under the watchful eye of West, Nan's personal maid, were kept rushing up and down stairs to receive callers either leaving cards or appearing to take tea and peer at the new child at appointed hours.

Topsy and Toby were naturally intrigued by the sudden existence of a new baby brother. Topsy or 'Toppy' as her mother sometimes called her, was now six years old, a pale child with red-gold hair like her mother's. She was fascinated by the perfection of Denys's tiny hands and feet. Her constant remarks regarding these miniscule limbs, 'Isn't he small, so TINY', were so often heard that before long he was nicknamed 'Tiny' by the whole household. His elegantly spelled Christian name, derived from Dionysius, Greek god of revelry and wine, was abandoned by the family who did not call him Denys until he went to Eton and then only sporadically. Within weeks of Denys's birth, Murray became 12th Earl of Winchilsea and 7th of Nottingham upon the death of his gambling half-brother and was now faced with the formidable task of scraping together what was left of the family fortune. He inherited a few of the paintings, among these the famous portrait of the dancing Chancellor Sir Christopher Hatton and a number of the more important pieces of furniture, but also an alarming list of debts to be settled. However, the 'wicked uncle' as the 11th Earl became known to the younger generation, left something more enduring than a trail of financial embarrassment and ruined properties. He also had a talent for writing verse – which he claimed to have inherited from his blue-stocking ancestor, Anne Finch, Lady Winchilsea the seventeenth century poetess satirized by Gay. When George was not fabricating schemes to settle his gambling commitments he was compiling rhymes, among them a paraphrase of The Book of Job. Later Denys became interested in the stoic philosophy of this work and brought it to the notice of Karen Blixen who, like Denys himself, was greatly influenced by it.

When Denys was six weeks old, Nan moved back to Lincolnshire with her children to live in one of the dower houses at Ewerby (within the precincts of Haverholme estate). That August Henry recorded in his faithfully kept journal his approval of his wife's ability to resettle their young family in his absence. Nan's resilience and sweet knack of companionship are captured by his jottings and so is his obvious need to be with her again: 'letters from home. My darling Nan I thank. Everything seems happy and cosy at Ewerby. I do long for her so dreadfully.' Lonely without her, the few concerts he arranged to fill in time only served to emphasize the distance between them. Playing 'moosic' – Topsy's expression – was 'very jolly but oh, who can compare with Nan for accompany-ment.' As 1887 drew to a close, Henry dismissed the year with a final lament, 'I hope 1888 may bring more luck in store for all of us. It has been a vile year on the whole, away from Nan and bothered with station affairs and mines anxieties, mostly alone.' In England, with less depressing pangs of regret Nan drank a toast alone to her husband with a glass of Champagne just after midnight and made her first entry in her diary for 1888: 'I hope "Brownie" (Henry) is a little warmer this year and less rheumatic.'

From the earliest possible age Denys Finch Hatton experienced a feeling of total security. He was surrounded by a large and loving family, tended by a string of retainers employed to smooth the path of their existence. Nurses, nannies, maids and butlers ensured unquestionable order within the house. Game-keepers, grooms and gardeners looked after the estate – their duties were essential facets of the way of life into which he had been born.

In the way that a fish is confident of the buoyancy of water and of its relationship within this element so were the servants and their employers at Haverholme entirely sure of one another in their appropriate roles. This was supported not simply by duty: there is evidence of genuine affection. When Henry returned from Australia the men on the estate welcomed him home with touching spontaneity by ringing the bells of Ewerby Church for him on the September evening of his arrival at Haverholme.

Denys's childhood was marred by only one isolated incident. When he was about four years old the children were in the care of a sly, bad tempered creature whose cunning had escaped the notice of either parent or 'Westy', as they called their mother's maid. After Denys had committed some childish impropriety the woman threw him on to his bed in the night nursery and started to beat him with a stinging bamboo switch. To muffle his cries she covered his head with his feather pillow, successfully stifling his screams of outrage. Topsy, though diffident by nature, watched the battle of wills from the start and, now outraged, took her opportunity to expose 'Nanny'. Without ceremony she burst into the drawing-room shouting indignantly, 'She's beating Tiny, she's

killing Tiny! . . . she's killing him!' Nan and Henry rushed
upstairs and caught the 'orrid Nanny' about to inflict
another blow on Denys's buttocks which were now red
with weals. Henry coldly dismissed the woman and as a
result of this episode 'Westy' now took charge of the
children until the boys went to West Downs Preparatory
School.

Naturally Topsy was protective of her youngest brother,
and this act in which she played the heroine seems to
have sealed a lifelong bond and tacit understanding
between them which grew in strength as they both
matured. Invariably it was to Denys rather than to Toby
that Topsy turned for advice later, and for comfort, for
she seemed to feel closer to him in spirit. It was Denys
and Topsy who shared their birthday and anniversary
gifts; Toby was the one who stood alone yet strangely
leaning on the other parts which formed this triangle.
Perhaps their parents' stock phrase of approval, voiced
whenever Topsy achieved any small measure of success,
'The girl's a marvel!' unintentionally undermined her
confidence and emphasized the double standard they subconsciously applied in their attitudes to boys and girls.
Neither Denys nor Toby seems to have inherited their
father's love of horses. Though they learned to ride
proficiently as a matter of course, they seldom sought
out their ponies voluntarily, and Toby actually harboured
a dislike for them, considering horses to be 'dangerous
from every corner!'

Nan taught Topsy to play the piano – she gave all three
children their first music lessons. 'Moosic' became an
integral part of their young lives. Singing was as natural a
sound as conversation – regarded as a birthright – in the
Finch Hatton household. It is difficult to understand
now, when entertainment is universally and instantly
obtainable, the effect which both the ballet and opera

had in England on the late Victorian audience, whose musical experience had been limited previously to the drawing-room. A new dimension was added to the realm of music. Nan seldom missed an opportunity to visit London when there were performances of either. Her favourite operas were *Don Giovanni* and *Faust,* and she performed as often as possible in the many soirées held at the Royal Academy of Music. It is not surprising, then, that the first indication Denys had in early childhood of his mother's return from London was the sound of her Broadwood piano. Nan set the ubiquitous nursery rhyme 'Twinkle, Twinkle, Little Star' to music for her children and that, as well as many other nursery favourites, were included in a book compiled from her own compositions entitled *Tunes for Tots* dedicated to Topsy, Toby and Tiny in their young days. The early awareness of those first musical notes enlivened Denys's inherent love of music and were no doubt unconsciously responsible for the whimsical way in which he often announced his own presence as an adult. When visiting friends it was his habit to slip into the house unseen and either set the gramophone going or play the piano. With some amusement he would await the reaction of the inmates – women found these spontaneous recitals particularly appealing.

Through their father, the children learned to appreciate the beauties of nature. He encouraged in them a sense of natural history, identifying the birds for them, explaining the reasons for their migratory flights and telling how the abundance of wild birds around Haverholme had almost been done away with, long ago, by a group of artful peasants. In Henry VII's reign, the avarice of the fen slodger had brought about the necessity for 'close seasons'. In those days, fowling was the slodger's trade and his sole means of livelihood. At a certain season the slodgers mustered in great force and drove the young ducklings into imprisoning nets before they were fully fledged and able to escape on the wing. They beat the poor creatures up and out of the marshes in wide tracts, capturing as many as two thousand birds at a time until they were so reduced in multitude that the king passed a law: 'An Acte agenste the Detruccyon of Wylde Fowle at such time as the sied olde fowle be mowted and not replenyshed with fether to flye nor yonge fowle fully fethered perfyctly to flye and the closed time between the last day of Maye and the first daye of August.'[1] As a result of this act the lands around Haverholme, which were considered to be one of the principal shoots in Lincolnshire,[2] still teemed with hare, pheasant, woodcock, pigeon, snipe and great coveys of partridge. The children, encouraged by Henry, became keen birdwatchers after these first lessons in conservation. Even green and golden plovers could be found and, in bad weather, huge flocks of wild geese, their necks outstretched in purposeful flight, while sometimes the occasional swan would take refuge on their three-hundred-acre estate.

When they were old enough they helped their father collect the 'cans of stuffed birds' after a fine day's shooting, in the season, at Bloxham. Proudly they boasted that out of three hundred and forty birds their father had shot three hundred and eight of the bag, though there were seven guns. The great feathered carcasses would hang line upon line, like some thickly spotted and barred curtain, secreting the flesh destined for raised game pies. Goudie the cook made them, her arms floured to the elbows as she rolled out the elastic still-warm dough. Indulgently if they were 'good' she rewarded them with snippets from the bows of raw pastry she used to garnish the pies.

Denys was now allowed to visit the gun room with Toby and their father: a sacred place with its steely weapons of death set strictly side-by-side in ever gleaming readiness for sport. They and cousin Maidy, who was a frail little boy, learned the rhyme by heart

> Never, never let your gun
> Pointed be at anyone
> All the pheasants ever bred
> Don't make up for one man dead.

And during a tenants' shoot which their father had arranged on the estate they escaped disaster narrowly themselves.

Henry had placed his children in a dog-cart at a safe vantage point to watch the event. In those days a shoot entailed certain occupational hazards – guns were still muzzle loaded and in the general excitement it was not unusual for ramrods to be left, accidentally, in the gun. A hare had been put up between one of the tenants and the children's vehicle. He missed his target but to Henry's horror succeeded in peppering the dog-cart and virtually torpedoing it with the forgotten ramrod. It penetrated one side, passed miraculously between the three pairs of legs and emerged on the other. Henry's anxiety overcame his usual English control as he shouted with feeling: 'My God, man, if you must kill off my children, then pick one of them, but don't brown the whole lot!'

Despite Murray's determination to cut expenses, Edith and her mother Lady Susan Harcourt, mother of the eccentric Aubrey Harcourt,[3] who now lived permanently at Haverholme, employed not only a resident nurse but a doctor too. The grounds of the estate were littered with invalid chairs, a phenomenon which once prompted a villager to comment in passing, at the sight of the pair muffled in blankets: 'What I say is, what's the use of wealth without 'ealth.' Aunt Edith deplored extravagance and lack of discipline in others yet at the slightest whim abandoned the safety of her yellow bath chair to visit 'La Tour Eiffel', a folly endlessly fascinating to her. She hired her own train carriage for these visits, adding each time to her private collection of 1st Class carriage keys. On her return she declared with satisfaction if inappropriately, 'Paris is such a quiet little place I always maintain.' Then, this 'belle époque' traveller, as if to justify her indulgent journeys, predictably offered her sole contribution towards economy. These were huge bolts of brown corded velvet. This 'Corde-du-Roy' as it was originally known, would be allotted to each member of the family for their tailors to make up as per instructions. It seemed indestructible, but if it did show signs of wearing there was always a ready replacement. In the majority of portraits Nan made of her beautiful children they are clad in this serviceable fabric donated by Aunt Edith. Nan's preference for theatrical detail may be detected in the design of the stylized jackets, waistcoats and caps. The loose fitting knickers stopped just before the boys' knees above their cocoa-coloured worsted stockings. As if they were twins, these ensembles were always identical and were completed by blouses fashioned from biscuity shades of tussore. To soften the severe effect of the material for Topsy, her dresses were trimmed with ample buttons, small diamanté buckles, pleating, crochet work or frills. Denys and Toby hated being 'dressed up' for the endless, time-consuming photographic sessions. Tough and energetic, they resented the hours of patient control required to produce good portraits and longed to be out of doors playing or climbing trees searching for rooks' eggs with Maidy. Their cousin, however, lacked their own robust health. Aunt Edith fussed continually over her only son and was fiercely protective over him. Once after little Vita Sackville-West had been staying with them, she felt impelled to write accusingly to the small girl's mother complaining 'Vita was very rough with little Mountjoy'.[4]

One of the favourite haunts of the Finch Hatton children was the old Monastery Garden. Denys and Toby were fascinated by the eeriness of the dark shrubberies where they would boldly go in search for traces of the graves of the medieval monks who had been the first inhabitants of their home. The Cistercian men from Fontaine who had first come to live at the priory on Candlemas Day (the feast of the purification of the Virgin Mary) in 1139 had allegedly been so displeased with their Gothic lot 'Halfreholme' that they had complained to Alexander, Bishop of Lincoln. He gave the discontented abbot Gervase and his men another site, offering Haverholme instead to his former confessor Gilbert of Sempringham. The Gilbertine monks were more diligent. They toiled over the land until its cultivation produced enough for their humble needs though initially they suffered great poverty. In 1164, Thomas, Archbishop of Canterbury, found sanctuary at Haverholme when fleeting the Council of Northampton. Later during the disturbed reigns of Edward II and his son in 1357, a group of men broke the banks of a dyke in a vicious act of vandalism, flooding the monks' three hundred acres of meadowland, ruining the crops and drowning their small herds of cattle. Shortly before the Dissolution of the Monasteries, Haverholme had apparently 'boasted many fine manuscripts and printed books'.[5] It was understandable that the history of their home intrigued the three children, adding authenticity to the weird games of fantasy played out in the dank undergrowth where they found relics of these gravestones protruding above the moss-covered ground.

Every Sunday the Finch Hatton children walked with

their parents to Ewerby Church as the bells chimed and echoed in its imposing broach spire which towered one hundred and seventy feet above the rise on which it stood. Church was never missed except in cases of genuine illness, and if the weather was considered too inclement to venture out of doors the ritual was performed within Haverholme itself. Even on the sunniest of mornings inside the small church the light shone at best a frail greenish grey, a subterranean hue cast by its old stained glass windows. The service was followed by a visit to the family graves and a walk across the deer park. The air here was moist and pervaded by the fresh smell of watermint from the river. Afterwards they took luncheon with Uncle Murray and Aunt Edith. Only on miserable wet days was one of the carriages used. Sundays at Haverholme were given over entirely to religion. Long passages from the Old Testament were read aloud during the afternoons, and learned. Denys had a naturally retentive memory and from an early age was able to recite these Biblical passages with ease. Interminable arguments and discussions took place, sparked off by the 'wicked uncle's' paraphrase of The Book of Job, and comparisons were made with the version in the Old Testament. The adult members of the family fully endorsed this stoic philosophy, believing implicitly that it was through man's own endeavour to rise above miseries, despairs and evils that he would achieve an understanding in the goodness and justice of God's ways. Ideally men should seek to acquire a control of the passions. Through such exemplary piety – and the resulting indifference to pain and pleasure – their reward would be the revelation of God's greatness. In turn this would instil an unquestioning acceptance of His mysterious intentions with grace in the knowledge that everything which lives must suffer and overcome, and from this knowledge win an inner peace. Job himself had, despite his lamentations, learned austere self-control and, through affliction, gained the humility to bow his head to the relentless hand of fate. God is therefore not God the supernatural but eventually becomes an attitude to the entire existence of the human being, offering each one of us the individual opportunity of affecting our own destiny.

During these endless discussions the children were expected to sit as still as rocks. The views exchanged by their elders must have seemed overwhelmingly remote and quite impossible to emulate – if they understood the greater part of these discussions at all. The best part of their young Sundays were the Bible stories read by their mother, but as they grew older they were expected to participate fully, contributing their youthful ideas to the adult conversation.

Like most young children, Denys loved to listen to his mother telling stories. Whether she read *Fairy Tales from Grimm* or *Aesop's Fables* or simple poetry, they all held his rapt attention. Just before he went to school she introduced him to The Rime of the Ancient Mariner whose theme of sin and expiation held him enthralled as the story unfolded about the shipmates in their 'sore distress'. Denys was so persistent in his request that his mother should read Coleridge's poem to him that she bought him a copy as a gift from which he quickly memorized the entire work. Toby associated The Ancient Mariner so strongly with his brother that he eventually chose an extract from the work for Denys's epitaph. Synonymous with the memory of Denys, and epitomizing his agnosticism and reflecting his personal creed,

> He prayeth well, who loveth well
> Both man and bird and beast

was engraved on the commemorative brass plaque in Ewerby Church and for the obelisk which Toby erected in his memory on the Ngong Hills in Kenya.

When Denys was seven years old he learned that prayers and morality, pious Sunday readings of the Bible or good behaviour bore little relation to survival. It was so cold that winter that Aunt Edith decided to avoid the annual bouts of influenza at Haverholme to which Maidy always succumbed by taking him off to Cannes. Muriel, Grandmamma and Uncle Murray went with them. Suddenly, unaccountably, Maidy fell ill; the French doctor decreed a diet consisting solely of asses' milk. After a month, reduced to skeletal proportions, Denys's cousin died while his bereft family watched helplessly. Topsy, Toby and Denys were spared the memorial service at Ewerby, but the shock of their cousin's death was profound. He had been a close companion, more like a brother, and they had shared most of their young lives with him. Only six weeks earlier they had opened their Christmas presents with him under the candlelit tree at Haverholme. There seemed no reason for it – he had been good and obedient.

From the time of Maidy's death it was impressed upon the Finch Hatton children that Toby would one day become the Earl of Winchilsea and Nottingham. Henceforth, when Nan photographed her sons, Toby as the heir was always placed on the right. The relaxed and intimate portraits she achieved of the three of them indicate a total unselfconsciousness. They obviously learned great patience and self-control, for in those days the photographic process was infuriatingly slow; they had to keep perfectly still 'watching the birdie' until the demon flash proclaimed a few minutes' relaxation. Nan posed them on chairs, against watered silk or damask covered walls, or perched them on small buttresses of the house with a rug placed between them and the stone, to ward off all risk of chills to the kidneys or piles. Her persuasiveness – a beguiling quality which Denys inherited from her in full measure – is also captured by the pictures she made of her 'brats' as she fondly called them. Readily they had agreed to mother's request to hold hands or snuggle up to one another for these portraits. Yet the effect Nan achieved was that of spontaneous affection. Her skill is proved by the timelessness of her results. They do not look posed. Yet posed they were and most of their outfits mirror the theatrical interests of the photographer. In one picture Nan has her sons gazing angelically into a heavy silver chalice – as if on the brink of some sacred ritual – an impression heightened by their matching, hooded cloaks. But their happy consent to these sessions did not survive puberty when they became naturally rebellious and made awkward models, and when Denys was about twelve he protested at being dressed like Toby. Perhaps his need for originality of dress was the result of this imposed uniformity in childhood. Toby, true to his more conventional nature, became more conservative in his choice of clothes as he grew older, while Denys selected highly individual items, in particular, his hats. Essex Gunning, their cousin and daughter of Sir Charles and Lady Gunning (née Finch Hatton), remembers her relatives considering this branch of the family to be 'very bohemian' with a total unconcern for the stir they sometimes created with their strange attire. On one occasion they were staying with her at Weldon and arrived to go cubbing clad in Norwegian national dress, 'looking like wild men from the woods in their tam-o-shanters'. Essex recalls feeling distinctly embarrassed at having to admit that the extraordinary-looking trio were her cousins and later when she and Topsy attended balls together facing the same dilemma when she tried to separate

Topsy from a thickly knitted peasant shawl. Her dress though elegant enough was ruined by the unsuitable garment draped about her shoulders. Topsy seemed oblivious to this; it was Essex who had the problem of removing it before she could be ridiculed.

West Downs Preparatory School, to which both boys were sent, was founded in the autumn of 1897 by Lionel Helbert and was situated on the outskirts of Winchester. When Denys arrived there in 1898 there were thirty boys in attendance and it was here that he experienced his first freedom from family ties. Denys, while a friendly child, was not gregarious. He wore an air of solitariness which could not be confused with loneliness, and he needed to seek out quiet places. Essex Gunning remembers that her cousin seemed to epitomize the cat who walked alone from Rudyard Kipling's *Just So Stories* – 'But the wildest of all the wild animals was the Cat. He walked by himself, and all places were alike to him.' This quality which distinguished him from the crowd in childhood increased in maturity. He was also inclined to 'fits of vagueness', appearing to be preoccupied with a universe he could not share, an infinity beyond his family's comprehension. His eyes carried an even deeper wistfulness than Topsy's and the sensitivity of his expression was like that of a wild creature, liable to startle easily at the slightest jarring note. However, his responses, even when he seemed to be daydreaming, were remarkably quick and lucid. Gradually Denys began to take the lead in everything he did at school. Toby, far from being resentful, appeared content with Denys's supremacy and just as their father depended on their mother, he began to count on Denys, as if gaining a strength and bravado lacking in his own make-up from him.

In the spring of 1897 the children's cousin Muriel married Artie Paget, the son of Sir Richard Paget. The

Winchilseas were opposed to their daughter marrying
into the Paget family, whom they regarded as 'very small
fry' though eventually they gave their grudging consent.
The wedding was postponed twice through Edith's feigned
illnesses, then finally took place on 31 May at St Peter's
Church, Eaton Square. Aunt Edith shocked the family by
arriving dressed entirely in white like her own daughter. A
fortnight later, during the annual Ewerby Feast for the
villagers and tenants, Muriel and Artie Paget paid a visit
to Haverholme which was unforgettable. Denys, Topsy
and Toby stood among the tenants lining the road which
led up to the great house. Along its carriageway, the
Pagets' team jogged and, when they reached the park
gates, a group of men greeted the newly married pair and
'took out the horses and drew the carriage to the front
door. There followed a feudal feast with the roasting of
an ox, sports and games which included the climbing of a
greasy pole to win a pig!'[6]

Denys was ten years old and the act of homage to his
cousin Muriel impressed him greatly. As an adult he
recounted his vivid recollections of that day to Karen
Blixen and she chose to weave the anecdote into two of
her tales. It appeared initially in 'The Dreamers':

When after the first performance of *Medée*, the people of the
town out-spanned the horses of my carriage, in which she was
driving, to draw it themselves, she did not look at the Ducas,
who put their noble shoulders to the task. No she wept a rain of
warm tears . . . [7]

On the second occasion it was used in *Anecdotes of
Destiny,* which was not published until twenty-four years
after 'The Dreamers'. Lady Muriel Paget's charitable
works for which she became famous are also referred to
in the tale 'Babette's Feast'.

She would, he said, rise like a star above any diva of the past or present. The Emperor and the Empress, the Princess, great ladies and 'bels esprits' of Paris would listen to her, and shed tears. The common people too would worship her, and she would bring consolation to the wronged and oppressed. When she left the Grand Opera upon her master's arm, the crowd would unharness her horses and themselves draw her to the Café Anglais, where a magnificent supper awaited her.[8]

Denys's and Toby's first long summer holidays the following year were spent at Haverholme but were dominated by the death of Uncle Murray, who collapsed suddenly with a heart attack and died a fortnight before they came home. Their father now succeeded the Earldoms and Toby became Viscount Maidstone. Aunt Edith, histrionic to the last, requested 'a bright and cheerful funeral' and ordered 'huge quantities of the blackest writing paper available'. Shortly afterwards she went to live in the dower-house occupied by Nan and Henry, who now moved back into Haverholme Priory. If sorrow marked the beginning of the holidays it had deepened by September. Muriel's first baby contracted infantile gastritis in an epidemic said to have been spread from 'fly-contaminated milk'. He died a few days before the children were packed off on the train to school. There must have been a considerable sense of relief in their young minds as they left the ambience of Haverholme that summer. Like their Elizabethan forebears, known as 'the funereal Finches',[9] they would have more than qualified for the title in their time.

3
1900–1905 – Eton

'My Tutor'
(A chill rumour has reached us that 'my tutor' is beginning
to be known as 'the man')

In future O Etonians remember when you can,
Not to hurt 'your tutor's' feelings by calling him 'the man'
. . .

You'll horrify the 'school yard' by calling it 'the quad'
The 'school yard' where our fathers and our fathers' fathers
  trod,
Let's do away with upstart names composed by foolish folk,
We'll speak the good old Eton slang, the slang our fathers
  spoke,
And now we'll make no effort to change the present plan,
And now to put the moral, I will end as I began
We'll talk about 'my tutor' and not about 'my man'[1]

Denys was just thirteen years old when he entered
Eton. He was now as tall as Toby though less inclined to
pudginess. He went in at the same time as Julian Huxley
(who was almost, to the day, a month younger himself).
But the grandson of Professor T. H. Huxley, the eminent
scientist and author, went in as a Colleger whereas Denys
entered as an Oppidan. He settled into Eton with few
pains and a great deal of prankish merriment. He immediately liked his tutor, Mr Tatham, whose gusts of laughter
offset the discipline necessary for teaching and control of
twenty rumbustious boys. Miss Skey, his sympathetic
house dame, was a kindly, red-haired freckle-faced
woman to whom the boys felt they could turn in moments

of loathing for tapioca pudding, knowing she would not force them to eat the glutinous stuff. They took their chilblains and their home sickness to her with similar confidence. Denys who now quite evidently exuded his mother's quality of charm, had also learned that he could exercise it for all manner of purposes. He could divert 'm'tutor's' attention on the slenderest and most unlikely of pretexts. On one occasion he pretended to spy a mouse when Mr Tatham had summoned him to give him extra work. Denys pointed out the darting rodent's course so convincingly that his tutor ended up on the floor searching for the fictitious beast armed with a poker. The ruse worked splendidly until he upset a jug of milk during the chase. At this point the miscreant, unable to contain his laughter a minute longer, burst into a fit of giggles revealing his fraud at once. 'M'tutor' fortunately had a sense of humour and all was forgiven, but Denys had achieved his aim and through this digression escaped his extra work.

Long before his name became famous on the green sward of Agar's Plough, Denys was well known for his mischievous nature. He conducted a teasing vendetta with the unshorn poodle Henrietta who belonged to Mr Warre the headmaster, and frequently caught her in some crime for which he deemed she should be punished. 'No but really, that dog! You wouldn't believe what she's been up to now . . .' he declared with mock exasperation as he delivered the untidy hearthrug of a dog back to her owner. If he devised some new schoolboy torment for the 'immortal Bunko' of Little Browns, to which the boys made hungry pilgrimages for provisions, the way in which he carried out his pranks was so infectiously full of fun that she could not be cross with him. She reprimanded him tolerantly, 'Now, can't you be'ave like a gentleman, Mr Finch 'atton?' But she adored him and he could get away metaphorically with murder as he replied with a cheeky lift of his chin, that he could not, 'Not before 11.15 schools'. His flippancy always fell short of insolence in the same way that his teasing never approached bullying or cruelty. He seemed to possess an inbuilt meter which prevented him from overstepping the mark and causing hurt or offence. Denys had a strangely magnetic quality at the age of fourteen with an ability to charm all those with whom he came into contact from whatever stratum of society they came. At the same time, his personal popularity never generated malice or resentment in his contemporaries or competitors. There is no evidence of rivalry or jealousy from Toby, who was overshadowed by his younger brother; at home Denys was his mother's favourite child and Topsy's preferred brother and this bias alone must have been hard to swallow when the agonizing pangs associated with adolescence are considered. Toby himself did not lack charm. He was elected to Pop for one half. But he could be hurtful and pompous and he lacked the aura of enchantment which accompanied his brother.

By the time Denys was fifteen he was taller than Toby and surpassed him in strength as well as intellectually. His limbs were long, yet he seemed bridled by an indolence of surety, a leonine laziness which was almost jestingly displayed. He appeared all the while to be holding himself in reserve for some undefined but important role. The quality made him unforgettable, yet was also impossible to pinpoint.

During the summer half Eton splits into two main categories. The Wet Bobs and the Dry Bobs – Slack Bobs are excluded from either universe and are few. The Wet Bobs are those whose lives revolve round the softly flowing Thames 'kissing away the buttercups which thrive on Brocas'. The Dry Bobs are the cricketing fraternity – the faction to which Denys belonged. In summer he was often seen loping across the immaculate Timbralls with his 'peculiar, slouching, almost rolling gait'. 'The Field', as the Timbralls are known in the Michaelmas half, is where he developed the qualities which gave him his colours.

In October 1903, a sad year for Eton marred by a terrible fire which broke out in Mr Kindersley's house, when two boys were burned to death, Denys was mentioned for the first time in the *Eton College Chronicle*. 'At the Wall', a game peculiar to Eton: 'Good kicks by Finch Hatton and Macmillan[2] were the chief features, outside Finch Hatton was excellent, repeatedly coming through.' But in a later edition of the *Chronicle* he was summarized more shrewdly during the football season under 'Characters of the Eleven' – 'The Hon D. G. Finch Hatton, when not charged is apt to be careless, uses the left side of his foot as if his leg were a golf club and kicks short. When charged, he rises to the occasion and is very hard to get past.' That last sentence was a remarkably acute observation of a trait repeated throughout his life.

Denys's tendency to use his leg like a golf club perhaps reflected in the coaching he had received from Uncle Harold, who was a superb golfer and frequently played in amateur competitions. The 'Avunculus Hector', as Denys called him, was High Sheriff of Merionethshire, and his house 'The Plas' at Harlech overlooked one of the finest golf courses in the country. Denys was always ready to regale his friends from a fund of fascinating tales connected with 'the Avunculus' – a staunch empire builder and his favourite relative, whose life excited Denys to emulation. His ability at field sports, his unerring eye as a marksman and his extraordinary collection of boomerangs were well known to Denys's friends – not to mention his wit and extravagant practical jokes. Denys was a born mimic and revelled in taking off Uncle Harold. He might explain how, in a recent golf competition, his uncle had got into a ghastly bunker and shouted out melodramatically:

'Oh my God – Help me!' adding with perfect timing as he lifted his eyes to heaven in mock supplication:

'And don't send your son. This is no boy's work!'

His ability to throw the boomerang 'with all the skill of the black man' gained Harold Finch Hatton as much fame in London as 'the Bottom story'. Denys's admiring group of listeners could hardly fail to be impressed by this huge burlesque, when the Avunculus Hector had joined forces with his friend Horace de Vere Cole a man renowned for his mad pranks. They arranged a lavish banquet at one of the largest London Hotels and hired a toastmaster to announce their guests, who were all the persons they could muster bearing the surname 'Bottom' – Winterbottom, Sidebottom, Bottomley and so forth. None of these unsuspecting guests was known personally but most accepted the gilt-edged invitation. Horace de Vere Cole and Uncle Harold derived their pleasure and amusement from watching the incredulous expressions on the faces of the vast 'Bottom family' as they were loudly announced one by one and gradually realized that they were the victims of an extravagant practical joke!

When Denys was sixteen, sadness and death impinged on Haverholme once more. On 16 May 'the Avunculus Hector', having completed his daily early morning run round the park, collapsed with a heart attack, literally on the front doorstep of his London house, 110 Piccadilly, where he died. He was only forty-eight years old. The whole family was shocked and heartbroken as they gathered at Haverholme for the funeral. Mr Tatham broke the news to Toby and Denys and they returned home at once, spending the weekend with Aunt Edith who, in describing the event to Muriel, wrote:

It was very nice having Henry and the boys till Thursday night, when they had to go back to Eton. Denys is over six foot now and a wonderfully good-looking boy . . . I do hope they won't be spoiled, but it is bad for boys to be so good-looking as they both are.[3]

After Harold's death, the Winchilsea family were down in London a great deal. Topsy, after a series of governesses, attended Kensington High School for a while before taking up the violin as a student at the Royal Academy of Music. She had to give it up eventually; she suffered from an acute sweating of the palms of her hands, induced by the action of her fingers over the strings. She remained a shy but very sensitive girl, reserved rather than withdrawn, in a world dominated by men of privilege. Though not given to practical jokes like Denys, she had a fine sense of humour and was full of fun. Her very delicate colouring served to emphasize a feminine fragility which counterbalanced a tendency towards heaviness in her above-average height. Toby left Eton at the end of the summer half in 1904, he had gained his shooting eight, passed his exams and was going up to Magdalen College, Oxford.

From the age of sixteen Denys emerged on a broad front. He had joined the Eton Musical Society in 1903 and now became its secretary – a post which he held until he left and managed with great efficiency. It was apparent that he had inherited the Finch Hatton flair for organization. He performed as well as handling the administration and he liked to entertain his audience with Madrigals from a book of sixteenth-century lyrics, given to him by his mother. His training in the Haverholme drawing-room now stood him in good stead. He was quite unselfconscious before a crowd of onlookers, a point made by the *Eton College Chronicle* when he won a prize in a singing competition: 'it has been whispered that the

lack of entrants is due to the lack of moral courage,
necessary to sing alone. The second prize was won by
Denys Finch Hatton whose clear articulation gave pleasure to all.' For this he was awarded a Dictionary of Music.
He became Keeper of the Oppidan Wall, a position which
he held for two years in succession. This strange game
with its extraordinary built-in lessons of endurance, poise
and balance preparatory to life, is played by tradition on
St Andrew's Day. Denys introduced his own variation by
persuading both teams to play an extra mural game during
which they were clad in pyjamas – a habit which endured
until he left Eton. As traditional as the match are the
interviews which precede this day of days. A reporter
was sent to track Denys down and interview him before
the match as one of the Keepers of the Wall. Having
drawn a blank at Mr Tatham's house he was advised to
seek out Denys at 'Little Browns' or Mr de Havilland's
house library, to which Denys, an avid reader who
'hankered after literary excellence', subscribed. This is
how he was finally discovered:

On rounding Keates Lane, the first thing that attracted my
attention was a pair of orange coloured slippers in the middle of
the road just outside the window of the library where I had
hoped to find my interviewee. As I stopped to examine these
curiosities, two voices called out simultaneously: 'Thank you,
shoes' and 'Leave them alone'. In great perplexity I decided to
compromise and throw one in, which was greeted with a shriek
of delight and a shower of imprecations on my head. However I
screwed up my courage and entered the library where I was
greeted with 'look at the appalling man! What on earth d'you
want in here?' This from a stalwart gentleman with a green
waistcoat, a hat on the back of his head and an Eton lower
arithmetic in his hand.

This reference to Denys's headgear is the first in a
series of incidents during his lifetime connected with hats.

It was an item of dress from which he seemed quite inseparable whether in Kensington, on the golf links at Harlech, at Haverholme, on safari or taking a stroll round Nairobi, in an aeroplane or under a car tinkering with the sump. Denys's choice of hat was invariably sufficiently quaint to warrant comment, and he gave the impression to friends that he was strangely anomalous without one. One of his few personal mannerisms was to push his hat towards the back of his head absentmindedly during conversation. This habit is recorded in almost every photograph taken of him, unfailingly his hat is tilted upwards as though he had pushed it back from his brow seconds before the picture was taken.

The interview continued:

I enquired if I had the honour of addressing Mr Finch Hatton. 'Don't mention it my man. Anything I can do for you?' I stated the object of my visit. 'Look here N*rm*n this man wants to interview me.'

Thus addressed, a small rather dark gentleman whose chief characteristics were a fine moustache and a beautifully tied tie, looked up from the paper which he appeared to be perusing and said 'Are you the fool who wrote that rot about the school being without the service of their well known back?' I denied any such expression as having emanated from my pen.

'Oh then you're no good, get out and let me learn my Euclid.'

The second Keeper now took pity on me. 'Well what d'you want to know? I'll answer any questions you care to ask.'

I replied that I wanted to know something about the Wall game on St Andrew's Day.

'Something about the Wall game on St Andrew's Day? Did you ever see such a man. Isn't he awful'. This somewhat personal remark was greeted with laughter from two other individuals in the room.

'Shut up! Its not funny' this from the gentleman addressed as N*rm*n.

'Well' pursued the Keeper of the Wall 'I don't know what to tell you except that the Oppidans are rather a hot side and ought to win, though I can't say that they're a pinch. We've got good seconds and behinds but all our outsides, including myself, have been crocked up most of the Half. I shall probably burst myself before the day – I've still got water on the knee – see' (he rolled up his trouser leg and showed me what looked like an ordinary knee-joint).

'There's nothing wrong with you my man' remarked one of the other occupants of the room.

'What lip! Come along N*rm*n we'll have to – ' But before anything further could happen the offending gentleman left the room and hurried upstairs precipately and peace reigned again. Mr Finch Hatton broke the silence.

'Well, is there anything more you want me to tell you?'

'You've not said anything about yourself or your achievements yet Mr Finch Hatton,' said I. 'What are the other games at which you have won distinction?'

'Oh is that all? Oh well I play the Field Game when I'm not broken and have the honour to represent the old Coll in their matches. Next half I play Soccer occasionally and amuse myself with such pastimes as Putting the Weight, Throwing the Hammer and Boxing. At cricket my style is considered unique; I should have undoubtedly played at Lords had not the Keeper of the 2nd Upper taken exception to my unerring aim with loaves of bread and to my method of fielding in matches. I sing a bit sometimes and am exceptionally brilliant at the Society's debates on Friday night. In fact I smother the arguments of those on the opposite side. I spend the greater part of my time thus being pursued by Dempster, intent on massaging my knees. I ought to be up with him now.'

'Oh shut up and come to school. I'm sick of this man!' said the other gentleman.

'But can't you tell me something about the Wall?' I protested as they prepared to depart.

'It's made of bricks and mortar!'

'Wit! Go upstairs and tell the Editor of the *Chronicle* to go to . . .' With that parting shot the interviewer was left to reflect on the paucity of his copy.

That first interview clearly shows Denys's flippant approach to life. The nonchalant façade served to protect him from all attempts to bring him down to earth or take life seriously. He took small knocks and rare moments of defeat with equanimity and, though he excelled at athletics, they were never his preoccupation or his ambition but taken in his stride. Once he came second in Putting the Weight, beaten by 1 foot 9 inches. Exerting himself only slightly, he won the next competition by a clear 6 feet 4 inches.

His real Eton life was in his friends, his mock antipathies, his laughter and his jokes, his catchwords ('Not a fool at all of course!') and his escapades . . . and underneath one always had the feeling there was something fine and spacious. How else could he have dominated the school as few boys can ever have dominated it before or since? Nor was there any need to go deep to discover his love of beauty or his reverence for heroes. Music and poetry touched him nearly . . . Denys was a great figure not only to Masters and Boys, but to the Eton population at large, human and animal; to the dignitaries and the scallywags, to the Fusees, the Holy Pokers and Jobies; the Sandies, the Fritzes and the Henrietta's . . . His recklessness and buccaneering ways always stopped short of doing any living creature harm.[4]

As he matured Denys did not suffer fools gladly but his innate kindness prevented the use of sarcasm or his sometimes biting wit on those blessed with fewer brains or of a timorous nature. The friendships which Denys formed at Eton endured a lifetime, and whenever possible during his life he always managed to gather together a few contemporaries to celebrate the 4th of June. During the First World War, in deplorable conditions, he conjured up a bottle of Champagne from nowhere to the astonishment of his compatriots. He remembered this anniversary with a persistence and gaiety which could only stem from a great affection for his 'alma mater' and a loyalty that never dimmed.

Philip Sassoon,[5] who entered Eton two years after Denys, benefited from his kindly and sensitive nature when he first arrived in Mr Tatham's house. Philip was extremely self-conscious of his Jewish connections, added to which his lisping impediment made him a natural butt for malicious bullying. Immensely wealthy but genuinely generous, he held large tea parties in his room providing friends with huge quantities of sausage rolls from 'Little Browns', schoolboy feasts that were microcosmic fore-runners of the lavish banquets he eventually became famed for as an adult. Naturally shy, with a passion for beautiful things, Philip, like Denys, was not one of the herd; but Philip lacked the self-assurance required to carry off the unconventionality for which he yearned. Denys would not allow Philip to be bullied – nor any of the other young boys for that matter. But in gratitude for this protection Philip sometimes displayed an embarrass-ingly ardent admiration for the older boy which roused his strongest disapproval. On one of the rare occasions when Denys was 'crocked up' in the sickroom, with an injured knee (to which he refers in the St Andrew's Day interview) Philip visited him, bearing rather extravagant gifts; first he presented him with a pair of diamond cufflinks, next a set of ruby shirt studs. The munificence of these offerings apparently offended Denys to such an extent that his immediate impulse was to hurl them into the grate disdainfully – only to retrieve them a little later to hoard them secretly, and eventually give them to Topsy as keepsakes. Denys had a strangely influential quality which drew the best from those with whom he came into contact – even when dissimilar from himself. Philip's admiration and gratitude for the kindness Denys showed him at school was never forgotten. Later, when he lived in Africa and needed an aeroplane to fly, it was Philip who generously put his own at his disposal.

Young, old, black or white, men and women fell under the mysterious quality of his spell. Elspeth Huxley described him precisely – 'The Legendary Finch Hatton, a man never forgotten or explained by his friends who left nothing behind him but affection, a memory of gaiety and grace'.[6]

While Denys was the Keeper of the Oppidan Wall he was also a member of Pop, the exclusive debating society which consists of only two dozen members. As this is a self-electing oligarchy membership is considered a great honour. Denys was elected for six halfs and was President for two of them. He used his powers with integrity and equilibrium. He was scrupulously fair and so direct that he instilled confidence and complete trust in 'the beaks', as Lord Cranworth testifies:

Having been two years in the XI and three years in the field, as well as being President of Pop, he was naturally a hero in the eyes of his school contemporaries. What however was astonishing was the unique (and I believe for once that is the correct adjective) position he attained amongst the masters. The headmaster used . . . not infrequently . . . to consult him on matters concerning the conduct and well-being of the school . . . during his last summer, he gave a supper party on a house-boat on the river, contrary to every known rule and that more than one master accepted and enjoyed his hospitality.[7]

The members of Pop are as easily distinguishable from the black and white throng as a peacock among magpies. The flamboyant waistcoat is the essential mark of distinction. Denys favoured a brilliant emerald green, elegantly punctuated by a gold watch and chain. Tailcoats were discreetly trimmed with black ribbon, and a stick-up collar with a white bow tie was also worn. Denys introduced 'sponge bag' trousers during his Presidency, and they have remained 'de rigueur' since. Sartorial distinction was completed by the wearing of a flower in the button-hole. In his weekly speeches, Denys's presidential role enabled him to draw on appropriate passages in the classics with wit and vicarious wisdom. Faultlessly he quoted huge chunks from Euripides, Bacchae or Demosthenes, from Vergil's *Aeneid* or Spenser's *Faerie Queene*. He was equally at ease with Shakespeare or the American poet Walt Whitman, whom he had just 'discovered', and was particularly fond of *A Midsummer Night's Dream* which he came to know almost by heart.

Eton with its proudly histrionic atmosphere admirably suited Denys's temperament. The establishment nurtured individuality but it counter-balanced this indulgence by its stringent tone of understatement and encouraged self discipline. Denys's personality attracted many friends from the gifted knot of Collegers – many of whom became famous although their flowering was brief. Nearly all perished in the First World War, yet curiously their names lived on. Among them Patrick Shaw-Stewart, Billy and Julian Grenfell, Charles Lister. Alan Parsons and H. J. W. Norton survived. Julian Huxley also formed part of this clique at Eton but broke away once up at Oxford in pursuit of serious study. Ronald Knox, later to become translator of the Vulgate and a famous Monsignor, was reputedly one of the cleverest boys in living memory at Eton. His inability to comprehend mathematics did not prevent him from becoming Captain of the School, and as such he was automatically admitted to Pop during Denys's presidency. Charles Lister, Lord Ribblesdale's younger son, used his persuasive and organizational abilities to set up a trade union amongst the Eton shop assistants. Ungainly and allegedly unpredictable, he once threw himself on to the ground during a stroll with Julian Huxley and screamed without warning or explanation for his strange behaviour. He confided loftily to Huxley that he was the only one of his crowd free from the guilt-ridden practice of masturbation. Denys, Philip Sassoon and Ronald Knox often entertained their élite and rowdy circle of friends with talented mimicry. Knox could take off 'old Warre' beautifully, voicing his dictum.

Dere's an evil elephant [element!] come into this school. Nobody saw it come in and it came in bit by bit. But we must stamp it out and destroy it. It's de elephant of betting and gambling.[8]

Guy Buxton, the grandson of Sir Thomas Fowell Buxton[9] was another of Denys's school friends; his older brother Geoffrey had been a companion of Toby's. Denys loved to spend part of the holidays with Guy and his large family at Dunston in Norfolk. Like Denys, who played the violin and piano, Guy was a member of the Eton musical society and played the harp. By this stage Denys's parents had moved to North Wales, so the times spent at Dunston were perhaps doubly appreciated.

Lord Winchilsea had moved to Harold's house 'The Plas' at Harlech in 1905. It stood in the shadow of Harlech Castle and commanded a magnificent view over Tremadog Bay. At the turn of the century, Harlech was noted for its healthy climate – a good enough reason perhaps for Winchilsea who suffered from persistent rheumatism to consider living there. By this time Toby was also causing concern: his heart showed signs of a murmur. The garden of 'The Plas' overlooked the Morfa (marsh) of Harlech where land and sea met and which contained the Royal St David's Golf Club. Richly green and impressive below, the Morfa contrasted dramatically with the Castle 'which standeth on a very great rock' and towered above the house. Despite Harlech's beauty Denys always retained his love for the horizontal spaciousness of Lincolnshire. His cousin, Essex Gunning, associated days of 'great happiness' with 'The Plas', which she much preferred to 'dreary old Haverholme – so beastly and flat'. But Denys found the fen appealing with its dark-soiled fecund land traversed by pollarded willows. On a crisp winter day their spindly branches seemed to create a summer mirage, vibrating against the vast skies uncurbed by hilly confines. He was fond too of 'dreary old Haverholme' for all its draughts and tendency to produce ailing inmates.

Dunston was also huge, cold, rambling. Typically Victorian, it was run by a fleet of servants. Its rigidly pious towers reflected the high moral purpose of the society and times in which it had been built, when comfort was scorned. Though it had fifty bedrooms only two bathrooms were deemed necessary. Toby stayed at Dunston occasionally. Geoffrey Buxton had not gone to University but was planning to go out to British East Africa, where, if he found the continent tamable, he planned to settle and farm. Since the turn of the century there had been much talk of 'the lunatic line' as the Uganda railway line had been nicknamed in Parliament. A good deal of publicity had been given to the opportunities available for prospective settlers. Hugh Chomondeley, Lord Delamere, had bought up miles of virgin land in the Colony, which he was now painstakingly developing into wealthy farms.

British East Africa seemed an ideal destination for a young man in search of the kind of adventure which Stanley and Livingstone had immortalized. Geoffrey was planning to go out in 1906. The discussions at Dunston on the subject must have roused Denys's curiosity and interest. Toby, in complete contrast, loathed travel of any description and considered that 'the black men started at Calais'. But Denys declared to Essex shortly after going up to Oxford, 'England is small – much too small. I shall go to Africa. I need space.' At Dunston, Denys and

Guy spent hours plodding across the East Anglian land captured in *A Midsummer Night's Dream*:

> The fold stands empty in the drowned field,
> And crows are fatted on the murrain flock,
> The nine men's morris is filled up with mud.

Guy's sister Rose sometimes joined the boys. Seven years younger than Guy she at once developed an admiration for Denys whose teasing banter provoked laughter rather than tears. She trusted this towering friend of her brothers whose ready wit entertained the grown-ups. Later Rose was to find Denys of great comfort during an anguished phase of her life when she turned to him for advice. Being so much younger than her four brothers she led the life of an only child and was always excruciatingly shy. Her happiest hours were spent with 'Munny' – Sir Alfred Munnings[10] – whom her parents employed as her art-master when they detected her natural gift with the pencil. Under his guidance she learned to sketch horses in charcoal – a technique in which he specialized.

During 1905 it was thought that if Denys exerted himself he stood a fair chance of winning a scholarship to Balliol. But he was fully committed to extracurricular activities and becoming a little conceited before the eulogies of his contemporaries. His bumptiousness comes surging through his replies to the interviewer singled out to talk to him before the St Andrew's Day match.

'I understand that you number among your accomplishments, singing, puzzles of the Chinese and Mouse-in-Clover type, billiards, boating, tricycling and piladex.'

'Oh yes, and don't forget that Balliol scholarship!' . . .

[At the end of the interview] Mr Finch Hatton fell to laughing so helplessly that he collapsed against a neighbouring broken-kneed cab horse, who stood the shock as well as may be expected. Our readers will be relieved to hear that Mr Finch

Hatton was not hurt . . . (He now weighed thirteen stone and five pounds.)

Irreverent to the last Denys obviously did not extend himself in the examination although he must have known that he was competing against a formidable bunch of boys, Knox and Huxley in particular. When they sat for the scholarship each candidate dealt with the questions allied to their own particular subject but all were asked to write an essay on 'What would you do if you had a million pounds?' Denys began by announcing that before anything else he would pension off all the Oxford Dons. The examiners were not amused; his unorthodox and facetious approach utterly spoiled his chances for a scholarship. Julian Huxley's answer won him the Zoology Scholarship. He suggested that the money should be used to buy up as much of Britain's unspoiled coastline as possible in order to preserve it. Curiously, conservation later played a part in Denys's life. He realized as a hunter how easily man could misuse the rights granted through game licences and did what he could to control this abuse.

Despite the fact that Denys had had every advantage, a tutor whom he admired, valuable competitive stimulus, the seclusion of his own room in which to study, encouraging parents who had complete faith in his abilities and the necessary intelligence the Balliol scholarship marked his first serious failure to come up to expectation. It was the first instance of that 'sense of power and determination and yet behind it all, indefinite but ever present, a feeling of waste.'

Suddenly Denys's future, which had seemed so full of promise, was obscured by doubt. Henry was hard pressed financially and could not now count on the aid of a scholarship. Success had seemed so easily within their youngest son's reach. After all, to coin his own pet phrase, he was 'not a fool at all of course'. Arrangements were made for him to enter Brasenose in September 1906 and he returned to Eton to complete classical Sixth, one of the Oppidans who remained there longer than anybody else. He seemed almost reluctant to leave.

His 'magnificent physique' and 'striking features' continued to elicit open admiration at Eton. Julian Huxley recalls in his autobiography: 'Finch Hatton by the way was without doubt the handsomest boy in the school. I remember seeing him on my return from a before-breakfast run, standing on top of College Wall in a red silk dressing-gown. An unforgettable Antinous.'[11]

Denys was thirty-two years old when he met Karen Blixen. Perhaps she chose to compare him to Hermes because he reminded her of the bronze statue found at Herculaneum – the forward leaning posture gives a conflicting impression of alertness and melancholy and there is a marked similarity in the shape of the ears (Denys's were noticeably pointed). The heroic ambience which surrounded him, sensed by mentors and comrades alike, was oddly unscathed by this recent failure. He suffered all his life from adulation. 'Suffered' because although he left nothing tangible to prove that it was warranted the impression persisted. As if defying mortality people still speak of him in almost hallowed terms. To be likened to a Greek god has been the ultimate compliment for over two thousand years. The hunter, the hero, the god and the lover have manifested themselves in the slender hipped, smooth bronzes of Greece for aeons. Denys's broad brow, his wide set, sensitive eyes, noble profile and stern chin softened by a mobile and sensual mouth epitomized the former slave boy to whom Julian Huxley refers. Denys's humour was renowned. So was his affectionate spirit, but he also displayed the seriousness and wistful melancholy so often defined in representations of the handsome youth from Asia Minor. His separateness, an impression of solitude was due to the isolation so often found in the ultra-sensitive personality. An ambiguous vulnerability attracted both men and women strongly to Denys throughout his life. His strange evanescence made him a candidate for lavish praise. Phrases used to describe him carried the echo of a fable. In a sense they caused an element of doubt for he sounded almost too good to be true. Curiously, too, his colleagues found it difficult to interpret the deep and lasting affection which he inspired and they would plead with intriguing repetition an inability to explain his formula. Karen Blixen accounts for some of his qualities thus: 'what they really remembered in him was his absolute lack of self-consciousness or self-interest, an unconditional truthfulness which outside him I have only met in idiots.'[12] A friend of the Winchilsea family, Lady Alastair Innes-Ker, said of him 'I have never known anyone with such complete freedom of spirit and mind.'

But perhaps it was more than any of these things. Possibly the combination of complete lack of pomposity or guile, a sense of fun tempered by kindness plus absolute irreverence for stolid convention. His sensibility could be likened to the flow, the delicacy of limpid water which within moments can suddenly become active, adventurous, taking the curve of the pebbles over which it runs. Essex Gunning recalls that he seemed to have 'immense reserves of affection' which she felt would one day be capable of 'giving out great love to the right person'. Relatives came to look on him as 'a recluse' yet he did not withhold himself from them.

At Eton when he wandered around barefoot during summer in a perfectly ordinary reach for comfort he was unaware that this simple act was transformed by him, in others' eyes, into 'a bohemian practice'. The curious thing is that this is even remembered.

In his last match against Winchester at Lords, Denys 'never bowled better' and with the traditional 'moping' and a genuine pensive nostalgia he prepared to leave Eton and its ghosts of Wellington, Grey and Gladstone, Shelley, whose poetry Denys particularly loved, Disraeli, Greville and Horace Walpole. Like him they had in their time clustered at the east end of College Chapel at the end of each half. A boy four years younger than Denys remembers an incident in College Chapel when the choir was singing 'O for the wings of a dove'. After the line of the title there is a considerable pause during which the 'unmistakable voice of Finch Hatton called out "Look under the door!"' His mocking advice was inspired by the flurry of pigeons pecking about in the courtyard.

Denys had loved Eton deeply, and characteristically he did not turn his back on his alma mater when her usefulness was exhausted. He returned often: to play in old boy matches, visit his tutor, support his nephews on red letter days and to take simple pleasure in the weathered beauty of the noble old buildings which engendered so many good memories for him. But he did not confine his visits to formal occasions. Once while dancing with a girl at a party he suggested that they go for a drive. She readily agreed: it was a lovely night – the moon full – a silver disk which often lured him out at very late hours. Careless of the direction he had taken she was surprised when they pulled up at Eton. They sat in silence looking up at his old school for some time. Then gently as if not to break the spell, Denys spoke three words only. 'Beautiful, isn't it.'

4
1906–1910 – Wales and Oxford

In 1906 an unprecedented number of Etonians went up to Oxford, seventeen of them to Balliol. Public schools reckoned their status by the numbers of their scholars admitted to Balliol – which the 'Avunculus' had attended in his day. But Uncle Harold had been ambitious, an adjective which would never be applicable to Denys, now going up to Brasenose.

Whether his personal lack of ambition sprang from a conscious determination to preclude the concept of 'a regular job' from the outset – if when interpreted that meant an office life – or if he totally lacked ambition, is a moot point. Any commitment which enforced his running with the herd would have been intolerable. Certainly he proved himself capable later of great singlemindedness, a quality which, if used mainly to keep himself apart, gathered momentum as he matured. Whenever he decided to achieve an aim, he succeeded against unreasonable odds and was difficult to dissuade from his course.

But he must have had misgivings in retrospect. Karen Blixen touches on his feelings, the twinges of conscience which he shared with a friend in a similar position – that of self-imposed exile – Berkeley Cole.

It was a curious thing about Berkeley and Denys, they were so deeply regretted by their friends in England when they emigrated, and so much beloved and admired in the Colony – that they should be all the same, outcasts. It was not a society that had thrown them out, and not any place in the whole world either, but time had done it, they did not belong to their century. No other nation than the English could have produced them, but they were examples of atavism and theirs was an earlier England, a world which no longer existed. In the present epoch they had no home, but had got to wander here and there and in the course of time they also came to the farm. Of this they were not themselves aware. They had on the contrary a feeling of guilt towards their existence in England which they had left, as if, just because they were bored with it, they had been running away from a duty with which their friends had put up. Denys, when he came to talk of his young days – although he was young still   and of his prospects, and the advice that his friends in England sent him, quoted Shakespeare's Jacques [sic]:

> If it do come to pass
> That any man turn ass,
> Leaving his wealth and ease
> A stubborn will to please . . .

But he was wrong in his view of himself, so was Berkeley, and so perhaps was Jacques [sic]. They believed that they were deserters, who sometimes had to pay for their wilfulness, but they were in reality exiles, who bore their exile with good grace.[1]

Denys entered Brasenose to read modern history under the tutorship of Dr Butler. Toby was already in his last year at Magdalen. Before Denys went up to Oxford he spent a few months in Wales with his family. Their London house had been in Upper Wimpole Street but they now moved to Harley Street – within easy reach of the Royal Academy of Music. There were visits to the theatre, ballet, opera, and musical evenings in fashionable drawing-rooms. Exposure to country life and urbane occupations in equal measure ensured an equipoise and polish in Denys. He met a wide variety of people from all walks of life and in town these were predominantly theatrically orientated. Nan's close friends, Mrs Patrick Campbell and Ellen Terry, whose affectionate and expansive nature now embraced Topsy as a young

woman, were regular visitors. A letter from Ellen Terry
to Topsy captures the intimacy of her relationship with
the Winchilsea family:

                                        Glasgow
Sweet Topsykin –
  A little wee bird tells me you are going on well altho' you are
weak – I just send my love to you and tell you I am delighted
you are better. *You must not write* or do anything your nurses
tell you not to do or you will grieve the Beautifullest lady in the
world and that is (NOT 'H.M.' but) your beloved mother. I
enclose a picture (which I think is not in your collection). It was
taken a century ago when I was *comparatively* young. This
noisy Glasgow is almost as noisy as Pittsburgh in America – but
I am in a very quiet lodging where I can think of you and some
other nice things. I will not write more. Your loving old friend.[2]
                                        E.T.

  The photograph shows Ellen Terry bending to admire
the tall lilies for which she had a passion. Her great
partnership with Henry Irving dominated the London
theatre for twenty years. Her loyalty made her a valued
friend. When Oscar Wilde was spurned by his so-called
friends during the scandalous trial involving the Marquis
of Queensberry and was released from Holloway on bail,
it was Ellen Terry who, heavily veiled, took posies of
violets to Oakley House and left notes of encouragement
to cheer him during that harrowing period. Denys's
mother composed lyrics for this great dramatic actress,
but Ellen Terry experienced some difficulty in singing
one piece Nan had created specially for her in *The Cup*
which ran for one hundred and twenty nights at the
Lyceum:

Lady Winchilseas's setting of 'Moon on the field and foam'
written within the compass of eight notes for my poor singing
voice, which will not go high nor down low was effective

enough, but the music as a whole was too 'chatty' for a severe tragedy. One night when I was singing my very best:

> Moon bring him home, bring him home
> Safe from the dark and cold

someone in the audience *sneezed*. Everyone burst out laughing and I had to laugh too. I did not even attempt the next line![3]

Because Denys had been introduced to the highest standards of theatre he had a loathing for amateur dramatics which never abated. Many years later he was inveigled into going to an atrocious amateur production at the Theatre Royal in Nairobi. His hostess, quite sure of his 'interest in the theatre', had already purchased a ticket for him. The acting was so bad that it amused him by its awfulness and perversely it remained in his mind. A character with great black moustaches was enquiring of a timid little curate 'a little red or a little white wine?' The red wine, labelled POISON was turned to the audience for the benefit of an unsubtle laugh. 'A little whaite whain,' replied the actor/curate in an effeminate voice with his little finger poised high above his glass in the classic 'genteel' manner of affectation. Ever after when he was lunching or dining and the question of wine selection occurred Denys leant forward with a theatrical leer and asked in an emasculated and highly affected voice 'A little red or a little whaite whain?'*

Essex Gunning cherishes memories of time spent with her cousins at Harlech. She places much emphasis on Denys's relationship with Toby and Topsy ('those three were always so close to one another') and the strong

---

* Years after Denys's death visitors to Hugh Martin's house were astounded at the African butler there who, though speaking very little English, proffered white wine to guests in this very manner. The servant had not realized that Denys's catchwords 'whaite whain' were a joke and believed he was behaving as a perfect English gentleman.

sense of family affection which was neither oppressive nor cloying. 'They were a wonderful family – quite unlike anybody else.' Essex, whom they christened 'S.X.', was treated more like a baby sister than a cousin. Descended from the mid-eighteenth-century beauties 'The Miss Gunnings', she was a slender girl, three years younger than Denys, with dark swinging hair and a lively rebellious spirit which gained confidence under the roof of her Finch Hatton cousins. Her rapport with 'Cousin Henry' was special and very close. Closer than Topsy's. She found no difficulty in confiding in the man whose own children were hesitant in his presence and likened him, affectionately, to 'an old walrus'. Later his grandchildren found him loving, indulgent and with a fund of delightful stories for every occasion. Recollections of holidays spent at The Plas possess an idyllic quality. Essex and Topsy were always together.

Cousin Nan photographed me in the other house [Nan's studio] over the road. How I hated being posed with Old Man's Beard draped in my hair. Cousin Nan had a lovely figure which Topsy inherited. She always wore a very wide belt to show off her slim waist. She never emerged from her room until midday. She used to distill scent from verbena and lavender gathered from the garden. It stood in large bottles in her studio, then would be decanted into smaller bottles for the guest rooms – the fragrance from these perfumes permeated the house inescapably. We used to go prawning . . . so silly, we girls, even if we were allowed to take our shoes off had to keep our stockings on. But it was at Weldon that I remember Denys best.

Essex recalls her father dispensing port one evening after dinner, beneath a huge cherry tree in the garden at the Rectory. 'Why is it,' said Denys, 'that the bubbles always travel up the glass? Why don't they go down the glass instead?'

'Denys had such understanding and sympathy,' 'Toby

had great charm too but he could hurt.' Essex mentions the brothers' devotion to each other and this is strongly echoed in Toby's diaries. These, though laconic, repeatedly convey an almost childlike happiness and pride of sharing quite inconsequential events with Denys. No occasion was too small to overlook. Each game of golf (Denys beat him persistently), all shooting and walking expeditions, gardening, long bicycle rides round Oxford, ferreting or, as on one wet afternoon, the making of some excellent toffee in the attic. However Topsy's predicament was rather criticized by the rest of the family, who felt that 'she led a rotten life socially at Harlech and spent far too much time alone'. This aspect of the Finch Hatton children's upbringing remains baffling. Nan and Henry who seemed generally such excellent parents, occasionally spoiled this image by a stubbornly bigoted attitude towards their only daughter. The men she met at The Plas far from being eligible bachelors were golfing companions of her father's openly considered by him highly unsuitable candidates for marriage. The role of paterfamilias he played was heavy handed, melancholy and often dominated by acute rheumatism. But 'the beautifullest lady in the world' who epitomized the real life model of a perfect Beatrice counterbalanced her husband's severity by enchanting people wherever she went. Dover Wilson has written of Beatrice that she was 'the first woman in English literature to have a brain and delight in its constant employment', a judgment which aptly fits Nan's personality. Her spirit seems to have been uncannily Elizabethan and it could be said of her, as Beatrice says of herself: 'There was a star danced and under that I was born.' The whole household willingly revolved round her yet she was unselfish, and Toby's diaries show that the affection and deference accorded to her was a simple response not a duty. It is doubtful whether her real-life Benedick played verbal sparring partner in 'their merry war', but there is absolutely no doubt as to Henry's adoration and devotion to Nan.

Denys and Toby now became involved in the technical aspect of photography, helping their mother in her dark room at Harlech. They still posed for her, though reluctantly, while Topsy was arranged for elaborate portraits with all manner of 'props'. Sheets of music, sprigs of lily-of-the-valley, ears of corn or stuffed nightingales, balanced somehow on her long fingered hands. She and Denys were strangely alike – their limbs borne with a certain languor. A similar underlying strength could be felt in their presence, like something carved from the same whole timber, such as oak, while curiously retaining the resilience of willow. Their hands were markedly alike. Toby was the one who differed. Essex remembers 'he had remarkable eyes – with stars in them' but his humour and his spirit were perhaps overshadowed by Denys's. He was conscious of his position and was less imaginative than his younger brother.

Their Welsh home, The Plas, was a long white building with a verandah running along its entire front. Gabled and roofed in slate, the steely hue was echoed by its windows outlined in green paint. From its narrow terrace overlooking the silent, wrinkled sea, Llyn – the curved spur of Caernarvonshire – could be seen. Essex Gunning's reference to 'the studio on the other side of the road' explains the route to Porthmadog and Tremadog which divided their garden. Shelley is said to have written much of his 'Queen Mab' near Tremadog and to have walked into the dining-room of his home there stark naked to 'assert before his guests the belief in man's natural virtue'. Denys's enthusiasm for this poet's work eventually communicated itself to Karen Blixen. When she wrote *Out of Africa* she chose Shelley's opening lines from his 'Hymn of Pan' – 'From the forests and highlands, we come, we come . . .' to set the tone of her first chapter. Later in the book, emphasizing the tragic denouement of her life in Kenya, she chose 'Gods and Men we are all deluded thus' from the same poem.

It was at Harlech that Topsy met Osmond Williams. Nicknamed 'Ossie', he was Toby's friend. Though Ossie was slightly older they had met at Eton. He lived a few miles from The Plas at Castell Deudraeth, Penrhyndeudraeth, and was the son of the first Baronet of Deudraeth and grandson of the first Liberal MP for a county which had been returning Tories since the Commonwealth. Initially this political bias did not appear to interfere much with Ossie's acceptance socially at The Plas, though Topsy nicknamed him 'Billic' after her 'beastly common terrier' – a mongrel which shadowed her during her solitary ramblings over Harlech Castle ruins. Tall, classically good-looking, Ossie was 'a brilliant horseman' with dark hair and surprisingly blue eyes. He played golf regularly with Henry and the boys – a fine rapport developing between the younger men. Ossie often walked over to visit them, lingering on to stay the night and joining in the family activities. He accompanied them to church, participated in comic operas, parlour games, such as Dumb Crambo,* which they always played at Christmas, shooting, skating or prawning and often stayed with them at their town house.

In London, frequent expeditions to the zoo simply followed the pattern of their childhood visits, when they had regularly made pilgrimages to see Uncle Murray's pet lioness.[4] On this innocent pretext – no chaperone was

* A game originating in the sixteenth century in which one side must guess a word, a rhyme to which is given, by representing other rhymes to it in dumb show.

needed – Ossie and Topsy now went to view her progeny.
When Toby wrote in his diary, 'Went to Deudraeth for
lunch. Saw Ossie who seemed fairly perky,' in January
1906 his observations were simply explained, for Topsy
and Ossie had fallen in love. The attraction was as strong
as it was inevitable. Though Topsy had been presented at
Court, she had been deprived of wide masculine contact.
Unlike many debutantes she found the necessities of the
social whirl overwhelming so that her retiring nature gave
her no cause to complain – the peace of the countryside
seemed to reflect her basic serenity of character. Now,
everyday exposure to Ossie guaranteed an eager response
in a girl of twenty-three who not only found him attractive
but who had had little chance of meeting 'a good match'.
How either of her parents could have overlooked the
possibility of this friendship deepening into love under
the circumstances is puzzling. But it brought about a
crisis in the family. A distinct air of disapproval now
hung over The Plas during Ossie's visits, yet he had been
totally acceptable in every way before as Toby's diary
entry indicates: 'December 8th. Topsy's birthday. Ossie
to breakfast. Gave Topsy a ring on condition she gave
me my umbrella back.' When Nan and Henry discovered
the seriousness of the situation, Topsy's father put his
mid-Victorian foot down. No daughter of his was going
to marry 'the son of a mere country squire'. As a staunch
Tory the idea of the marriage was unacceptable and
distasteful on political grounds alone. Denys's and Toby's
sympathies lay entirely with their sister and Ossie. Their
support did not sway Henry in the least. He refused to
tolerate the watering down of their noble blood or a
political division in the family. He took to referring to
Ossie deprecatingly as 'that Welshman', an unkindness
which only strengthened Topsy's resolve. A battle of
quiet wills now followed. Topsy defied them by becoming

engaged to Ossie. With a stubborn conviction, her unerring spirit carried her through the next six years of
frustration while the problem simmered.

Denys took to Oxford with the same cool imperturbability as he had entered Eton but where Eton had laid
claim to a permanent place in his heart Oxford did not
touch him so nearly. His attitude was one of flippancy.
Jest provided a protective façade. His sensibility was
applied to others. Essex Gunning appreciated Denys's
kindness and understanding 'combined with a great sense
of fun. His voice was musical and soft – quite lovely –
and his brown eyes were hazel and laughing. He had light
brown hair with golden highlights in it.' Already, at
Oxford, Denys's hair was beginning to recede, and was
of the wavy texture inclined to crinkliness. His cousin
described a soft, almost dove-like gentleness that could
not be mistaken for weakness. His prowess was essentially
masculine but his Byronic lustre made him irresistible.
His poetic quality contrasted intriguingly with a masculine
aggression and typically English flair for sang-froid in a
dangerous situation. Courageous actions for which he
became renowned in Africa were shrugged off casually,
he never needed to raise his voice in anger: a word or
look was enough.

Alan Parsons, who named his first son after Denys
and was at Oxford with him, recalls a rare occasion of
aggression:

Under a guise of laziness and even slovenliness Finch Hatton
never let his keen brain rest idle for a moment. Though he did
not appear to take games seriously yet his golf was good enough
for him to play at Oxford. The only time I saw him rouse
himself and that cynical smile leave his remarkably handsome
face (his premature baldness had not then appeared) was in a
street fight at Abingdon. He set about his opponents for
twenty minutes or so and enjoyed himself hugely, gigantic and

triumphant. Yet that evening he spent an hour in the organ-loft of Brasenose chapel. Like his brother Lord Winchilsea, who was a good violinist, he loved music passionately. He told me the last time we met, he had come all the way from East Africa to hear 'La Boutique Fantasque' – it was perfectly true . . . London always seemed rather too small for Denys Finch Hatton . . . I had known him intimately for nearly thirty years and I always thought that the twentieth century did not suit him either. Even as a boy he was utterly different from other boys of his age. It was not merely a question of unconventional attire (he turned up as best man at my wedding in an ancient shooting coat) but of unconventional outlook. He was like one of his Hatton ancestors of Elizabethan days – a man of action and a man of poetry.[5]

Again the usual superlatives are employed to describe Denys, while Toby, in contrast to his larger-than-life brother, is overshadowed apart from a single reference to his musical accomplishment. It must have been easy for Toby to lean on Denys psychologically, but though Denys showed a genuine affection for his older brother he was totally independent of him. The way in which he did not confide his movements to Toby reveals an almost unconscious determination to break away under a guise of thoughtlessness. Toby constantly refers to 'meeting Denys unexpectedly at stations, or on the train home', during the brothers' Oxford days. Obviously no previous mention has been made as to his plans or movements. Once when Toby returns to The Plas for Christmas, he records his crestfallen surprise in his diary 'arrived home 1 A.M. and heard of Denys's departure for Vienna tomorrow'.

Denys's migratory tendencies were now manifesting themselves, as can be seen from Julian Grenfell's letter to his mother. Lighthearted rebellion was the mood.

The great amusement this term is lying in the quad and singing from 8 to 1 every night. Charles has been away for a week canvassing for Russell at Wimbledon; he played cricket the other day in black trousers and black boots. Bones has (literally) shaved his head with a razor because he says there is no one here he wants to please. Denys has taken a season ticket to London and spends all the time in the train. Everything is going splendidly and I love this term . . .'[6]

It seems to have been something of a cult at that time to shave the entire head though the motivation may have been different with Denys and Toby. On the eve of departure for a fishing holiday in Norway, they shaved their hair off too. When they returned regrowth seemed decidedly sparse and their father set about finding a specialist who dealt with hair restoring. After discussion with this gentleman, Toby went into one cubicle, Denys to another for an application of some unguent which would guarantee a healthy new thatch. Henry waited outside. Suddenly with a bloodcurdling shriek Toby shot across the room in one direction practically colliding with Denys who emerged just as rapidly from another. The barbers had applied neat ammonia to their pates. Denys's hair never really recovered from that drastic removal by shaving. It continued to diminish until, but for a narrow strip of hair which could be seen from beneath his hat, he was completely bald.

Toby held his place in life with a painstaking charm and solidarity. He loved dancing, parties and balls were happy social commitments, and he could clearly be seen conforming to the roles of future Earl and ideal husband. Reliable, sensible, courteous and impeccably turned out, his lack of glamour is somehow captured by his own pen: 'First night O.U.D.S. Great success though personally bored to tears. Had to stand half an hour in an archway with a broken sword in tights!' He met Winston Churchill and thought him 'the worst man I ever saw anywhere'. Though Toby had better shaped teeth than Denys's, which were irregularly placed, he also suffered his mother's bugbear of troublesome teeth and, even at the age of twenty-one, complained frequently of rheumatism. Next came a series of effervescent baths for his enlarged heart which, for some inexplicable reason, Aunt Edith insisted Denys should take as well.

There was at Balliol while Denys was at Oxford a coterie of prize winners dubbed 'The New Elizabethans'. They came from Eton, were athletic and academic and kept themselves apart even from their other Etonian contemporaries, who were referred to somewhat deprecatingly as 'the Plebs'. Yet this Balliol set 'an especially rumbustious and flamboyant one . . . a self appointed aristocracy'[7] admitted Denys to their fold. Headed by Ronald Knox, who was now aided and abetted by an unrepentantly socialist Charles Lister, the 'new Elizabethans' included the cream of the Eton boys: Daniel Macmillan; Julian Grenfell, who would be remembered for his war poem 'Into Battle', Billy his younger brother, who was quite capable of flattening an assailant at a single blow but was gentle and scholarly beneath this somewhat aggressive exterior; Alan Parsons, whose Italian Renaissance good looks and intelligent mind captured the heart of Viola Tree* whom he eventually married, and Patrick Shaw-Stewart the less monied son of a General who, though brilliant, was not as ambitious as the rest, and who fell in love with Julian and Billy Grenfell's mother.

Knox was considered to be the wittiest President the Oxford Union had ever known, though Lytton Strachey, who was a close friend of Ronald's brother Dillwyn, disagreed on this point. He in some fit of pique dubbed him 'a Christian, a prig and, a self-sufficient insignificant

---

* Herbert Beerbohm Tree's eldest daughter.

little wretch'.[8] The author who coined the title for this exclusive group, E. B. Osborn, argues that the last thing any of the New Elizabethans were was priggish: 'for Eton has always been kind to all those whose philosophy of living whatever it may be does not issue in priggishness and snobbishness – two of the modern deadly sins which were unknown – nay unthinkable – to all the New Elizabethans.'[9]

The fashionable young 'bloods' who formed this set would virtually take over 'the Anna' as the Anningdale Society was called. Its dinners often culminated in 'waterfalls of crockery down a fourteenth-century staircase'[10]; or they could be heard chasing nonentities out of the quad. Philip Sassoon, who could not hope to compete athletically or intellectually (he was at Christchurch), was one of their victims when he incurred the wrath of one of Lord Desborough's sons, whose tendency to bully contrasted strangely with their dazzling conversation at Society dinners. The sound of the coach horn heralded their rowdy progress at night. In mitigation for this obstreperous behaviour, they at least paid for any damage done in these wild moments.

At Brasenose Denys lived in College on the third floor in a room reached by a spiral staircase which overlooked the quad. Toby, whose digs were quite distant, often stayed the night with him. Denys joined Vincent's, a sporting club exclusive to the University Blues, Bullingdon's and the Phoenix Club. This was a dining and debating society attached to B.N.C. which met on eight Tuesdays of the year, a function which Denys never missed. It was restricted to twelve members but each was expected to bring a guest. One of Denys's frequent guests was a certain Philip Page whom Gerard Goschen also brought along to the Phoenix. Gerard, who was the son of Lady Alexander Goschen, had known Denys at Eton and they spent Christmas together in Vienna one year.

Whether it was Philip Page who gave Denys the copy of *Peter Pan* illustrated in the softly muted manner of Arthur Rackham or whether it was Philip Sassoon whose aesthetic tendencies (Denys defined an aesthete as a man wearing a hair shirt and sandpaper trousers) and stubborn yet hopeless admiration for Denys are sufficient reason to believe he could have given him the book, is not known. Written inside its cover is:

> To Denys from Philip. February 1907
>
> The stars shall fade away, the sun himself
> Grow dim with age and nature sink in years
> *But Thou* shall flourish in immortal youth
> Unhurt amongst the war of elements,
> The wreck of matter in the crush of worlds

Next to the two words in italics on the third line whichever Philip donated the book has drawn a small arrow towards 'Peter Pan'. Whatever the hidden reasons for this tender inscription and whatever inspired the writer to pluck Joseph Addison's lines from the classical tragedy and pattern of a stoic man, *Cato,* they can only have been the result of an intense admiration. Perhaps in those few lines of dedication there emerges an intrinsic truth about Denys: did he, like the legendary Peter Pan, never want to grow up entirely? He never shirked responsibility, on the contrary, but neither did he seek it. One of his nieces recalls that he persistently feared growing old. He liked to be thought of as eternally young.

As the second son, a fact which had been impressed upon him throughout his upbringing, he would inherit nothing of great importance. The responsibility of bringing forth an heir could be left to Toby. Denys was bored by the social round; like Julian Grenfell, though not as intolerant, he was uninterested in the common herd.

'What a far better thing it is not to get married,' Julian wrote to his mother. 'Marriage is such a short odds gamble, and the funny thing is that the real gamblers and chancers have the sense to leave it alone knowing that it is a bad bet, while the careful ones, who know neither the form nor the odds, plunge and go down.'[11]

The rigid underpinnings of the state of marriage held no attraction for Denys either. Added to which, the depressingly dull nature of debutantes whose finest recommendation was a good pedigree put the 'season' on a par to the annual blood-stock sales at Newmarket. Denys preferred his uncurbed freedom, which, with charm, he found surprisingly easy to achieve. With an instinctive, almost political dexterity, he found he could proffer sufficient attention to everyone in the right place at the right time, appeasing their need so that his own liberty could be achieved. In this way he caused neither hurt nor offence to anyone.

And he had learned to recognize the span of life as an ephemeral thing. He had seen relatives, playmates and friends die and had attended many funerals. He was determined to live life to the full and enjoy it intensely and in the present. Guy Buxton's tragic death can only have strengthened his private resolutions. Guy had been salmon fishing with his father in Scotland, and the latter, seeking a better spot, had wandered downstream. Guy had a salmon on the line but somehow lost his balance on a loose boulder, and the ghillie, seeing the young man fall, panicked; instead of rushing to the boy's aid he ran downstream to call his father, shouting incoherently in his fear. It took several minutes to establish the urgency of the drama and by the time they reached Guy he had drowned – apparently the fall had knocked him senseless.

Lord Cranworth (Bertie) recalls an incident from Denys's Oxford days that reflects a combination of his inherited Finch Hatton and Rice humour, both brief and pithy.

At Oxford the same ascendancy over his fellows continued. He gave up serious cricket and football and played golf for the University with success though his attitude towards games may be sensed by the following. . . . He gave his opponent in the Varsity match, a yard putt and when an ardent partisan remonstrated with the remark 'Remember, you are not playing for yourself but your University' he rejoined, 'And perhaps you might remember you are playing for neither!' With his grand physique and slow crooked smile he was enormously attractive to women. Indeed nature presented him with more gifts than were the fair share of one man.[12]

Denys's dry riposte was typical of the mercurial delivery of his wit. There is a strong resemblance to his Uncle Murray's reaction at his first political rally and also to the humour of his grandmother's brother, one of eight in the Rice family, who was a General. When asked by some tiresome relations what his occupation actually was, he replied, 'I knit.'

Lord Cranworth's observation regarding the attraction felt by the opposite sex for Denys is not exaggerated. Possibly his innate air of aloofness, giving the impression that no woman could capture and hold him, supplied that essence of provocative challenge which makes seduction more exciting, particularly since he was able at the same time to appear to give himself in rapt attention to whomsoever he happened to be speaking.

For the greater part of his life he remained uncommitted and very selective. It bored him to discover that he was repeatedly in conversation with subjective females whose chief concern was the impression they were making on him. In the same way in which he sought a life of adventure, he required the tacit sentinel of danger, the possibility of failure, to rouse his ego and excite his interest. But his looks undermined his requirements by attracting the majority. He was handsome enough when he went to Africa but after several months of exposure to the sun, which bleached his hair and bronzed his skin deeply, with his velvety brown eyes and his slow rakish smile of greeting, the effect was apparently devastating. His height alone – he was six foot three – was enough to make an impact on people meeting him for the first time.

There is no evidence of any great love in Denys's life at Oxford, though he was very impressed with one girl he met through his friend Gerard Goschen's sister Vivienne.*

Their cousin, Catherine Bechet de Balan, came to live with them from the age of sixteen. Four years older than Denys she was imaginative, intelligent and extremely vivacious. She was French, spoke English and German fluently, and made a gay companion when she stayed at The Plas. Denys and Toby spoke French well and were having private lessons in Italian at the time. In 1904 she toured Morocco, dressed in native costume. This theatrical outfit complemented her dark hazel eyes and olive complexion to give her the zest of a Romany gypsy, a brilliant contrast to the watery, English hybrid type of girl Denys met all too often. In August 1905, when Denys was just nineteen, Nan invited Catherine to stay, insisting that she bring along her peasant costume so that a portrait could be made of her. 'Pussy' as she was generally known, though Denys always called her Kitty, looks in these studies as if she has strayed by chance from a passing

* The author Vivienne de Watteville, who wrote *Out of the Blue*.

caravan serai into Lady Winchilsea's little damask-lined drawing-room. The photographs capture this whimsical girl in all her dark-eyed allure. In the fleshiness of her underlip and the slight protrusiveness of her fine, white teeth is a promise of sensuality which would be interesting for a man to call to account. Her Moroccan dress with its gaudy metallic trimming would have looked vulgar on anyone less sure of their own individuality but on her the result is intriguing, not cheap.

Four years later Denys was considered to be, briefly, one of her suitors but she married an older man, Lieutenant-Colonel Wilfred Lucas. When their second son was born, she insisted on christening him after two of her old 'flames'. One was Denys and the other a Roman Catholic – Cecil Trafford*, and both became the child's godfathers. He was christened Denys Cecil Lucas on 22 January 1915 at St Mary's, Cadogan Gardens, Chelsea. Kitty Lucas and Denys remained close friends. They wrote to each other, and Denys always made a special effort to see her when he visited England. In 1927, when he was having a safari vehicle built to his own specification and purchasing equipment required for his relatively new profession as a hunter, he tried to persuade her to accompany him back to Kenya for a holiday. Despite his highly romantic approach (he called Africa 'the-great-keep-it-dark-Continent') she declined the offer though it was perfectly serious as far as Denys was concerned if somewhat unorthodox by pre-thirties standards. Kitty, a little nonplussed by the offer, was living at Stowmarket at the time. She was perfectly happily married with five children. One evening at about midnight she heard the sound of their piano being played. In disbelief she crept down to

---

* Brother of Ralph Trafford, who became headmaster and later Abbot of Downside.

the drawing-room from which this unsupernatural sound came. Upon opening the door she discovered Denys playing away as if it was the most natural place for him to be in the world. To the end of her days Kitty never found out how he gained entry to the house. It was this type of stratagem which added delicate weight to his mythus and set him apart from his contemporaries. His singlemindedness commanded respect and countermanded the ethereal quality, so that in truth it could be said of him: 'Denys always seemed to do everything he wanted to do and never do anything he did not want to do. Anyone else leading such a life would have deteriorated.'[13]

His personal choice of clothes now played a part in the general romantic image. He selected softly tailored shirts of fine material with self stripes, and was often seen wearing a loose foulard tie in the manner favoured by Rupert Brooke whom Denys met several times on visits to Cambridge and whose poetry he admired. He might once have disdained Philip Sassoon's expensive presents at Eton, but now, he ornamented his hand-made shirts with pearl tiepins or cufflinks of his own choice which heightened his *fin-de-siècle* air. This polish was not sustained, however, and if he stood out amongst the point-to-point set of Bullingdon's he occasionally appeared so ungroomed and negligent that one could hardly credit the contrast. He would carelessly fasten his jacket on the wrong button, forget to polish his shoes or leave his socks to concertina round his ankles in acts of pure slovenliness; almost always his hat was askew.

Philip Sassoon, slender and impeccable, now discovered that he was acceptable to the formidable new Elizabethans only on the common ground of Bullingdon's – he enjoyed fox-hunting, Denys seldom rode to hounds. Oxford was not a happy place for Philip. His lisp had become more pronounced since his Eton days and his

lack of interest in games did nothing to help his image.
He tried to compensate for his vulnerability by holding
lavish parties and exploiting his gift for mimicry. But
even these ploys back-fired and he once so enraged Julian
Grenfell with his extravagance that at the first opportunity
'he turned on Philip and drove him round the Tom quad
with his big Australian stock-whip, double-cracking it
within inches of Sassoon's sleek head . . . no doubt he
could have hit him with perfect accuracy. It did not
lessen the victim's humiliation.'[14] Philip's opulence was
sometimes flaunted to an insensitive degree, and though
it stemmed from an almost pathetic need to make up for
his personal inadequacies, it was not acceptable to those
aware of poverty. Anyone who mixed with Lord Ribblesdale's son Charles Lister could not fail to be persuaded
by his views on the subject. He was 'the embodiment of
comradeship in whatever society he found himself . . .
the way men lived filled him with curiosity' and became a
rabid Trade Union agitator. He even roused the girl-
workers at the Clarendon Press to strike on one occasion.
Oddly enough, he entered the diplomatic world after
taking his first in Greats, having become so disillusioned
and intolerant of his fellow socialists that he gave up the
fight as far as a career was concerned.

During Christmas 1909, when Denys visited Vienna
with Gerard Goschen, he was lucky to escape the usual
family gathering, for it wasn't especially happy. Henry
was recuperating from an operation, Nan was suffering
from agonizing bouts of toothache, and although Toby
did his best to lift his parents out of the doldrums there
was little he could do to cheer Topsy who had been
separated from Ossie since 1907 when he had left England
after the engagement drama. He went to work on the
railways in Chile and Bolivia, where he remained until
1911. The rest of the party spent Christmas in London.

Toby took his father for small outings in their motor car if the weather was not too bleak, despite the fact that he too was unwell. Palpitations and catarrh marred his enjoyment: he got 'beastly cold' while having his portrait painted, and the jottings in his journal echo depressingly those his father made on his voyage to Australia in the year Denys was born.

During Ossie's absence Topsy discouraged all the tardy ploys of her parents to bring her into contact with eligible bachelors. She shied away from their arrangements and was even known to have crawled under the table at one function when Ossie was present rather than dance with anyone but him. In a book* Denys gave to Topsy in his last half at Eton he wrote within the gift: 'There is no good arguing with the inevitable. The only argument available with an East Wind is to put on your overcoat.' While the significance of the present and its inscription remain a mystery it might be that Denys and Topsy had reluctantly accepted the futility of reasoning with their parents on her behalf. She had had her bedroom at the top of the house at Harlech and its furniture painted completely in white which suggests Syrie Maugham's influence but perhaps reflects a stubborn virginity while emphasizing an invincible faith in Ossie. When he returned to England in 1911, she ignored all threats of severance from the family and married her Welshman. This act of moral courage won high praise from Denys. Truly 'the girl was a marvel'.

In view of his parents' attitude towards Ossie Williams and Topsy, Toby probably delayed the moment of announcement that he had already met his future mate. He had fallen in love with Margaretta Drexel the

---

* *School of the Wood* (some life studies of Animal instincts and Animal training) by William J. Long 1902.

daughter of the Philadelphia banker Anthony Drexel. He had met her at a party at the Berkeley Restaurant the previous summer, and in her he was to find the glamour and verve lacking in his own make-up. The general opinion was that Margaretta who was statuesque with dark hair and camelia pale skin was 'ravishing'. If Nan and Henry had objected to Topsy marrying 'a middle-class country squire' it seemed logical that they would find the idea of an American questionable as the wife of the future Earl even though she was immensely wealthy. Her grandfather had founded the Drexel Banking Company of Bankers with J. Pierpont Morgan and she had certainly been brought up with every advantage that money could buy. The Winchilsea family were financially strained; an injection of money would help to maintain the remnants of their once vast estates; and if there were doubts they were swiftly dispelled. 'Maidstone' (later 'Maisie') as his future bride insisted on calling Toby, married her at 'a terribly American function' on 6 June 1910. In London. Topsy and Essex were bridesmaids and Toby naturally expected that Denys would be his best man. But, to his everlasting hurt and amazement, Denys declined the honour with the remark that he 'couldn't be fagged'. Perhaps this rebuff, tantamount to an insult, was intended as a show of loyalty to their sister but the effect was the same. Denys had loyally defended Topsy when their parents had priggishly and unnecessarily offended Ossie who was a dear friend. He now found it impossible to come to terms with his father's attitude as all impediments to his brother's marriage dissolved like snowflakes in sunlight after they met Margaretta. It was assumed that all who met her would be 'bowled over by her exquisite profile and good looks'. Denys observed her shrewdly while Toby awaited his opinion anxiously. After she had spent a weekend with them all at The Plas Denys finally proffered his opinion. It left Toby fuming and his parents astounded. 'Well, at least she's got good manners,' he commented briefly on his future sister-in-law.

5
1910–1911 – Africa

Apart from announcing that he found England too small there is no evidence that Denys might go to Africa before May 1910. Possibly he was encouraged to do so by his cousin Muriel and her husband Artie Paget. He stayed with them from time to time and they had been to the Sudan in 1909. Geoffrey Buxton's enthusiasm for the country may have convinced him that he should explore British East Africa. Many acquaintances were going out at the time, lured by the promise of wealth and adventure. The Pagets planned to visit South Africa in the autumn of 1910 and it is more than likely that Denys saw this as an ideal opportunity to investigate the possibilities of emigrating, for he travelled with them.

When Lord Winchilsea wrote to the Bursar of B.N.C. on Toby's birthday – 28 May 1910 – he mentions nothing of his youngest son's intention of going abroad though he manages to convey his own frail state:

Dear Sir,
I enclose a cheque for £17.1.9 pence in payment of my son's battels. I am anxious to explain that the delay is not due to him but to me. He gave me by my request, all his accounts on leaving Oxford, but I have been unable to attend to them hitherto, owing to ill health.

Yours faithfully,
Winchilsea.

A week earlier Denys had written to his tutor from Liverpool where he was staying with his old friend Norman Tod (mentioned in the first St Andrew's Day interview at Eton):

c/o W. N. Tod,
Dry Grange,
Allerton
Liverpool.

May 10th 1910.

Dear Dr Butler,

I shall be coming up to Oxford on the 26th of this month and would like to take my degree on the following day. I am told that I may obtain information as to the particulars from you. I expect to be out of England during most of the next six or seven years so I shall be taking my name off the books. I trust you are well and Mrs Butler.

Yours sincerely,
Denys Finch Hatton.

Denys took his degree but once more fell short of expectation: he only achieved a fourth.

After Toby's and Margaretta's wedding in June Denys went to stay with Muriel Paget during an exciting aviational event which she and Artie were in the throes of arranging at Wolverhampton. Artie had always nurtured a secret longing to fly and had promised himself he would do so before he died. Now as Chairman of the Organizing Committee of the Flying Meeting in July 1910 his dream seemed within reach. Like everyone, Denys was impressed by Blèriot's achievement in 1909 when he had been the first man to fly the English Channel and now he had the exciting prospect of meeting the Frenchman, for Muriel had arranged a large houseparty for the week of the meeting. Among her guests at 'Old Fallings' were Claude Grahame-White, Captain Scott the explorer and his wife Kathleen, and Charles Rolls. However, the wayward English weather messed up the event for the majority of the time. A freakish wind sprang up though after tea it usually dropped and the pilots could take briefly to the air.

There followed the customary chapter of accidents – accidents in which, as was then not uncommon, the machines suffered more than the pilots until soon, aeroplanes were to be seen in fragments at all corners of the ground. Grace's 'Wright' hit a railing and lost its propeller; Radley's 'Bleriot' rose twenty feet then dropped like a stone; Ogilvie and Gibbs both crashed and damaged their machines . . . Grahame White was the hero of the day, winning, with an aggregate of one hour and thirty-three minutes in the air during the whole week! the £1,000 endurance prize.[1]

Denys and Muriel seemed to have inherited the same quality of fearlessness, for during the Flying Meeting, Muriel, daring, impulsive and with a complete lack of concern for her own safety was suddenly spotted by her husband and cousin 'sitting on the front edge of the lower plane (on Grahame-Whites' machine) with her feet dangling in space and was maintaining this rather insecure position by holding onto the vertical interplane struts!' The spectators were breathless with admiration – no passenger flights had been scheduled and women were considered doubly dangerous because 'their hats were apt to blow off and become entangled in the propeller'. Muriel was ecstatic; 'It was simply splendid,' she told the reporters, 'the feeling as one sails smoothly through the air is most exhilarating . . . I had every confidence in Mr Grahame-White. He talks to you all the way and I was not a bit nervous.' A French admirer later wrote to Muriel that this pilot claimed it was his greatest hour when he flew with 'the most fascinating of earth's fair daughters at his side till the angels with their wings of azure were almost jealous in the deep blue sky. Bravo Mu!'[2]

Evidently, like Denys, Muriel inspired lavish admiration and in several ways these cousins possessed parallel qualities. Their need to wander was apparent (Muriel

travelled constantly, devoting her life entirely to charitable works and returning only for brief intervals to her
family). Both were persuasive and had inherited the Finch
Hatton talent for organization – though Denys's powers
were less tangible they were harnessed to an ability of
inspiring self-confidence in others. Perhaps when Karen
Blixen speaks of his 'reverence for values outside other
people's understanding' it gives a clue to his power. He
seemed to provoke others to exploit their best qualities,
and it was the indefinable force of this catalyst which
induced love and admiration from those close to him. In
return they seemed to strive only to win his friendship
and approval – as an acknowledgement of their own
existence. An incident concerning a cousin typifies this.
As a girl she came up against 'Henry's darkest disapproval', because he felt the match she proposed to make
highly unsuitable and did not believe the man of her
choice could make her happy. Denys's father tried to
persuade her to break off her engagement several times
and was scorned. When the subject inevitably came up
for discussion a few months later Henry unwittingly used
a threat when he commented, 'You know I shall have to
tell Denys about this . . .' That remark was so strongly
effective, 'like a whiplash' across her mind, that the girl
broke off her engagement immediately. The marriage she
made eventually was entirely happy and successful. Essex
Brooke reiterates the power of Denys's approval. 'He
was such a *good* influence on people' concluding, at the
age of eighty-five, 'he was extraordinary. I never met
anyone like him before or since his death.'

His dormant boldness appeared later. His physical
reflexes were as mercurial as his mind and he could be
relied upon to act with expediency in a crisis which
demanded incisive thinking. Under pressure he carried
himself with an air of effortless ease – possibly it was this

as much as anything which gave his deeds the quality of chivalry. The amazing part was that in the midst of heroic acts, as ready master of a situation 'he always found time somehow to spend in small acts of kindness for the most unlikely people of any age or any type'. It was this last quality which earned him his wide reputation for greatness and made him so loved.

Exemplifying all these characteristics is an incident which occurred in 1930 when he narrowly escaped death while motoring from Isiolo to Nairobi, at Nyeri – ninety miles from the capital. His safari car skidded in thick mud as he crossed a very narrow bridge, overturned and dropped into a ravine eighteen feet below. The river was in full flood – the rains had come – the waters swirled rapidly over the vehicle pinning Denys and his Somali servant, Billea Issa, on the river bed. It was already dark and there was no help available:

Mr Finch Hatton, however, was a man of great physical strength. He raised the body of the car on his shoulder and succeeded in crawling free after which he raised the car again and managed to extricate his servant. Neither was hurt but Mr Finch Hatton was far more concerned by the loss of his quaint and well-known blue hat (somewhat like a bowler) than about his narrow escape. He borrowed a hat from a nearby house – indifferent to the fact that the hat was of a type usually worn by ladies and made it serve his needs until he could get another of his 'bowlers' from the special stock he kept.[3]

At the Wolverhampton Flying Meeting it was a miracle in view of the weather and the venue (the racecourse) that there were no serious accidents. But some sort of weird doom followed all those who ate Artie's great, rum-filled sugar cake designed like an aeroplane in their honour. 'Rolls went on to a similar meeting in Bournemouth and was killed: Cecil Grace flew out to sea and was lost and two years later Captain Scott and his companions met their death in blizzards of the Antarctic.'4 As for Denys, he must have decided there and then that he would one day have an aeroplane of his own and fly high above the world in that still magical unknown. It is ironic too that this was the moment which marked his own destiny with death.

Denys sailed with Muriel and Artie to South Africa in the autumn of 1910. On arrival he stayed with the eminent politician Dr L. S. Jameson whose fine political career had long eclipsed the infamous and abortive Jameson Raid of 1896,5 and Muriel's first meeting with Sir Starr brought about a lifelong admiration. She called her only son, born in 1914, after him. Artie Paget's younger brother was on the staff of Herbert Gladstone, who had recently been appointed first Governor General of the Union of South Africa; so the Pagets stayed at Bishop's Court, his house just outside Cape Town. Regular visitors were Smuts, Botha, Hertzog and Merriman. But interesting politically, wealthy and topographically beautiful as it was, this part of Africa lacked the excitement Denys was seeking. Its thin veneer of urbanity could not disguise the underlying strata of provincial affectation. Nor was he in sympathy with the South Africans' discriminatory policies. He sailed for British East Africa and reached Nairobi on 18 March 1911.

From the moment Denys sailed into Kilindini Harbour to disembark by rowing-boat in Mombasa he sensed the romantic air of adventure. The gigantic baobabs (quite unlike any tree in Europe) clustering at the harbour entrance to the island are strange in their purplish solidity; the bustle of the port, its multifarious population scuttling barefoot in flowing garments, evoked scenes from the Arabian Nights. The old Portuguese Fort Jesus rises from the bluest of seas to link water to azure sky in an untidy rectangle of apricot. Its apparently innocent, crenellated structure gives no clue to the long and bloody sieges associated with it in the late seventeenth century. Denys's love of history, his quest for adventure, his appetite for both were whetted as soon as he came ashore. He had one day to explore the maze of scruffy narrow streets. Coffee vendors crouched beside their shining brass pots dispensing measures of a bitter brew in tiny handleless cups. The men ruminated betel-nut, a leaf which when chewed with the parings of areca nut stains the teeth an ugly brown reminiscent of great age or of hags and witches. Mangy cats of all sizes sunned themselves, or scavenged for food in the open drains by the fishmarket. Women peered from their black shrouds of purdah, the traditional bui-bui, seeming to melt into their own modesty in the shadows; their nutmeg-dark faces turned away from the intrigued gaze of men. Muslims, Arabs, Africans, Christians, dhow captains and traders went about their business with a peaceful resignation.

In the old port, pervaded by the stink of dried fish, lay the ancient vessels of the sea, the dhows, their course controlled by the benevolence of the monsoon. Its force filled their graceful lateen sails to bring them annually to Mombasa. Easter was the time for repairs and careening. The huge brown timber hulks, usually hidden in the marine depths, now lay sequestered on their sides at Pwakuu, resembling at low tide, gigantic, newly-hatched moths. The men scrambled over them, stopping leaks with sheepfat and lime, and they seemed to be lying in wait with furled wings for the whisper that the monsoon had changed. Then as they spread their canvas it would blow them on endless quests for cargo that had continued since the time of Solomon and Sheba.

In these sights Denys could see verses from the Bible re-enacted before him. 'Once in three years came the navy of Tharshish bringing gold and silver, ivory and apes, and peacocks.'[6] If the cargoes were less opulent in 1911 they were not less exotic. The smell of spices and cloves from Zanzibar mingled with the less appealing odour of fish. The trade was in skins and ivory, Persian carpets, copal, opium, salt, long terra cotta 'boriti' or mangrove poles and ancient Arab chests, brassed heavily, defying a mantle of corrosive verdigris.

This animated, oddly Biblical tapestry was as far removed from Haverholme and its religious concepts as the planet Mars.

Denys caught the train at Mombasa station at 4 o'clock the next day. From the coast the train draws away inland and upwards to Nairobi 5,500 feet above sea level, Mazeras is crossed first, its lush vegetation thick with coconut palms and banana trees, then later, the contrasting Taru desert. There scrub, cruel and thorny, springs from the red earth. The sunset comes almost too quickly in Africa, lowering itself upon the obstinate, untamed bushes, effacing within half an hour all views. This makes the newcomer impatient for dawn to see the splendour of the plains, pitted with narrow game tracks and dotted with the animals themselves.

In those days the train stopped while passengers dined at the small 'dak' bungalows, built at intervals along the 'iron snake' leading to Nairobi. Out they would get to stretch their legs and meet fellow travellers. New impressions, the alien sounds of the first African night, its unfamiliar smells, generated a friendliness common to new immigrants and were shared with excitement. Cicadas seemed to drill into the darkness. Fireflies signalled to each other in minuscule bursts of light. At daybreak, the most impressive sight of all is awaited: the great mountain Kilimanjaro. If the clouds deign to expose its snowy reaches they are bathed in a rosy suffusion as the sun comes up.

Denys came to love the sun with its basking warmth, to long for it when away. He suffered horribly from the cold, and Essex remembers, as an adolescent, going to say goodnight to him in his room at Weldon, to find him swaddled and hunched in a thick Shetland shawl over his pyjamas. From now on he frequently complained of the English climate on his visits home.

Just before Nairobi the Athi plains are reached, rolling pastures of silvery green seem to unfold endlessly. Here and there the sun shines through a veil of grass seeds to catch the curve of a low hill. Daylight reveals great herds of gazelle, among them giraffe and ostrich grazing peacefully. The giant birds resemble pert chorus girls in dull feathers. The abundance of wild life in 1911 is legendary. To the uninitiated the first glimpse was of disbelief. Dark herds of buffalo roamed ponderously while the lesser plains game darted about, flicking their scuts, constantly driving off the maddening flies. Others stood gazing watchfully across the plains with luminous eyes, beyond the grape-blue outline of the Ngong hills.

Nairobi had grown at the railhead haphazardly, a haste mirrored by its scruffiness, not helped by the tall blue-gum trees which towered above the patchwork of tin roofed shacks with an unkempt look.

But if it was ugly and unpromising to the urbane eye its novelty and the many divisions of race and creed made the amalgam fascinating. The rickshaws symbolized a certain decadence while the devout missionaries rep-resented religious hope for their hedonistic passengers. Above the motley characters the peculiarly red dust drifted up from the pot-holed streets – if the dirt tracks could be called streets at all. The first sight of a native woman walking with a bottle on her head with the unconcern of an Ascot belle in the latest creation from Paris is amazing to the European eye.

Denys stayed at the Norfolk, the Claridges of Nairobi, which announced its amenities with great pride in the only newspaper: 'Suites of Sitting and Bedrooms. Private Villa Apartments for Safari Visitors. High Class Cuisine. Billiard Room. Special Terms for Settler Residents. Spacious Grounds. French Laundry. Hairdresser', and luxury of luxuries, 'Hot and Cold Baths always Available'. Among his fellow guests that week were the Marchioness of Donegal, General and the Hon Mrs Peters, Mr and Lady Margaret Loder, Major Armstrong, Count and Countess Chorinsky and four guests who, like Denys, became well known Kenya personalities: Captain J. Riddell, W. Zimmerman, D. Russell-Bowker and A. C. Hoey. Lord Kitchener had just left.

Great excitement was caused that week by the number of antelope seen wandering round the township. As *The Leader* explained, 'like March hares, Kongoni appear to go mad at this time of year and their vagaries cannot otherwise be explained unless it is in the scare of lions'.[7] While in the social column it noted that Count and Countess Chorinsky 'have been at the Tana [river] and had a record bag among which are counted a 53½" buffalo and a 49½" buffalo, a black-maned lion and 23 other species'. The measurements refer to the span of horn from tip to tip.

Denys wasted little time in Nairobi. Impatient to see more of this extraordinary land of contrast he made arrangements to look at a farm for sale up-country. He went as far as Eldoret where there was a tiny settlement on the Uasin Gishu Plateau – commonly known as 'Sixty-Four', the distance in miles from the then railhead, which only went as far as Londiani, and consequently the survey number. This area was freshly opened up and was then

expected to be one of the principal centres of coloniz-
ation. Land values were soaring with each new influx of
settlers so that time became an important economic
factor. Denys, given to swift decision, bought a farm at
'Sosiani', as Eldoret was then known.

With a shrewdness which became characteristic he
went into partnership with a pioneer who had already
established himself in the district, Herbert Wreford-
Smith. The land though fecund was uncultivated, but
they planned to grow flax on the farm which was traversed
by the Sosiani river. Wreford-Smith owned a flourishing
transport business plying between Londiani and Eldoret
which was an additional asset to the partnership. There is
no record of where Denys found the money, though
Essex Gunning remembers he had inherited a small legacy
from a relation along with a piece of land in Norway. For
the most part his finances remain a mystery. Thereafter
he earned his living through dextrous trading.

Herbert Wreford-Smith also owned Sosiani Store in
partnership with MacNab Mundell. They were Official
Brokers, Auctioneers, Produce, General and Hardware
Merchants, in short, true pioneers able and willing to
turn their hand to anything, to grasp fortune as it came
their way. There were fifteen British and Dutch residents
already in that area engaged in very primitive hunting
and farming. Like MacNab Mundell and Wreford-Smith,
Denys realized the potentialities of the country and before
long he invested in the little trading store when it acquired
the dignity and importance of becoming the Post Office.
Of wattle and daub it was almost certainly the strangest
building in which His Majesty's mails were ever handled.
The mails, such as they were, were conveyed between it
and Kipigori by native runners. Elspeth Huxley in one of
her many books on Africa wrote of Denys and this
particular process of communication: ' . . . once, when

he was on safari in the very farthest, wildest regions, many days' march from contact with mails and telegraphs, a cable from London forwarded by relays of runners with cleft sticks, caught up with him in the bush. Its content was brief. "Do you know George Robinson's address?" Back went the reply as it had come, by relays of runners travelling for weeks with cleft sticks. It was even briefer. "Yes." [8]

The Sosiani Stores, which did a roaring trade for miles around, was actually best known for the little bar hidden away at the back of the premises known as 'The Rat Pit'. At three o'clock one morning its door was broken down by someone with an urgent thirst and when it was not replaced for a whole year the few white settlers helped themselves to the stock of beverages whenever they pleased and left payment either in cash or IOUs. Not a cent was lost nor was the sporting trust of the proprietors towards their customers taken advantage of in any way. On another occasion 'a big burly man with a very strong personality that was destined to effect great influence in Kenya, arrived at Mr Mundell's store calling authoritatively for a table and chair and established himself on the verandah and proclaimed with éclat that the local branch of the Standard Bank of South Africa was there and then opened!'[9] He was J. C. Shaw.

Here in The Rat Pit, directly behind the Standard Bank, the local population sat and gambled while their ox-carts and buggies were loaded with nails, canvas, twine, paraffin, flour or ammunition and sufficient supplies to keep the purchaser going for the next month or so. The little gatherings broke the monotony and the great distances between human contact. A meeting with friends whose common problems could be helped by an exchange of views broke the fatigue of a journey, and destinations were always uncertain then. The caravan road between Eldoret and

Londiani was hazardous at the best of times and its travellers lay at the mercy of the weather.

Increasingly groups of ox-wagons – albeit sporadic – crossed this stretch, loaded to the brim with settlers and their chattels. These small cavalcades of brave families had purchased land, putting their faith in the totally unknown in exchange for a possible fortune. Pioneers had increased notably since Sir Percy Girouard became Governor in 1910, and the passage of new immigrants had prompted the Hon Berkeley Cole, a settler who had followed his brother Galbraith in 1906, to set up a small hotel at Londiani.

Berkeley Cole's partner in this venture was another enthusiastic settler, Bertram Francis Gurdon (better known as Lord Cranworth), who had fallen in love with the country in 1905 when, despite the most basic conditions, he immediately brought his wife and young family out. Travellers could be stranded for days at Londiani, depending on the state of the road across the Uasin Gishu Plateau. It was little better than a cart track and in the rainy season totally impassable. The idea of the Londiani Hotel seemed so good to the partners in theory that they also set up a similar hotel at Nyeri which they called The White Rhino, but in practice the hazards of running a small hotel were trickier than either had imagined. The bar made splendid profits when the road was transformed into a muddy red-river by the rains but the debts incurred for vast rounds of drink on the then thriving 'chit system' were high and very often unpaid. There were only three resident Europeans in Londiani at the time and they could hardly support the hotel with their thirst.

Naturally the bar was our most prominent feature . . . an extremely attractive one . . . when newly erected also a dining-room and sitting-room and perhaps a dozen bedrooms, some in the main building and some in separate huts. The latter were the more to be recommended. The worst feature of the wooden house, is that sound travels through the walls and one bitter complaint from a lady who spent most of the night listening to the two occupants of the adjoining room discussing herself, her clothes, her family and her probable morals. She had not apparently had sufficient initiative to retaliate in kind . . . if you were anywhere near the bar you could not expect to get any sleep until a late hour. Later some of the wood warped which made privacy even more precarious.[10]

At the Londiani Hotel the bills were more often settled than at the Nyeri one. At least the defaulters had no alternative but to travel back along the same route and this gave the proprietors a chance to extract payment. The White Rhino suffered badly because the Central Line could be reached via Rumeruti and invariably was. This venture ran at a terrible loss and Berkeley Cole and Cranworth were forced to sell out in a couple of years.

Denys broke his journey at the Londiani Hotel and at Soysambu, Lord Delamere's estate overlooking Lake Elmenteita. This was the beginning of his close friendships with the people he later introduced to Karen Blixen, who immortalized them in *Out of Africa* and *Shadows on the Grass*. 'D' as Lord Delamere was called by friends, and his wife Florence lived in a knot of Kikuyu rondavels, traditional red-mud huts, thatched, primitive and of the cheapest possible construction which served as their home. Florence died when she was only thirty-four, but her wit and courage lived on in many people's hearts. Famed for her hospitality, she was one of the many unsung women who struggled beside their husbands as they established those first farms. She was Berkeley and Galbraith Cole's sister and like them she was red-haired and determined, but they all suffered poor health. Florence and Berkeley had defective hearts and Galbraith was the crippled victim of arthritis. Before it bedevilled his life, he had trekked over the Rift Valley escarpment in 1904 when he first came to Kenya, by completely dismantling his wagons at the bottom of the escarpment and carrying them piecemeal to the top. He then reassembled them and went on his way. He was the first white man to reach Thomson's Falls after the explorer who gave his name to them twenty years before. Indefatigable, hard, undaunted by fate, his nature is explained by a man who worked for him for four years, the author and philosopher Llewelyn Powys: 'God with his clumsy grip can break his back but never his spirit. Haughty, arrogant, reckless, magnanimous, it goes to its doom asking no mercy.'[11] Like most of the pioneers the Coles and the Delameres were imbued with a tenacious courage which accepts defeat and tries again. It is true that land was bought cheaply by people of great wealth. But as they grappled with problems, watched great herds of imported, pedigree cattle dwindle with new viruses which they could not counteract, the coming to terms with nature's stern rules was an arduous and sometimes hopeless process. It took a special brand of perseverance to cope with disappointment. Flocks of sheep which had taken years to rear were wiped out by heartwater, crops suffered drought, and if the herds were enormous so were the losses when rinderpest took its toll. Later when the pickings were rich they were abundantly rich, but in the beginning resilience was the pioneer farmer's sole resource.

Like Denys, Berkeley Cole was an adventurer at heart 'whose spirit chafed unconsciously at convention and discipline'. He 'carried himself extremely erect with a little Artagnesque turn of the head to the right and left, the gentle motion of the unbeaten duellist'. Berkeley's farm on the lower slopes of Mount Kenya took up most of his time, but he was also the Elected Member of the Legislative Council for Western Kenya for five years. He pressed for, and achieved, better rail communication in that area and urged the Government to recognize the need for African education. This motley pair – Denys towered above Berkeley – resembled old Elizabethans shadowed by their blackamoors when their personal Somali servants, Billea and Jama, followed behind for the white men flung their Somali shawls about their shoulders in a way that suggested the flow of cloaks. In Africa, Denys and Berkeley lived at the leisurely pace of a forgotten era, in strange contrast to their kindred need for the excitement of the unknown. Berkeley's weak heart impinged on his life to the extent that he felt he should not marry. But it was said that he kept a Somali mistress at the Somali settlement of Ngara, just outside Nairobi and conveniently situated on the road to Muthaiga Club. It was he who was mainly responsible for the building of Muthaiga Club, where Denys and Karen Blixen would first properly meet. One evening in an unusual outburst of respectability Berkeley had declared that he was 'sick of being treated like a pig at the Nairobi Club'. On the tide of this outrage Muthaiga Club was born, and when it was built underlined a social split in the young community. Nairobi Club was associated with the Government Officials who viewed 'the settlers' with the suspicion the élite accorded them.

Within four weeks Denys had travelled hundreds of miles, purchased land, formed a partnership and met the leading personalities of the Colony. He was firmly convinced of the country's bright potential and his future in it.

One of his favourite Welsh haunts had been Ystumilyn Marshes, a desolate and beautiful stretch upon which a chain of pools lay scattered, like huge forgotten pearls. It was renowned for its wildfowl, and in this place he had found peace when it was becoming apparent that freedom, space and independence would become mainsprings of his life. His ever-increasing need for a sense of infinity must have been realized when he looked over the brim of the Great Rift Valley for the first time. It is an incredible vista of rock, sky and space lying 2,600 feet below. The extinct volcanic hills lie unscathed by time, bleached by a merciless sun. Upon their unconquerable faces, the ancient tears of lava have fossilized in their course. In the Rift, the deceptive mirages are dispelled only by immense violet shadows from the clouds floating against its lid of cerulean blue. The extinct volcano of Longenot emerges, seems to lord it over the lesser peaks, a colossus set to guard the lower plains and the game which nibbles and manures the vanilla-pale grass. Into these grasslands three lakes are set, Naivasha, Elmenteita and Nakuru, the two latter trimmed in pink by their dense flamingo population. A smell of soda hangs on the air, from the crusty mineral lying on the margin of the brackish water. This ingredient is essential to the birds' diet; they scan the water-surface for plankton and strange creatures which intensify their colour. Beyond Nakuru stands the Mau summit crowned with its dark cap of richly foliated forest and in between the undulating farmland of Njoro. Against this panorama the birds whirl at twilight removing the band of pink colour from the gunmetal mirror of each lake to beat the air with their wings. First they melt into the sunset sky then, turning, reappear, paler and banked in sharp relief against the promise of rain-filled clouds.

Clouds in Africa have an importance unimagined in England. They are not threats but herald a deluge for which farmers scan the horizon weeks before they arrive. The smell of rain over a dusty plain in Africa is as intoxicating as a happy seduction. There are two wet

seasons known simply as the 'long' and 'short' rains.*
When they start all people, even townsmen, rejoice in
the promise of rebirth. Crops will flourish and cattle
fatten before the sun rules once more. They are essential
for economic survival and must penetrate a ground which
will have to endure four more months of dry weather.
Then the parched earth will crack again in silent supplication for the next essential downpour.

Denys had fallen under Africa's spell. It is the allure
of a mysterious woman whose magnetism beckons yet
defies all reasonable explanation. Her moods may fluctu-
ate with the wind, sometimes balmy, dazzling or cruel
but never dull. The taste for Africa gets under the skin.
So Denys began a lifelong affair. He would leave again
and again for months at a time, but like a wave whose
sole destiny it is to flow back he would return. His
wanderlust could be given free reign without fear of
saturation. He never seemed to tire of exploring her
crevices, of trying to learn the secrets of her vast, earthy
metabolism or of crossing her deserts on foot. His
mother's antecedents had been seafarers whose incessant
wanderings had taken them across the world on water.
In Denys lay the same dark restlessness which tugged at
the soul. He was a nomad, an itinerant aristocrat and
heroic vagabond. Perhaps a little of the illegitimate blood
of Margaret Finch – Queen of the Gypsies who died at
Beckenham in 1740 – was responsible for his wanderlust.
She 'after travelling over various parts of the kingdom
during the greater part of the century settled at Norwood
whither in her great age the fame of her fortune telling
attracted numerous visitors. From a habit of sitting on
the ground her chin resting on her knees the sinews at

---

* Long rains, early March–June; short rains, mid November–mid
December.

length became so contracted that she could not rise from that posture. After her death they were obliged to enclose her body in a deep square box. She died at the age of 109 years.'

It has been said that throughout Denys's life Toby tried coaxing him to return to help to run the estate but was unsuccessful. Many felt that the second son's abilities had fallen on stony ground. Lord Cranworth's view was similar: 'with his vast talents he might doubtless have made a success in public life, but it just bored him. I remonstrated with him in later years for his apparent lack of ambition and the more than partial burial of his great talents but he was quite unrepentant and pointed out that one had but one life and that he reckoned that few people had had more out of it than he . . .'[12]

As an inherent migrant, Denys was fascinated, felt an affinity with the Maasai tribe at once. Later he came to know them well after setting up a series of trading stores in their reserve. It is difficult for the European with an eye for beauty not to be impressed by their lithe bearing. Their coiffures, intricately plaited under a lacquer of red mud, the coating of ochre smoothed over their burnished limbs, give them a sculptural quality. Denys believed that they had reached their cultural goal through their warrior spirit, refusing in their dignity to either accept or give tenderness. He found that the smile with them was rather an expression of triumph than of greeting. Habitual thieves of cattle, their arrogant bearing seems to have been fused into them through their diet of milk and blood. It has produced strong bones, healthy teeth and ability to walk great distances. Their indolence of bearing ratifies their fearsome reputation. Like weird human storks, they can stand on one leg, the other tucked behind its knee, for hours. So impressed was Denys by the shape of their feet that, after some scrutiny, he decided that square-toed shoes should be worn to cultivate the same highly desirable standard in Europeans and proceeded to have all his shoes, by Peals of London, made to specification. These were 'entirely straight along the sides and quite square at the toes'. Topsy's son Michael remembers the day when he bumped into Denys on his last visit to London outside Harrods: 'One could not forget that tall figure in the dark-blue town suit and black Homberg hat, wearing a Shetland shawl over his shoulders and highly polished, what seemed to me, boats on his feet.'[13]

The Maasai proved their manhood through directly confronting and slaying a lion with only a spear for protection. Exposure to such danger has deprived them, in a sense, of the ability to show sympathy. Lord Delamere though a fiery man indulged their covetousness despite losing many cattle in their raids. Their cunning amused him; he came to his own terms with them and they loved and respected him in return. Galbraith Cole was less tolerant of their marauding stealth. When he caught three Maasai skinning one of his sheep he arrested them and killed one as he tried to flee. The stock thieving on his farm had increased and he was provoked into taking the law into his own hands. He was tried for manslaughter and acquitted, but under a direct order of the Secretary of State in England was subsequently deported. It was the result of his honesty and moral courage. He had refused to perjure himself at his trial. When Karen Blixen lectured at Lund University in 1938 she gave an example of Galbraith Cole's unswerving conviction, which a man of less fibre would have easily betrayed. Like the Maasai he had killed, he paid his price without question:

The Judge said to Galbraith, 'It's not, you know, that we don't understand that you shot only to stop the thieves.' 'No,' Galbraith said, 'I shot to kill. I said that I would do so.'

'Think again, Mr Cole,' said the judge. 'We are convinced that you only shot to stop them.'

'No, by God,' Galbraith said, 'I shot to kill.' He was then sentenced to leave the country and, in a way, this really caused his death.

But this case lived for a long time afterwards among the natives. I often heard them talking about it and they called Galbraith Cole, 'Debr Lao'. 'Debr Lao,' they would say, 'He had but one tongue in his mouth.' Cattle die, kinsmen die, in the end we ourselves die. One thing I know that never dies: judgement on the dead.[14]

Galbraith Cole's heroic honesty was typical of the greatness which Denys expected of his friends, a standard to which he rose himself with a complete lack of all sham. When Karen Blixen speaks of being 'blessed with heroic friendships' – three were undoubtedly Denys, Berkeley and Galbraith.

Slim, handsome and as vain as ebony peacocks the Somalis were the other tribe. They were born traders and kept a wily eye on the main chance. They were easily distinguishable to the untutored eye by the colourful turbans which marked their religion. This headdress avowed their orthodox Mohammedanism. Their erect, haughty bearing made them unacceptable to many settlers, but Denys found he admired their unservile attitude in the same way as the Cole brothers, Lord Delamere and later Karen Blixen did. Denys's Somali servants became indispensable to him; he trusted them as friends and faithful retainers. He knew he could look into their dark intelligent eyes and expect a response of equality, for their Arab ancestors had infused in them a sombre pride of race.

Before leaving Nairobi Denys opened an account at the Standard Bank of South Africa which also served as a temporary postal address. The shabby embryonic town was a strange pot-pourri of unconvention struggling against itself in an attempt to conform to standards which were alien to its climate and conditions. Normally a small but bustling centre of trading with one station and a couple of hotels it became overloaded with guests on race weeks, accommodating the great incoming tide of settlers in tents. In this informal atmosphere gatherings naturally turned into parties. Some people could only get to Nairobi once a year, so it is not surprising that boisterous humour often got out of hand as the picaresque characters competed for attention to sustain the hilarity. Elspeth Huxley, who grew up in the country, gave an accurate description of the town that would develop into a capital city:

. . . it looked like some humdrum little South African 'dorp' straggling rather listlessly in the sun and occupied for the most part of the year by a handful of European Officials and storekeepers, a mob of Indians packed into the insanitary and smelly bazaar and a drifting population of all breeds of natives. Two or three times a year it would suddenly fill with tattered settlers in broad-brimmed felt hats and revolver holsters. At such times there was something of the eighteenth-century spirit about the place. Aristocrats in fancy dress (or so their costumes would appear to a visitor fresh from England) paraded the streets or lounged over their drinks on the verandah at the Norfolk hotel . . . there was a certain robustness about the evening carousals in the bar which carried the traditions of the tavern.[15]

On Saturday, 22 April 1911 – two days before Denys's twenty-fourth birthday – it was announced in the 'local rag' as he called *The Leader,* 'The Honourable Denys Finch Hatton, who has now left for England, has purchased a farm in British East Africa and will shortly return to take it up.'

In complete contrast to the scene he had left behind Denys now rejoined the English circus of social events. Those two years prior to the First World War were prosperous and gay. Perhaps they were spawned by an uncanny instinct that it could not last, for the frivolity was almost ominous. Denys plunged into this frenetic whirl on his return. He attended the Coronation of King George V on 22 June 1911 at Westminster Abbey with his parents, Topsy and Toby. Margaretta was now expecting her first child.

There was a surfeit of parties and balls that summer because of the Coronation and the release from official mourning. Two or three parties a night were the rule rather than the exception. In contrast to more formal entertaining – like Denys, Muriel could be relied upon to be different – she and Artie and Sir Philip Burne-Jones gave an unconventional soirée in his house in Egerton Crescent. The guests, 'only about two hundred and fifty', had been asked to 'a small jolly' which proved to be a harmless bohemian frolic held in a suite of chairless and flowerless ateliers. After the pomp of the Coronation functions it was found refreshing . . . the distinguished guests sprawled upon rugs on the floor and helped themselves to beer from the barrel wreathed in green hops; the men smoked churchwardens while the more advanced women lit cigarettes and all joined 'in a free and easy manner' in the choruses of popular songs. There followed Miss Maggie Teyte and other soloists, a Greek mandolin band and finally a most unbohemian Gunter supper of langoustine, quails, ortolans, red caviar and vintage wines. The '*Daily Chronicle,* under the headline 'QUEER SOCIETY PARTY SUPPER FOR DUCHESSES SERVED ON THE FLOOR', described the evening as 'different', 'remarkable' and at moments decidedly 'comical' only refraining from overt disapproval in consideration for the distinguished company present. It was hard work keeping up with the Burne-Jones's![16]

Denys probably found it diverting enough but at the

same time the silliness of 'the season' must never have seemed more ridiculous in his eyes. The women were expensive dolls, gowned elaborately in ruffles, feathers and jewels, their sole aim to attract a wealthy and noble husband. Their conversation seemed to consist of inconsequential chatter. Fashion led the assembled herds by the nose as entertainment grew in lavishness. One band for an evening seemed meagre – three more fashionable. The days of wine and roses were in full bloom. Music drifted from illuminated balconies into elaborately staged gardens. In a happy nimbus of sound it encircled the innocent young men without a hint of the slaughter which would follow.

During 1911 the theatre, ballet and opera were bursting with new and exciting productions which were not to be missed. Granville Barker's memorable production of *A Midsummer Night's Dream* was one that stood out in importance for Denys. The costume designer had, with a stroke of genius, literally painted Titania, Oberon and the fairies in gold in order to differentiate on sight between them and the ordinary mortals when they appeared simultaneously on stage. It was a simple ruse but it created an instant fairy-tale element which was remembered by all who saw it. He also went to a particularly fine production of *Don Giovanni* by Mozart.

The Russian Ballet's effect and influence on London in 1911 is well known and was no figment of the imagination. Diaghilev, Fokine and Nijinsky excited balletomanes with *Petrouchka, L'Oiseau de Feu* and *Le Sacre du Printemps,* and these productions were a revelation to audiences who, at best, had been used to rather stereotyped performances of classics, such as *Giselle, Swan Lake* and *Coppelia.* The earlier appearances of Pavlova resulted in Arnold Haskell's declaration 'The story of the English ballet begins with Pavlova and Diaghilev.' These Russians were fine grist to Count Benckendorff's diplomatic mill. As Ambassador he became the most popular foreign envoy in London and his country's influence was felt even in the world of fashion – Cossack hats and exotic Siberian peasants began to appear in the social and artistic scene as these ballets, backed by Stravinsky's music, burst into life on the stage.

Denys was deeply impressed by Nijinsky's rendering of the straw-filled puppet Petrouchka. Nijinsky captured all the impossibility of sloughing off his jerky dependence on the strings. *Petrouchka* became his best loved ballet and one of his favourite pieces of music as well. When the twelve-inch records became available he bought a set and gave them to Karen Blixen as a gift. Like 'The Rime of the Ancient Mariner', the ballet *Petrouchka* became synonymous with Denys and after Toby learned of his brother's death he forbade the playing of the music in his house. It evoked too many keen memories. He was so emphatic about this particular piece of music that through the deprivation Toby's daughters linked it with Denys as well.

That season Denys also went to *L'Après Midi d'un Faune,* choreographed by Nijinsky but set to Debussy's soft melodious music. It was in direct opposition to the violent concatenation of Stravinsky as the composer strove to bring to life the full implication of the pagan spring festival, but Denys equally enjoyed romantic music which stirred the emotions.

Though when he sang madrigals Denys might have come from a world of knights and paladins or from the age of Elizabeth when lavoltas and galliards were danced at the Inns of Court, his real taste was for the most modern creations of his day. Karen Blixen told how they disagreed on this subject:

Denys and I, however, did not agree in our tastes. For I wanted the old composers, and Denys, as if courteously making up to an age for his lack of harmony with it, was as modern as possible in his taste of all arts. He liked to hear the most advanced music. 'I would like Beethoven alright,' he said, 'if he were not so vulgar.'[17]

All the same their search for the wild and the new had been a separate but common quest. Denys had 'seen what men of imagination cannot help seeing in a dream of a country like Africa'.[18]

How Denys's parents reacted towards his intention to emigrate is not known. If Nan felt a natural maternal alarm at the prospect of seeing her favourite son (an acknowledged bias) only for brief and unspecified intervals in the future, she would never have disclosed this private fear. Her intuitive ability will have enabled her to realize that clinging or the slightest hint of possessiveness would drive him away for even longer periods. After his first departure, her letters indicate an intense but curbed affection. While she calls him 'my very very dear one', 'my dear heart' or 'my own mite' she seems in the very next phrase impelled to apologize for this intimate indulgence, lest the hollowness she experiences at the thought of another leave-taking shows. As a compensation Topsy is mentioned: – things wouldn't be so bad if she were nearer but 'that cannot be helped either'. Henry probably recognized the futility of trying to dissuade Denys from his course. All three children respected their father but their deepest affection was unquestionably for their mother. They were concerned about Henry's health; the comments Nan makes regarding her husband's ability to come to terms stoically with his lack of robustness display relief rather than spontaneous warmth: he never seemed to be free of aches and pains for very long: 'I am glad you thought father better in himself and hope he really is so' Nan wrote to Denys 'but he does *try* to be so cheery and hide his troubles and aches.'

On 2 August 1911 Margaretta's first child, Christopher, an heir, was born which brought great joy to the entire family. Topsy, still pining for Ossie, had shown that she would never marry anyone else. At the end of the year arrangements were made for her marriage to Ossie when he returned to England. Neither parents of the families attended. And it was Margaretta who sweet and independently American insisted that Toby gave his sister away despite the overriding disapproval of the Winchilseas. Essex recalls that Toby was 'very much the future Earl that day' asking rather affectedly 'Essex, have you seen my wife?' to whom naturally she was always 'Margaretta'. But his pomposity was felt by outsiders rather than within the family. This remark contrasts strongly with his witty explanation to his children of their social standing, 'But for a series of unfortunate deaths, all you children, would have been born to an impoverished parson.' Flora Finch Hatton, another cousin, and Denys completed the wedding party. Ossie and Topsy were married on 5 February 1912. No wedding photographs were taken outside the church. Somehow one of the newspapers learned of the event and published the following bleak report in its social column:

Mr Osmond Williams, who was one time in the 19th Hussars, and Lady Gladys Finch Hatton were married very quietly on Monday afternoon. No invitations were issued for the wedding and there was no reception afterwards. The bridegroom is the eldest son of Sir Osmond Williams. The bride is the only daughter of Lord and Lady Winchilsea and sister of Viscount Maidstone.

Topsy secreted this clipping amongst her papers but it was not discovered until after her death. She had always disliked her official names and the stark, if correct, announcement did not endear them to her any further. A studio portrait, one of the few not made by her mother, taken on her wedding day shows a remarkably serene woman. Her beauty bears the lasting quality of marble and oak. Any private bitterness or hurt is hidden by a wistfulness. There is no feeling of revenge in the sweet full curve of her mouth. Perhaps her mother's private sympathies for their absence from the marriage had softened any resentment she could have harboured. Nan's parents had both been dead at the time of her own wedding, but if she understood her daughter's disappointment she would never have gainsaid Henry's decision. Ossie and Topsy 'spent a bitterly cold honeymoon in Bude in Cornwall' and shortly after left for Canada where Ossie worked as a ganger on the Canadian Pacific Railway. In 1913 Ossie went to Mexico which was not considered safe for Topsy, who, expecting her first child, returned to stay with her parents-in-law at Castell Deudraeth to await its birth. Denys left England towards the end of 1912 to settle in British East Africa.

6
1912–1914 – Pioneers

In September 1912 a large banquet was held in London at the Connaught Rooms in Great Queen Street to honour the outgoing Governor of British East Africa, Sir Percy Girouard KCMG and to welcome his replacement Sir Henry Belfield CMG, who would take up his official position at the end of the year. His term was held until his retirement from the Colonial Service in 1917. Denys and many of the prominent settlers and overseas investors were guests and it was at this gathering that an association of settlers was first suggested. Another meeting was held, at Carlton House, Regent Street, attended by Viscount Cobham, a director of many estates in Kenya, Lord Cardross, Lord Hindlip, Major the Hon H. Guest, Dr W. S. Rainsford, Captain Ewart Grogan, Captain Riddell, A. C. Hoey (after whom a bridge was named beyond Eldoret*) and Denys among others, where the East African Association was formally founded. The object and aim of the association was non-political and was intended to keep fellow settlers and prospective investors in touch commercially and socially while visiting London.

When Denys returned to Kenya there was considerable dissatisfaction fomenting with the Government – mainly because the Land Bill discussions had dragged on since 1909 yet had still not reached any satisfactory conclusion. Lord Delamere's chief concern was to gain recognition from the Colonial Office of the settlers' undeniable right to vote and elect their own representative in the Legislative Council.

* Hoey's Bridge – now Moi's Bridge.

As there were now about six thousand already resident it seemed a not unreasonable desire and this was the issue throughout 1913. Lord Delamere felt it to be an imperative move and the second step towards ultimate self government. Had the War not intervened there is little doubt that he would have succeeded in pushing through the grant of electoral rights as early as 1914. It was clear that the British Government was not developing the country rapidly enough; its system could not cope with the rapidly changing conditions as droves of settlers arrived. This tardiness created the atmosphere of discontent and apprehension to which Denys returned in November 1912 so unlike the happy-go-lucky mood of the land which he had left in early 1911.

On 14 December *The Leader* announced: 'The East African Exploration Development and Mining Co Ltd is now in the process of formation. The first directors are G. K. Watts (Chairman), Mr D. Beaton, Mr A. E. Fawcus, the Hon Denys Finch Hatton, Mr S. H. Montagu and Mr Fred Marquodt (Managing Director).' The following Saturday the same newspaper carried a rather grand half page vertical advertisement declaring the Capital of the Company to be 450,000 Rupees and inviting the public to buy shares. The venture attracted a good deal of comment and attention and the paper backed the purchasers of the advertising space with an editorial on the subject. It seemed that like the Avunculus Denys was going into the mining business.

Bulletins reiterating the worthy nature of the company's Managing Director appeared spasmodically, and it is clear from the reassuring tone of these items that the rush for shares had fallen considerably short of expectation. While the articles aimed to allay public suspicion they seemed to have the opposite effect; the political climate was unsure, and when the investors were unforthcoming the intended seriousness of the enterprise dropped to that of a music hall farce. By 1 February Mr Marquodt had 'located and pegged a very important mica proposition, a few stations down the line . . . not far from the rail.' The mounting pressure of apprehension brought about a face-to-face interview in *The Leader* which concluded on a note of rising hysteria: 'It would seem that the opportunity of acquiring an interest in the East African Exploration Development and Mining Company is one which is riskier to ignore than accept.' The overall feeling of doubt, however, was not unfounded. A month later the surprising doom-filled headline appeared 'THE LATE FRED MARQUODT' – the company never got off the ground before the gentleman 'upped and died'. The edition which published Marquodt's Obituary on 24 May 1913 also reported, in the 'Local and General' gossip column: 'We learn that Mr McMillan has sold his "Parklands" property including the dwelling house and grounds to Mr Finch Hatton – we understand the price he paid for it was £4,000.' The strange coincidence was that after Denys's acquisition of the McMillan property, the McMillans purchased 'Chiromo', the house where Lady McMillan told Karen Blixen of Denys's death.

Denys must have written to Julian Grenfell inviting him to Kenya for he planned to join him there in the summer of 1914. Nicholas Mosley comments: 'In 1912 it was still the dream of young men to get out of England; but they carried their patterns of mind around with them. Neither Julian nor Denys Finch-Hatton [sic] quite escaped these. Finch-Hatton survived the war but . . . He was like Julian an individualist, and often haunted by depression.' The New Elizabethans may have been more intellectually inclined than Denys but oddly enough it was he they most admired: 'The only member of the Eton and Oxford Group who seemed to be making much of a life for himself was Denys Finch Hatton'. He, as Julian described it later, 'made a lot of money by shipping timber from his place in Norway and bought a palace from an American millionaire where he entertains the countryside on champagne and caviar.' Julian thought him 'such a tonic after all these deadbeats'.[1]

That May, the roads around his new property at Parklands a little outside Nairobi were 'ankle-deep in mud'. The long rains transformed all the byways into red quagmires. The potholes were so bad in Government Road in Nairobi itself that a bunch of irate settlers indicated how they felt about street maintenance by planting a banana tree in each small crater on its surface! So heavy was the deluge that the Norfolk Hotel provided its rickshaw boys with heavy canvas capes, which at least afforded some protection and which distinguished them from the five hundred or so rickshaws plying for trade in the town. Motor cars were a rare sight (there were about half a dozen in the entire country) among the camels, ox-carts, mules and horses intermingling with the pedestrian traffic in the oozing thoroughfare known as Sixth Avenue.*

Denys did not even consider hunting as a source of income until 1925. When he hunted it was for the love of the sport, the fascinating and wily art of tracking and outwitting the game which held him in suspense. Besides, he enjoyed the solitude of the bush. The fear of what to many men would have seemed isolation was with him a love of infinite space and peace. The same year that he became a 'white hunter' in the accepted sense of the term he was also appointed an Honorary Game Warden. He favoured photographic safaris and was one of the early activists against wanton killing. He wrote articles, which appeared in *The Times,* on the joy of stalking game with

* Delamere Avenue now renamed Kenyatta Avenue.

a camera as opposed to a gun. In a series of heartfelt letters to *The Times* he deplored the misuse of licences and the unmitigated slaughter revealed by rotting debris the vandals left behind. His repeated complaints to the appropriate Game Wardens had proved ineffectual (in Tanganyika* they were virtually ignored). He hoped that, by publishing his findings in *The Times*, he might coerce the officials concerned into taking immediate preventive action. His anxiety was chiefly directed at the use of cars 'from which the wholesale destruction of game had been taking place for . . . three years'. To this extent Denys may be considered a valuable protagonist of better methods of game preservation, in support of those actively establishing game reserves and hunting control, such as Akely, Percival, Stevenson Hamilton, Hobley, Hingston and the Chief Game Warden in Denys's time, Archie Ritchie. Had Denys lived longer he would undoubtedly have been drawn into the working field of conservationists.

An American client, Frederick B. Patterson, whom Denys took on safari in 1927 tried to discover how Denys had become involved in professional hunting: '"How did you get into this sort of thing?" I asked him in the middle of our first conversation. He smiled amiably, "Oh, it just sort of happened if you know what I mean." '[2] Patterson had been surprised at the breadth of Denys's knowledge of Africa. After he returned to the States he published a book on their shared experiences. The veneration which Denys consistently elicited comes across as Patterson recalls their first meeting in London.

It was the Duke of York who recommended me to my white hunter, the Hon Denys Finch Hatton. I could have found no better person for the job. He was a true sportsman, a fine

---

* Now Tanzania.

companion and a fair dealer with the natives: a man fearless in
the face of danger and most considerate at all times. I met
Hatton in London on my way out. There we discussed what
African game I had better try to get and where was the best
place to look for it. I found Hatton a walking encyclopaedia on
such matters. He could rattle off the names of all the animals
and tell to a quarter of a mile where one could find them on
the map. He knew their habits and how to circumvent their
treacheries.[3]

It also 'just sort of happened' that Denys became
involved in cattle trading with the Somalis. But his
reputation for this occupation, as usual, became magnified
via the grape vine:

Finch Hatton had been on a trip to Arabia . . . he had bought a
million cattle at half a crown a head and was about to drive
them, presumably miraculously, across the Red Sea and sell
them for £150 per head in Nairobi. Then he was going to grow
cotton. Don't you think it would be great fun? They have never
grown any there yet, and the soil is most unfavourable to the
growth of the same, but that only really makes the experiment
more interesting.[4]

The quantity of cattle and money and the venue may
have been distorted by distance but the spirit, the sense
of surmounting challenge, remains true. The Somalis also
drove horses from the Northern frontier to sell.

Two of Denys's friends, the indefatigable Dr Burkitt
and a tea planter from Kericho called Butterfield,
indulged in horse coping as a sideline:

When Dr Burkitt knew that Butterfield was coming to Nairobi,
he would assemble as many horses as possible from which to
make selection outside his consulting room in the road. Butterfield would be mounted on these horses and made to trot up
and down in front of the Post Office, while Burkitt watched
their action. He secured an old bowler hat from Denys Finch
Hatton, inside which he would rattle a stick in true Irish fashion,

to make the horses trot. Then the bargaining began. All medical work would be held up for this event and patients who arrived would be invited to join in the fun.[5]

Denys now purchased a substantial piece of land at Naivasha on which to ranch cattle and attempt to grow pyrethrum. The Eldoret farm was being successfully managed by Wreford-Smith and he was obviously not needed to assist but 'While he naturally took up land, farming was not in his blood and he infinitely preferred trading . . . as a source of income. The very best of company, he was the life and soul of any convivial gathering at which he was present. Yet he was far from dependent on company, and, as an instance had just previously to the War been entirely by himself on a six-months cattle trading trip to Italian Somaliland and he told me that he never enjoyed six months more.'[6] Somalia was to become one of Denys's favourite places and he was on his first visit to bring back cattle and ponies in 1913 when a new pioneer arrived in Nairobi, he was Baron Bror von Blixen-Finecke.

This aristocratic Swede comments 'Nairobi in 1913 was more like an empty old anchovy tin than anything else. I cannot say that the town and I fell in love with each other at first sight – even if I was received in the kindest manner by, amongst others, the multi-millionaire McMillan who then reigned over a wide demesne in East Africa.'[7] Even since Denys had arrived Nairobi had developed. The owners of the old Stanley Hotel had acquired land and built a much larger hotel which they called The New Stanley.* It had just opened and diametrically opposite

---

* The original owner, Mayence Tate, had thought that when she sold the first Stanley Hotel she could retain the name for the next development. But there was a court case over the matter and the name New Stanley was the outcome of the matter.

stood a new three-storey building, the first to be elegantly
constructed in stone, called Nairobi House. Like all
travellers to Nairobi, which means in Maasai 'the place of
sweet water',* Bror von Blixen arrived by rail. Like
Denys he was twenty-five years of age, of noble lineage
and an adventurer who would become a fine hunter; but
there the similarity ended. They both had charm but
were otherwise entirely different. Baron Bror von Blixen-
Finecke had

. . . the most delightful of smiles, caught, like a strip of sunlight
on a familiar patch of leather, well-kept leather, free of wrinkles
but brown and saddle tough . . . gay, light blue eyes rather than
sombre grey ones and his cheeks were well rounded rather than
flat, his lips were full and generous and not pinched tight in
grim realisation of 'What the wilderness can do'. He talked and
was never significantly silent. He generally wore a khaki bush
shirt of 'solario' material, slacks of the same stuff and a pair of
low cut moccasins with soles – or the vestiges of soles. There
were four pockets in his bush shirt, though he never carried
anything unless he was hunting, then only rifle and ammunition.
He never went around hung with knives, revolvers, binoculars
or even a watch. He could tell the time by the sun and if there
was no sun he could tell it anyway . . . He wore over his closely
cropped hair a terai hat, colourless and limp as a wilted frond.[8]

Blixen's own words are best used to describe what
brought him to Africa. In their ebulliency is a good
measure of the man himself:

I was born at Näsbyholm in Skåne, the family estate where the
best shooting in Sweden is to be found . . . the freedom of the
fields and woods, the joy of wandering at will, without compul-
sion and observing wild things and scenery causes a strange
singing of the blood – it is a tune one never forgets, which no
school discipline can drive out of one's mind . . . The daily
grind of the classroom cannot fail to be minor hell for a boy

---

* Literally translated, Uaso Nyarobe means 'The cold river'.

who has grown accustomed to roam about under God's sky without let or hinderance. Master and pupil parted without tears of regret . . . Alnarp. Things went better there but . . . I was always on the wrong side when there was a difference of opinion as to the solution of a disciplinary problem. I learned so much about agriculture that they were bold enough to make me responsible for the tenant farm of Stjärneholm, on the Näsbyholm property . . . the result was not bad and it is not inconceivable that I should have been living in Skåne a well to do farmer . . . if something rather important had not happened – I got engaged to the girl whom I called Tanne, but whom the whole world was to know many years later as Isak Dinesen, authoress of *Seven Gothic Tales*. The human imagination is a curious thing. If it is properly fertilised it can shoot up like a fakir's tree in the twinkling of an eye. Tanne knew the trick and between us we built up our imagination in which everything but the impossible had a place. The promised land which hovered before our eyes was called Africa and our golden dreams included a large farm teeming with fine fat cattle. . . . Behind our imaginings lay a reality named Aage Westenholz an Uncle of Tanne's. This excellent man was among other things the owner of a rubber plantation in Malaya. 'What would you say for exchanging Stjärneholm for my rubber plantation . . .' he asked me one day. It was like asking a horse if he would care for some oats. I accepted gratefully without a moment's reflection. At twenty-five one does not search one's conscience anxiously before undertaking a new task; tapping the trees for rubber was no more difficult than cutting rye when it is ripe, and the rubber market was particularly good at the time . . . our confidence was unbounded. The fact was that another uncle, Count Frijs, had just come home from a big game hunting expedition in Africa and was so brim full of impressions of his trip, that he could hardly talk of anything else – which was quite understandable . . . 'A well run farm in East Africa just now ought to make its owner a millionaire' Mogens-Frijs said one day. 'More quickly than a well run rubber estate in Malaya?' I asked. Quite possibly.' 'In that case,' I said and I looked at Tanne. She nodded. And so our course was clear. For Penang we read Nairobi; for Malaya, East Africa. We would milk cows and grow coffee . . . and the only anxiety was how I should be able to put all the money in the bank . . . after voluminous correspondence with Africa, a farm of seven hundred acres was bought. The gold mine was ours. All we had to do now was extract the rich ore.[9]

Bror's reaction to Mombasa was enthusiastic. 'Is there not a flavour of negro mysticism about the name itself? . . . after the uniformity of the sea one was almost blinded by the swarm of fantastically variegated Oriental costumes.' But the beauty of the country and the diversion of the train journey was dominated by his acquisitive hunting instinct, 'With all respect to the scenery there is something which is bound to make a greater impression on the traveller – the fauna. . . . Opposite me . . . on one trip sat a gentleman who did not seem very much at home in Africa. He looked longingly at his gun, which lay in the rack.'

Bror soon discovered that the gold he was seeking could not be made out of stockbreeding. 'Gold meant coffee. Coffee growing was the only thing that had any future; the world was crying out for coffee from Kenya. I . . . sold my seven hundred acres and bought instead from Mr Sjøgren the Swedo-African Coffee Co, owning 4,500 acres near Nairobi and about the same near Eldoret.'[10]

Bror von Blixen-Finecke was actually a second cousin of his bride-to-be, Karen Christenze Dinesen. She was almost two years older than her fiancé and it was intended that she should join him in British East Africa when he had settled his business transactions. It was, in fact, a curious relationship from the start, based on the shifting, deceptive quicksand of an unrequited love. Her brother Thomas Dinesen told Donald Hannah, who has written an impressive literary criticism on Karen Blixen, that 'she and her husband had utterly different temperaments, and the measure of their divergent interests is perhaps sufficiently indicated by a remark she made years later

that Bror Blixen was a person who did not know whether
the Crusades dated from before or after the French
Revolution.'[11]

Karen Dinesen was born on 17 April 1885 at Rungstedlund near the little fishing village of Rungsted which lies
fifteen miles north of Copenhagen, close to the sea. She
had one older sister Ea and a younger one called Elle
and she was always known by her family as 'Tanne'.
Ingeborg Dinesen, her mother, then produced two sons,
Thomas who was to become closest to Tanne in their
maturity and a last child, Anders. The father of these five
children, Wilhelm Dinesen, was a restless military man
whose active brain gradually drew him into politics:
eventually he became a member of the Danish Parliament. That he had settled down at all to domestic life is
surprising: his adventurous nature had involved him in
several European wars including the Prusso-Danish
conflict of 1864, but before that he had lived in self-
imposed exile among the Chippaway Indians in the
Middle West of America. A personal tragedy had been
the motivating force behind his need to shun his immediate world in favour of the absolute necessity of survival.
This was the death of the girl he loved, Agnes Kral- Juel-
Vind-Frijs, who had died at the age of eighteen while on
holiday in Italy. Although she was Wilhelm Dinesen's
cousin, he had hoped to marry her. As he lived and
learned the Chippaway's creed, their fundamental culture
and the skills of trapping he eventually came to terms
with his loss sufficiently to return to Denmark, where he
married and reconciled himself to a dull but orderly
family life. He was comfortably off and for a while ran
their small farming estate but they could not be considered landed gentry despite a collection of noble
relations who looked upon this branch of the family as
upper middle class Danes.

Tanne was devoted to her father, who encouraged her to join him on walks when he would tell her some of his adventures and talk to her at great length on the role of nature, stressing and explaining the goodness of the less civilized races and enlarging on his own family background which fired her imagination. Although he refused to take himself seriously as a writer, Wilhelm Dinesen's creative drive produced several works: *Jagtbreve (Letters of the Hunt)* which was published in 1889 then, three years later, *Nye Jagtbreve (New Letters of the Hunt)* under the pseudonym 'Boganis' and a more serious work which was based on personal experience entitled *Paris Under the Commune.*

It is not difficult to imagine the trauma which Tanne, an intelligent and adoring daughter, experienced at the age of ten years when she learned that her father had committed suicide by hanging himself in a room of the boarding house in Copenhagen which he inhabited when the Danish Parliament was in session. Though the reasons for this drastic action are clad in a certain amount of mystery, Tanne believed as an adult that her father had discovered he was a victim of a venereal disease and had chosen death incisively rather than bring shame on his family, but these suspicions have not been substantiated. The scars caused by this immense shock ran very deep in Tanne for she had lost not only a father, but the one person in the household who had sensed, with all the empathy of an artist, this one daughter's above-average intelligence. He had guided, personally nurtured her needs from the first moment of recognition. When asked at the age of seventy by Parmenia Migel, a biographer, if she remembered the event Tanne replied – 'It was as if part of oneself had also died.'

After her father's death the atmosphere in the home was dominated by women. Her mother donned sombre widow's weeds, which she wore until she died, and proceeded to meet the unenviable challenge of bringing her children up without a husband. But Ingeborg Dinesen did not undertake her task alone. Her mother lived conveniently near Rungstedlund, at Folhave which now became their second home. Her sister Bess Westenholz a spinster with a will of iron reinforced by her belief in the Unitarian Church of Denmark, also lived at Folhave. It was with this maiden aunt that Tanne had her first head-on collisions of temperament in adolescence. In a speech that Tanne made in New York in 1959 she touches on the life she led as a child and the need in those days, to create one's own amusement:

Children of my day, even in big houses, had got very little in the way of toys. Toyshops were almost unknown, modern mechanical playthings which furnish their own activity, had hardly come into existence. One might, of course, buy oneself a hobby horse, but generally speaking an individually selected and individually knotted stick from the wood upon which imagination might work freely, was dearer to the heart. We were not observers such as children today seem to be from birth and on their own, and not utilisers, as they are brought up to be, we were creators. Our knotted stick for all working purposes, in appearance and as far as actual working horse-power went, came nearer to Bucephalos and eight-hoofed Sleipnir or to Pegasus himself than any magnificently decorated horse out of a smart store. In a similar way we liked to christen an enterprise or epoch . . .[12]

Tanne started writing small stories as early as seven years old and often her recreational hours were absorbed by the production of sketches and simple plays she had written for her brothers and sisters who, like herself, loved to dress up and pretend to be other people. Before long the stuffiness of her aunts with their suffocating ideas fed by books on either politics or religion became oppressive. So claustrophobic in fact that Tanne's 'discovery of Shakespeare' at the age of fourteen is remembered by her as 'one of the first really good events in my life'. In retrospect she explains, 'I was like my father's family, my grandmother did not understand me, she liked my sisters better. I was very unhappy as a child.'[13]

At the age of seventeen she had a year's private drawing tuition through which she gained entrance to the Royal Academy of Fine Arts in Copenhagen. Later despite continued opposition from Aunt Bess she persuaded her mother to allow her to go to Paris to further develop her sketching and painting. Her underlying need during this period when she found she was torn between painting or writing, was for freedom. She longed to break away from her matriarchal surroundings and petit bourgeois cautions against everything enjoyable. Her taste of real liberty came through being allowed to go with Ea, her eldest sister, to Oxford in 1904 to an establishment run by a Professor Carlyle. There with other foreign students who had also come to perfect their English they spent the summer. Tanne had learned the language from her mother but it was here she gained the Oxonian assurance that was later reinforced by life with Denys and exposure to his literary tastes and classically scholastic English background.

When she was fifteen Tanne went to stay at Frisenborg Castle in Jutland. Here and at Katholm where her cousins lived, she was given a glimpse into a different way of life, one which contrasted sharply with the earnest ambience of Rungstedlund. Her Dinesen cousins filled their time with parties, hunting and endless streams of visitors: she felt that void of inadequacy – so painful in adolescence – the lack of suitably fashionable clothes compared to theirs, emphasized by the insouciance with which they pursued their lives. 'They were quiet in their manners and least of all self-centred but they radiated turbulent content, and their pride in being alive was almost vainglorious.'[14] When the time came to return to Rungsted Aunt Bess Westenholz's Lutheranism and grim disapproval for Tanne's flights of fancy and vanity only stressed the difference between herself and her nobler cousins and made her yearn all the more for pretty clothes and the immutability of the lives they led.

In Paris she became friendly with Mario Krohn, an art historian who was to be one of her first intellectual male friends. He encouraged her literary talent and tried to dissuade her from diffusing her creativity and concentrate on writing. He even offered to marry her and publish anything she wrote but Tanne refused though she still maintained a close friendship with him and saw him frequently in 1910. When she returned to Denmark, as though reaching out subconsciously for her dead father's approval, she became engrossed with the Frijsenborg and Skåne set. Clara Kral-Juel-Vind-Frijs, who was the sister of the girl Agnes her father had loved so passionately but lost, had married Baron Frederick von Blixen-Finecke of Näsbyholm, Skåne; and their twin sons Hans and Bror now became the object of Tanne's romantic interest.

Hans was a spectacular young man. He had once won a horse race at Klampenborg, flown his own plane across the sound to Malmö and won another race there all in the same day. But Hans took no notice of Tanne and it was Bror who courted her with persistence until eventually he became the metaphorical door through which she could escape the irritations and cautious prudence of her family. Ironically it was her barely concealed admiration of his brother which provoked Bror's tenacity and brought about her final acquiescence after his third proposal. Had she accepted with alacrity, been an easy conquest, he might well have lost interest before it was too late to

retract. Parmenia Migel suggests that class-consciousness
and grandiose ideals instigated her strange compromise
with reality for 'the satisfaction of being addressed
"Baroness".' But Judith Thurman, another writer, puts a
more delicate construction on what might be dismissed as
pure snobbism:

Had they [Tanne's family] actually had a title she would perhaps
have been spared a certain yearning, a certain reverence for the
aristocracy which could be disconcerting at times – like a mole
on a particularly fine nose. It gave her a curious pleasure to
hear herself addressed as Baroness or to hear a great name
announced in her drawing-room . . . And her idea of nobility
was of 'largeur' rather than 'hauteur'. But she had a poetic
delight in the names.[15]

Karen Blixen's own recollections of those days are
recorded in a speech she made in 1959 before The
Academy of Arts and Letters in America. Obviously
these views had by then had time to gain perspective and
some of the origins will have dimmed. It is doubtful if her
feelings on the subject of sailing to Africa were either so
palpable or so unblurred, for at twenty-eight she was still
imprudent enough to marry a man she did not truly love.
Perhaps as much as to free herself she married on the
rebound. But at seventy-five she was wiser and more
articulate. When she talks of 'Mottoes of my Life' which
had influenced her since childhood her memories obviously contain a modicum of accuracy. As she takes each
'motto' and examines it, it is as if, having rediscovered a
trunk of discarded but once-loved clothes, she is holding
each to the light or against her own body allowing her
memories to flood back with great freshness of colour
and texture, as each garment comes up.

On the covers of old exercise books, now found in attics,
mottoes in red and blue pencil come and go. The one that most

often returns is a highly laudable maxim: 'Essayez'. Others in Latin which I have unfortunately now forgotten. 'Still I am unconquered' or 'Often in difficulties, never afraid', I take to have been written down in some kind of bitterness or rebellion against higher powers sitting on the child – our governesses most likely, for I have never gone to school but we were taught . . . at home, to which circumstances I owe, I think, the fact that I am totally ignorant of many things . . . Other mottoes, . . . I take to have been picked for the sake . . . of the beauty of the words themselves. 'A sicut aquila juvenescam'. It will, . . . I think have been at seventeen, I got my own way and was studying painting at the Royal Academy of Copenhagen; that the richness of possibilities consolidated into one and that I chose for the first real motto of my young life, 'Navigare necesse est, vivere non necesse'! The audacious order was flung from the lips of Pompeus to his timid crew of Sicily which refused to set out against the gale and the high seas to bring provisions of grain to Rome . . . To me myself it became natural to view my enterprise in life in terms of seafaring, for my home stands but a hundred yards from the sea . . . The Paradox of Pompeus, for a paradox it is, . . . to young people who think in paradoxes, comes as the true, clear logic of life. No compass-needle in the world to me was as infallible as the outstretched arm of Pompeus. I steered my course by it with unswerving confidence, and had any wiser person insisted that there was no earthly sense in my motto, I might have answered 'Nay, but a heavenly!' and have added perhaps 'and a maritime.' Before this . . . gale I was swept, on the eve of the first World War under all plain canvas to Africa. I was at that time engaged to my cousin Bror Blixen, . . . In the true spirit of Pompeus 'It is necessary to farm, it is not necessary to live,' we set out.

Genuine simplicity of heart at all times, will call upon expected indulgence in the governing powers of the Universe . . . The Goddess [Nemesis] might have answered me 'All right, have it your own way. Sail on and give up your idea of living' this I take it was her answer to the Flying Dutchman. To me her answer came differently 'Bless you, you fool! I shall set your sails, I shall turn your wheel and I shall have you sailing straight into life.' Under the flag of my first motto I sailed into the heart of Africa and into a Vita Nuova, into what became to me my real life.[16]

Like a bird fluttering bravely against the golden wires of a cage, she had yearned for freedom. All her longing is captured in a poem called 'Wings' (*Vinger*), and if she prayed for the sort of liberation conjured up by the images in that verse, she was in for a monumental shock. Thomas believes that this was probably written when Tania was about eighteen.

'Written in Danish it reads as follows when translated:

> In its prison my heart sings,
> Only of wings, only of wings,
> None of the world's lovely songs,
> Echoes so sweetly in the ear.
> Even birds, born in a cage
> Soar freely in dreams to the skies,
> And in its prison my heart sings,
> Only of wings, only of wings.
> High are the heavens, deep and limpid,
> A well of blue, sparkling with light,
> High will I soar without dizziness,
> See the earth fade behind and sport with the winds,
> In summer the rose unfolds its buds,
> And the world is wondrously beautiful.
> And in its prison my heart sings,
> Only of wings, only of wings.'[17]

It is said 'When the Gods wish to punish you they answer your prayers' and in Tanne's case this axiom amounts to one of blistering prescience. She had set herself a challenge and this was the masochistic proposition of sharing her life with a man who, at best, could be compared to one of her later mirror images. Her acceptance of this extraordinary premise parallels her father's compromise with life. The intricacies of his and his daughter's relationships resemble a complex, finely embroidered piece of seventeenth-century stump work. It is as if a wall-hanging has been prepared in the space of two generations as a legacy and warning for a third. The similarities and contrasts between Karen Blixen's first affairs of the heart and her father's bear the mark of a private and delicately preordained template on a canvas which only they could see. It is as if Tanne's father, with his foreshortened life, had been unable to complete the colours and highlights of this three-dimensional tapestry and had only had time to fill in the monotones, and that Tanne, with her vivid imagination, must take up the threads for him and sew over the canvas in bright twines of possibility.

Perhaps because of her immaturity, the subtlety of nuance which would become apparent later in her writing was too impulsively defined at the age of twenty-eight, almost as if in her haste to continue where her father had broken off, she must impose bizarre whims upon his pastoral background.

Observed in retrospect, Bror seems curiously like a ghostly forerunner for one of her characters in the story 'Roads around Pisa' the first 'fabliau' in her first collection of stories *Seven Gothic Tales*. He was like a distorted looking-glass reflection about which she was to write with an accuracy which could only have been learned through bitter experience. Describing the foolishness of belief in mirror images she wrote: 'So your own self, your personality and existence are reflected within the mind of each of the people whom you meet and live with, into a likeness, a caricature of yourself, which still lives on and pretends to be, in some way, the truth about you. Even a flattering picture is a caricature and a lie.'[18]

In that same passage is enfolded all the infinite regret she felt about her marriage even after twenty years. 'Love ought to be even more so. It ought to mean, along the roads of life, the companionship of another mind, reflecting your own fortune and misfortunes, and proving to you that all is not a dream. The idea of marriage has been to me the presence in my life of a person with whom I could talk, tomorrow, of the things that happened yesterday.'[19] The emphasis of her 'ought' is as wistfully sad and deprived as her opening lines from *Out of Africa*: 'I had a farm.' Throughout that book, just as it is mirrored in her works of fiction, she has shown herself a master of paralipsis.

When Tanne met Bror in Mombasa she was only moving towards the reflection of the man she loved. That was her paradox. Probably for this reason, she has never chosen to give the world a physical description of her husband or anything which would substantiate his existence as if she had recoiled from the recollection. That he married three times is sufficient proof, when his many girl friends and mistresses are taken into account, that women found him irresistible, but it is difficult to see him through Tanne's eyes or mind, before the crushing disillusion manifested itself. In January 1914, Bror had thoughtfully arranged for a Somali servant, whom he had employed and who spoke English to meet his future bride at Aden. His name was Farah. The gesture was considerate and imaginative – on a par with Tanne's exotic concept of Africa itself. She has since written long passages of adulation on the merits of Farah Aden, her major domo. One of the clearest starts her book *Shadows on the Grass:*

As here after twenty-five years, I again take up episodes of my life in Africa, one figure, straight, candid and very fine to look at, stands as doorkeeper to all of them: my Somali servant Farah Aden. Were any reader to object that I might choose a character of greater importance, I should answer him that that would not be possible.[20]

Tanne's journey on the D.O.A.L. ss *Admiral* had been a pleasant one as it steamed through the Mediterranean, the Red Sea and on into the Indian Ocean. She had become friendly with one German passenger in particular, General von Lettow Vorbeck. He like Tanne was engaged to be married but he was sailing away from his fiancée Frau Margarethe Walbrath whereas Tanne was sailing towards the end of her betrothal. Prince Wilhelm of Sweden was also on board but mainly the passengers consisted of British settlers. None of them (except perhaps the General) could foresee that in eight months they would be at war. The safari which Lettow Vorbeck and Tanne planned to make together and the offer she made to find breeding mares on his behalf would all come to nothing and all that Tanne would be left with apart from her happy memories of the voyage was a signed photograph of the General and the cold British shoulder of suspicion.

When she disembarked at Kilindini on 13 January 1914 Tanne must have made a romantic picture. Her entourage consisted of Farah, Dusk, her elegant Scotch deerhound, and Bror who had rowed out to the ship to greet her. In those days there was no quay and the last hundred or so yards of their journey had to be undertaken in a small rowing boat. Tanne was not very tall, which subtly emphasized Dusk's rangy conformation as he clung to her side, while Farah walked suitably distant (the dog is considered unclean by Muslims), tall and ebony coloured in her wake. January is one of the hottest times of the year in Mombasa so that the slight breeze which teased her long skirts was welcome: with her future husband at her side, the prospect, under the heat of the great brass sun, can only have seemed optimistic.

They were to be married the next day by the Swedish Consul Åke Sjögren at the District Commissioner's office and Bror's best man was to be Prince Wilhelm of Sweden. Bror had travelled down from Nairobi with the Swedish Consul from whom he had purchased their land at Ngong and with Sir Northrup McMillan and Mr Stanley the traffic manager of the Uganda Railway as part of the official welcoming party in honour of the Prince. Happily all the arrangements had coincided with Tanne's arrival; now they had also been invited, as man and wife, to join the Royal party on the last stage of the Prince's journey – on the special train placed at his disposal by the Governor Sir Henry Belfield.

The glamour, not usually associated with civil marriage ceremonies, created by the wedding party making its way across Treasury Square to the DCs office on 14 January 1914, must have turned a number of inquisitive heads. The square itself was impressive with its central garden shaded by mango trees. Their leaves, dark and fleshy, seem too heavy to be stirred by a breeze; and in their lush stillness they are as precise as a painting by Henri Rousseau. The solemnization of their marriage must have far exceeded any of the notions in Tanne's imagination at that time. After the formalities they wandered down the gentle slope towards the sea to look at the stout walls of Fort Jesus. In this small but distinguished gathering she must have had the feeling that she was walking within one of her fantasies. For nothing could contrast more sharply with the adverse conditions of the European winter she had left behind. Before her stretched a warm sea, clear and blue and delineated only by an endless white ruffle from the waves as they broke over the secret coral reef; thick baobabs[21] abounding with superstition, the barefoot pedestrians, robed in kanzus or half naked, and the babble of strange tongues gave the whole atmosphere the insubstantiality of dreams.

There were no dhows to set her imagination sailing but there was the plaintive, sacred call of the muezzin from his mosque in a bid to bring the faithful to prayer, five times a day. No music or images embellish Islamic devotions. Shoes are cast off in humility, prayer mats unrolled and heads bowed in submission to the will of their God. The sound of the muezzin is weird, haunting to the Western ear, penetrating the mind long after it has been heard for the first time.

Bror and Tanne entrained for Nairobi at four o'clock the following afternoon. The first phase of the journey has been described by Bror (though not this occasion) in his book *African Hunter*:

. . . the train journey between Mombasa and Nairobi is a matter of eighteen hours. . . . For the first bit one can give oneself up with a quiet mind to the pleasures of the table in the dining car, and drink a bottle of African burgundy, which is not so bad by any means, for the scenery is not worth looking at – dreary bush which can give no pleasure to anyone . . . but at the break of dawn you must be on your legs with eyes wide open! Kilimanjaro – [22]

The usual stops were made but Bror and Tanne benefited from the rather more gracious meals and wines served for a royal palate. On arrival at the station in Nairobi, the party was welcomed by the Governor's ADC. Captain Winthrop-Smith. Bror and Tanne were staying at the Norfolk Hotel but were included in the invitation, at Prince Wilhelm's request, for the luncheon party given by Sir Henry Belfield at Government House. If Tanne remembers meeting there a tall, English noble-man whose hair seemed to have receded rather prematurely there is no record of it. As a bride of only three days it would be understandable if she overlooked his presence. Yet, she would one day write of him with an authoritative confidence in her knowledge of his forebear, Sir Christopher Hatton:

If Berkeley were a cavalier of the Stuarts' day, Denys could be set in an earlier English landscape, in the days of Queen Elizabeth. He could have walked arm in arm there, with Sir

Philip or Francis Drake. And the people of Elizabeth's time might have held him dear because, to them, he would have suggested that Antiquity, the Athens of which they dreamed and wrote. Denys could indeed have been placed harmoniously in any period of our civilisation, 'tout comme chez soi' all up till the opening of the nineteenth century. He would have cut a figure at any age, for he was an athlete, a musician, a lover of art and a fine sportsman. He did cut a figure in his own age, but it did not quite fit in anywhere. His friends in England always wanted him to come back, they wrote out plans and schemes for a career for him there but Africa was keeping him.[23]

It was not until almost the end of the War that she wrote and told her brother Thomas, in Paris, that she had at last met her perfect ideal of a man. After the luncheon, *The Leader* reported, 'the Prince and his party proceeded to the residence of the Honourable Denys Finch Hatton, who has kindly placed his house at the disposal of the Prince'. The gesture takes on an air of courtliness suggestive of the laying down of an Elizabethan cloak for the Queen to tread upon. If Tanne had had time to read the 'local rag', which is dubious, she might have been amused to note that she was mentioned in two different columns in the same edition of *The Leader*. Under the 'Social Column' the copy ran 'The Baron and Baroness von Blixen-Finecke arrived in Nairobi on Thursday. They travelled from Mombasa with Prince Wilhelm on a special train and were among the guests of the lunch given by His Excellency in honour of the Prince.' The second appearance of her name occurred in the Shipping Section: amongst the list of disembarking passengers is mention of a 'Frau Karen Dinesen'.

The bulletin in the social column contains all the elements of the society depicted in *Seven Gothic Tales*. Shortly after they were published she explained her reason for setting them in another era: 'I moved my stories back into a really romantic time, when people and conditions were different from today. I could become completely free by doing this.'[24] Her notion of liberty reflects a feeling that not only had she voyaged out to a new life but had simultaneously sailed back in time. The pattern of life in Kenya then recalled an era of aristocracy and feudalism from before the Industrial Revolution. It is not unreasonable to believe that she experienced her first heady flight to freedom in the brief metamorphosis from 'Frau Karen Dinesen' to Baroness von Blixen-Finecke. The worlds conjured up in the images of those names are light years apart. She was rarely called Karen: to strangers she was known as 'The Baroness': those who claimed to know her and referred to her as Karen merely revealed their snobbish aspirations. To Bror she was always Tanne as she was to her family and immediate circle of friends until she met Denys formally in 1918 when he christened her 'Tania', the name she most used until she died.

Muthaiga Club was officially opened during the week that Tanne and Bror arrived in Nairobi. It was to become *the* social centre for dances and parties and offered 'all the recreations common to first-class clubs throughout the world'.[25] It boasted two motor cars complete with European chauffeurs, tennis courts, a croquet lawn, a golf course with a European instructor in permanent residence and 'a very spacious motor garage erected with up-to-date stabling occupied at present by the horses of our local sportsman's racing stud.'[26]

As soon as they were able, Tanne and Bror moved out to the farm. Their first home was an unassuming bungalow comprising four square rooms set in four thousand five hundred acres of land. It was not until 1917, when they acquired the Mbogani house, built from blocks of dressed Nairobi stone, with columns and shady verandahs, that Tanne began an unwitting period of gestation as the future author of *Out of Africa*. And just as she makes no mention of her husband in her book it also contains no reference to their marriage or their first dwelling together in Africa.

Immigrants may be divided into two basic categories: there are those who come to a country to give and others who come with the explicit intention of taking away as much as possible and in the shortest possible time. Tanne belonged to the former group and she now immersed herself completely in becoming a coffee farmer. With all the generosity of the true artist's soul, she stretched herself out willingly to meet the country on its own, sometimes harsh, terms. She reached for the advantages and tried to ignore its inadequacies, the scruffiness and the small irritating problems which so often punctuate an African day. Perhaps this very essence of giving it what emanates beyond the printed word from the pages of *Out of Africa*. Long after the book is closed it lingers in the mind, set apart from hundreds of other books which have been written about the same expanse of territory. In it she has embodied infinitesimal beauties of the mind which apply to race and creed and nature. These observations spring from an ineffable love and come from twenty years of sometimes harrowing commitment. Today the book is her posthumous act of generosity which will stand as an immortal witness to the depth of her perception. When writing of her father Georg Brandes* once commented: 'He loved war for its own sake with the love of a soldier and an artist . . . and thinks nothing embellishes a landscape more than soldiers fighting.' An inherent spirit led his daughter to believe with equal fervour that nothing embellished a landscape in Africa more than coffee trees in flower. In the chalk-white blossom lay the pollen of dreams and Tanne was a dreamer. One who was almost

* The Danish writer.

determinedly enraptured by all the new impressions flooding into her mind.

In those few months before the outbreak of war she learned to shoot, to farm, to hunt and to live as a wife. But Bror was a 'coureur' whose insatiable need for fresh conquest made him repeatedly unfaithful. At first she did not detect his infidelities but when she did the tremors of insecurity were both understandable and predictably disastrous in a marriage based on such slender means of survival.

Tanne's description of Nairobi is conciliatory 'All the same Nairobi was a town; here you could buy things, hear news, lunch and dine at the hotels and dance at the Club. And it was a live place, in movement like running water and in growth like a young thing.'[27] When a few pages further on she explains the solitude she so often experienced she is not referring to her married life with Bror, she is telling of a later period of her life when she was involved emotionally with Denys. 'At times, life on the farm was very lonely, and in the stillness of the evenings when the minutes dripped from the clock, life seemed to be dripping out of you with them, just for the want of white people to talk to. But all the same I felt the silent, overshadowed existence of the Natives running parallel with my own, on a different plane. Echoes went from one to the other.'[28]

In the husk of those interminable evenings lay the germinating seeds for the stories which would one day become *Seven Gothic Tales*.

7

1914–1918 – War

'Neither I, nor anyone else,' Bror wrote, some twenty years later, 'who lived through them, will ever forget the first days of August 1914.'

The day before the official declaration of war, a few Swedes assembled at Tanne and Bror's house in order to discuss their position in relation to the political situation. They were Erik von Otter, who was known as 'resase moja' (a Swahili epithet meaning 'one cartridge') because of his unerring aim with a gun, Helge Fagersköld, Nils Fjastad and Emil Holmberg.

Tension had been mounting for weeks and on 5 August Martial Law was declared. Although there were still only rumours to go by, their discussions were based on the premise that Sweden would sympathize with Germany. Bror remembers: 'We discussed our position in the event of an alliance between these countries coming about and agreed that the only thing we could do was to offer our services to England, our adopted country, with the reservation that we should be freed from military service if Sweden joined Germany.'[1]

Having decided on this rather delicate question, Bror and Erik von Otter bicycled into Nairobi the following day, to investigate further and report at the recruiting office which had just opened. They found the small town in an absolute turmoil. Nairobi House buzzed with rumour and had now become the centrepoint of enquiry. Perhaps its stone solidity rendered it the natural target for concentration, conversation and military gravity; everyone seemed to have forgotten Government House, the seat of Administration perched on the hill . . . round Nairobi House a seething mob of people boiled and bubbled, and as became a pioneer country the influx was armed to the teeth.

Some of it carried rifles, old shot-guns, or revolvers and bushman's friends. It demanded that it should be allowed to fight. In due course a gallant band of mounted warriors descended upon the capital. The spectacle was a never-to-be-forgotten one. Armed with long bamboo canes, upon which knives had been affixed and with fluttering pennants, making a brave show in the highland's breeze the 'Lancers' invaded Nairobi. The Lancers might have passed but what was one to say of the mules? And the donkeys? And the non-descript assortment of apparel. The stress, the tension of the first days of war, broke under the spectacle of this gallant band of Lancers and Nairobi laughed.[2]

The white population numbered about seven thousand, half of them able-bodied men. The Protectorate's sole military force consisted of one battalion of the King's African Rifles. There was no reserve of troops. Excitement quickened and brought more men pouring into Nairobi when the news seeped through from German East Africa that two British cruisers had shelled Dar es Salaam on 8 August. A description of the volunteers' extraordinary diversity of battledress is recorded by two of the recruits themselves:

They came in shorts . . . in breeches, in helmets, in stetsons, in double terais, high-laced boots, in shoes or puttees, in leggings, in tunics, in khaki shirts open at the neck displaying brawny chests. They arrived in buggies, on horseback, on muleback, on motor cycles, motor cars of every make, kind and age, push bicycles and ox-waggons, by train and on foot. Great hefty giants from the Uasin Gishu Plateau, Dutchmen . . . tall blonde Norwegians, Swedes, swart Italians, lean muscular British settlers all gravitated at the call. In due course The East African

Mounted Rifles was born. From the humble nucleus raised by the stalwart pioneer . . . Mr Russell Bowker, Bowker's Horse (or B squadron as it was to be latterly called) blossomed forth. There were mules, donkeys and racehorses for mounts; well bred and ill bred men for riders. This was part of the first line of defence. Sir Ralph Willies transferred activities from Nairobi House to Hunter's Buildings opposite the New Stanley Hotel, where the Nairobi Defence Force came into being. The army looked ridiculous and fought superbly – it took pianos and settees up to the front and went into action without any training.[3]

Bror enlisted with Bowker's Horse; Erik von Otter went into the East African Mounted Rifles and Denys joined Berkeley and his proud band of Somalis which came to be known as 'Cole's Scouts'. This fine-boned man, small of stature and capable of buffoonery to the point of overplaying his hand had persuaded eight hundred Somalis to offer their services to the Government. He assumed the 'complete brisk cheerful carriage and expression of an efficient young officer' and his understanding and sympathy now stood him in invaluable stead. The Somalis would prove ideal trackers through the experience of their sheer necessity to survive and unlike many of the volunteers they were used to the hardest conditions of the desert. Despite mettlesome command – or perhaps due to it – they found discipline was hard to accept and their arrogance eventually provoked mutiny. Lord Cranworth found that 'the Somalis loved drill and ceremonial, and we spent long hours, mounted and dismounted at machine-gun work, surely the dullest of all human occupations. They got fairly smart and efficient but fire discipline was the trouble. Once they began to shoot . . . their eyes lit up and they became almost unrestrainable.'[4] A crash course of training was necessary to instil some sort of army drill into these raw recruits who were established at a camp on Nairobi Racecourse.

Bror was commissioned by Captain Woosenam, Head of the Intelligence Department in Nairobi, to arrange communications between himself and Lord Delamere, who was patrolling two hundred miles of unguarded frontier along the German Masai border. He, Ture Rundgren, Nils Fjastad and two other Swedes were to keep the line of communication operating so that Nairobi was constantly fully informed. Motor cycles were used on the worst roads and native runners over more difficult ground. Extreme distances and hazards were initially overcome by carrier pigeons but these were found to be impractical in face of the law of nature:

They were troubled by hawks. If the pigeons encountered a hawk near home, they would turn back and fly for their lives, sometimes darting into their wooden tower so close to their pursuer that the hawk would crash against the wall unable to check its flight. One day two pigeons turned up completely plucked, as bare as roast chickens, from the hawk's attacks. They recovered and grew another set of feathers but in the end all the pigeons were killed in active service and communications had to be established by heliograph stations.[5]

Bror found his assignment rather dull, the only satisfaction being that he could guarantee 'the punctual arrival of letters'. Even worse in his opinion was that 'unluckily for me Woosenam was transferred . . . and I had to pay out of my pocket for the supplies I had obtained for the expedition'.[6]

The patrols were gruelling in the early part of the campaign. Lion abounded and menaced the messengers. Tanne displayed a remarkable act of courage when she defended herself, unarmed and single-handed, against two marauding lions. She was assisting Bror by running a sub-station at Kijabe – a relay point between the Masai German border and Nairobi.

Of necessity Lord Delamere was always on the move so that Bror's marches tended to be haphazard. On one occasion, when it became imperative to follow hastily, it was

. . . impossible to take the whole camp with us at once: I hurried on ahead while Tanne, my wife, took command of the transport wagon, drawn by sixteen oxen which had to follow rather more slowly. On the third evening just as they were preparing to pitch camp, there was a fearful disturbance among the oxen, which had been left quite alone for a few moments. Tanne hurried up and saw two lions, each of which had jumped on to an ox's back. It need not be said that the teamsters had disappeared like phantoms and my wife faced the two lions alone and unarmed, for through an oversight, the rifles had been carefully stowed away among the baggage. But she had the heavy stock-whip and with it she literally whipped the lions away from the oxen. My wife made light of this incident. 'What else could I do?' she asked. 'If I'd had a gun I'd have used it of course; but the stock-whip is not to be despised as you see.' One of the oxen had been so severely mauled by the lion in those few seconds that it died of its wounds, but my wife's care succeeded in saving the life of the other.[7]

When Tanne became a writer she touched on that incident, dismissing it modestly as 'one of my many great adventures with lions'. Through the perspective that time or distance bring to all things, she manages to transform the confrontation, reducing the heroism of the act to the point of distortion with slow descriptions of 'the smoke curling under the constellation of stars that came up from the East,' which dissipate the original, frantic sense of nightmare fear and the urgency she must have felt. She superimposes a dreamlike atmosphere on the episode and there is no hint of the paralysing moment of terror in the brief seconds before she took up the stock-whip in defence, like a cornered lioness herself grasping at her one means of survival. Nearly all those couriers encountered lion face to face but few acted with such bravado. One horrifying incident concerned a Boer called Postma, who was scouting for Lord Delamere, and who also showed great courage when he came upon five lionesses:

The horse shied badly and Postma got off and one lioness that had cubs came for him and got him down, biting him badly in one thigh and clawing him badly on the other. The lioness was dragging him along when he managed to kill her with his revolver. He was alone as he was riding ahead of his boys, but he managed to get his pony and made Morgan's camp. I have dressed the wounds and intend taking him to Nairobi via Lumbwa.[8]

Nils Fjastad wrote that report and showed an impressive example of Swedish endurance by bicycling one hundred and fifty-miles to the nearest station 'in a record time of twenty-four hours . . . a mule cart was sent out and the injured man's life was saved' – Fjastad's achievement is all the more admirable when one remembers that he was travelling across absolute bush.

It is possible that Tanne underplayed her experience with the lions because she associated it with a time of discomfort, she felt alienated and 'was somehow on the wrong side and was therefore regarded with distrust and fear by everybody'. In *Out of Africa,* she actually compares this aura of suspicion with the unease she felt encompassing her on the day of Denys's death, of which she is still ignorant. She obviously felt deeply shunned: 'This nightmare was in reality a reminiscence of the time of the war. For then for a couple of years, people in the Colony had believed me to be pro-German at heart.'[9] In fact there was not an iota of truth in the gossip but several human whims perpetrated by Tanne herself in all innocence now conspired against her. The atmosphere leading up to the declaration of war had not helped. From 4 August all cables had been censored, and German nationals and suspects arrested. Muthaiga Club had suspended their membership simultaneously. So it was hardly diplomatic to carry on her person a signed photograph of General von Lettow Vorbeck. Rather naïvely, Tanne had been persuaded by Farah to carry it on all journeys for he felt it might prove useful – even save her life – in the event of capture by the Schuzctruppe. While Bror was assisting Lord Delamere, she had also personally employed a young South African, whose surname was Klapprot, to accompany the ox-wagons. On a routine search this man was believed to be German and, because he failed to produce identification papers to clear himself, he was arrested in error. It was through his arrest that Tanne came to be in charge of the expedition when the two lions attacked her oxen. A final piece of evidence formed the ballast which convinced the English settlers of the rumour which was rife – that Baroness von Blixen-Finecke was pro-German. Just before the outbreak of war she had been negotiating the purchase of horses at Naivasha for General von Lettow Vorbeck and was arranging to send these ten Abyssinian breeding mares down to German East Africa by rail. Her final transaction had been prompted by the General himself, who reminded her of her promise, but the mares never reached their intended destination. Though the sale was finalized, the declaration of war decided the issue. Ruefully, Tanne admits in *Out of Africa* 'Still I could not get away from the fact that I had, at the time, been buying up horses for the German Army.'[10]

Those coincidental facts provided ample grounds for the patriotic observers, mainly women, to draw their own conclusions and they gave Tanne a wide berth which caused her much personal unhappiness. Their self-righteous discrimination was strengthened by the tone of the tune their men sang as they marched off, loyally to fight for their adopted country – a bowdlerized version of 'Marching to Georgia':

> Hurrah, hurrah, the standard of the free
> Hurrah, hurrah, the mistress of the sea
> Draws her sword to indicate her children's liberty,
> Death to the tyrant invader!

Such was the curtain raiser on the theatre of war in British East Africa. Berkeley and Denys with a handful of other officers moulded their band of pugilistic Somalis with determination into a viable fighting force. Grim reality soon replaced the vivid and slightly comic scenes of a pioneer community at war, caused by disorganized fervour as much as anything else. Soon the battles raged with the same violence encountered on the European front; many men were killed in action and others died of disease in quite deplorable tropical conditions which they were too ill-suited to surmount, either by training or birth. Four harrowing years and fifty-thousand lives later (double the number of men lost in the Boer War) German East Africa became Tanganyika but Tanne's General von Lettow Vorbeck eluded his enemies with the infuriating skill of the great soldier he was and even at the end retired undefeated. The Englishmen who fought against him acknowledged his brilliance and concluded that though he was severe he was a just man whom they held in their highest esteem as a General. As the British lumbered on in their pursuit of this arch enemy throughout the war, they were likened to 'a lepidopterist on the hunt, with holes in his net, for a butterfly which kept turning into a wild bee'.[11]

A trooper who, before enlistment and after the war was considered Galbraith Cole's[12] best farm manager, remembers seeing 'Denys escorting the Big Brasses round, always surrounded by maps, etc . . .' Lord Cranworth, who was with Denys, Berkeley, Erik von Otter, Donald Seth-Smith and Tich Miles in the East African Mounted Rifles, remembers that Denys could not have been less interested in 'sodjering' as he called it – 'he made no secret of the fact that warfare bored him to distraction but needless to say he made a success of it . . . never in my experience did anyone in his comparatively lowly position achieve such influence, more perhaps than any other member of the staff. Yet such was his charm that I never heard anyone grumble at his ascendancy.'[13] If warfare 'bored Denys to distraction' he broke the monotony that first Christmas, by hurling a few plum puddings requisitioned from the Officers Mess over the enemy lines. For this schoolboy prank he apparently received a smart rap over the knuckles though it did little to repress his sense of the ridiculous or his mirth tinged with cynicism at the idea of fighting during a season associated with 'Goodwill and Peace Unto All Men'.

Some time later, after the disbandment of Cole's Scouts, Denys fought alongside Major-General Reginald Hoskins while he was commanding the First Division under General Smuts. He had been the Inspector-General of the King's African Rifles in August 1913 and Denys greatly respected this tall (an inch smaller than himself) roman-nosed officer who took over from Brigadier Seymour Sheppard. He had been serving in France until, in 1916, he was chosen by the C in C, General Jan Smuts, to take over the First Division, Smuts knew him personally and trusted his judgement and knowledge of bush warfare. During an ambush at Handeni in 1916 when the Major-General's ADC was killed Denys saved Hoskins' life and it was this gallantry which allegedly earned him his Military Cross. Though he was mentioned in despatches there was no citation. Erik von Otter was awarded an MC during the same manoeuvre when they were trying to cross the Lukigora River. Denys subsequently replaced Captain McMillan as Major-General Hoskins' ADC and remained with him until he was posted to Mesopotamia near the end of the war.

From February 1915, the Germans had been successfully cut off from further supplies and reinforcements but the British desperately needed more men to hold this advantageous position. By May, Nairobi was seething with Indian troops and officers and by summer these were backed by battalions from Rhodesia and South Africa. Denys kept in touch with friends and family by letter as and when he was able. All his life he showed a complete disregard for the writing materials he used, irrespective of the recipient's rank or relationship. Graph paper, scratchy nibs, thick wax crayons, pencils, lined pages torn from cheap exercise books, headed vellum from Haverholme Priory, army issue economy paper which blurred and smudged on the application of ink or stationery from 'The Conservative Club', they were all the same to him. He used whatever came to hand and every bit of space on it including the margins. One of the oddest instruments for writing which he ever possessed was an almost phallic black pen with a one-inch retractable gold nib. It looked as if it could accommodate a whole ink-well of ink and was about eight inches long – resembling an obscene, if slightly obscurely designed, weapon of defence. It bore his own name, unhyphenated, and that of White's Club. It is almost impossible to tell whether Denys used the hyphen in his surname because he tended to run the Finch and Hatton on, either in indolence or haste. Essex Brooke remembers her grand-father becoming 'incensed when the hyphen crept into their name' and its use is something of an enigma though the present family, and the titular head, favour the spelling without the hyphen.[14] In *Burke's Peerage* the hyphen appears consistently but on the memorial plaque which Toby had engraved for Denys it has been omitted.

At the beginning of September 1915, he wrote to Kitty Lucas (née Catherine Bechet de Balan) in tardy response to a letter of hers earlier that year, announcing the birth of her fourth child and asking him to become one of its godfathers. The boy was christened Denys and he was delighted to accept the honour. In lurid, red ink and on flimsy lined paper, he describes to Kitty some of the problems he has encountered:

Nairobi
September 12th 1915

Dear Kitty,

I know you will forgive me for not answering your long and very acceptable letter of many months back. The fact is that I have been moving about a good deal since war broke doing patrol and scouting in this large and very difficult country. Most of the fighting has taken place in dense thorn scrub in waterless, fever-ridden country so that it has not always been too pleasant. The size of the country, we have a front of five hundred miles and a most vulnerable railway running through the thick brush country to protect, renders operations extremely difficult with the comparatively few troops which are at present available. If the initial attempt of the expeditionary forces had been success-ful, the Germans would have probably given in very soon, but unfortunately, as you know, it was a fiasco owning to over confidence. As it is now, they are rather pleased with themselves and are giving as good as they get. They have the advantage that their troops are African and know the country whereas the bulk of our forces are Indian, are unused to this country and go sick very easily. The Germans too have the advantage of short lines of communication along their border, whereas the border is a long way from our railway in most places. I am up here now to arrange with HQ for a scouting job in a new piece of country. One hopes that the war will soon be over as everybody's affairs are going to rack and ruin – But I do not wish it to finish before the Germans have had a taste of what they have given Belgium and France. I am much flattered at hearing that I have so distinguished a Godson. I shall have to present him with a German scalp to commemorate his birth. I was so sorry not to be able to go and see you when I was in England but I was tremendously rushed just at the finish and you insist in living in such an ungetatable place. The Russians seem to have been fighting a magnificent retreat and now news comes that they seem to be checking the Germans very successfully. The Germans must realise by now that they cannot hope to win in the end this time. Let us hope that we shall never give them a chance again. Well, goodbye Kitty and give my love to Denys Lucas and to his father, I hope we shall all meet again in happier days.[15]

Denys signed his name in full, a habit which he adhered to during correspondence throughout the war, possibly as a security measure.

His remark about 'conditions being none too pleasant at times' is a masterpiece of finchhattonymous understatement. Conditions were deplorable. There wasn't a field hospital within three hundred miles of the German East African border; when the rains were not teeming down the dust caused by the trampling columns coated the soldiers thickly and the land itself required taming before the enemy; the sick were victims of dysentery or malarial fever and in certain areas the stench from the bloated carcasses of the horses, oxen and mules which lay rotting where they had dropped, rose foully and clung to the air they breathed. Supplies were on the wane and the poor oxen, bitten by tsetse fly, were doomed to die. They were used to traverse land quite unsuited to lorries and necessity kept them between the traces to be worked till the last minute. Essential loads of boots and socks for the troops were the luxuries these pathetic and sickly animals carried. Across thick sand rivers, ten oxen per cart staggered beneath a load of two thousand pounds on their final march to death. The men, besides being tired and often hungry, were plagued by ticks, and 'all kinds of creepy crawly things imaginable, huge spiders, large lizards, puff adders and ants that bite and sting like hell . . . it keeps one cheerful. There are also lions, leopards, herds of giraffe, wildebeeste, wild boar, etc. It's a great country' commented one soldier.

A bewildering variety of topographical features impeded their progress; swamps, mountains and blistering desert belts had to be manoeuvred by the porters. Without the essential service of its Carrier Corps, the army could not move a yard. The European officers more than appreciated the importance of these lowly men, for the African forces were in no way concerned with the whys and wherefores of the campaign. They were inadequately trained but they made immense sacrifices in the common cause – none greater than the humble porters who died in large numbers without the glory accorded to askaris or soldiers.

Morale was low as disheartening news trickled through from Europe. Denys learned that the nucleus of his brilliant friends from Eton and Oxford had been obliterated in quick succession. All the stench and ugliness of war reinforced his belief in the brevity of life. Julian Grenfell died at Ypres, Charles Lister was killed at Salonika after being wounded three times. Patrick Shaw-Stewart (in love with Julian's mother Ettie Grenfell) survived Gallipoli only to fall at Cambrai; the laughing studious Billy Grenfell was killed within a mile of his brother on the same day. Nicholas Mosley writes of this group, including Denys, in his biography of Julian Grenfell: 'they and others formed a group which, after they were dead, was taken as almost mythical, in that it seemed a brilliant culmination of an Eton Tradition.' Rupert Brooke, a morning star of poetic promise, died in April 1915 leaving, as a legacy for future warriors on the point of departure: 'If I should die, think only this of me . . .' Perhaps the bitterest news of all for Denys to accept was that his friend and brother-in-law, Ossie Williams, was dead. He had been one of the original officers and the first Commanding Officer of the Prince of Wales Company of the Welsh Guards, which had only been formed on 26 February 1915. He died of wounds received at the Battle of Loos on 30 September 1915. Perhaps the saddest aspect for Topsy was that had he lived just a little longer he might at least have seen his one-month-old daughter, Anne, just once. Denys's greatest concern was for his sister whose brief term of happiness had been curtailed so meaninglessly. With Ossie's death she returned to a life which seemed inevitably touched by solitude. She never married again and devoted herself to bringing up her two children. Ossie was mentioned in despatches and awarded the DSO: Queen's South African War medal (5 clasps); Mons Star and, posthumously, the 1914–18 Campaign Medal and Victory Medal but all the honour bestowed or recognition in the world could not bring Topsy's beloved 'Billy' back or give her children the father they would never know.

After the battle of Mbuyuni during which Denys fell asleep from sheer exhaustion, under a thorn bush, an incident occurred which proved he did have a temper though he rarely showed it. By this stage most nerves were frayed and he had reached the point of weariness where rage manifests itself before there is time to master it, when he wandered into the mess tent unexpectedly. Here he caught a junior officer whom he had treated as an equal and a friend, writing what appeared to be a diary which he tried but failed to conceal from Denys. The man had been seconded to Cole's Scouts from the Loyal North Lancashire unit. Denys demanded to see what he was furtively trying to hide. It transpired that he had been keeping a detailed record of everything that was discussed in the mess tent and despatching the verbatim reports every week since his arrival to the headquarters of his battalion. Disgusted and angry with this breach of loyalty Denys turned white with anger. But his ire had not rendered him speechless. The sound of his raised voice was so unusual that it attracted Cranworth, 'Tich' Miles, and Berkeley Cole to the scene. They arrived to find the offender cowering in a corner of the mess tent with Denys towering above him.

'Good,' he shouted loudly, 'I'm glad you've come. I want you to see what this bloody little bastard has been doing for us ever since he's been attached!' And with that he threw the book containing the closely written results to Cranworth. That the entries were unflattering was the least important aspect as far as Denys was concerned. He was livid at the act of violated trust which he considered so ignoble that he insisted on sending a fiery despatch, reporting the matter to HQ. The man was returned to his battalion immediately. Cranworth and 'Tich' Miles would have waived the incident but Berkeley backed Denys to the hilt in the matter.

Life was not all unrelievedly grim however. Opportunities to shoot game presented themselves and the general gloom was lightened by the stoic comradeship of brother officers. Major A. C. Miles, known as 'Tich' on account of his minute build, was so often with Denys and Berkeley that they were known as 'The Three Musketeers'.

Like everyone else during the war in East Africa, Denys had his share of lion adventures. Once when they were encamped in what was normally a game reserve, in the dry season, a large pride of lions came too close for anyone's comfort. It was pitch black and the alarmed sentries dared not shoot for fear of revealing their position to the enemy. The sounds indicated that the marauders were closing in on the camp. Denys insisted on taking Lord Cranworth out to have a look at them more closely while refusing absolutely at the same time to take a loaded rifle. 'Denys, of course, took nothing but a torch,' Lord Cranworth recalled. 'Steadily the roars approached until they seemed all about us and I broke into a cold sweat. There came a minute's pause and an awe-inspiring roar boomed off right against us and the hair rose on my head. Denys switched on his torch and focussed it full on the tawny brute, certainly not ten yards away. "You can stay and be eaten if you like, I'm off to the mess." '[16] His nervous friend retreated with caution and Denys, as relaxed and intrigued as the Biblical Daniel, laughed and followed with the greatest reluctance. They counted twenty lions round them that night.

Usually when Denys took leave he accepted Galbraith Cole's open invitation to stay at Keekopey their thirty-thousand-acre estate at Elmentieta. Galbraith, the acknowledged authority on sheep, had imported the first merinos in the country on to this farm. Berkeley however preferred cattle raising and preferred horses to either. Galbraith's wasting arthritis prevented him from active service and while his manager, Will Powys, became a soldier for the duration of the war, he used the help of Will's brother Llewelyn to assist in the running of his farms. Llewelyn had been staying in the country for reasons of poor health when war was declared. Later he became a writer of some standing, like his brothers John Cowper and T. F. Powys. It is interesting to read his lyrical description of Denys in one of his earlier books,

Black Laughter. In one particular chapter all the characters are dubbed somewhat guardedly by alphabetically ordered initials. 'A' is Galbraith: Denys is 'B':

'B' was another character I admired. He could best be likened to a sinuous-limbed dog-puma indolently sunning himself under the swaying palm-trees of the Amazon till such time as vigorous action is imperative. One got the impression that he could bring anything he undertook to a fortunate issue. He had the same quality of courage as 'A' but was far less reckless, combining the audacity of some old-time Elizabethan with the wisdom and foresight of the son of Laertes. I saw him first fingering a pistol in a Nairobi gun-shop, fingering it with the casual interest that men of action will show for such toys and well I liked the look of his scholarly appearance, which had also about it the suggestion of an adventurous wanderer, of a man who knew every hidden creek and broad reach of the Upper-Nile, and who had watched a hundred desert suns splash with gilt the white-walled cities of Somaliland.[17]

The intriguing aspect of Llewelyn Powys's personal impression of Denys is that it bears a marked resemblance to a character called Morten de Coninck who appears in the story 'The Supper at Elsinore' from *Seven Gothic Tales*. The words, of course, are as different as their authors but the qualities are there, attributed in real life to Denys and embodied in Isak Dinesen's fictitious hero:

He had no need to exert himself. When he came into a room, in his quiet way, he owned and commanded it. He had all the beauty of limb and elegance of hands and feet of the ladies of the family, but not their fineness of feature. His nose and mouth seemed to have been cut by a rougher hand. But he had the most striking and extraordinarily noble and serene forehead. People talking to him lifted their eyes to that broad, pure brow as if it had been radiant with the dimaond tiara of a young emperor or the halo of a saint. Morten de Coninck looked as if he could not possibly know either guilt or fear. Very likely he did not.[18]

A man who hunted with Denys commented 'When he came into a room conversation stopped momentarily and you were always aware of his presence, his ineffable charm. He did not have to do or say anything to hold or make a bid for your attention, for you to know that he was there. Everyone looked up to him'. Again the same quality manifests itself, through different words, but comparable to the spirit of Morten de Coninck. The reference at the end of that passage to de Coninck's lack of fear or guilt, undoubtedly points towards Denys's family motto as much as to his physical courage. The inscription on his crest 'nil conscire sibi' – conscious of no guilt – he always jokingly declared to mean 'totally unconscious' implying a hefty intake of wine. Tanne openly preferred to acknowledge an older motto of the Winchilsea family. She spoke of it in her address 'mottoes of my life' to the American Academy of Arts and Letters, more than twenty-eight years after Denys's death. This was 'Je Responderay':

I liked this old motto so much that I asked Denys . . . if I might have it for my own. He generously made a present of it and did even have a seal cut for me, with the words carved in it. The device was meaningful and dear to me for many reasons, in particular for two such. The first . . . with its high valuation of the idea of the answer in itself. For an answer is a rarer thing than is generally imagined. There are many highly intelligent people who have got no answer at all in them. A conversation or a correspondence . . . is nothing but a double monologue, you may stroke them or you may strike them, you will get no more echo from them than from a block of wood.[19]

In that extract, Tanne, who could justifiably claim to know him better, with a greater intimacy than anyone outside the realm of family relationships, has put her finger on the pulse of his magnetism. It was the power of his response which affected people: his ability to communicate sensitively with his fellow human beings, bringing out the best in them with dignity and affection.

At Keekopey, Denys enjoyed brief respites from the bloodiness of war. Long discussions, ranging from theology and literature to Darwin's theory of evolution, soothed the disturbed mind of the inner man. Both farmers, cut off from direct confrontation with battle, savoured Denys's visits. Llwelyn Powys speaks here of Galbraith:

. . . his was a witty intellect, free from cant and many were the quips he would let fly when there was a good bundle of olive wood on the hearth . . . The divine art of fireside conversation, of poetry, of philosophy was in his opinion, merely a charming accessory to life, the serious all-important occupation raising fat wethers for the market.[20]

Denys, Galbraith and Llewelyn in sympathy, loving the wild, shared 'the moaning of the wind through the ant-eaten thorn bushes of Laikipia', and Denys, far from the artillery, the shells, whose lethal passage sounded like tearing silk, found peace and regained his equilibrium before returning to the misery which fighting engenders in humanity.

'A friend of mine is staying, one Finch Hatton,' Galbraith wrote to the girl he would later marry. 'He is on Hoskins' staff who is in command in place of Smuts. He is up here on leave and is busy trying to learn to play the guitar – seeing a guitar here again makes me think of your songs.' Denys persevered with his self-taught guitar lessons and later, when the war was over he used to serenade Tanne by the fireside at her farm at Ngong.

By the middle of 1916 Major-General Hoskins' Command, the First Division, was a mixed bag of Imperial contributions. It consisted of Indians, Rhodesians and

British with a measure of King's African Rifles and East African Mounted Rifles tossed in for good luck. Each division in the next important manoeuvre formed in effect a tentacle stretching out far beyond the nucleus of operations.* The Dutchman, General van Deventer, was in charge of the Second Division which, like one of the prehensile limbs of this gigantic military octopus, reached one hundred and fifty miles southwest of Moshi† as the British troops attempted to envelop – contract rather – round the German forces. The entire success of this operation depended on the decoying tactics of Brigadier-General Sheppard and the exact timing and secrecy of the affair. Sheppard, who was commonly known as 'Ha Ha Splendid' (due to his repeated comment 'Ha Ha splendid, lots of fighting, lots of fun' whenever a crisis presented itself), was supposed to make an assault on the bridgehead on the river Lukigora and divert the German's attention sufficiently to allow Hoskins to envelop them from the left while moving up stealthily on the enemy at

* 22 May 1916 'The flanking march down the Pangani was one which the strategy of Smuts dictated, and its performance was entrusted to the First East African Division, a force of which the units had already proved their worth not only in the infinitely trying months of our long defensive, but in the battles for Kilimanjaro earlier in the year. While the bulk of the First Division moved down the Pangani by forced marches . . . its second Brigade under Genral Hannyngton, should press directly down the Tanga line . . . a third mobile column mainly of the King's African Rifles struck across from M'buyuni [sic], past Lake Jipe to either N'galu or the Gonya gap, the only passes in the unbroken chain of the Pare Mountains. . . . In three months time they had not only freed the Tanga line of a stubborn enemy, but had swept through the heart of a savage and waterless country and struck again at the Central Railway, isolating the capital, Dar-es-Salaam.' Francis Brett Young who wrote *Marching on Tanga* commented: 'I do not think that so great a military movement had ever been made before through the heart of tropical Africa.' *Marching on Tanga* (pp. 32–4). Severn Edition published by Heinemann, London 1935.

† In present-day Tanzania.

the same time from the rear. Sheppard was reinforced by the British armoured car detachment which was voluntarily set up and financed by Major Sir John Willoughby. (He had once been jailed for complicity in the Jameson Raid and although too old to qualify for services in France had obviously retained an aggressive zeal which had abated little since his younger days.)

The troops of Hoskins's flying column marched for twenty-four hours without making a single halt, and it was planned that they should attack the Germans at once on arrival.

'Perhaps to their surprise, they did just that,'* Buchanan recalled. 'I have never seen men more utterly tired and woebegone than the Fusiliers at the time of their approach to the Lukigora river . . . and yet, when they went into battle all fatigue was forgotten – or they were careless of further physical trial – they fought like madmen.' In fact the Fusiliers borrowed a page from the Schutztruppe in this action, storming the German positions in one of the wildest bayonet charges yet seen in the campaign, whilst the Gurkhas of the Kashmir Rifles swung their kukris like berserk vivisectionists on another sector of the line. It was all over in a matter of minutes. At long last a Smuts envelopment had been brought off without a hitch. Except that the Germans got away again.[21]

At the beginning of 1917, General Smuts decided that Major-General Hoskins should succeed him as Commander-in-Chief. General Smuts, a hero in England, had so far managed to occupy three-quarters of German East Africa and had gained control of the railway system and harbour installations; in fact he was the only Allied Commander who had had the enemy in full retreat, which was no achievement to belittle. He was now invited to

---

* Captain Angus Buchanan MC author of *Three Years of War in East Africa* (p. 110).

the Imperial Conference in London, which he accepted in a cloud of glory.

Major-General Hoskins and Denys learned of this promotion as they were breakfasting at Kabata on 20 January 1917 while Hoskins was still in charge of the First Division. He and Denys rode twenty miles before being transferred to a waiting car which drove them to Kilwa. There they were picked up by plane and flown to the British HQ where Hoskins received his orders. In six hours, they had covered two hundred miles, in today's terms slow but in 1917 remarkable. The only trouble was that the army and operations which Hoskins took over were in a sorry state through disease, starvation and irremedial transport and communications difficulties. For all practical purpose they were a defeated army, added to which that January the rains were not only premature but the heaviest in recorded history. There was small consolation in the fact that the Germans suffered the same overwhelming problems of water-logged warfare.

The task Hoskins now faced was that of virtually rebuilding his army from the ground up. At least his appointment was a popular one, not only because it put a British officer back in charge but he was known to be an ideal administrator who would extend his organizational powers fully. Denys admired the way his commanding officer took up his challenge with a will to succeed against all odds but when General Smuts declared publicly in London that 'the campaign may be said to be now over' it was a harsh blow to the morale of everyone. Those left behind in British East Africa were not only astonished but highly indignant. The elusive von Lettow was still at liberty, the forces inadequate and the climate was adding to the deplorable conditions. Yet, their late Commander-in-Chief had dismissed the facts as he grew in heroism and treated Hoskins' urgent pleas for guns, medical supplies, bayonets and reinforcements with ridicule. The army was reduced to half the size of when it had taken Taveta. The Carrier Corps now literally became beasts of burden and had to move everything on two legs; the porters had numbered seven thousand five hundred, now a hundred and thirty-five thousand were necessary. Hoskins ordered the expansion of the King's African Rifles, increasing it from thirteen to twenty-two battalions, which were then formed into seven regiments giving the force a combined strength of twenty-four thousand men. He spared no effort to gather every remaining asset so that by May the British were in a vastly superior position. Hoskins was now prepared to bring the campaign to an end. The Germans were lumped together at the south-east corner of their Colony and, providing the British pressed forward east north and west they no longer had a way of escape. But the British Expeditionary force never fulfilled its drive under Hoskins. With as much warning as when he had been appointed, quite inexplicably Major-General Hoskins was relieved as Commander-in-Chief by General van Deventer, who was to be the sixth General to attempt to beat the one-eyed General von Lettow Vorbeck.

On 6 June 1917, after Denys had managed to see Berkeley who was desperately ill and 'reduced to nothing', he attended a formal parade, where among fluttering banners and a guard of honour, Major-General Hoskins made his farewell. At Nairobi railway station, the acting Governor, the Hon Sir Charles Bowering, waved them off, as the bugles sounded the general salute. Despite the pomp it was a bitter personal retreat for the departing General, who had the full sympathy of his tall ADC, Captain Finch Hatton, who left with him.

The following account was written by Galbraith Cole,

who went to Nairobi to see Denys off, but in it Denys's views are not difficult to detect:

. . . all the military folk are very disappointed and surprised at Hoskins being taken away and are one and all depressed beyond words at the prospect of the change, more especially the South Africans. Hoskins has done so much to make his men enthusiastic under the most trying circumstances and with his personality appears to have won the goodwill of everyone who came into contact with him. Things were I believe in a state bordering on chaos when he took over and he has made prodigious efforts to prepare for a final effort and now on the eve of his advance, he is superseded. It may, this transfer of command, be necessary from a purely political point of view but from a military one, it does not appear to have anything to commend it.

Towards the end of the war when von Lettow was still eluding his enemies with infuriating cunning Denys wrote to Kermit Roosevelt on the subject in a mood which reflects his personal feelings clearly enough:

Von Lettow has now re-crossed the Rovuma [river] and is again in German East Africa. If van Deventer was not a Boer this would certainly procure him the very choicest raspberry, but I suppose he will be allowed to blunder on ably assisted by Sheppard his C of Staff until Lettow takes Nairobi, unless the defeat of Germany in Europe puts an end to hostilities in BEA. As Smuts gave van DV [Van Deventer] a KCMG for allowing Lettow to escape south of the Rovuma, the least he can do now is procure him a Grand Cross of the British Empire for letting him escape north of that river again. If they had left Hoskins there I firmly believe he would have finished off the show by the end of 1917 in spite of being handicapped with Sheppard.[22]

In the summer of 1917 Denys returned to England for about eight weeks, his first visit home since he had settled in British East Africa. His parents were living once more at Haverholme Priory and he was happy to be in the familiar surrounding of the place where he had grown up. In the midst of writing a bantering letter to Kitty Lucas, who had carelessly omitted to advise him of her current address, he received his orders to proceed to Mesopotamia with Major-General Hoskins.

Curiously enough, though freedom of time and space appeared to be essential conditions of Denys's life, he was always punctilious about informing family and friends of his whereabouts and his immediate plans. He always left forwarding addresses for mail when he was on the move and invariably left alternative suggestions as to how he could be contacted or located. His letter to Kitty, on the pale grey folded page used by the inmates of Haverholme Priory, displays a gentler side of his teasing compared to the sarcastic wit reserved for so-called heroes of war. He addressed himself to his two-year-old godson Denys Lucas:

> Haverholme Priory
> 8–8–17

My dear Denys,

I was very glad to get your letter this morning, as I have been wanting to write to your mother for some days. Will you convey to her as delicately as possible, that it always makes it easier for her correspondent to answer her letters if she gives him her address? Your dear mother Denys, is not altogether free from a hereditary weakness of her sex – namely of expecting a little more than it is possible to give. I have found it to be so in most countries I have visited including Africa, the great 'Keep-it-dark' continent. However, I have with my accustomed resource – your Godfather has no modesty – already discovered a means of getting a letter to your mother in spite of her reticence as to her whereabouts. I had what is called a brainwave Denys and sent it to ROYCROFT to be forwarded to your ma. Please calm her with this information. I have not complied with your rather thoughtless invitation to send you a telegram. Economy Denys! War time economy! I am saving up all the money I generally spend on telegrams to buy you a tin mug as some sort

of Godfathering present. I had meant to try for a handsomely
chased, heavily embossed solid gold George III punch bowl,
but I have just received news that all my cattle in East Africa
are dying with Rinderpest; so – no more of that! Dear Kitty, in
the midst of this nonsense I have just been handed a telegram
telling me that I shall be starting for Mesopotamia about the
middle of next week, so I fear I must shirk you. I am going up
today and shall have to be with my man on and off till we start.
Write Conservative Club.[23]

In the midst of the letter he had made a few, light inky
smudges, to these he added, as an afterthought, minute
arrows attached to the word 'tears', indicating that he
was weeping over the loss of his cattle. In this case not
only had he utilized the margin but the centrefold too,
making the letter a puzzle in terms of continuity.

By the end of that year Denys formed a new friendship,
with a young American Captain attached to the Motor
Machine Gun Corps, British Expeditionary Forces, whom
he met on the outward-bound journey to Mesopotamia.
He was one of the sons of the former President of the
United States of America, Theodore Roosevelt. Kermit
wrote a book entitled *War in the Garden of Eden* which
was published in 1920, and illustrated by his own photographs. The following passage gives an idea of the conditions under which they met. They were aboard the ship
Taranto:

We laid up two days in a harbour on the Albanian coast,
spending the time pleasantly enough in swimming and sailing
while we waited for a new escort. Another night's run put us
into Navarino Bay. The grandfather of Lieutenant Finch Hatton,
one of the officers on board, commanded the Allied forces in
the famous battle fought here in 1827, when the Turkish Fleet
was vanquished and the independence of Greece assured.[24]

The journey was bearable until they entered the Red
Sea by which time they had transferred to another ship.

It was August and when one talks of the Red Sea in August there is no need for more to be said. The *Saxon* had not been built for the tropics. She had no fans nor ventilating system such as we have in the United Fruit boats. Some unusually intelligent stokers had deserted at Port Said and as we were in consequence short-handed it was suggested that any volunteers would be given a try. Finch Hatton and I felt that our years in the tropics should qualify us and that the exercise would improve our dispositions. We got the exercise. Never have I felt anything as hot and I have spent August in Tuma, Arizona and been in Italian Somaliland and the Amazon Valley. The shovels and the handles of the wheel-barrows blistered our hands. We had a number of cases of heatstroke and the hospital facilities can never be all that might be desired.[25]

Aboard the *Saxon* Kermit witnessed their first military burial at sea, which they found deeply moving. The short classic burial service was read as a lane of 'Tommies' stood with their rifles reversed and their heads bowed; then the body swathed in the Union Jack was slid over the stern of the ship 'then the bugles ran out the haunting, mournful strains of the Last Post and the service ended with "Abide with Me".' Denys recalled Shakespeare's lines on this complete and beautiful evolution through death in *The Tempest*:

> Full fathom five thy father lies;
> Of his bones are coral made;
> Those are pearls that were his eyes:
> Nothing of him that doth fade,
> But doth suffer a sea change
> Into something rich and strange.

They sweltered on down the Red Sea and entered the Indian Ocean. They wanted to disembark the many sick on board at Aden but their orders were to sail on without touching. Duties were light and they spent the time 'playing cards or reading'. Kermit Roosevelt was a slightly

built, pensive young man, with fairish hair and a subaltern
moustache who never went anywhere without a volume
of poetry or one of the classics in his pocket. Denys and
he became engrossed in 'Layard's Early Adventures'*
Kermit had 'Ninevah' and 'Babylon' with him on this
voyage. As the *Saxon* entered the 'Garden of Eden' they
were amused by one of the 'Tommies' who was so
disgusted that he exclaimed 'If this is the Garden of Eden
it wouldn't take no bloody angel with a flamin' sword to
turn me back!'

When they docked for the night at Amara Denys and
Kermit decided to go ashore for a stroll in the cool of the
evening. As they proceeded down the bank Kermit caught
sight of a sentry walking his post before the bridge whose
appearance was 'so very important and efficient that I
slipped behind my companion to give him a chance to
explain us'.

'Halt. Who goes there?'

'Friend,' replied Finch Hatton.

'Advance friend and give the countersign.'

Denys started forward determinedly followed by a
very suspicious and uncertain Kermit whose nervousness
turned out to be reasonably justified when they were met
with a threatening lowered bayonet and the aggressive
remark that there wasn't any countersign!

At Kut they came across a gruesome sight even for a
battlefield. A group of desert looters, 'who do not clean
up as thoroughly as the African hyena . . . had paid the
penalty through tampering with unexploded grenades and
"dud" shells and left their bones to be scattered around
the dead they had been looting. The trenches were a

---

* Sir Austen Layard, 1817–1894, British author and diplomatist and
the excavator of Ninevah. His two books *Ninevah and its Remains* and
Discoveries in the Ruins of Ninevah and Babylon were highly praised.

veritable Golgotha with skulls everywhere and dismembered legs still clad with puttees and bootes.'[25]

Denys and Kermit were stationed together at first in Mesopotamia but Denys now grabbed at the opportunity he had been waiting for since the Flying Meeting at Wolverhampton; with Major-General Hoskins approval Denys found a replacement ADC and applied to train as a pilot with the Royal Flying Corps. By the time the news of his acceptance came through Denys and Kermit's friendship was firmly established. Thereafter they kept in touch by letter, meeting in London if their visits coincided. They played chess and bridge together, shared interests in photography and literature (Kermit actually had *Plutarch's Lives* dropped to him from a plane by Denys) and these common bonds were fused by a love of the wilderness. Kermit knew Kenya to a limited extent for he had accompanied his father on the famous 'Roosevelt Safari' in 1909. Companions with whom one had such a complete rapport were particularly valued during the war years. The day the news came through for his flying course, Denys scribbled a note to Kermit with a black wax crayon, on a torn ear of graph paper:

Dear K,
  I have orders to proceed Basra at once en route for Egypt. I hope for a day or so in Baghdad but may not get it. Also I hope I shall not be pushed into transport direct from Egypt but I am afraid I shall. I shall stay with ? tomorrow night. I am leaving by the 2 P.M. train. I have found a substitute to take my place with Hoskins. Forbes-Adams 34th Pioneers. Hope your new mates aren't altogether too pricelessy.
                                Denys Finch Hatton (signed)

The expression 'pricelessy' refers to their recent spate of gambling. Denys had just paid Kermit a cheque for £7.10.0. Unused to being beaten he immediately challenged Kermit to a return game. The note attached to the cheque however sounds rather a reference to medical care than the next rubber!

Dear K,

  Herewith your tie and your ill-gotten gains. I may be station-wards about ten – if so I'll bring a pack and rub you properly in the break – you perfectly priceless old thing.

DFH

Unfortunately before Denys started his flying course, he heard that his partner, Jack Pixley, who jointly owned the farm at Naivasha and shared interests in a trading firm they had established, had been killed in France. Pixley's death made Denys's return to Kenya imperative to make alternative business arrangements – though the name of the company 'Finch Hatton and Pixley Ltd' survived until 1931. Denys's application for leave was granted.

It was during this three weeks that Denys met Tanne von Blixen for the first recorded time. Among her notes is a chronology of dates all connected with Denys, that, as will be seen, appear to have guided her pen in the writing of *Out of Africa*. The first entry is small but significant: 'Saw D. 4.4.1918' and noted on another page in her large slanting writing is in Danish against the same date: 'Traf først Gang Muthaiga' – Met for the first time Muthaiga.

8
1918–1919 – Wings

When Denys returned to Nairobi he stayed at Muthaiga Club. The Parklands house was probably requisitioned during the war and sold afterwards to recoup some of his heavy financial losses. The Club had all the facilities required by a bachelor pressed for time, and it was the perfect meeting place for the floating population – a state imposed by war. In those days members dined at one long table rather than individually, engendering the festive air of one large dinner party rather than fractured groups of acquaintances. Among non-members beyond its French Renaissance façade the club had acquired 'a darkly intriguing reputation for bacchanalian revelry. Dinner was an invigorating preliminary in the long crowded dining-room.'[1] Outside the country its fame was even more exaggerated – 'a sort of Moulin Rouge' as one settler described it. But the escapades behind its select doors were spontaneous displays in the release of cooped up spirits after months of loneliness or hardship trebled by war, a temporary escape during four years of dreariness, yet they provoked an unreasonable longing in the uninitiated to be able to identify themselves with 'the Muthaiga Club crowd'.

Denys was on the brink of his thirty-first birthday. Tanne, whose birthday was a week earlier, was almost thirty-three. She and Bror had been married for only four years but she had already learned that marriage was no childhood tale of living happily ever after. Whilst Bror was an affectionate husband he was also an incorrigible philanderer. He made ready use of the opportunities for affairs at a time when women were left alone indefinitely while their men were engaged in battle. After the personal slight of being suspected of being pro-German, the trials of establishing a coffee farm, about which, despite their enthusiasm, they knew nothing, Tanne next learned a fearful lesson in private humiliation. She discovered with horror that she was infected by a contagious social disease, for which she had to return to Europe for a cure.

Clara Svendsen, who became Tanne's secretary for fifteen years, and Frans Lasson, joint authors of *The Life and Destiny of Isak Dinesen* were the first writers to disclose that: 'After the first year of marriage, Karen Blixen had to go home to Denmark to be treated for a venereal disease which she had contracted through no fault of her own. Too much time had elapsed before she set out; and when she arrived in Denmark it took time to make discreet arrangements, which Karen Blixen insisted on, in order to keep her mother, with her Puritan upbringing, in ignorance of the situation. Karen Blixen herself believed that the long, hard years of illness she had to endure later in life were a result of this disease. It was with open eyes that she entered upon the same fate which she thought had threatened her father.'[2]

Clara Svendsen recalls that when 'the Baroness' told her many years after she had been in her employ 'Then it happened, after I had moved to Africa . . . that I contracted syphilis from my husband' her employer's eyes contained 'a crucified expression'. According to her brother Thomas it 'became absolutely necessary for her to receive more prolonged treatment. At the hospital in Nairobi, they advised her to seek help in Europe and at the beginning of June 1915, she returned to Denmark after an extremely difficult journey through war-torn France, Switzerland and Germany. Two long spells in the National Hospital in Copenhagen, three months in all, helped her a great deal, but she only gradually recovered completely, if indeed she ever did.'[3] Her secretary also refers to Tanne's later life as consumed in her 'heroic fight against the overwhelming odds of illness . . . like one human being trying to stem an avalanche'. Because of the persistent loyalty of those who loved her, her brother Thomas, in particular, although the world is now fully conversant with the fact that she suffered from 'a venereal disease' it is no wiser about its specific nature or the crippling effect it may have had on her relationships with the opposite sex from then on. The natural loyalty of her family is acknowledged and admired but having revealed the matter in principle the once laudable motives behind this impenetrable fog of secrecy appear now to have outgrown their usefulness. Her medical history is now of interest in the academic sense and it is hoped that future biographers will be able to define this delicate question in a professional manner and with professional assistance. It could explain that unexpected facet of her personality, the discrepancy which fanned a possessive demon into positive, destructive action as her relationships with men progressed, particularly in later years. The vague idea that her association with Denys was platonic is due as much to the use of the word 'friend' as to the emphasis on friendship and the lack of an open declaration of love. But as will be seen, there is another reason for this for Tania was manacled by truth. Because of this private integrity, the link which has coupled them so strongly (and enigmatically) has been forged by her own pen and subsequently those who wrote about her. Yet Tanne and Denys's closer friends scorn the idea that their relationship was so unearthly that the love between soul and soul precluded the need for physical expression. The question remains loaded because the lovers remain on their ethereal pedestal – unsullied by pain, desire and the impetus of touch. Ingrid Lindstrom has stressed Tanne's health, her energy in the twenties. Could it mean that like other victims of venereal disease at the beginning of the century, she was pronounced cured perhaps to learn later that this was not so? Did the subterranean ravaging continue to work against her despite the fashionable applications of the medical profession at the time – of mercury, arsenic or bismuth? It was not an uncommon predicament and would account for much. Alternatively it is possible that her later illnesses were the consequence of these early 'cures'. Thomas explains Tanne's abundant personal courage as that of one who was prepared to 'defy unhappiness and pain . . . she undoubtedly wished to meet and to overcome almost insuperable difficulties . . . Her illness could easily have brought her to the edges of despair, but she took her sufferings in quite a different way as if thinking "now I've endured that too. Now I'm even nearer to experiencing really great things." '[4]

Thomas Dinesen's fraternal observations are succinct and are borne out by an apparent underlying masochism – a quality which seems to haunt nearly all his sister's situations.

Tanne's problems with Bror when she returned to Kenya early in 1917 were made more difficult as she realized how thoroughly irresponsible he was – especially with money. Bror seemed impervious to their debt of honour to the various members of their families who had put up the money in order that they might realize their dream, a shabby repayment for the faith vested in them. But for all his roguery he was unrepentingly charming; friends waived his transgressions, dismissing him fondly as 'a jolly good fellow'. Metaphorically he could get away with murder and invariably did. Loud and blustering, his facile and rather conceited manner swept women off their feet. His frank sexuality induced exactly the lusty response his aggressive masculinity demanded. Tanne had obviously lacked this requisite (indeed, when the terms of their marriage are re-examined it would have been surprising if she had not) so that he was driven by this need in constant search for adulation. A craving which gave no regard to Tanne's sensitivity as a wife impelled him to seek as best he could. He was indiscreet and his insatiable desire for fresh conquest earned him such a dubious reputation that when friends learned he was taking mutual acquaintances out hunting, if there were women in the safari party the married men were 'advised to take a spare woman along in case he popped into bed with one of their wives'. His type of bravado is exemplified by the occasion when, while standing at the door of Muthaiga Club, chatting to a friend, he was all the while eyeing a pretty young American girl of obvious wealth who had come out on safari with her father. After ten minutes, assured that he had caught her eye in open flirtation, he swaggered forward a few steps, turned ostentatiously to his male friend and declared loudly, jerking his head in the girl's direction:

'You see that – well, that's mine for tonight.'

Later Bror boasted openly in the men's bar of his successful prediction – the girl had simply been a reassuring notch to his ego.

For Tanne, an acutely observant and aesthetically discriminating woman, it must have been very painful indeed to tolerate such behaviour publicly. There is little doubt that she is describing her own chagrin, Bror's indiscretion and an aspect of her marriage in her story 'Tales of Two Gentlemen' which appears in *Last Tales* published in 1957:

He . . . within the first two years of their married life acquired two supreme decorations at his native and foreign court. But when he and his wife had been married for three years he observed a change in her. She became pensive . . . stirred by some new mighty emotion obscure to him. It . . . seemed to him that she would now prefer to show herself in the world on such occasions where he was not with her, and to excuse herself . . . where she would have to appear by his side. 'I have spoilt her,' he reflected . . . 'her ambition – her vanity now make her aspire to outshine her lord, to whom she owes all?' . . . on an evening when they were alone together he resolved to take her to account. 'Surely my dear,' he said to her, 'you will realise that I am not going to play the part of that husband in the fairy tale who, owing to his connection with higher powers, raised his wife to the rank of queen and empress, only to hear her in the end demanding to have the sun rise at a word. . . . His wife for a long time did not answer him; in the end she rose from her chair as if about to leave the room. . . . 'My husband,' she said in her low sonorous voice, 'surely you realise that to an ambitious woman, it comes hard, in entering a ballroom to know that she is entering it on the arm of a cuckold.'[5]

Although there is a typical Dinesen sex/role exchange here, for Bror was the cuckolder rather than the cuckold, this passage possesses many of the elements of her situation with Bror – the timing within the span of their marriage – her lowlier origins, the title he bestowed upon her and the inevitability of their changing relationship. The comment at the beginning on the 'native and foreign court' is probably a *double entendre* and Tanne's oblique reminder of Bror's indiscriminate coupling with African girls and European women. The room which the wife dreaded entering is the dining-room at Muthaiga Club and the scene taken as a whole captures her artistic ability to transform a personal and rather ugly experience into a passage of literary merit.

Tanne's deepest feminine pride had been bruised very badly by the time she met Denys. The gossip Bror generated left stains, uncomfortable reminders of his breach of accepted social codes; Tanne felt implicated even when she was not present, as if in some way she was responsible for his behaviour. He drank heavily and ran up debts; at one stage in order to elude irate creditors, he retired to a cave he had found in the Ngong Hills; while in hiding his staff were instructed to inform anyone who pursued him out to the farm that he was 'on safari'. Yet while he lived with Tanne he continually gave parties at the New Stanley Hotel or Muthaiga and among his guests were a preponderance of glamorous women. On more than one occasion *The Leader* flattered him by singling out the most chic of his entourage, commenting on their fashionable clothes; it was not easy either for Tanne to accept the fact that in these instances she was over-shadowed, in favour of more *soignée* women.

When Tanne met Denys at Muthaiga Club on 4 April 1918 she was ripe for the release from her misery that the reassurance of an '*affaire de coeur*' may bring; she needed to escape from her loneliness – her trampled aspirations of happiness. If possible she needed the attention of a man who was superior, not only socially but publicly, intellectually and physically, though that last quality prob-ably played the least important role in the self-rescue of her battered personality. She needed someone reliable and responsible: a sensitive man who was capable also of taking her hand and flying with her to her enchanted realms of fantasy through imagination. Denys fulfilled all these sub-conscious yearnings at the precise moment in time when she was most vulnerable as a woman. Though she probably could not have sensed the immensity at this meeting. Denys's presence in her life was not merely an '*affaire de coeur*' he was to be the *grande passion* of her life.

Before knowing him, her creative drive and fecund imagination had been immature – diffused and confused. Rudimentary schooling and snatches of education had produced prolific jottings since childhood – mainly unfinished – of small plays, poems and paragraphs of prose which gave way to adolescent painting and semi-serious study. These were explorations but they were tentative interpolations of the endless possibilities that life has to offer. Denys acted as a valuable enzyme in her development as a writer. She may have yearned desperately for wings to carry her away when she set sail for Africa and married but so far her flying had been reduced to crawling through her first escape hatch (marriage to her cousin) and the seeds of her immense literary talent still lay in the fleshy pod of undevelopment. Denys leavened her life, opened up new worlds through new languages, literature, music and religion. The gifts which he brought acknowledged her own bright existence. His kindness and gentleness in contrast to her husband's aggressive approach to life became balm to her wounded pride and his total disregard for convention sheltered her against the chattering hurtful sounds which reverberated about her failed marriage causing her such deep shame. Now those silently pointing fingers directing disparaging innuendos at her alliance and her 'oddly close dealings with the natives', would gradually fall away as she gathered strength and became an accepted part of Denys's world. His friends, Berkeley and Galbraith Cole, Hugh Martin, Lord Delamere, Uncle Charles Bulpett, Frank Greswolde-Williams, Rose Buxton and her brother Geoffrey, became hers too. Denys's poetic appreciation of the land and its people for whom she already cared deeply, lifted her into a world which she could now share on a different plane but which she had begun to believe existed only in dreams.

Denys and Tanne's first recorded meeting was conventional and brief – an evening of good food, wine and conversation which flowed easily against the light operatic background of Chinese paper lanterns – and there was one other rendezvous before he returned to Egypt. Optimism had arrived at this particular time with the heavy drops of the rainy season which drummed insistently on the roof. Patiently everyone waits for the African deluge, appreciating the smell as it touches the dust. The din as it falls on a corrugated-iron roof or spills over the guttering can almost obliterate all sound of conversation.

In a markedly erotic but brief chapter in *Out of Africa* Karen Blixen wrote: 'It is a lovely sight when the roads of the farm have all been turned into streams of running water, and the farmer wades through the mud with a singing heart. . . . He cries to the sky: Give me enough and more than enough. My heart is bared to thee now, and I will not let thee go except thou bless me. Drown me if you like, but kill me not with caprices. No coitus interruptus, heaven, heaven!'[6]

'I will not let thee go except thou bless me' was taught to Tanne by Denys from the little Bible his mother gave him when he was six years old and which today is at Rungstedlund, Tanne's last home in Denmark. It comes from the book of Genesis: 'And he said "Let me go, for the day breaketh" and he said "I will not let thee go except thou bless me."'[7] Later on in that same short chapter she comments 'The friends of the farm came to the house and went away again. They were not the kind of people who stay for a long time in the same place.'[8] On those two pages her writing is libidinous and is perhaps motivated by her secret knowledge of the first seduction.

Whether or not Denys and Tanne became lovers in the true sense at this time is not known. Though it may be purely coincidence, a high percentage of Tanne's seduction scenes in her stories are prefaced by rain or by other natural elements which might make the face of a lover damp: snow melting against warm skin, salt spray, mist or even tears. The strong physical attraction Denys felt for Tanne was undoubtedly mutual. He may have been drawn to her initially by the striking similarity she bore to Kitty Lucas. She was of an even height, about five feet three inches, and of a similar build. Tanne's complexion was less olive but otherwise their colouring was the same, each had beautiful sloping shoulders, and an eagerness to live life to the brim seems to have been caught in the timelessness of each of their faces. A photograph of Tanne swathed in a length of stockinette taken for a passport in 1936 bears a subtle sameness to the one of Catherine Bechet de Balan in her Moroccan outfit taken as early as 1904. Yet another taken of Kitty when presented at court is so like that of Tanne at about the same age they might be mistaken one for the other, particularly as each subject is half-turned in opposite directions. One almost has the feeling that, if they turned simultaneously – could be mysteriously animated – their full-face images might blur for a second, gain focus and melt into one and the same person. The dressing of their hair, the neckline of the style of each dress contributes to the general effect but it is the bearing of each girl, the fleshy underlip of each mouth, the demure but promising eyes, the breadth and balance of the facial features which strike the viewer. This uncanny likeness is a separate thing from that of identical milestones in well-bred young womanhood of the late-Victorian era. Denys admired in women beautiful hair, perhaps compensating and being more aware through his own increasing lack of it. Tanne apparently did not have very good hair and as she grew older wore scarves and hats to disguise it.

But whatever the attraction was it was reciprocal and it was strong, for Denys, who was basically a selfish creature and determinedly selfish at that, was also too energetic in his quest for adventure and too elusively independent to have taken up the first phase of their relationship on his return from the war, the following year, unless he had very much cared to.

Tanne was now about to embark upon a period of intoxicating experiences taking the form of fractured episodes of intense living. Soon, long months of solitary existence on the farm when Bror was off hunting or ivory poaching were compensated for by weeks of great joy when Denys came to Nairobi. And eventually after she and Bror separated he moved out to live with her on the farm at Ngong.

Eudora Welty, one of the literary critics writing on Isak Dinesen, has defined very precisely a feature of Tanne's work which might be described better as a quality: 'She made a story of an essence; of an essence she made an elixir and of an elixir she began once more to compound the story.' The very craft of Tanne's taletelling so shrewdly assessed in that sentence was actually a reflection of a whole new pattern of existence for the rest of her life in Africa. It was to be a protracted exigence dictating her life for the next thirteen years. As mistress of her craft as a story teller, she became a mirror image of her own *mélange* of sorrow and rapture; the inevitability of each parting from Denys was accepted with an almost masochistic pleasure in the knowledge that each long moment spent apart from him could only bring his return nearer.

There was only one small blemish like a worm within the apple, unseen through the appetizing, wholesome skin at first glance. Tanne was at heart a stubbornly possessive creature; it was more of an affliction than a greed, and it later developed into a sickness of sorts. It was a weakness for which she could not be blamed entirely, a state to be viewed with compassion, for her need grew from childhood when a starvation of love and paternal affection had become an overwhelming deficit. Only an unreasonable amount of attention from the opposite sex could assuage her. Unfortunately possessiveness seldom diminishes. It grows and spreads like a cancer, tingeing all the extremities of living and every aspect of it, and it appears where least expected.

There is a luminosity about the maxim 'I will not let thee go except thou bless me' which is the epitome of generosity and idealism. But there are few human beings who are capable of living out that truth of truths. Tanne used it quite often in her tales and freely for her chapter on rain in *Out of Africa* perhaps because it was to become a significantly bitter lesson in her own character formation. But she was frugal. Ironically, as with all writers, no experience is too virulent to be discarded; everything can be used and exploited in the end. Eventually she turned the disadvantage of her possessiveness and destructive self-knowledge, for which she was to pay such an inestimable price, into advantage. Recognizing her mistake – though all too late – she took it and laid the blame on the shoulders of the make-belief heroines running demoniacally through her fantasy tales, relentlessly pursuing boys, young men, husbands and lovers, running on and on and on in order to escape.

Early in May 1918 Denys and Berkeley went to greet Galbraith Cole and his bride Nell as they returned from England after their wedding, at Nairobi station. They had 'a fearful time sorting all the luggage . . . and Berkeley finally suggested they pitch a tent on the station for the night.'! But they eventually got everything together and Nell [Lady Eleanor Cole] invited Denys down to stay after he had finished his business dealings in Nairobi. He bought an old Ford car so that he was mobile and decided he would drive back to Cairo by the Nile route, which he calculated would take him about a month – if things went well he could just make it by 23 June when his flying course was scheduled to start.

His next problem was to find Billea Issa, his Somali servant; it was like looking for the proverbial needle in the haystack – they had lost touch at the outset of war. After much cabling, a means of communication which Denys frequently utilized despite his joking admonitions to Kitty Lucas on the subject of wartime economy, he managed to retrieve 'my Somali by frantic wiring to all the heads of GEA and PEA' and then he accepted the newly married Cole's invitation and went to stay at Keekopey for three days before setting out for the Sudan. Nell Cole wrote to her mother Lady Balfour about the visit.

Denys Finch Hatton stayed for three days last week on his way to join the RFC in Egypt. He was going via Uganda to the Sudan. A very attractive person with a delightfully wide range of interests. We went 'pigging' with him several times but the pig were very wild and he was not shooting well so we got none. We got three buck one day – meat for the boys who badly wanted maize meal or posho as it is called and is very expensive owing to the shortage in this country and the two boys are kept to a minimum allowance so are glad of a bit of meat.

Denys left Gilgil on 14 May 1918 and travelled overland, reaching Shepheard's Hotel Cairo on 21 June, which he thought was 'pretty good going'. The following day he learned that he had just missed the start of the new flying course and would have to kick his heels until the next batch of training. He wrote to Kermit at once, regretting the haste he had made while crossing the Sudan when he could have lingered and savoured the journey 'I wish I had had longer but I was hurrying to get here in time to report on the 23rd. Quite a nice piece of country between Nimule and Rejaf which one walks (about a hundred miles). I heard elephant all one night but I had to leave them without a visit to push on and catch the boat at Rejaf.' After explaining how he tracked down Billea he goes on, 'I have him with me now, though I may have to part with him as I am going to school and it seems a shock to them that anyone can want a servant of his own. However I shall make a pretty determined attempt to retain him. I hear Hoskins is in Ismailia; I am going to find out today for sure.' Of his recent trip to BEA he comments: 'It was nice to be in the country again and I covered wonderful distances across country in an old Ford 'sufferia' [the Swahili term for a simple tin cooking pot] which I eventually sold for £50 more than I paid for it . . .'

His gleeful satisfaction at his profit on the car is evident but there is no hint of the friends whom he has relocated, no mention of where he has been staying nor any indication that he has met anyone of particular interest. But Denys was not given to exposing details of his personal life either during conversation or in correspondence. In fact he habitually destroyed letters from friends and in a curious act of caution urged them to follow suit. As a result, hardly any of his letters survived this elimination process. This facet of his personality does not quite measure up to the fabulous but tragic nobleman friends revered – but it only occurred with those few to whom he wrote. His determination not to become imprisoned by his own hand is clear in his instruction to one girl to whom he wrote poetry: 'Never keep anything in evidence.' Those words portray an instinctive fear of commitment. Possibly under this influence, even Topsy burned all of Denys's letters to her, two or three years before she died, destroying the record of a lifetime's exposure of personal feelings. The notion may have been an extension of his concept of privacy which, like his idea of freedom, was sacrosanct. But equally it mirrors the shirking of a certain responsibility. The trait is not altogether appealing, it suggests an inability to fully grow up and come to terms with possible actions provoked by the written word, almost assuming the role of an escape clause for himself.

In the same letter to Kermit he reveals his dread of being pushed into a tent with complete strangers and how he planned to delay this moment until it was imperative to reach Aboukir Depot for the start of the next batch of training: 'where we will be eight in a tent I suppose and *such* an 8 probably!' Having finished his letter Denys retired to bed 'with a touch of fever'.

Denys had been replying to a letter from Kermit that had been awaiting him in Cairo. The friends had been out of touch for nearly four months and now Denys learned that Quentin Roosevelt, Kermit's older brother, had been killed. He offered kindly sympathy and the hope that the news may not be final and as a double insurance that Kermit received this letter he contacted the consul in Alexandria with a copy which could be relayed: 'I was very sorry that your brother has been killed but I have seen since that he might be alive and a prisoner. I hope this is right.' However the American Diplomatic service were unable to be of much help except to advise Denys that Kermit had left Egypt for France to 'join the American Forces there. He was to meet his wife somewhere in France or Italy.' They suggested as an alternative that Denys might like to contact Kermit's father-in-law, The Hon Joseph Willard, American Ambassador in Madrid. Though this matter is insignificant enough it is the type of gesture which earned Denys the heartfelt gratitude of those who knew him and set him apart. Many would have written the first letter of condolence but few would have gone to the lengths of ensuring its ultimate delivery with its simple message of concern and sympathetic hope. Actually Denys and Kermit did not discover one another's whereabouts until the end of the year when Denys was hospitalized.

Back in Kenya, Tanne clung to the dream of her farm's success in spite of her spoiled marriage and with a stubborn will to succeed. At that time, hope was all she had left and as a mariner might cleave to a plank which was once part of his ship, she placed her cumulative faith in the success of her next coffee crop. But her moods vacillated with the wind. There were too many 'shauries' (a wonderful all embracing Swahili word meaning troubles or any complication of an adverse nature and which, in a word, saves the victim all necessity of recounting the tedious and harassing details to the listener) for her to remain equable.

If only she and Bror had realized at the outset that the farm was to present them with so many difficulties but as with most pioneers this vision was withheld from them. To produce the valuable harvest which they needed so badly they required a certain rainfall. Tanne has explained that 'height' was chiefly responsible, but the most serious determining factor for the ultimate failure appears to have been inadequate rain.

But like all pioneers they could only experiment and courageously try again when things failed; with each flowering of the pretty acrid blossoms hope rose. There was such promise in the sight of the chalky cloud of flowers whose virgin aureole Tanne likened to spring in Europe.

But she was in Africa; her metabolism works at an entirely different tempo and it takes time to learn her inimitable rules for survival. The native has it; he is born into her way, which may seem puzzling to the immigrant, a yoke of patience bordering on folly. But it is not folly, it is resilience and an acceptance of fate, of slow hard conditions which have driven into his being an unlimited capacity to bow before failure. In some things, such as parturition, there are no short cuts, and instinctively the native will accept that only time will decide.

There are no seasons in Africa which can compare to those in Europe and consequently there is little respite. No gently falling rains, instead deluges, waterfalls, even rivers for a while and then comes the unrepentant sun. It bakes the land for months on end and extracts every vestige of moisture. It has no remorse. It dries up rivers and muddy dams, turning them into sandbeds or crevices of dust, and the transient benison of fresh green grass covering the earth becomes slowly bleached and eradi- cated again. Reality is reached when the intermittent clumps of ivory appear; these are the worldly remains of the parched herds of game. The bones picked clean by the efficient vultures are the true evidence of weakness and they announce the fact that breaking point has been reached. It is nature's way of winnowing her herds. Those creatures once so fleet of foot have simply failed the test of Africa's stern rule of subsistence. It is almost as if the Gods of the two elements, Jupiter and Apollo, are incessantly arguing which of their powers is the greater at the expense of earthly existence. Human sympathy accorded under more temperate conditions is misplaced. Above all, Africa demands tenacity and by that ability everything stands or falls.

Tanne, less logical than a man, as all true women must be, had then only loyal determination by which to honour her debt to her family and the eye of an artist like stars in the night to guide her. She was forced to turn to the family frequently for money and by the end of 1930, when the bank foreclosed on her, she had borrowed a formidable sum in the name of a hopeless attempt at turning a dream into a reality.

In June of 1917 Tanne's optimism was high but she had injured her leg and the wound would not heal for a long time. She was concerned that she might be scarred for life (her fears were realized) and it must have been very painful for it was sufficiently bad for her to require treatment and stitching under chloroform twice, yet still it refused to heal. While she was resting this leg she wrote to Thomas, who seems to have been more of a confidant than anyone else in her life apart from Denys, about the farm and casually mentions Denys for the first time. But it is not as casual a reference as it appears – she has saved it till the last for inclusion, as a child will hoard a sweet. Furthermore her facts are not quite correct, which means she wishes to imply that she knows more than she actually does and that she intends to draw him into Tommy's life too if she can. Oddly enough, Denys was in a similar condition at exactly the same moment in Helonaus; his leg was up because of complications caused by a septic toe.

                                                      7.11.18 Ngong
My Dearest Tommy,
        . . . at last we have had rain and everything is blooming and promises the best for this season. The farm looks excellent and I really hope and pray that you will soon receive a higher interest . . . It's no joke having the responsibility for other people's money – especially that which you have in all friendship entrusted to me. . . . My leg has not yet healed yet I have a horried scar from knee to hip which I am very sorry about (Bror hopes that not many people will be allowed to see it). . . . If you come to France as a pilot, then you might possibly meet a person called Denys Finch Hatton, who is also a pilot on the French front, and that would please me greatly. In my old age, I have had the good fortune to meet my living ideal in him, and it would be nice if you two could meet.[9]

Denys found that first nine weeks of his flying course 'rather boring' and 'not unlike being back at Oxford except that one's companions are rather different and one has to attend the lectures'. Which leads one to believe he did quite a bit of skiving as an undergraduate. But the moment he started the actual flying he loved it and was rather disappointed that the medicos would only pronounce him fit as a pilot in warmer climes. He spent two days' leave exploring Jerusalem and Bethlehem with General Hoskins and he wrote to Kermit that he had taken some good photographs and had 'liked the Omar mosque and the wailing wall, where I got a magnificent photo of a ridiculous Jew, wailing in a Charlie Chaplin bowler'. The course was apparently tough in terms of hours – 'they work us morn to morn here' – but this was compensated for once in the air. They 'slipped'* in Cairo, which gave him the opportunity to wine and dine well at the Turf and Sporting Club pretty frequently. He hoped to be fully fledged by the end of the year. And he was. Unfortunately, though, he damaged his right foot in September, and the treatment from his own description was hardly conducive to improving the situation. He was now forced to stay in bed, which he loathed, but he had time to catch up on his correspondence and he wrote a long letter to Kermit, from the Grand Hotel in Helonaus.

2.11.18

Dear Kermit,

This place has been converted into a hospital and for my sins I find myself in it. Two months ago I ran a piece of barbed wire under my R. big toe nail; the toubibs after chopping and burning it about for some time eventually reduced the unfortunate limb to such a condition that they hastily rushed me into hospital and tore off the nail. That was in Cairo: I was then sent here to

* An aviation term for night stopping or landing in order to change crew.

convalesce where they succeeded in allowing my toe again to go septic; it is not yet healed up and it begins to look as though the war will be over now, before I am fledged. I have just heard from East Africa that the Government has again shown itself in typical colours by stirring up trouble with the Masai in the most senseless manner. It appears that they settled that the Masai ought to contribute 250 moran to be enlisted and sent an official to collect them. The Masai objected and after having a good few killed by maxim-fire they split up into marauding parties. Government then panicked and sent for Delamere who seems to have gone down with a boy and a cook and settled the whole thing, so Lady Colville writes. But not before one party succeeded in looting a trading store we had at Lemek, where they burnt all the building etc, and stole all the stock and trade goods, hides and skins etc, to the value of over £5,000 and I expect they have similarly served other farm stores. I trust that we shall be able to obtain compensation eventually but you may be certain that the Masai will not be keen to pay up and Government having now probably got the right wind up, will try to shirk responsibility in their usual manner. I enclose a rather bad letter from Berkeley Cole on the subject, published in the local Nairobi rag. It is disjointed and far too long and becomes foolish towards the end. I got your 'Stamboul Nights' some days before your letter and knew that you had sent it. I like several of them; the author is an understanding man evidently. The Bosch in defeat is making it plainer than ever that he possesses neither a sense of humour nor of dignity, e.g. he has just announced through the Swiss Gvt that he wishes to make arrangements by which both sides shall cease to bomb behind the lines: and then his delightful note to the Czechoslavs reorganising them as a nation and saying that Berlin will be delighted to welcome their Ambassador!!! Bosch humour is another name for horse-play and Bosch dignity is another name for bombastic pride. I hope that the war is treating you well: but I expect conditions in France must be damnable. It is marvellous the way we have been advancing and now it looks as though we must catch a lot of the Crown Prince's crowd. Here the weather is delightful and if my toe had not let me down, I should be well on my way towards completing. As it is the next few days may see a German collapse and with it the end of any point in my remaining a 'sodjer', and as things are pretty messed up in BEA. I shall probably settle to get out as soon as possible. I shall have to go to England on business first anyway. Remember to let me know if you are there, a wire c/o Winchilsea Ruskington will always discover my whereabouts. . . . I am very glad that Marshal rounded off the Mespots show so neatly and that we walked into Ninevah, that great city. I think your president has been very satisfactory lately – opinion about the Germans has hardened very much in America for which we ought to be most thankful as it will serve to brace up what Maxse* described as 'the Westminster Invertebrates'. What in the name of Kaiser II, George is plunging England into a General Election for with 7 million women voters, just at the end of the war is more than I can fathom. Why not get the war over first; but perhaps we shall! Keep well, it must have been nice having your family with you in France.

Denys

The incidents leading up to the uprising of the infuriated Maasai are fully described in Elspeth Huxley's *White Man's Country* but a short extract will explain their reaction and the circumstances under which Denys lost his trading store at Lemek.

Within the next few days, over fifty stores in the Mara district were pillaged and burned and several of the unarmed Indian owners murdered. The damage was later estimated by a Commission at £24,000. The telegraph line from Narok to Elmenteita was cut. All Somali traders and their sheep ordered out of the reserve. Settlers along the boundary applied for police protection and their Kikuyu labourers started to desert in fright. A system of mounted patrols was improvised. Several stores belonging to Europeans in the reserve were attacked and burnt. The moran population was quivering with resentment and on the verge of revolt. Every purko moran was on the war path with his spear greased and ready.[10]

---

* Leopold Maxse, Editor of the *National Review*, who was married to Katherine Lushington the original of Virginia Woolf's Mrs Dalloway. The spelling of Masai that Denys and his contemporaries used was then the accepted form.

Lady Colville's information in her letter to Denys was correct. Had it not been for the tactics and persuasions of Lord Delamere, the Government would have had a widespread Maasai rebellion on their hands. Berkeley Cole's feelings on the subject aired in this 'rather bad letter' are fair and are of interest from a sociological aspect. It also gives the reader a first hand glimpse of Berkeley's own character as observed by Denys and Tanne. When he mounted his high horse 'the shadow of it began to move and grow falling into a haughty and fantastical canter . . . '

Sir:

It is with surprise I learn of the recent disturbances in the Masai reserve. Surely with all the wars and rumours of wars all over the world a little more tact could have been displayed by the powers that be, to keep the peace in the very centre of a British Protectorate. The history of these natives during the last 16 or 17 years is roughly as follows (I am open to correction on the matter of details and dates): When the Uganda Railway arrived in the territory known as Masailand they did not feel inclined to meet the inhabitants as enemies and the Masai on their side, partly because of a certain prophecy of one of their elders (M'Batian) and partly through a respect for rifles and impedimentia they had never before seen, were quite willing to fall in with the Government's views and allow the Railway to proceed unmolested and without interference and consequently an agreement to this effect, was made between the Government and the Masai. Some few years later it was found expedient to get them to withdraw to Laikipia, this they did without more than a murmur of discontent at leaving their favourite grazing grounds. Later again the Government quite rightly found it necessary to move them a second time, in order to allow for European expansion to the north. The Masai were removed to a reserve in the south where they were told they could remain for all time. This was met with a certain amount of protest in the course of which, I believe it was ruled, that these people were not British subjects – however the move was effected. When the war broke out, many of these people volunteered for

service, but their abhorrence of discipline was well known and
they were not taken on, more than in small numbers, as scouts.
Being extremely rich they practically kept the country in meat
for the first three years of the war, the meat being comman-
deered from them at a price far below market prices. However,
at whatever price it had been taken for, it would not have
compensated them for their loss, as they have very little use, if
any, for money, the possession of stock being one of their only
desires. Two or three times they raided the neighbouring
German natives with varying success and no reproof from the
Government. On the fourth time, however, they were suddenly
fined no less than 2,000 head of cattle from one section alone.
This I know, soured them in a way that few would believe, and
a feeling of exasperation crept into them which was more than
a passing affliction. The natives themselves have been little
understood or sympathised with by the various officers put in
charge of them from time to time since the death of Mr Collyer,
and their consequent aloofness from anything to do with our
Government has probably led to this fiasco. It was recommended
that they should be conscripted, the reason is hard to see (a)
admittedly they made indifferent and intractable soldiers and
(b) they are not British subjects; however had they been wanted
badly and were necessary to our welfare, a little tact from some
person or persons they would listen to, would have certainly
brought them out. As it is, the order is issued peremptorily and
backed by an armed force – and a refusal is the result; was the
next step taken to endeavour to secure the ring leaders, in the
process of which, one or two old women and a few cows got
shot? If this were so, it would be sufficient to open the ball
from their point of view and their subsequent attack on the
armed force. As a result they were speedily to learn that maxim-
guns and rifles are 'not good enough'. What is the next step?
They break up into the bush and doubtless will become gangs
of modern bush rangers; not a very pleasant thing to have in
our midst! Especially for farmers struggling to keep cattle
diseases at bay and their farms in close quarantine. Happily we
hear that Lord Delamere has been asked to go and clean up the
mess and I trust he will be able to do so.

'Should end here' Denys marked at this juncture but
Berkeley continued on his high and mettlesome hack like
Don Quixote on the wretched jade Rozinante:

I cannot see why these people should not be left in peace after considering their past history and conduct. Bibles and bottles have apparently proved useless so now it is bullets, all for the sole reason that they are extremely conservative and do not care about our inestimable civilisation. I cannot also imagine how soldiers recruited as aforesaid can be of any service to the nation; rather I should think an additional extravagance in food and clothes; add to this they die like flies when taken to a tropical country. I am told the military position today is 'well in hand' this I never doubted but what about the civil population and those who depend on these people for herding their stock, their herd boys will now be in a great fever wanting to go off and see the damage done to their friends, relations and possessions, leaving us all at lambing time with a blue-eyed Kikuyu, his knowledge of herding beginning and ending with 'Shepherd's Pie'. In conclusion can anyone tell me what the inordinate craze of every officer-in-charge of the Masai Reserve is, to make them DO SOMETHING?[11] [The cutting is torn off here.]

By December 1918, however, the recruiting of the Maasai by the KAR for soldiering was no longer necessary. Germany had renounced all her overseas possessions to the Allied and Associated powers by Article 119 of the Treaty of Versailles and the First World War was at last terminated. The frayed ends of everyone's lives became tendrils of hope during peace, vesting faith in the rebuilding of a new and prosperous future. Denys was awarded the MC as well as Pip (1914–1915 Star) Squeak (1913–18 Campaign Medal) and Wilfred (Victory Medal 1914–18).*

* Dubbed after the *Daily Mirror* strip cartoon.

9

1919–Tania and Denys

Before Denys left Egypt his foot healed well enough for
him to qualify as a pilot and he was fit enough to indulge
in a private safari via the wilds of the Sudan on the
homeward journey to Nairobi. Obviously something
made him change his mind about going straight to
England on business before returning to Kenya. There he
lingered on, after attending to farm problems, in order to
take Tanne on safari before making his trip to Europe.

Upon reaching Namasagali on 27 January 1919, he
learned that Theodore Roosevelt had died on 6 January.
He wrote at once to Kermit:

I am on my way from Cairo to Nairobi and yesterday we met
the papers from BEA in which I learned of your father's death.
I am very sorry: it is a great loss for the right cause just now
when the next three or four years will demand much clear
thinking of the leaders of civilisation and I know how much it
means to you.

I have had quite an amazing trip through and am feeling
quite healthy again in this comfortable climate. The Nile played
up quite according to the guide books, as regards game. I saw
four lots of elephant at different times, one very big herd; and
one morning we came across a lot crossing the river, about 20,
and a young bull got swept down below a proper landing place
and could not get out and as we passed by, he drowned and
sank before our eyes.

Old Kitchener came through with me; he arrived at Rejaf
with a bed, a blanket, a shot gun, 2 tins of 'petit beurre' and a
set of false teeth to walk across to Nimule, so it was just as well
that I had a certain amount of stuff and a couple of chairs with
me! We had a great time getting across from Lake Albert to
Masinde Port to catch this boat across Chioga – furious wiring,

relays of porters, an old motor lorry which took us the last thirty miles on the iron rim of one back wheel and just caught the *Speke* which barged through the Sud and transferred us to the *Stanley* yesterday morning and here we are at Namasagali about to entrain for Jinja. I see in the BEA papers that the Government has a scheme for giving free grants of land to fellows here who served in the war. You ought to take some up and come out and settle here. I believe there will be a Committee in London who will deal with the application there.[1]

Besides picking up 'old Kitchener' in Rejaf, Denys had found a new servant; a cook and 'a real old Swahili ruffian of the old safari type, with a huge black beard; the name he gave me is Hamisi but I notice his associates call him "Simba"* on account of his mane no doubt.' Denys could not believe his luck at finding such a gem in the Sudan desert 'who devils chicken á merveille and is an expert baker – so I intend to retain him if he will bear with me'. He need not have worried about Hamisi tolerating his idiosyncracies – like Billea Issa and Kanuthia, Hamisi stayed with him for the next eleven years. They were devoted servants, did not resent his stern maxims and sometimes pithy criticism, but took pride when he praised their efforts. Billea went everywhere with Denys – in Africa it is better to travel across the bush (essential for survival in many cases) with another person.

In February 1919 Denys, like the von Blixens, had a renewed burst of faith in the Colony, and the von Blixens' coffee farm at least was not hampered by neglect. Their shiny trays of seedlings and young coffee trees presented a reassuring sight. Elsewhere choking weeds and rusting machinery were a depressing but familiar spectacle. Had Denys's income depended on his farm alone his problems would have been more severe, but even as a trader his

* 'Lion' in Swahili.

losses were considerable and his cattle herds had been reduced by rinderpest while the farm in Eldoret had suffered too through the conscription of men for war. Now the enthusiasm of peace encouraged settlers to urge relatives and friends to take up opportunities which seemed abundant in the Colony after four wasteful years. Even so Denys had misgivings in recommending it to married people – though convinced that Kermit's wife, Belle, would like Kenya he was diffident on the subject of settling as 'I am never quite sure of it as a country for white women and children'.

The 'free grants of land to fellows who served in the war' were made under a scheme mapped out briefly by the War Council as early as 1915 for settling ex-soldiers on the land. The reasoning behind this idea was predominantly strategic. The War Council were convinced that the East African Campaign would have an unsettling effect on the indigenous population, that the general white prestige would be shaken by war amongst them selves. The insurance for safety lay, they thought, in numbers; and a hefty influx of Europeans, in the form of a 'soldier settlement scheme' would provide an excellent all round solution.

When Denys met Tanne the year before, Bror was already playing an active part in raising money from Swedish bankers who had been invited to put up Swedish capital for this scheme. By summer 1918 the issue had come to a head so far as the Swedes were concerned. Bror had crossed swords with Lord Delamere over the viability of certain data he had submitted. Lord Delamere retaliated by challenging Bror publicly to substantiate certain figures he had proffered for successful crop returns, dismissing these categorically as unworkable. The final confrontation took place at Nakuru in mid-June.

The Swedish proposals were condemned as Lord Delamere took Bror's scheme apart proving that he was not only backing a dubious venture but perpetrating a swindle from which he would personally benefit, if it came off.

An extract from *The Leader*'s account of that meeting shows how Lord Delamere viewed the subject:

If any of the promoters are here present, we would be glad to hear from them and it was with this idea that Bror Blixen was invited to meet us here today. . . . If his figures are correct, I would be glad to hear if he is prepared to base his selling price on the farms on these figures. It will be noticed from the correspondence in *The Leader* of Saturday May 25th, that a certain Eckman, presumably one of the financiers, was willing to accept three times the fifteen years crop as purchase price, and considered it sufficient. . . . Let us see what Eckman was satisfied with, adopting again the Baron Blixen figures at the same estimate of expenditure; it would show a return of 35%. Quite a modest investment. Much has been made of the company's return of the fifth year not being a normal one. How does Eckman propose to provide for this out of his profits? He could hardly be able to do it . . . Is he really satisfied with his 35% or what? He is not a philanthropist, therefore we cannot take him on trust. Is it, that he knows the published returns of his figures are too low – for any higher figure would change his modest 35% to 102% – or is he calculating on the catch crop of flax which would enable him to recover his capital in one year and leave with, according to Baron Blixen's figures, £1,710, or mine £6,150 for shepherding his own sources of income![2]

Bror bluffed his way through the meeting with characteristic charm and braggadocio, but his ruse to recoup some of his losses through his participation in the Swedish Settlement Scheme had been detected and foiled. It is unfortunate that he did not take his own forthright advice on coffee growing: 'Any experienced coffee farmer will tell you that the altitude above sea level influences the growth of coffee trees to such an extent that the variation of 1000 ft will show a difference of two years bringing it to full bearing.'[3] But he seemed incapable of shifting from coffee to a crop more suited to the rainfall and altitude of his land or of taking incisive action by selling up and buying land elsewhere. However the selling of a farm, into which one has immersed oneself, is not as simple as that. Tanne explains the problem years later, when she had come to accept her own pig-headedness without making vapid excuses: 'the land was in itself a little too high for coffee and it was hard work to keep it going; we were never rich on the farm. But a coffee plantation is a thing that gets hold of you and does not let you go, and there is always something to do on it; you are generally just a little behind in your work.'[4]

In 1919 in spite of Tanne and Bror's marital and financial difficulties they still figured predominantly in each other's lives. Ironically the harvest of coffee that same year was the best they had achieved since they purchased the farm. In an early letter to the British Legation in Copenhagen, Bror puts his proposals for the farm at Ngong and at the same time touches on Tanne's wretchedness at the suspicions of the British community of her pro-German leanings:

As to my own interest in the proposition, I cannot . . . work for anybody but the Karen Coffee Co, and I would therefore be glad, if you could use your influence to persuade the financiers to farm out the ultimate work on contract and I would then see a chance to have some profit for my shareholders utilising the experience we now have of local conditions. I furthermore think it would be unwise if someone was brought out from Home to conduct the work out here without such experience. We have had a bad year out here owing to reduced shipping and the extraordinary seasons, which has influenced estimates, but now we seem to be on the right side. With your knowledge of the Dinesens and their anti-German feelings you can understand it has been very hard for my wife being looked upon as pro-German.'[5]

In 1918 Bror had tried to attract the attention of Sir Charles Bowering, the acting Governor, towards his Swedish Settlement Scheme but was apparently thwarted because of 'certain rumours . . . accusing me of introducing German money into this country and hinting at me being a Hun myself. I asked the acting Governor . . . for an explanation and assistance, but the only result was a law prohibiting transfers to foreigners of property here.'

Tanne and Bror felt slightly bitter about this, which is understandable. When Tanne wrote to Thomas, whom she is convinced will share her own enthusiasm for the country – she is determined that he will come out to settle – she refers to the matter. They had already discussed the possibility of taking up a five-thousand-acre farm and Tanne had tentatively reserved Crescent Island, on lake Naivasha, for her brother which she thought she could get 'for as little as £100'. But later she wrote, ' . . . about the farm at Naivasha. It's still not sold, but as a foreigner you can't get a transfer on it. Generous England! and now that the war is over you must come over yourself, there is no point in my buying anything you haven't seen.'[6]

Just before Christmas Tanne learned by cable that Thomas had been awarded the Victoria Cross. She was justifiably immensely proud of him. But the impressive report of his splendid gallantry served a deeper purpose than the simple fulfilment of either sisterly or phyletic pride. It finally cleared her in the eyes of the predominantly British population. After they had read the heavy black headline on the front page of *The Leader* on 21 December 1918 BARONESS BLIXEN'S BROTHER GETS VC and absorbed the following news item, they could no longer question her fidelity:

Those who have the privilege of knowing Baroness Blixen the charming wife of our Swedish Settler Baron Blixen will learn with pleasure that her brother, Private Thomas Dinesen, Quebec Rifles, has earned a VC as set out in *The Times* list as follows: 'for most conspicuous and continuous bravery displayed during the hours of hand to hand fighting which resulted in the capture of over a mile of strongly garrisoned and stubbornly defended enemy trenchment. Five times in succession he moved forward alone and single-handed, put hostile machine guns out of action accounting for 12 of the enemy with bomb and bayonet. His sustained valour and resourcefulness inspired his comrades at a very critical stage of the action and were an example to all.' It is interesting indeed, that no fewer than 15,000 Danes have fought for the Allies in the ranks of the British Army.[7]

Early in 1919 the ex-soldier settlement scheme was taken up in earnest for the second time – although Swedish participation was discreetly dropped. The Land Commission now proposed that land already surveyed for alienation should be thrown open for this project; by May the Commission and Government had settled the terms of application, which had changed from the original concept quite basically. Rather than give the land away, it was agreed that it should be purchased by ex-soldiers under very easy terms. Applications flooded in. A draw which bore all the importance of a raffle at a parochial fête took place at The Theatre Royal in Nairobi in June. Two tin drums filled with named and numbered tickets revolved and dictated the future of fifteen-hundred future settlers. Those who were the lucky winners were allocated lands. When the *Garth Castle* deposited its keen bunch of immigrants at Mombasa in November the local press dubbed them 'The Mayflower People'. Like the original pilgrims they nurtured high hopes for prosperity but were to learn that hardship and disappointment go hand in hand with 'trial-and-error' living in a new land.

There was a severe shortage of flax in England and this now became the crop which held the promise for the quickest return. Denys's land in Eldoret was ideal for flax, so that he took his next gamble with confidence while the price was good. By the middle of 1919 it was fetching as much as £300 per ton and was still increasing in value. He and his partner set their labourers to plough and till their land with patient sloe-eyed oxen and waited with certainty for the flax flowers to clothe the farm in an exquisite shroud of blue. They were not disappointed when in 1920 the price for the crop rose to reach almost double in return for their capital – even tow fetched as much as £340 per ton. The beauty of the harvest was almost as beguiling as its income – but the price plummeted in 1921 to less than £100 per ton. Ingrid Lindstrom, Tanne's much loved friend, and her husband who had been at school with Bror, came out in 1920 with the intention of growing flax at Njoro only to find that the bottom had dropped out of the market before their first crop was ready.

At the opening of her idyllic chapter 'Wings' in *Out of Africa* Tanne states that 'Denys . . . had no other home in Africa than the farm, he lived at my house between his safaris and he kept his books and gramophone there'. But this did not apply in 1919 when he first took her on safari. She is referring to a later period when he came to live on the farm after Bror had left and divorce proceedings had already been instigated. On his return to Kenya after the war Denys rented a small cottage attached to Muthaiga Club which he shared with Lord Delamere when he came up to Nairobi. Overlooking the golf course it afforded more privacy than the clubhouse itself. Denys's journeys were so frequent and his restlessness such that he never stayed anywhere long enough for it to be termed 'home' in the true sense of the word, other than Haverholme or The Plas, until he went to live with Tania at Ngong.

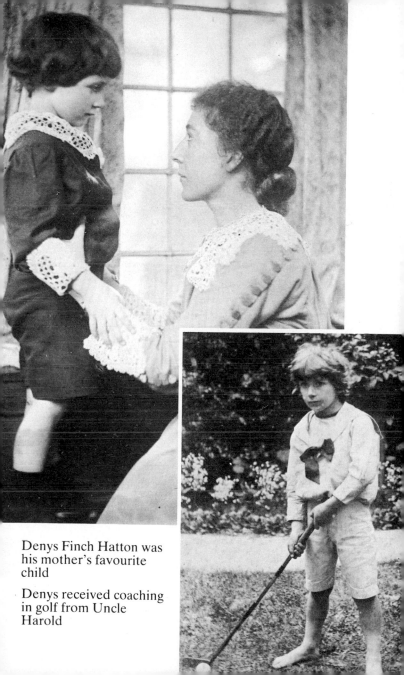

Denys Finch Hatton was his mother's favourite child

Denys received coaching in golf from Uncle Harold

Julian Grenfell and Denys Finch Hatton entertaining the members of POP – Eton 1904

Toby had great charm ...

Topsy on her
wedding day ... one
of the few
portraits not taken by
her mother – 1912

Denys admired the courage of
the Masai . . .

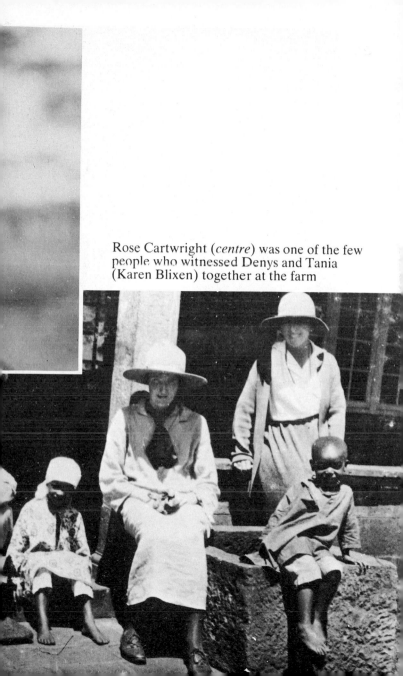

Rose Cartwright (*centre*) was one of the few people who witnessed Denys and Tania (Karen Blixen) together at the farm

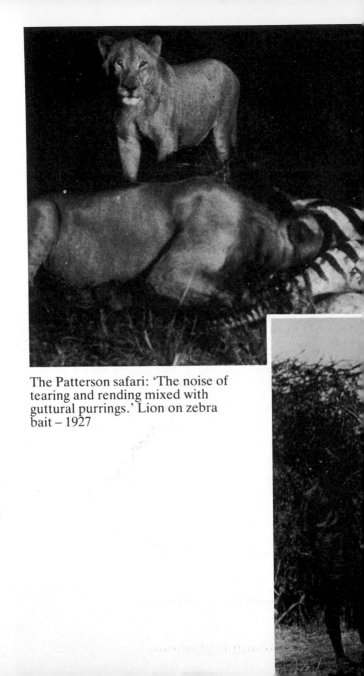

The Patterson safari: 'The noise of tearing and rending mixed with guttural purrings.' Lion on zebra bait – 1927

'There was just time to
jump to one side as the
buffalo rushed by ... Finch
Hatton's bullet found the
beast's brain with a timely
aim that saved my life'

On safari with the Prince of Wales – every afternoon they stopped for tea at four o' clock

'Tania', the name by which Denys knew Tanne, was subsequently adopted by all their friends. It is clear from her own annotations (though they were made after his death) that he was of the utmost importance in her life from the date of their first meeting. But is unlikely that he established his whim of calling her Tania until 1919. If he wrote to her from Egypt, no letters have survived and it seems likely that the habit started during their first safari together. It was an abbreviation of 'Titania', inspired by the enchanting qualities of the Queen of the Fairies in Shakespeare's *A Midsummer Night's Dream*. To Denys Tania evoked all the charm of a woodland deity; her aura hinted that anything might or could happen with her quicksilver mind.

Amongst Tania's papers, torn from an old notebook, is a list of relevant dates; mainly they refer to Denys or her own whereabouts in relation to his. Each entry seems to form a link with him, his travels, the death of his mother, the various clients he took on safari, and together they seem to have formed a working backbone, a personal chronology for the writing of *Out of Africa*. The first date records her first meeting with Denys at Muthaiga; the second gives the dates of their first safari together thus: 5.3.19.–14.3.19 *'rundt om Kenya m. Denys'* (round Kenya with Denys). The safari lasted nine days. Under that notation is 'went home in summer' and *'saa Denys i. London September'* (saw Denys in London in September). Throughout the list each entry is emphasized by his initials.

Yet at a first reading or even after a second, she gives her readers little clue that Denys was her sheet anchor and the 'grande passion' of her life. However, once the key has been turned in the lock of the door which they themselves seem to have shut with some deliberation in the face of a curious world, the clues are all there. They are subtle and tender allusions which, once that door has been pushed ajar, just a little, are not difficult to recognize or to understand. They abound in all her works and are her private salutations to this very significant existence. It was Denys who introduced her to most of the characters whom she has so lovingly recalled to tread the pages of *Out of Africa*. From the very first line, so sad and ominously, 'I had a farm in Africa', she acknowledges the quintessence of his being. On the second she drifts as gently as the glider she is predicting would 'be lifted upwards by the currents, over the mountain top' and as noiselessly, into Denys's realm of the sky and hills. Here they rode, picnicked and camped together and even chose the site of their graves – the Ngong Hills which they particularly loved. Its forests secreted their 'pet' herd of buffalo. They had walked on its game tracks at full moon. Like its eagles, they had flown together over the summit and they shared its view from the verandah of her house where they drank their early morning tea and where 'you woke in the morning and thought: Here I am, where I ought to be.'

Throughout her tales of fantasy Tania has insinuated small clues, like a preference for certain wine, food or literature, or personal gestures and quotations which invoke the memory of Denys. *Shadows on the Grass*, a slender sequel to *Out of Africa* written twenty-three years later, is a store-house of tender allusion. Possibly these were too fresh, too painful, to include initially but they allow Tania's readers a discreet step closer to their relationship. The references to Denys here give him a new dimension, put flesh on the word, instil a practicality of character which has been suffocated, if not lost, in the myth. It was he who introduced Tania to the efficient agent of whom she says in this book: 'From the time I left Africa . . . I sent out a small sum of money to my old

firm of solicitors, Messrs W. C. Hunter of Nairobi.'[8] W.
C. Hunter handled all Denys's business matters in his
absence and was the Chairman of Muthaiga Club while
Denys was on the Organizing Committee. The President
was Charles Bulpett – 'an English gentleman of the
Victorian age' living as the permanent guest of Sir
Northrup and Lady McMillan at Chiromo. Hugh Martin
– another close friend, had been up at Oxford with
Denys. Tania's inclusion of these characters, the presence
of these clues, verify Denys's powerful effect on her life.
They do not commit her yet at the same time dispel any
question that *Out of Africa* is basically the story of their
life together. Certain omissions will be understood when
the circumstances of his death are revealed, and word-
lessly substantiate two of her convictions: 'things are not
what they seem, they hardly ever are' and 'it is not a bad
thing in a tale that you understand only half of it'. She
has skilfully employed the tactics of a mistress-woman;
the participant of an illicit affaire, prevented by social
convention from venturing into open reference. But she
has woven their private jargon and their shared private
pleasures into her work with all the craft of a weaver bird
creating a nest from grasses and strands of human hair. It
was a posthumous act of complicity – if a little one sided
– that complemented her choice of pseudonym 'Isak',
'the one who laughs', to perfection.

Friends who knew Tania and Denys well – few were
privileged to observe their relationship closely – concluded that they fully intended to perpetuate the aura of
mystique which from the start has served to swathe
and protect them in an enigmatic smoke-screen. Even
Thomas, Tania's closest confidant, was excluded from
those precious weeks when Denys came to the farm,
during his own protracted visit to Kenya. If Tania received
word that Denys's arrival was imminent, she immediately

contrived all manner of small safaris or visits Thomas could make to up-country friends. In the end she admitted rather lamely that she expected Denys at any time and wanted to be alone with him. There was this same defiant demand for monopoly in Tania's relationships later in life with young men of letters and intellectuals whom she favoured. She repeatedly dismissed her secretary or anyone else who happened to be around, in order to be alone with these individuals, even if she had to create fictitious errands as decoys.

Later, after Thomas had met Denys and returned to Denmark, he learned to detect Denys's comings and goings from the tone of his sister's letters. Overwhelming 'shauries' with the staff, rows with managers, and despair at the financial pressure generally indicated that Denys had just left or had been away for some time. When her letters were full of joy and hope, bearing the air of Elysian happiness, Denys was staying or about to arrive on the farm. In the matter of love this is understandable. Byron has it that 'friendship is love without its wings' and Tania's moods soared with optimism when Denys was near.

A female observer who admired them both recalls: 'Tania and Denys were both very elusive and meant to be', adding thoughtfully, 'as for Denys, one would have gone to the ends of the earth for him'. That rider perhaps gives a clue to his enduring magnetism. His fascination, which lived on beyond the grave, perhaps explains why Tania's life as told in *Out of Africa* appeared to begin and end with him, but mysteriously is never fully explained. From the time she met Denys she managed to eradicate most aspects of her life with Bror; this obliter-ation could form part of her fight for survival without bitterness – she did not have a very happy time with Bror after the first year. Yet she was always loyal, before and after the divorce, helping him if necessary when he was unwell and never really disclosing how much she had been hurt, over and over again, by his lack of sensitivity.

She seems to have had an infinite capacity to frame and heighten each moment spent with Denys, to draw from an almost perfect relationship a lifetime of appreciation. In the way that a connoisseur never gulps a vintage wine but sips it slowly almost with reluctance delaying its intake to savour each drop, she eked out her life shared with him. After his death the years before her must have seemed like a life-sentence. But through those years of loneliness she learned to spin out her private recollections. She used them as literary caresses or anonymous souvenirs to a memory which she cherished.

Kamante, who takes the lead in her second chapter in *Out of Africa*, came to her on Easter Sunday that same year, a diseased and emaciated little Kikuyu boy whose suppurating sores had never been diagnosed and whose task was to herd his family's goats. She sought a cure for him, then employed him, and he is now another immortal. He has risen, through her kindness and generosity of spirit and through his own in-built philosophy, to bestride a world of literature which he neither recognizes nor comprehends. It is likely that he does not even know that it exists. Yet he has become part of it. He rose in Tania's household from 'dog toto' to gifted cook and today remembers 'Mr Pincha Hattern he was a good man' with grey-haired nostalgia for things long past. Tania had a profound, unbiased understanding for all her African servants but her deep appreciation of Kamante's predicament springs from an understanding within herself when she writes of him: 'He was a thoughtful person. Perhaps the long years of suffering that he had lived through had developed in him a tendency to reflect upon things, and to draw his own conclusions from everything he saw.'[9]

Tania had the same capacity. And in neither of them is a feeling of martyrdom or sickly malcontent.

In March 1919 when Denys first took Tania on safari the journey was as much devoted to exploring each other's minds as to visiting the favourite haunts and hunting grounds. A safari can be a misery if the organization is slapdash. Denys possessed a practical ability, the foresight to arrange expeditions that went off smoothly. Avoiding the unhappy results of haphazard packing he made it a rule to cover every eventuality without overburdening the porters with loads of superfluous kit. He likened a safari to being marooned on a desert island. 'Method,' [sic] he declared 'maketh man':

Remember [said Finch Hatton] that the real secret of ordering stores is to know how long each tin of sardines, so to say, will last you. You have to work it out by the law of averages. These mathematics will teach you that one pound of tea lasts one man a fortnight . . . a one pound tin of marmalade will last the same man a week and ten days to finish a tin . . . of plum jam . . . the whole art of buying stores lies in being able to estimate the 'life' of a tin of sardines.'[10]

No detail during Denys's preparation for safari was too small. Tents were inspected for rents, missing ropes or poles, and each had to be at least eight feet high 'so that a man of some inches may stand straight in it and be at ease'. A tent bathroom he felt was 'a most necessary annexe in which not only to bathe but to keep cameras, rifles and other dearer possessions'. His efficiency was motivated by a natural desire to have things running smoothly so that he could relax and enjoy himself fully. Forgetfulness was dangerous for 'it is no unusual thing to arrive late in camp . . . too tired but for an impromptu meal. . . . But where is the tin opener? The tin opener is in Nairobi . . . though your servants can . . . open a tin given time . . . it will not be before your temper is fairly frazzled. It is easy to forget things . . . easier to remember them.'[11] Denys's client Frederick Patterson concluded that 'one of the most arresting items of an African journey is the new kind of technique the traveller learns', and noted Denys's ability to 'hunt up some corner of the world and make it more English than the home island itself'. Denys did not force this ability or his opinion on others, though he felt sound advice 'from an old hand' was always worth consideration. On the subject of clothes he decreed 'the fewer the better' adding 'you will learn what suits you by personal experience only' – 'remember it is not everyone whose skin is tough enough to wear shorts in the sun . . . or to stalk in.' He favoured long khaki trousers himself, bush shirts with adequate pockets for oddments and sometimes a drill waistcoat. Usually he sported a faded red scarf, loosely knotted at the neck, to which he occasionally affixed a jewelled pin. His ensemble was unfailingly completed by one of his quaint collection of hats – generally a blue 'bowler' supplied by James Lock & Co, St James's St, London. Amongst this extraordinary selection were topies, bowlers, double terais, Hombergs and one silken collapsible opera hat.

Tania preferred riding breeches and supple, hand-made leather boots, for protection against the sharp thorny scrub. To protect her eyes from the glare she wore a wide-brimmed hat, with a highish crown, to which she sometimes added a soft cockade of feathers. When she was slender (her weight fluctuated considerably) she looked almost absurdly chic for the bush: one of her favourite photographs of herself was taken in 1919 on the farm just after their return from this first safari. Denys probably took it, for the distinct air of the professional behind the camera comes through the picture itself. It is the one she chose for *Shadows on the Grass*. She stands completely happy and relaxed yet with all the awareness of a model who is confident in her physical presence, or like some lean, prized, thoroughbred race horse, disdainful of the crowd. In her hands she holds a single rose. Pania, her Scottish deerhound, clings to her side, turned away from yet part of her, combined as they are by the dapple of sunlight and leaves. The composition and symmetry of this picture make it a timeless portrait. It is taken with an agapistic lens and could, even today, have slipped from a fashion portfolio. (Anita Loos the Hollywood screenwriter compares Tania's presence to that of Queen Alexandra – 'She was slender and dressed with much more chic than was necessary – than royalty had any need for.' Like Isak Dinesen . . . Alexandra in her eighties possessed a charm that actually amounted to sex-appeal.) Tania's presence, fascinating and enigmatic did not diminish either with age.

Bror had given Tania the first taste of the hunt. She wrote to Thomas in October 1914 about it. The excitement is all there:

Bror gave me a 256 rifle, with a telescopic sight, a wonderful weapon which I was terrified to use at first, but which I gradually learned to handle. Bror is an excellent teacher . . . I used a hundred cartridges to kill forty-four head of game. One is easily tempted out here to shoot at too great a range, but Bror sternly stopped me and he's very clever at getting you close to the game. But I've put a bullet in the hearts of Wildebeests and Topis at over four hundred meters range. I shot twenty different kinds of game.'[12]

There is little gentleness in that letter, it is predatory in true response to the man she temporarily loved and then admired. Bror's hunting skill is acknowledged by fellow hunters, Denys included. Both their reputations survived mortality. But Bror's approach was the ferocious assault of life. (He could drink a bottle of gin at night, wake at dawn and hunt all next day.) His power, his own prestige, drove him into a world of raids and fortifications. At Denys's side, under his influence, Tania learned the incorporeal facets of the chase; she changed her outlook after Bror left and in assuming responsibility she admits: 'Before I took over management of the farm, I had been keen on shooting . . . when I became a farmer, I put away my rifles.'

With Denys, Tania dared to dream again. And in her Denys discovered a woman whose intellectual capacity, if untutored, was fecund, and whose imagination was as lively as a *capriccio*. They were romantic – poetic seekers. Tania speaks of his qualities and powers of observation with tenderness in *Out of Africa:*

Denys had watched and followed all the ways of the African Highlands, and better than any other white man, he had known their soil and seasons, the vegetation and the wild animals, the winds and smells. He had observed the changes of weather in them, their people, clouds, the stars at night. Here in the hills, I had seen him only a short time ago, standing bare-headed in the afternoon sun, gazing out over the land and lifting his fieldglasses to find out everything about it. He had taken in the country and in his eyes and his mind it had been changed, marked by his own individuality and made part of him.[13]

Her nostalgia for the closeness of their relationship is revealed by the phrase 'standing bareheaded in the afternoon sun'. If Denys was vain at all, the one thing he regretted and was conscious of was his lack of hair. By the time he was thirty-eight he was almost completely bald. Only closest friends were aware of the fact – he was never seen hatless out of doors – and the rim of hair which showed beneath his hat was convincing enough to fool strangers. When his car overturned in 1930 and he and Billea almost drowned 'Mr Finch Hatton was far more concerned about the loss of his quaint blue and well known hat' . . . he borrowed one . . . 'indifferent to the fact that the hat was of the type worn by ladies.' Tania used the bones of this little incident for a fragment in 'The Roads Around Pisa', sub-titled 'The Accident', for her first story in *Seven Gothic Tales*. As usual she has freed herself by setting the incident back in time and changing the sex of the passengers. The car becomes a carriage driven at great speed (Denys tended to drive too fast) which overturns.

A broad young woman . . . now began disentangling herself with loud lamentations. The old man turned his eyes upon her. 'Put on my bonnet,' he said. The maid . . . after some struggle got hold of a large bonnet with ostrich feathers and managed to get it fixed on the . . . bald head. Fastened inside the bonnet was an abundance of silvery curls, and in a moment the old man was transformed into a fine old lady . . . the bonnet seemed to set her at ease.[14]

In that short passage the reader can appreciate Tania's gift for fancy and her ability to transform real life fabric into fantasy which still bears the stamp of truth. The vulnerability of the man exposed, his confidence shaken by the loss of his hat, far from being ridiculed is comprehended fully. The victim in the story (and his original in real life) would rather wear a woman's hat than disclose his baldness.

For Tania Denys's mysterious reserve, in contrast to Bror, heightened his magnetism. The unknown in the man held her captive. With him she could sit 'into the small hours of the morning, talking of all the things we could think of, and mastering them all and laughing at them'. In 'The Dreamers' she makes a discerning observation. One can almost feel her turning over Denys's attributes in her mind, weighing them against Bror's. Her husband's personality is embodied in the role of the seducer Baron Guilderstern of Sweden, while Denys's disinterest in competing, his polish and need for solitary independence, come through also.

But in the case of the Baron it was clear that the point of gravity had always been entirely with him. . . . It appeared from his talk that all his ladies had been of exactly the same kind, and that kind of woman I have never met. With himself so absolutely the hero of each single exploit, I wondered why he should have taken so much trouble – and he was obviously prepared to go to any length of trouble in these affairs – to obtain time after time, a repetition of exactly the same trick. To begin with I was, being a young man myself, highly impressed by such a superabundance of appetite. . . . Life, to him, was a competition in which he must needs shine beyond the other entrants. . . . I thought it silly to exert myself about it just because it happened to be the taste of others. Not so this Swedish Baron. Nothing in the world was in itself good or bad to him. He was waiting for a cue, and a scent to follow, from other people, and to find out from them what things they held precious, in order to outshine them in the pursuit of such things. . . . When he was left alone he was lost. In this way he became more dependent upon others . . . and probably he shunned solitude as the very devil. . . . Yet he was no fool. On the contrary, I should say that he was a very shrewd person. He had adopted in life, the manner of a good, plain, outspoken fellow who is a little unpolished but easily forgiven on account of his open, simple mind. . . . As he was without nerves which make ordinary people feel the strain of things he had without doubt an extraordinary strength and stamina, and was held by himself and by others to be a giant in comparison with those who have imagination or compassion in them.[15]

Tania, the dreamer of daytime, writes of dreams in *Shadows on the Grass* and tries to recall whether she had been told or whether she had read somewhere that in a book of Etiquette of the XII Century, 'the very first rule forbids you to tell your dreams to other people since they cannot possibly be of interest to them'. Dreams it is true are above all private meanderings of the night mind, unfettered by logic, drawing the sleeper into the far sublunary spheres of beauty, transience and impossibility, into which the waking human is forbidden by his very consciousness to stray and from which it is sometimes irksome to return to reality. An old aunt of Tania's requested this epitaph: 'She saw many a hard day. But her nights were sweet.' But in reality, morning and its light always follows to break the flight of the night-enchanted captive. The dream that held Tania captive and of which she would never be able to speak, was the eternal hope that one day she would become Denys Finch Hatton's wife.

But Denys belonged to the wild nomadic world and he never intended to marry anyone. His need for time and space were pre-requisites to all his plans and had dominated his life since he had discovered their feasibility in Africa. He fled if he felt the pressures of social and personal attachments closing in upon him. Anyone, male or female, who attempted to rein him in or set limitations to his freedom would lose him. Like Blake's Job in his regained prosperity Denys kissed 'the Joy as it flies' and lived 'in Eternity's sunrise'. Marriage was a cage and cages did not exist in his world or his mind. Like one of the eagles he and Tania watched as it built its eyrie high up in the Ngong Hills, his noble air of authority and conviction, his individuality, carried him into worlds which were shut to those of a less fearless nature. Those who loved him accepted these fiercely defended beliefs – 'He who bends to himself a Joy, doth the winged life destroy.' Those who understood, treasured the rare moments when he allowed himself to be shared.

Married friends who dined with Tania and Denys on

the farm on one occasion recollect the vividness of the evening – the woman found Denys the most attractive man she had ever met because of the absolute magic about him which was quite unforgettable. His magnetism to both sexes was not unlike the quality of the Pied Piper. Like a meteor he arrived only to go off again, but he brought with him the enormous sky, the plains and forest. He wanted the wild. The settlers always hoped to get him into politics but he would not even consider it, disappearing into the bush to get away from it all.

The transience of life in the bush obviously attracted him, yet a camp is a home, no matter how temporary. It is an oasis and becomes the personal reflection of fundamental needs. Shelter from the wind, shade from the midday sun, water and privacy may be combined in a spot of great beauty. After the tents had been pitched on Tania and Denys's safari they had little to do but enjoy the days. Denys took care of the practicalities – he knew right down to the last piece of kitchen equipment that 'with half a dozen aluminium pots, one frying pan and one kettle an African cook can, under the stars make . . . the most sumptuous of dinners.'

After two or three days in the wild the senses sharpen again. Instincts buried for aeons under the yoke of what is termed civilization, reawaken. One lives again by the sense of smell – from dawn when the aroma of bruised grass exuded from the air by the tent pervades it – to dusk when the fresh dung of an unseen herd of buffalo is discovered. The ear strains to reach the million different sounds each telling a story of their own. The eye learns again to stretch its range of vision – to note the soundless messages of the bush. Vultures circling ominously speak without voice of approaching death. On the plains the news is relayed by their open invitation as they gather in anticipation and become a flock. They know they will be first to dine. The russet-tipped grass may be subtly broken and bent from the passage of some herd. Shadows at midday are scant but are always sufficient to camouflage three or four elephant standing as still as red earthen rocks, fused beneath a scruffy euphorbia. Strangely in their vastness they may be overlooked by the casual eye. There comes a rebirth of oneself in the discovery that such atavistic senses have survived. To watch a native tracker for the first time is to recognize the true craftsman – he sniffs out the lair of his quarry with all the characteristics of the animal itself. He finds the secret track it uses to reach water; the ground answers him in his quest for information.

Complicity is the keynote of those who hunt in Africa. The closeness, possibly framed by danger and the very savagery of the act, binds two pursuants irrevocably together. The tale of a day's chase may be retold round the camp fire at night – but like a dream recounted or a love affair described each telling diffuses the essence and excitement of the original. The listener may politely acquiesce but he is always an outsider. Big-game hunting is a severe test of compatibility. Everything is unpredictable. Adverse conditions, fear, ignorance and fatigue can act as tripwires in relationships. The weaknesses cannot be seen in advance but by introducing discord they can break the spell of unity. But for those who surmount and share the apprehension at the moment of death, the chafing from the day-long walk and the thorns, the harmony of this reward is rich indeed.

Tania has been called a woman of great courage and in Africa she was certainly physically tough and capable of walking great distances. At the age of sixty she spoke publicly of this resilience: 'I have been very strong, unusually so for a woman – able to walk or ride longer than most men, I have bent a Masai bow and have felt in a moment of rapture a relationship to Odysseus. The pleasure of having been strong is still with me, the weakness of today is the natural continuation of the vigour of former days.'[16] Ingrid Lindstrom admired Tania's physical endurance, recalling how 'she could ride for days on end across the Masai reserve, with no sign of discomfort, fatigue or pain – she was one of those people who were never ill.' Which is strange when the world has been led to believe through the oblique references to her illness that she was left physically weak and impaired for life. Most of the books written on her convey an impression of lingering weakness but this seems to have manifested itself after Denys's death. Obviously her mental resources contributed to her courage, but it is unlikely that, had she been suffering, she would have gone on that safari with Denys. He has been recognized repeatedly by friends as being 'a kind man' but he was also shrewd; he measured this kindness wisely, ensuring that he displayed his generosity within the bounds of his tolerance. He was no collector of lame ducks. Certainly he would never have considered taking a helpless or an ailing woman into the bush. In fact, Tania is the only woman he chose to take out on safari. The responsibility of a burdensome companion who might have endangered their lives in a crisis would have killed the irresistible lure of adventure. The risks were too great for Denys to contemplate an intrusion of this nature on his own pleasure.

When he was thinking of taking up hunting profession-ally he wrote to Kermit about his limits of forbearance: 'I am thinking of doing a bit of white hunting to earn an honest penny! . . . So if you know of any pleasant people who want to shoot put them in touch with me. You know the sort of people I should get on with *and* the ones I should *not*. Don't send any of the latter!' He was almost ruthlessly selective in his choice of clients. There is only one instance recorded of an unhappy safari under his guidance. And the discomfort was his rather than his clients', who consisted of an American, his wife and his daughter. Denys found their company so disagreeable that he re-routed his safari in order to escape them for a few hours. Arriving at Rose Cartwright's (née Buxton) farm at Naivasha, he introduced the American family, settled them into their rooms and excused himself abruptly. Later he took Rose aside, explaining to her 'they are too abominable for words' and begging her to excuse him from dinner 'If you could send mine to my room on a tray.' He apologized for inflicting them on her and Rose knew he would never have resorted to such behaviour without good reason. She took the clients off his hands and after a day's respite the group continued on its way without acrimony, nor were the clients any the wiser as to Denys's feelings.

Tania has writen: 'Camping-places [sic] fix themselves in your mind, as if you have spent long periods of your life in them. You will remember the curve of a wagon track in the grass of the plain like the features of a friend.'[17] Every day you look forward to returning to your temporary home. A bath or a shower after a day in the sun is an unimaginable luxury and takes on the feeling of something exclusive and rare, for water has to be carried by hand from the nearest water-hole, heated in 'debis' (old paraffin tins) and brought bit by bit to the canvas bath or shower bucket as required. So the very act of bathing takes on the atmosphere of a sacred rite through dependence on the servants who prepare every-thing for you.

All good hunters study the rhythm of the wild. Denys imposed this discipline upon himself and taught Tania to do the same. The strain is less after a while and it becomes possible to sit so still, so close to the ground, that the stirring of an insect in the grass takes on the volume of a tiny marching army. The tiredness from this strain of learning nature's way brings a muted tranquillity, and after their pastoral day they would sit about the fire replete with happiness.

Content steals over a camp at twilight; the trackers exchange tales of the day's adventures with the kitchen staff, the skinners whistle idly through their teeth as they complete their tasks for the day, salting the skins, preserving trophies temporarily until they can be delivered to the taxidermist in Nairobi. Knives are sharpened, cigarettes rolled and shared. The ends glow in the dark like red shooting stars as they are passed from hand to hand. They sip strong tea, as the smells of roast guinea-fowl, newly baked bread or coffee drift on air already spiced by trampled grass and wild flowers. Bats skim the edge of darkness. The last birdsong dies in the trees as the night sounds predominate in an atmosphere of great peace which is conducive to confession. The experiences shared by day are binding: there are no false barriers to prevent the unburdening of one's conscience. Memories from childhood spring up, inconsequential things – snatches of poetry, sadnesses. All these secrets steal almost imperceptibly from the depths of the soul in the dying embers of a camp fire without pain or the feeling of foolishness. They dined well but Denys never carted along bottled or tinned luxuries from Fortnum and Mason's to supplement his menus in the bush. In Hamisi's hands, the fillet taken from an Impala marinated and roasted in the blackened Dutch oven sunk into the ground was a delicacy in itself. They ate spurfowl which they shot at dawn; made soup from the bones – Denys especially liked thin peppery bouillons – or the roasted leg of the wild pig, combined with herbs and seasonings which provided more than adequate fare.

Tania was sufficiently interested in cooking during her first year of marriage to take a course in the art. She went to a professional chef in Paris – a Monsieur Perrochet – because she felt 'it would be amusing to make good food in Africa'. In Denys she found an appreciative gourmet who liked piquant sauces as much as poached fish masked in a parsley sauce – a bland delicacy which 'Goudie' their cook used to make for him at Haverholme. One of his favourite dishes was 'omelette à la chasseur' which Hamisi prepared from the tender livers of wild birds. Tania later taught Kamante Hamisi's recipe so that when Denys came back to the farm it could be made for him as a 'welcome home' treat. He had also retained a childhood passion for oranges – often carrying one in his pocket on walks or rides to chew on when thirsty.

After dinner while sipping the last of their wine their first long discussions began. Like Denys, Tania was a good listener. He related his solitary adventures in the Sudan or Somalia and under these starlit conditions his teaching began:

Denys taught me Latin, and to read the Bible and the Greek poets. He himself knew great parts of the Old Testament by heart, and carried the Bible with him on all his journeys, which gained him the high esteem of the Mohammedans.[18]

But when they spoke of God, Denys's concept was quite different from that enforced by Aunt Bess's rigid moral discipline and Unitarian beliefs. On coming to Africa Denys had purchased a Swahili edition of the Bible – 'Masahufu Mtakatifu wa Mungu' – to help him learn the language which he believed would be a useful aid in understanding the Swahili-speaking people as a race. He called them 'the children of Ham' and was intrigued by their interpretation of Christianity. He believed that the Bible should be re-examined as a work of literary merit, an epic in the form of a novel or incredible folk-tale, and that when seen in this light the repressive connotations of religion and the Bible would fade. Only if it could be judged in the same way as Chaucer's *Canterbury Tales* could it be freed from prejudice. He was not a deeply religious man. He was an agnostic. He did not fear death though he feared old age and dependency. He appeared to find the authenticity of life in the probable finality of death. Though he lived by a private creed of right and wrong he neither affirmed nor denied the immortality of man, nor acknowledged the existence of a supreme being. The Book of Job was the part of the Old Testament from which most of his allusions stemmed but they were essentially aesthetic or intellectual comparisons and comments, substantiating his idea that the Bible was literature, not religion.

To keep pace with this new mind was a challenge which surpassed all Tania's previous challenges. If Denys was not an intellectual in the true sense of the word, his interests were scholarly, he was erudite and well read but never pedantic.

Her own recollections of her father from childhood represented the same uplifting need to stretch her capacity to think. The subjects discussed with Denys covered the space between the two eternities. There were no confining bonds. Perhaps this frightened her a little, putting her on her mettle and alerting her creative force. It stirred her depths of intelligence into a state of discontent. In her doubt, she wrote to her brother in 1926 touching on these inadequacies of which she was now acutely aware. It is clear that exposure to Denys confirmed the shortcomings of her own education and all too often made her pitifully ignorant by comparison. But the fact was, she did have the average tutoring given to girls of her class. She was not exceptionally deprived but a victim of her time and sex. When Denys was away he sent her books, pictures, records or pieces of music, feeding her mind with notions they might discuss when he returned. In one note he comments 'This music is for a dance in a Lesbian ballet: and is danced by a very pretty little creature, Nikotina . . . The music is full of humour and raises many recollections.' From that communication it seems that Denys enjoys introducing her to new sounds as much as experiencing them himself. He seems to be promising a shared conversation, engaging her in recollection of the past. When she wrote to Thomas she was obviously considering writing as a way to redeem her wasted life and talent. It had taken twenty years for the same woman to change her mind: she had no intention of becoming 'a piece of printed matter'. Now she reveals all her qualms and frail aspirations when she writes in a moment of truth to her brother:

And here I sit in an idyll which is no idyll, except I shall make it into one! Oh, do you think Tommy, do you think I can still 'become something' or have I neglected my chances in life while there was still time, so that I have nothing left but to fade away and go to seed, to be patient and hope that others will have patience with me for being a complete failure? Naturally there will be dreadful, possibly insuperable difficulties over finding myself some kind of activity or some kind of job, because I know nothing whatsoever. However isn't it also dreadful that honourable people can allow a person to grow up, just because they are of the female sex without learning *anything at all*. . . . What did they think? Well, they probably thought of marriage as our future. . . . With all my endless drawbacks, I do have the advantage that conventional considerations mean nothing at all to me.[19]

Denys's influence can be felt strongly in that letter. She had been involved with him emotionally, for almost five years when it was written. With Denys Tania learned humility, but in her usual reflective way it is he, in her opinion, who was the modest one. Hers was harvested and grew into the widened horizon she applied to the most mundane aspects of daily life giving it dimensions which she had previously not contemplated. And Denys? 'He was happy on the farm; he came there only when he wanted to come, and it knew, in him, a quality of which the world besides was not aware, a humility. He never did but what he wanted to do, neither was guile found in his mouth.'[20] She shared his close observations, measured, calculated and tempered in his mind by an asceticism which few were capable of or prepared to share. But Tania was. And it was this that set them apart and served to stress, if anything, the remoteness of the true melancholic in his character.

One morning on that safari when the mist still clung to the hollows in the land, as if some gigantic bride had silently passed leaving her filmy train floating in her wake, they went in search of buffalo. Denys wanted to photograph them at close range. It was one of his ambitions to show these unpredictable bovines of the wild in an oncoming stampede; to capture them like Odin's valkyries transformed into beasts, with their horns magnified against their own silhouettes, against the immense sea of sky. They came upon a herd together, which seemed to materialize before their very eyes and counted one hundred and twenty-nine of them as they emerged, one by one, through the morning vapour. Tania writes of the moment in the very beginning of *Out of Africa*: 'As if the dark and massive iron-like animals with the mighty, horizontally swung horns were not approaching, but were being created before my very eyes and were sent out as they were finished.' Fascinated they watched the herd drift out onto the plain browsing as they went, and now Tania learned that the 'art of moving gently, without suddenness, is the first to be studied by the hunter and more so, by hunters with a camera. Hunters cannot have it their own way, they must fall in with the wind, and the colours and smells of the landscape, and they must make the tempo of the ensemble their own. Sometimes it repeats a movement over and over again and they must follow up with it.'[21]

Eventually Denys did get good photographs of buffalo, both moving films and stills, but it took many years of patience to achieve the results he wanted and considerable exposure to danger. The buffalo is a shy beast and difficult to approach; if annoyed it displays a formidable temper with which it is difficult to contend. An accurate bullet shot, the punctuation of life, is usually the imperative solution. J. A. Hunter* one of Kenya's most renowned professional hunters, recounts trying to film buffalo with Denys in the latter part of 1930, just a few months before he died:

We hunted quite a lot together, always exploring new grounds and trying ever unsuccessfully to get good motion pictures of charging buffalo. Denys pursued this object with intense devotion and we tried many times to get a single buffalo to charge our truck while Denys operated the camera. . . . But we were never able to overcome the difficulty of the clouds of dust raised by the herd. . . . In one instance the herd was so blinded . . . that a young bull ran straight into our truck. It straddled the bonnet. I heard the crumpling of metal and I jumped from my seat on the wheel to kill it with an immediate frontal shot before we found ourselves crushed beneath its weight. . . . We tried other tactics. There are clumps of reeds on the north side

---

* Hunter's Lodge on the Mombasa Road is named after him, and was his home.

of the Lake [Natron] offering ample cover for sneaking up on herds of buffalo. In addition, Denys and I camouflaged ourselves with long grasses. We spotted a bull with a fine pair of horns, he looked a real fighter, and headed him off from the main herd, knowing that as soon as he found himself pursued by the truck he would head for heavy cover. I drove the truck and pursued the bull across open country at a steady twenty miles per hour, not wanting to tax his strength. Then he turned off and headed for a solitary tree beneath which he stood facing us defiantly. Denys got his camera into action and I drove round and round the bull, hoping to get it into a charge, and although he made one or two feints towards us, he would not press them home, and in the end we had to give him best and drove off, with some good pictures but not the pictures of the charging beast that Denys really wanted. I wish we had tried harder on that occasion, for no other opportunity came his way.[22]

Though abortive, that encounter typifies Denys's patience and perseverance. He never gave up and was ever discontented with anything that fell short of perfection. If when he was teaching Tania something, she failed to come up to expectation he admonished her firmly but gently 'No, no, no, Tania – I'm afraid that's not quite right, come on, try again.'

Strangely, Tania and Denys failed to agree over the artistic merit of the camera. This small incompatibility is mentioned in *Shadows on the Grass*:

Nowadays great sportsmen hunt with cameras. The practice started while I was still in Africa, Denys, as a white hunter took out millionaires . . . and they brought back magnificent pictures, which . . . to my mind (because I do not see eye to eye with the camera) bore less likeness to their object than the chalk portraits drawn up on the kitchen door by our native porters. It is a more refined sport than shooting and providing you can make the lion join into the spirit of it you may here, at the end of a pleasant, platonic affair, without bloodshed blow one another a kiss and part like civilised beings. I have no real knowledge of the art – I was a fairly good shot with the rifle but I cannot photograph.[23]

Tania's comment implies that the very bloodlessness of an expedition in photography extinguishes and renders the act unimportant, the chase anaemic. But perhaps this hobby of Denys's impinged on an aspect of her relationship with him for she could not share entirely in the pursuit; she may even have felt excluded and superfluous in the matter. It was almost as if the camera, manipulated exclusively by Denys, his attention centred on it, obviated her existence causing real pangs of jealousy. The time he spent in the dark room developing the plates and completing the process also excluded her. One of his longest absences from the farm was a safari that lasted five months in the pursuit of good photographs. Platonic the gaze of the eye of the lens on the lion may have been, triumphant the result immortalized on film, but to Tania they represented the confirmation of another long absence and perhaps this prevented her from complete enthusiasm for the final product.

Some of Denys's photographs of buffalo appeared in *Country Life* magazine in 1928 where they accompanied an article written to coincide with the topical interest surrounding the visit to Kenya by the Prince of Wales. But his fascination with the animals never waned. He and Tania came to know the herd in the Ngong Hills which they looked upon as their own and followed with close interest. When Denys brought his plane to Africa they often flew up to 'watch the buffalo feeding in the hills' at sunset. On nights when the full moon floodlit the landscape with its cold metallic gleam, at Denys's whim, they drove up often after midnight to gaze at the restive creatures watering at nocturnal pools before seeking the safety of the forest glades by dawn.

10

1919–1921 – The Breaking Point

During the next eighteen months a significant shifting of places occurred within the circle of people who touched on the lives of Denys, Tania and Bror. After her expedition with Denys, Tania was brought back abruptly to the unpalatable reality of her domestic situation. Even had she not discussed her marital problems with Denys – which is highly unlikely – he was made aware of how difficult Tania's life with Bror must have sometimes been when he attended a Committee Meeting at Muthaiga Club on 18 April.

During their absence, Bror had behaved offensively towards a club steward and a formal complaint had been lodged. Though no details of his impropriety are given, it is clear that he was aided and abetted by a Mr Sheen and that the scene took place at a dance and was embarrassingly public. The matter was put before the Committee, which consisted of Charles Bulpett, W. C. Hunter and, among others, Denys. Presumably if he had chosen to use his persuasive powers he could have influenced the rest of the Committee to adopt a less arbitrary line, but he did not and 'the secretary was instructed to write to this member and ask for an account of the matter'. Denys was also at the meeting which acknowledged Bror's written explanation and apology sent by registered post, but he was now threatened with being 'posted' for non-payment of his outstanding account at Muthaiga. As an example, one of his paramours placed her pearls with the grocer during one crisis as security against an unpaid bill. The measure staved off the pressure. Later the pearls were retrieved. 'The trouble with Bror,' commented an old girl friend of his, 'was that he was always far too generous.' She added 'He was always spending his last cent to help someone.' But opinions differed as to his weaknesses: 'The trouble with "Blix",' (he was generally known as 'Blix', or 'Blicky' to Kenya friends) a male friend remarked, 'was that he was always his own worst enemy.'

Although Tania, and subsequently her biographers and critics, are vague and inconsistent on the exact date of the break up of her marriage it was about this time that all hope of salvaging the situation was lost. Nevertheless, she and Bror travelled together to England on 14 August 1919, sailing from Kilindini, Mombasa on the s.s. *Pundua* and spending ten days en route in Bombay.

Perhaps under the recent influence of Denys, who always travelled with a personal servant, Tania decided to take a young Somali boy with her to tend to her various needs; he was a younger brother of Farah her major-domo and his name was Abdullahi. Immediately before this leave she had attended her first Somali wedding with Denys who was the guest of honour. The groom was Billea Issa, and Tania was very impressed with this celebration, making no less than three references to it in *Out of Africa*. Towards the end of the book she recalls:

Bilea [sic] had been to England twice with Denys, had been to school there, and spoke English like a gentleman. Some years ago Denys and I attended Bilea's wedding in Nairobi; it was a magnificent feast that lasted for seven days. On that occasion the great traveller and scholar had gone back to the ways of his ancestors, he had been dressed in a golden robe, and had bowed down to the ground when he welcomed us, and had danced the sword-dance, all wild with the desperado spirit of the desert.[1]

In the same chapter she refers to it again, remembering 'The Rime of the Ancient Mariner' 'which was a poem Denys had much admired. I myself had never heard of it until Denys quoted it to me, – the first time was, I remember as we were going to Bileas' [sic] wedding.'[2] It was the perfect moment as they drew near to the exotic group, to recite Coleridge's opening lines:

> It is an ancient Mariner,
> And he stoppeth one of three
> By thy long beard and glittering eye,
> Now wherefore stopp'st thou me?
> The bridegroom's doors are open wide
> And I am next of kin
> The guests are met, the feast is set
> May'st hear the merry din.

Perhaps in this fabulous setting her imagination caught fire. Certainly from her own description of the event the reader can almost smell the incense and the spices, and appreciate the keen bargaining and trading which preceded Billca's nuptial feasting. First she describes the shack-like construction of the typical Somali house. Insubstantially nailed together 'to last for a week', – its architecture echoes the heart of their nomadic heritage. Then she speaks of the surprising contrast to be found within its shabby walls: 'so neat and fresh, scented with Arab incenses, with fine carpets and hangings, vessels of brass and silver, and swords with ivory hilts and noble blades . . . A big Somali wedding is a magnificent, traditional festivity. As a guest of honour I was taken into the bridal chamber, where the walls and bridal bed were hung with old gently glowing weavings and embroideries, and the dark-eyed young bride herself was stiff, like a marshal's baton, with heavy silks, gold and amber.'[3]

In a style which supports Parmenia Migel's claim in

Titania that Tania loved all her life to 'faire de l'effet' she arrived in London in 1919 with little Abdullahi, whose chubby face under his turban was as brown as a polished nutmeg. Immaculately suited he walked respectfully behind her wherever she went. She must have looked wilfully eccentric after the stringencies imposed by uniforms and wartime economy. A friend who remembers Abdullahi 'sleeping on one occasion in the corridor because there was no room for him' commented. 'She took Abdullahi with her simply to pack and unpack her clothes – a task which she taught him herself – it was really quite unnecessary.' In view of the fact that she was very short of money she could easily have forfeited this extravagant whim. But friends remember that 'even when she was desperate for money she still liked to dine at the Savoy'. Whatever motive lay behind her decision to take Abdullahi to Europe it ensured that she did not travel unnoticed. Perhaps as she disdainfully led the way on the grey pavements of London she imagined herself some richly endowed courtesan picking her way across the aged canvas of a Venetian painting while her blackamoor holds her silken drift of hemline from the mud. Since childhood, when she dressed up in her mother's clothes to act out her own plays for the amusement of the family, Tania had possessed an innate sense of the theatrical.

Abdullahi, self-effacing with natural powers of concentration, was a bright child of about twelve years old. It was not easy then to pinpoint the age of an African 'toto'.* Those born before the European education system invaded their world fixed their birth to 'the year of the locust', 'the drought' or 'the deluge'. Some tribes pin age to the year of circumcision (puberty); approximation is the only answer. Even now if you ask a man his

---

* Swahili for child.

age he will pause and answer with the preface 'I think I am . . .' As Abdullahi grew older he watched fascinated as Denys and Berkeley played chess. Standing absolutely still he worked out the moves for himself. When they asked him one day whether he knew what they were trying to do he replied that he knew the game. They took him on experimentally. He played in unbroken silence, never hesitating over his next move and, to their astonishment, after a few games was able to beat them. Denys, who considered himself a superior player and did not take a beating easily, was so impressed by the young boy's untutored intelligence, his obvious bent for mathematics, that he felt he should have lessons. He gave his old textbook *The Oxford Book of Mathematics* to Tania so that she could teach Abdullahi. Eventually she sent him to school and paid for his formal education in Mombasa. She lost touch with him after Farah's death but in 1955 the Danish author John Buchholzer came across him in Somalia when he was researching for his book *Africa's Horn* – a collection of Somali folk-lore and poetry. Abdullahi spoke to the writer about his Danish benefactress and Buchholzer put them in touch with each other again. Tania was delighted to have news of him – he had married Farah's widow Fatima (by family tradition if a Somal dies his younger brother takes his wife in order to raise up his seed). In *Shadows on the Grass* she tells how she sent him a typewriter as a gift and Abdullahi's response: 'It gave him, he says, a decisive advantage over competitors in the career and he owes to it that he has now for three years been holding the office of judge in Hargeisa. "I am," he concludes his letter, "carrying my official duties successfully, with dignity and popularity." '[4]

Tania always actively encouraged the education of her staff, her squatters and their children. Like so many of the pioneer women on farms she set up a small school as well as a clinic. The teaching and doctoring was rudimentary and practical, but more than counterbalanced small affectations like taking a Somali boy to Europe in her retinue. But unfortunately as she grew older Tania's intrinsic and unquestionable sorcery grew to become a two-edged sword. Eventually the disparity between the reality and the myth became so great that the myth precluded any allowance for human frailty – those small vanities of which all mortals are culpable in a common and binding sense. So by her very own magic and her driving force of creativity small actions of jealousy, possessiveness, vanity and paralipsis assumed an importance far exceeding normal proportion. Once Denys became firmly established in her world, the myth was enlivened by his own indefinable force and the gap between allegory and truth became even wider. Each small human fault afterwards became that much more unacceptable.

In practical terms, taking Abdullahi to Europe was the essence of prodigality and meant an extra return fare for his passage, hotel accommodation, food, a complete wardrobe of warm and suitable clothes for the society in which she intended to move, let alone incidental expenses. In terms of human experience and opportunity, however, it was a remarkable chance for the little Somali child whose parents had probably never ventured from the Northern Frontier, and philanthropically it should not be discarded or misconstrued. The lengths to which her obstinacy stretched and her iron-will worked for the benefit of her African staff and squatters on the farm are well known. Elspeth Huxley described the custom of squatting in *White Man's Country:*

A Resident Native ordinance was passed to regulate the growing custom by which natives voluntarily left their reserves with their wives and families, cattle and goats and all their possessions to settle as 'squatters' on the uncultivated parts of European farms. In return for free land, grazing, water, firewood, medical attention and so on, the hut-holder contracted to work for half the year at the ordinary rate of pay for the European farmer on whose land he squatted.'[5]

This fealty, the whole system of squatter and landlord and its concept, is evident throughout Tania's works of fiction, and as the 'lord of the Manor' she controlled, worked and handled the estate, played her part, responding to the full. She devoted herself to her people's survival, inspired by the very concept of Servant and Master dependency. She was not born to this way of life. It imposed itself upon her subjectively through her relationships with the aristocracy. But the results were the same. Her staff revered her and this feeling, which they recognized as a deep humanitarian concern for their well-being, encompassed all those who worked for her.

She was a woman of indomitable courage. [Ingrid Lindstrom recalls] I will never forget how at the end, when the bank foreclosed on her farm, she was desperate for money to pay her staff. She needed five thousand Kenya shillings for back payments alone, none of them had been paid for about three months. She disappeared into Nairobi early one morning and returned about three o'clock the same afternoon. I was very deeply moved when she came back from Nairobi, clutching two bags of silver coins, as happy as a schoolgirl about to pay off her debts. She called Farah and he set up a table on the verandah and there, sitting in the shade of the house, she counted out the money from the bags, shilling by shilling, to each and every member of the staff and casual labourers. I never to this day [1974] came to know how or where she raised that money.'*

During the von Blixens' absence from Mbogani Farm in 1919, Farah was left in charge of the coffee harvesting

---

* See note on Currency in East Africa p. 473.

at Ngong. Denys arrived in London in September. Presumably Bror was present occasionally but Denys and Tania went to the ballet, dined and were re-united with friends for the first time since the war. Everyone was determined to enjoy himself. Tania planned to return to Denmark to see her family, but she had not foreseen that this might be a problem. Post war conditions made passages difficult to obtain. Denys managed to arrange for Tania to travel on a small vessel which was sailing from Newcastle to Bergen. He drove her himself to the north of England to catch the ship. '"Don't forget to come home," was all he said as they stood there on the pier. But it was enough. The African farm was really home. They both knew it.'[6]

It is curious how one aloof figure amongst a group of friends can in a detached way and while still on the perimeter of a circle be responsible for coincidental couplings. Yet, like the professional puppeteer of a travelling marionette show, Geoffrey Buxton seems to have been the invisible manipulator in this milieu who pulled the string of fate. Geoffrey, quiet and unassuming, had moved out to Kenya in 1906 and remained a close friend of Toby's since Eton. His name hardly ever appears in the annals of those days yet his enthusiasm for the country, his confidence and persuasions regarding the future were such that many friends and a good many of his relatives came out and settled on his recommendation. There seems nothing very spectacular about him, he was tall, dark, 'good-looking' with a passion for horses, polo and gardening. He married, settled down and ran his farm. It was through Geoffrey, who organized a dinner party for a small group of friends in London in 1920, that Bror who was there briefly with Tania met the woman who was to become his second wife.

Her name was Jacqueline Birkbeck and at the time she

was married to Geoffrey's cousin, Ben. Neither Tania nor Denys were among the guests. It was an evening which promised a measure of gaiety, Geoffrey had booked seats at His Majesty's Theatre in the Haymarket for the musical *Chu-Chin-Chow*. Oscar Asche, who also appeared in the production, had leased the theatre from Herbert Beerbohm Tree and was so nonplussed at this highly successful adaptation of 'Ali Baba and the Forty Thieves' when it ran for 2,238 performances that he dismissed it as 'scented hogwash'.

Bror sat next to Jacqueline Birkbeck during dinner and at the theatre. Her recollections of that evening are clear. Bror, who was reputed to be 'never significantly silent' was as unforthcoming as a clam. 'I thought him awfully dull,' 'Cockie' confessed, as she elaborated with tenderness on their subsequent marriage. It survived ten years but, like their first marriages, ended in divorce. Generously she admitted her love for Bror and how after they had separated for good she would have married him again. Jacqueline Birkbeck, née Alexander,[7] was the daughter of a private banker and was 'brown eyed, plump, pert as a robin and appropriately nicknamed "Cocky" [sic] . . . her sense of fun seemed to bubble up from a source of mirth which could not be contained and overflowed when any degree of solemnity was required.'[8]

She had been to a fashionable day school as a child, run by a Miss Wolff in her private home in South Audley Street. Here Cockie had made friends with Iris Tree, the third and youngest daughter of the famous theatrical actor manager Herbert Beerbohm Tree. Cockie was always in Miss Wolff's black books for playing theatrical jokes and breaking rules. The complicity for such escapades between these two sealed a lifelong friendship and as they grew up they developed into equally fascinating though quite different types of woman. Cockie's friend

Iris was no stranger to the Winchilsea family – she had been included in weekend house parties at 'The Plas' during Toby and Denys's undergraduate days. When Iris was about fifteen Toby records meeting her in his diary, though his enthusiasm might have been reserved for a rather tiresome bundle of laundry: 'Caught train to Newport and I found on the train Miss I Tree, Mr and Mrs Buxton etc. . . .' Denys also knew Viola, Iris's older sister, quite well, she became a lifelong friend of Topsy's. They met when Viola was secretly engaged to Alan Parsons at Oxford. Subsequently Denys was best man at their wedding; their first child, a son, was named after him and he was made godfather. Viola Parsons recollects the beauty of Denys's godson at his christening: 'Denys was a month old, all robed in gold, lying on a golden brocade cushion given to us by the Kendals. He looked like a waxen Spanish image.'[9] It was Viola who wrote in *The Alan Parsons Book* – an anthology of her husband's favourite poems and sayings which she had compiled from his Oxford days – 'Julian and Billy Grenfell were things apart and so was Denys Finch Hatton.' Of her sister Iris she wrote: 'Iris was never far away, the first girl with bobbed hair who cut off and left her plait of Rheingold tresses in a train. She had my father's passion to be gay and never was out of love.'[10]

Iris, like Denys, had been a friend of the Grenfells, Patrick Shaw-Stewart and Charles Lister. Just that much older than she, they had assumed in her eyes the importance of demi-gods whose martyrdom was complete when they had fallen so wastefully on the battlefields of France. Her compassion and sense of loss are recorded in these lines she wrote about the Great War:

> For look! the gorgeous armies marching onwards,
> And look! the draggled line, the feet that lag,

The burning banner and returning homewards,
The pallid faces and the bleeding flag.

Denys also epitomized Iris's romantic notion of a hero
and it is hardly surprising that at one of the junctures
when they met up again during the mid-twenties they
found each other mutually attractive. Denys was drawn
by her restless and witty nature. In many ways they were
alike. Of Iris it had been said 'she was always called to
the unknown, to the road that leads on – the stranger at
the inn, the tune round the corner.' Again the social
circles overlapped through Margaretta and Toby in the
Anglo-American set, which embraced the Cunards,
Margot Asquith, Belle and Kermit Roosevelt and Iris,
who married Curtis Moffat, an extremely handsome
American photographer in 1916. A brief description of
Curtis Moffat describes the type of man Iris found irresistible: '. . . a physical grace and sartorial elegance, a
philosophic turn of mind, a felicitous manner of self-
expression (he was an entertaining talker and good correspondent and his handwriting was remarkably beautiful)
quick wits and powers of concentration (he was an excellent chess player and even invented a two-dimensional
[sic] chess board for his own use and amusement).'[11]
Osbert Sitwell remembers Iris in his book *Great Morning* 'she was possessed of a honey coloured beauty of skin
and hair that I have never observed in anyone else'.
Carrington,[12] who studied at the Slade with Iris, captured
all these qualities in a naïve oil painting of her friend as a
knight, astride a grey charger, leaping out of the picture.
In 1919 nostalgia for lost friends crept into the melancholy yet urgent need to celebrate. Denys learned that
Julian Grenfell's last words in Boulogne hospital were
'Oh for a deep and dewy spring, with rivulets cold to
draw and drink . . . Ah if I could.' Alan Parsons 'did not

like strangers, an unwise failing in 1919 and kept out of their way as much as possible, furiously compiling his scrapbook meanwhile. The war did not end with a shout of glory or joy but with the bleak outlook of a world without young men. Everyone felt a dull, feckless feeling . . . as if after a funeral . . . "And now what?" Duff Cooper alone of our [Alan and Viola Parsons'] contemporary friends survived and Denys Finch Hatton, going off forlorn to Kenya.'[13]

Iris became a living legend among her admiring friends, which included Lady Ottoline Morrell whose curious percipience strengthened a talent for collecting celebrities in embryo. Her generosity, when she kept open house at Garsington Manor, ensured a meeting place for a whole generation of writers, painters and poets of merit. Dora Carrington, the tantalizing 'child-woman' whose hopeless love and self-abasing adoration of Lytton Strachey ensured a place for her among the group of intellectuals who flowered in intimidating profusion around Bedford Square, wrote to Lytton of Iris's difficulty in coping with the bonds of marriage. 'Darling Lytton, I suppose Lady Tree's style is "old cheese" to you, but I was completely bowled over by her punning humour and high spirits. No wonder Iris is such a good humoured character, living with such a steel to sharpen her wits on, I am not surprised she prefers Lady Tree's company to any husband.'[14]

Again Carrington writes to Lytton Strachey in November 1919: 'The new ballet is exquisite [*Parade, The Good Humoured Ladies* and *Les Sylphides*]. I think you will like the tumblers. Iris [Tree] was there with her muff.' – which is a typical Carrington pun on Curtis's surname. Daphne Fielding's description of 'Iris's muff' sounds curiously like Denys: 'Shortly afterwards she [Iris] met . . . Curtis Moffat. . . . His looks and manner attracted her at once. He spoke softly and slowly and an air of indolence added to his charm. His eyes contained a quizzical expression and his smile was sometimes melancholy. His forehead was that of an intellectual and his fine dark hair was already beginning to recede.'[15]

But after four years of marriage Curtis's charm no longer held Iris's attention and she was on the point of departure. Denys took Iris flying when he was in England and she wrote a poem for him which eventually appeared, without the dedication, in her anthology *The Traveller* published in America in 1926. Denys loved this poem – Iris gave him a copy of the book which he took back to Kenya. He treasured this slender volume, a storehouse of Iris's memories, and often took it to read on safari.

> I saw grey geese straining over the flatlands,
> Saw them as I feel them, symbols.
> Felt my soul stiffened out in their throats.
> Iron rocks of the north by the wrinkled sea.
> When the spring corn piercing through.
> Ribs of a black boat rotting in the sand,
> Bones of a giant,
> In the endless wavering, surf-printed lines of desert dunes
> . . .
> I saw wild geese flying before sunrise
> Ancestral wings lashed to their windy paths,
> And the grey whiteness of them, ribboning the enormous skies
> And the spokes of the sun over the crumpled hills.*[16]

Like her friend Cockie Birkbeck, Iris was much in demand socially, but their charm was quite different. Iris evoked the fragile magnetism of fleeting rainbows and picnics. Cockie's vivaciousness glowed and smouldered with an earthy sex appeal which men found equally difficult to resist. Viola Tree remembers 'sitting in the

* The version of this poem which Tania used in *Out of Africa* is incomplete.

dining-room with pieces of paper and pencils reckoning up our inheritance from *Chu-Chin-Chow,* the play that, to my father's alarm and almost disgust, ran on and on at His Majesty's, making him golden eggs.'[17] Cockie's recollections of the show conjured up that golden lustre; the impression Bror made upon her was one of dullness. When she went out to Kenya later that year, Algy Cartwright, who later married Rose Buxton, insisted she must not accept an alternative invitation because 'you must stay and meet a fascinating man called von Blixen'. But she had been bored by him and went to the Nairobi Races in order to give him a wide berth.

During Cockie's visit Rose Buxton came out to stay with her brother and through him met Algy Cartwright whom she married in Norfolk in 1923. They returned to settle on his farm Melewa at Naivasha. Now, Rose's long standing friendship with Denys brought her into Tania's home. Infrequent though her visits to Nairobi were, she invariably stayed at Ngong when she ventured off the farm and was one of the rare individuals who saw Tania and Denys together. Perhaps because of her acutely shy nature she doubly appreciated Denys's sensitivity. She recalls with affection, 'Denys was *so* understanding.' Other friends placed emphasis on his intuitive ability, a concern outside himself for others. One woman thought this sensibility 'quite remarkable' on an occasion when she was lunching with him in London. She was going through a phase of great unhappiness and, though she had not mentioned the source of her problems, Denys adroitly steered the conversation round to the point where he could advise her without her having to commit herself. 'Remember,' he said, 'when you are sure in your heart that you have done everything you can to make your marriage a success, *in all sincerity,* and it still does not work, then you must leave as soon as possible, for it is merely weakness to go on trying.' Rose was one of the least flamboyant of Denys's female friends but for all that she was, even in her shyness, a remarkable individual. Hers was the gentleness (captured in her delicate silk embroidery) that induced field mice or birds to take crumbs from her hand without fear – yet she was a crack shot when it came to stopping a buffalo in its tracks. On the whole, though Denys attracted many, he sought out larger-than-life personalities as companions. In London these were considered bohemian, roving – their wealth allowed them the indulgence of being 'different'. In Kenya, however, the settlers generated their own essence of individuality, not conforming to any type or class. At a time when individuals were condemned, reduced on all counts by the pressures of a society opposed to anything but convention, a defiant disregard for its rules often placed those who broke away on a quasi-heroic pedestal.

Such bids against orthodoxy, the need to escape the rigid rules of society are often interpreted as 'running away' or regarded as a form of tribal truancy. The institution of marriage requires certainty as a basis for security, yet it is this essential ingredient which unremittingly undermines the sense of adventure. Slowly exposure demolishes the fragile qualities of fascination, excitement. The price for passion is passion. By some self protective instinct Denys seems to have preferred his relationships to flow to and from him while he, like a lonely headland, remained unconfined for they ebbed as surely as waves on an outgoing tide. To his friends he was a 'life enhancer', bringing his supreme self-confidence with him, affecting all those whose lives he touched for the better. An antithesis develops when one attempts to define his autocracy – a command untainted by conceit. But to crystallize the aura of myth can only be destructive. Denys habitually conformed when it came to allocating

time to the family while he was in England. As if
compensating for his continued absences he seemed to
share himself out in small pieces. In London he usually
stayed at the Conservative Club but at weekends he
joined his parents at Haverholme where the rest of the
family converged when he was there. Each time he left
for Africa his mother found that she was 'not particularly
courageous or unselfish' about his departures, explaining
that if she were she would not 'squeal as much or as
often'. Deliberately she shelved the date for his departure
in the back of her mind and on one occasion confessed
'did you realize my own mite on Sunday . . . that I had
not grasped that you were going for good . . . of late I
have not kept dates clearly in my head and I fancied you
were going next week and so might be coming down
again. It is horrid your going away but I am quite sure
you ought to go, as there is nothing to be said against it.'

The Winchilsea standards had not changed appreciably
when seen through the eyes of the younger generation,
who were much in evidence, often seven or eight of them
present including Muriel Paget's daughters. The carriages,
left over from Denys's childhood, were still used by the
indefatigable Aunt Edith:

The most prominent event in the day was the ritual drive to
Sleaford. 'The carriage is at the door M'lady'. The commotion
of getting into the Victoria the arranging of tartan rugs, cushions
'just so' and a huge bear-skin rug on top; 'little furries' round
her neck, her footstool, her umbrella, her minute instructions
to Florrie and Annie.

Her horses were chosen for their slowness and it was a
maddeningly slow trot . . . to Sleaford. The tradesmen were
called from their shops to take orders: marrow bones from 'Big
Clarke' and mackerel (their spines to be fried on toast) as
special treats for us.

Aunt Edith was now a strict vegetarian and lived on a
diet of oatmeal biscuits, wholemeal bread, honey, cream

and stewed fruit. Muriel's children also remember their visits to their Aunt and Uncle at the old priory with Gran Edith.

We loved walking with her to Haverholme across the deer park. The air was always damp from the river and scented with water mint. West, the housekeeper, with her high black dress and her chatelaine would receive us and take us along to call on Uncle Henry Winchilsea. . . . Aunt Anne, a pioneer in portrait photography, lay on the sofa in semi-darkness, an enormous puzzle on a table beside her. Uncle Henry was rather quiet and sad. . . . He liked taking people upstairs to a spare room where hoards of flies increased undisturbed until such time as he chose to demonstrate the efficiency of his new Hoover. He would unscrew the thing, emptying a mass of dazed flies on to the floor, where they would begin to sort themselves out![18]

The bond between Denys and Topsy had strengthened since childhood – in their unattached state his sister felt she could turn to him for advice and companionship without feeling intrusive in the acute awareness of her own solitude. Toby and Margaretta's world – brittle and fast-moving – overwhelmed her but with Denys she shared views on many things except that she was deeply religious though 'not oppressively so'. Denys took a special interest in her children (he nicknamed Anne and her girl cousins 'the virgin ladies') visiting Michael at Eton during boyhood. From the age of ten, Topsy's son looked forward to Denys's arrival from Africa, remembering how his uncle climbed tall elm trees to get rooks' eggs for him on one visit to Haverholme and advised him to 'read the Bible – its a good book!' Denys's tales of adventure were no less fascinating to his nieces and nephews than Uncle Harold's had been in his own childhood. He told how he had been attacked by a crocodile while crossing the Lorian Swamp in Kenya in 1927 and had had the presence of mind to insert his fingers into the reptile's eye sockets until it let go. In fact this is the only solution for an encounter with a crocodile – the eyes are the only vulnerable part of its armoured body. The wound took a fortnight to heal but he had saved the loss of a leg. Impressive feats like this were counterbalanced by amusing foolery. Diana remembers her uncle as 'a dreadfully funny mimic who could take off anyone to perfection'. This gift was not confined to oral imitations. In a letter to Kermit he writes of a meeting with a Scotsman whom he came across on safari. 'I had an amusing trip in Southern Masai in January and February – they have had a gold scare down there and I went over to have a look at the rush. I camped one night with a hopeful Scotch amateur who showed me a wretched little reef[19] with great pride saying it carried two pennyweight. I asked if 2d. wt. was a workable proposition. "Not too gude," he replied, "but et'll get beggerrr and betterrrr as she goes doon." The right spirit anyway!' Denys concluded in a kindly manner. The 'virgin Ladies' remember Denys announcing before his voyages back to Africa 'I think I will draw up a case of oranges and lie in my bunk until I reach Mombasa.' He found the sea voyage irksome.

After spending most of 1920 in Europe, Denys returned to Kenya, with Billea, on the s.s. *Dunvegas* arriving in Mombasa on 2 October. Tania was away too until the end of that year, sailing into Mombasa on the *Garth Castle* on 30th December accompanied by her brother Thomas. They were met by Bror and Farah, who rowed out to meet them in the customary manner – a quay had yet to be built at Kilindini. When they went ashore to spend the night in an Indian hotel before travelling by train to Nairobi the following day, Bror, like Jeremiah, began to regale them with pessimistic stories of the farm and all the disasters which had taken place during Tania's absence. They were suffering from drought and as a result both the coffee and maize crops were ruined; all prices had dropped catastrophically because of the world slump and their new flax crop was superfluous. The labourers had not been paid, nor was there enough farm-grown maize to feed them their 'posho'* Thomas sensed in Bror a feeling of unwelcome extending beyond the depressing facts and remembers his sister's stunned reaction to her husband's crushing welcome. 'Tanne sat as if paralysed. It was hard when seven or eight years' work, hope and faith are swept away in one blow like an empty illusion. She soon went to bed. I don't think she slept much that night.'[20]

Thomas Dinesen had detected in his brother-in-law a total loss of interest in the farm with its current problems and further suspected that Bror was exaggerating the situation for private ends. His suspicions were confirmed soon enough as he realized that his sister's marriage had foundered irreparably.

It was after this leave that Denys, while still living in the cottage at Muthaiga, brought back Walt Whitman's *Leaves of Grass* which he wanted Tania to read and it is Whitman's inimitable style in one of Denys's favourite poems 'Song of Myself' which can be felt in a paragraph from *Out of Africa*: 'I know a song of Africa, I thought, of the giraffe and the African new moon lying on her back, of the ploughs in the fields and the sweaty faces of the coffee pickers, does Africa know a song of me?'[21] Today the book containing that poem is listed among Tania's books at her final home, Rungstedlund, as so many of Denys's books and records are.

During this time Ingrid Lindstrom remembers first meeting Denys. The Lindstroms, like all the settlers, had been affected by the world slump. They owed money to

* Ground maize, not unlike polenta; the African's staple diet.

Algy Cartwright for their house and he was now pressing them for payment. Oddly enough Cockie and Ben Birkbeck had viewed the same house a fortnight before and thought they might buy it but Cartwright seemed unsure about the sale of it so they had not rushed any decision; Ingrid invited the owner for lunch in order to sweeten his temperament on the day he planned to discuss the terms of payment. Like the fatted calf, she slaughtered her best duck for luncheon but Algy never arrived. Two hours later he strode to the house dismissing all thought of a meal and settled down to business. Preferring to be away from this wrangle Ingrid wandered down to the stables where Algy's chauffeur was fixing a mechanical fault on his car.

'Have you had lunch?' Ingrid politely enquired.

A very cultured voice replied that he had thank you very much and eventually 'emerged to reveal the tall, and very handsome figure of Denys Finch Hatton complete with hat!' The incident amused them both and was the beginning of a sympathetic friendship.

Cockie went out to Bror and Tania's farm at Ngong just before she returned to England and remembers that Ingrid's husband 'Samaki' (meaning fish in Swahili), who was a quiet man, joined them at Bror's insistence for luncheon. They arrived at the farm, Tania was still in Europe, and there was not 'a thing in the house to eat'. Undeterred Bror sent Farah off to Nairobi by car with orders to shop for a meal. Round after round of drinks were consumed – Bror did most of the talking and Samaki sat sipping his gin until eventually Farah announced that the meal was ready. Bror paused significantly. 'When Samaki has finished what he is saying, I think we will go in for lunch,' said Bror. On Tania's capabilities as a coffee farmer Ingrid Lindstrom's opinion supports Thomas Dinesen's. Several years after his last visit to

Kenya he wrote 'in contrast to my sister, I never had any faith in the farm and before I left Africa for good, I had almost given up hope of its success . . . the genius of my sister as an author apart, she was perhaps the greatest woman I have ever known, but as a farm manager she was totally incompetent.'[22]

But in 1920 despite Bror's warnings the farm looked remarkably healthy on Tania and Thomas's arrival at Ngong. The economics of the venture were thrashed out and they concluded that to salvage the farm they must cable the Danish shareholders for £2,000. The response, thanks to Tania's mother who put up the interim loan, was immediate. They believed they could stave off bankruptcy until the next harvest. Bror tried to persuade Tania to grow Eucalyptus (Blue gum) for 'kuni'* as all domestic stoves and water heating relied upon wood for power but Tania would not hear of it. She was very stubborn and convinced of her own invincible success – quite simply she felt she could do the job better than any manager.

Thomas recognized his sister's strengths and weaknesses but seemed unable to dissuade her from her intentions. At times her unquenchable faith and optimism were hardly credible.

She was the manager of the company and the responsibility for the millions was a constant pressure on her. Her many letters to the board in Denmark express great anxiety every time the harvest threatened another failure. A good under-manager, an assistant to run the farm, was difficult to find and Tanne never found a truly satisfactory man. . . . The other astonishing capacity of Tanne's was the ability she possessed all her life to get her own way, to make all kinds of people bend to her demands and wishes. Time and time again, when running the farm, we were short of money for the wages . . . I [Thomas] had to go on my motor-cycle to Nairobi to try to get a loan

* Kuni – Swahili for firewood.

from the bank or from a moneylender – only £100. But no, impossible, everyone knew about the uncertainty of the company. Next day Tanne drove our ancient car into Nairobi and soon returned. 'They were nice; here's the money, £300.' It is a somewhat dangerous characteristic and it did not always work. When Tanne was a bit older, she would feel deeply hurt when her wishes were not granted, however great the objections in the way. She was the one who was right![23]

Bror remained on the farm for only four more months – Cockie occasionally went to the farm and recalls the devilry with which Bror casually introduced Denys: 'This is Denys Finch Hatton – *my* friend . . . and my wife's lover.' When Bror left Ngong he went to stay with Samaki and Ingrid at Njoro. She remembers with affection how 'right until the end Bror would do things for Tanne [Ingrid was one of the few in Kenya who always called her by her childhood name]; he was such a kind man, helping her always, unpacking things and doing everything for her. If an animal was sick, he would happily stay up all night to save it – even if the creature was not his own. He was reckless but charming and gave out a lot of himself.'

The Lindstroms were witnesses when divorce proceedings were instigated in 1922 after which there was a gay luncheon at the New Stanley Hotel. (A Swedish divorce was made absolute in 1925 – the news was cabled to Tania from Denmark by Thomas.) It was all very urbane and relaxed as Bror, Tania, Samaki and Ingrid sat at one table, while the lawyers involved lunched next to them. However the decision to go through with the divorce had been 'a difficult one for Tanne' Ingrid remembers. 'The family wanted it, Thomas wanted it, Bror certainly wanted to marry Cockie but Tanne did not want a divorce.'

Two minor but revealing incidents connected with

Denys – not Bror: they occurred at a much later date – disclose the depth of Tania's need for security – an essential requisite in all her relationships with the opposite sex. Both cast an illuminating backward light on what then appeared to be thoroughly illogical behaviour in her reaction to the thought of divorce from Bror. Both took place after Denys had established Tania's farm as his home for several years.

The first was a rare moment of self revelation when she admitted to Ingrid Lindstrom in an almost pitiful bid for reassurance after he had been away on safari for some time and while waiting for news of his return: 'As long as Denys's hat is hanging there in the hall, I know he will always be back.' It is sad to think that Denys's hat, to the general public an amusing quirk inseparable from his physical appearance, had assumed, through its tangibility, such extreme importance. It gives a clue to the incubus, the panic she felt at the possibility of his not coming back. It became a personal talisman, reassuring and consoling during his protracted absences. It contrasts strangely with his own casual attitude towards his hat – because it could always be replaced – leaving a feeling that Tania was desperately dependent on him, though this was the last thing she would have admitted. His own feelings about his headgear are illustrated by the occasion when, after breaking down during a safari, he made for the farm of friends in Laikipia. One of the daughters of the house remembers 'a tall and elegant young man, wearing a rather quaint bowler-type hat, which amused the children of the household so much that they captured it and played football with it.'

The second incident occurred when Tania was staying with Lady Colville at Naivasha in 1928 – again she was whittling away time while Denys was on safari. She confided to this friend that with Bror and Cockie due to return from Sweden as man and wife she was in a quandary about what to call herself, because 'there will be another Baroness Blixen'. Lady Colville reassured her immediately, as friends generally will under such circumstances, that there was no cause for alarm. 'When you come back from Europe, you will be the Honourable Mrs Denys Finch Hatton.' Upon which Tania was pale and silent.

Both these examples display Tania's pathetic day-to-day fear, a haunting trepidation germinated not purely by loss, but rejection and loss-of-face. Ironically this anxiety drove her to react in exactly the opposite manner required to ease an increasing tension in her later relationship with Denys. In fact she could not have chosen two men for whom the shackles of marriage were more intolerable. Perhaps this very element of individuality and independence of spirit attracted her, unconsciously fascinated her (in that it represented a challenge worth conquering) more than anything else.

When each facet of Tania's marriage to Bror is weighed and measured carefully; when each single disaster is considered, naturally enough, everyone expected her to be relieved to have disassociated herself from him. But, acknowledging Denys's elusive nature, remembering the swift and painful departure of her father from her life, understanding the hurt she can only have experienced over Bror's infidelities, her apprehension is entirely comprehensible. The breaches of self-confidence are hardly surprising. When the question of legal divorce arose, not since childhood after the initial and terrible shock of her father's death, had she felt so insecure. These subconscious fissures now reverberated again, not unlike a seismograph relaying danger signals connected with the idea of masculine deprivation to her psyche. Panic must have swayed all her decisions and influenced her action.

Clearly this talaesthesia went unrecognized by her family, who were mystified by her reaction, and it was probably inexplicable to herself at the time. And this seems to have been her one streak of pusillanimity, for there is no doubt as to the courageousness of her nature in every other way.

Tania's fear was that once the decree was made absolute Bror would emerge as the victorious partner, while she would appear stranded even publicly rejected in the eyes of an inquisitive world. Marriage and only marriage, amounting to an open declaration of Denys's love for her, was the one thing Tania privately desired more than anything else. Though she had boasted of her lack of need for convention it was the one convention she would not have scorned. In 1938 she wrote an unpublished lecture, which has been partially revealed in Donald Hannah's critical book *The Mask and the Reality* in which he comments with some shrewdness: 'the reader becomes sharply aware of what has been omitted from her printed work'. The extract from the lecture is even self-deceptive, in that she claims of Africa: 'Here at last one was in a position not to give a damn for all conventions, here was a new kind of freedom which until then, one had only found in dreams. It was like beginning to swim when one could stretch out in all directions, it was like beginning to fly where one might have left the law of gravity behind. One might get a little dizzy, it was a little dangerous as well, it took courage, as it always does to recognize the truth. But it was glorious, intoxicating.'[25]

True, it was unconventional, true it must have been intoxicating especially at first. But her implication of utter contentment with this state of things is tempered by a merciful perspective. She seems to have forgotten that in reality she was looking at a bright patch of sunlight, as though down a long dark tunnel, at the end of which is hope. But happy memories live on: remembrance is the Garden of Eden of the mind from which we harvest solace in old age. What has been omitted from all her printed work and published letters is her own vulnerability and the admission of her deep-seated horror of rejection, the source of her puzzling reaction to the idea of divorce. Unfortunately, as much as she adored and needed Denys, her anguish was founded on his cardinal need for liberty, which could ultimately only aggravate and undermine this lack of confidence even more.

Denys moved out to the farm after Thomas Dinesen returned to Denmark in the middle of 1923, when Bror left Mbogani. Gradually through indirect references in Tania's letters to her brother, Thomas began to detect her changing, strengthening affinity to Denys. In June 1923 Tania wrote, 'In 1915, I could have gone home without sorrow, and even in 1920 without it meaning the whole of my life. . . .' And another letter written in August displays a subtle change of tone and style a broadening of her intellectual spectrum. Her letters from this date are no longer dominated by farm problems or confined to domestic banalities. She offers philosophical opinions aired with an increasing conviction and authority which has not (at least in her published letters) previously shown itself. She now writes ebulliently of freedom and happiness being 'inner states', declaring with great assurance 'rules can't be made for what produces them'. At the end of the letter she informs Thomas 'I am expecting Denys here, perhaps today, anyhow this week, and so as you know, death is but nothing, winter nothing. . . .'[26]

She has exuded the sigh of relief, the surge of joy she felt when Denys returned each time, by shifting the elation which was personal to the response of the farm and its labourers. There is no trace of self pity: Tania knew that when Denys was in the bush anything might happen to harm or delay him resulting in agonizing terms of suspense while she was alone on the farm, waiting, waiting, waiting interminably for the sounds which would say he was home. The approach of his Hudson car or the sound of the record of Beethoven's Piano Concerto No 4 which he might set spinning on the gramophone he had given to her, a message from a runner or, indeed, any hint of his existence and wellbeing or imminent return.

When one of Denys Finch Hatton's long safaris was drawing to its end, it happened that I would find, on a morning, a young Masai, standing upon one long slim leg, outside my house. 'Bedâr is on his way back,' he announced. 'He will be here in two or three days.' In the afternoon, a Squatter Toto [sic] from the outskirts of the farm sat and waited on the lawn, to tell me, when I came out: 'There is a flight of Guinea-fowl down by the bend of the river. If you want to shoot them for Bedâr when he comes, I will come out with you at sunset and show you where to find them.[27]

It must be remembered that it was not sheer selfishness – though undoubtedly Denys had a strong measure of it in his personality – which prevented him from keeping in touch when he was on safari or of advising her of his exact date of return. The best that could be done was done to alleviate her misery but he was hundreds of miles from postal facilities and could only ever guess at his homecoming date. This uncertainty, the element of surprise, quickened her delight at each return, giving it greater emphasis, an importance which if preordained might have lost some of the excitement.

Every author draws from his or her own personal experience of life. Indeed, it is this very quality which gives their writing a valid touch, making a situation credible no matter what flights of fancy have been used to pad out the original idea. As Virginia Woolf says of her

intriguing Renaissance fairytale *Orlando,* 'Every secret of
a writer's life soul, every quality of his mind, is written
large in his works, yet we require critics to explain one
and biographers to expound the other.' Like Tania's
works of fiction, *Orlando* is crammed with fantasy, sexual
ambivalence, and motivating passion, and its author has
also liberated herself from personal implication by setting
the tale in another age. The influence Denys's existence
wrought in Tania's life, whether for better or worse, was
profound. Though the time he spent on the farm was
brief, the versatility of his mind, his exacting but self
imposed standards, his personal code of honour, his
philosophy and rejection of meaningless convention, his
magnanimous nature and the experiences Tania shared
with him made their relationship unforgettable. Commitment to another cannot be legislated for true commitment
comes from within not from outside any relationship that
is valid. Its effects, woven almost inextricably into her
work, are at the heart of the development of her own
ideas so that it is only possible to illustrate the more
obvious examples. Her associations with other people
influenced her too but not to the same extent. Perhaps
because her memories are not solely the result of lyrical
happiness but for other unexplained and nullifying
reasons, they carved a deeper pattern on the matrix of
her conscience. Perhaps, after his death, her hoarding
of his books, his records, inconsequential notes, even
telegrams expressing his concern that she was unwell,
assumed an importance beyond the relationship itself. As
proof of his existence . . . as examples of daily committal
. . . or tokens of what can never be taken away. Edgar
Alan Poe captures this idea in his *Tales of Mystery and
Imagination* when he writes that 'Either the memory of
past bliss is the anguish of today, or the agonies which

are, have their origin in the ecstasies that might have been.' As much as love for Denys, it was infinite regret too which made him the catalyst that changed the destiny of Tania's life.

11
1922–1931 – A Thousand and One Nights

Before Thomas returned to Denmark in 1923, Denys stayed at the farm for the odd weekend and occasional two- or three-day visits. Tania's brother commented 'Denys Finch Hatton was the only friend who meant anything to her and whom I soon learnt to value greatly' and who, during this protracted holiday 'only came at intervals for a few days' visit'.

Until 1925 and during this phase of his relationship with Tania, Denys could be considered a trader or merchant. Like so much of his life, his financial assets apart from generalization remain something of a mystery. The businesses in which he had vested interests were geographically widespread so that he was away a good deal attending to them although he turned this necessity to advantage, treating the great distances between his farms and trading stores as minor safaris. His string of 'dukas' (an Indian term for shop, a duka in Kenya tends to sell everything from chicken wire and hurricane lamps, to bread, bully beef, nails or blankets) were scattered across the Maasai Reserve. He was also Managing Director of Kipliget Ltd, formed originally to buy up land for development with Tich Miles and four others.* One of their first purchases was 611 acres of land on the northern mainland of Mombasa, which acquired the name of 'Shotgun Estate', for when they went down to inspect their newly acquired property they noticed that a small house had recently been built within a triangular hedge

* Messrs Milligan, Montagu, Lennon and Dashwood.

which enclosed about 15 acres. Slightly puzzled they approached the dwelling and when a man appeared one of the directors asked to see the tenant's title deeds. He disappeared into the house and came out brandishing his shot gun. 'This,' he said, slapping the gun, 'is my title deed.' Eventually the squatter's fifteen acres were excised from the rest of the land. Denys used Kipliget Ltd to assist Tania during a time of financial embarrassment when he arranged for the company to buy a first mortgage on her farm to ease the strain. However he was not prepared to commit his shareholders for more than £2,000. He was currently a director of the Anglo-Baltic Timber Company and he personally owned shares in a sisal estate thirty miles north of Mombasa island on which he owned a piece of land. Here he built himself a small house, placing it on the southern, seaward edge of the plantation which stretched as far as Kilifi creek. It overlooked the great blue Indian ocean and lay on the northern entrance to the deep water creek of Takaungu. He had bought it the year before the war ended when he was staying for a few days with his friend Ali Bin Salim – Wali* for the coast area. Just before he bought the land he mentioned going to look at it to Tania in a note asking for a road report to Ngong. 'I have a Hudson with me and I want to go up the coast for a few days to try to get a piece of seashore land. . . . I feel like a child out of school or convict released from prison after getting off that boat. I don't think I shall ever go to Europe again by sea. I am much looking forward to seeing you again.' Upon that piece of land was the dwelling place which he eventually suggested Tania might like to use when she 'began to talk of having to leave the farm, he offered me his house down there as he had had mine in the highlands.

---

* Arabic for foremost, therefore leader.

But white people cannot live for a long time at the coast unless they are able to have many comforts, and Takaunga [sic] was too low and too hot for me.'[1]

In those days Mombasa was still looked upon as 'the white man's grave'. It was true that while it was a most romantic spot under the full moon when 'the beauty of the radiant, still nights was so perfect that the heart bent under it' it was too isolated, too cut off from every comfort and too spartan by far for any woman to contemplate living there alone. But it was a perfect retreat when they wanted to be together for a few days and eventually when Denys brought his small bi-plane to Kenya it was easier to reach and they flew down as the whim took them.

The house was very small (basically two main rooms with a narrow passage dividing them) and was built of coral blocks carved out from the reef then plastered. A narrow verandah ran across the front, supported by four columns forming two, crude squared archways. At their base, low walls acted as 'baraza' seats. Here Denys and Tania could sit, using the little verandah as a third room which captured the breeze and commanded a superb view over the sea. The atmosphere in the rough hewn cottage was strongly Arabic; its thick walls ensuring coolness at all times. The windows, small to preclude all glare, made the main rooms dark. Denys had followed the Lamuan tradition of embedding mangrove poles in the plaster ceilings so that they were ridged, and high. Each door architrave was inset with carved Lamu beams and the doors themselves were as heavy as fumed oak upon which he had mounted solid brass bolts for security.

The approach to the house, then as now, was through a sisal plantation along a rough murram road. In maturity this crop resembles a green army, its tall flowers bayonets held regimentally perpendicular and alert for action. Here they seem to protect the hinterland of Takaungu from sea invaders. The first view of the house still is of crumbling Swahili ruins, projecting here and there from the tangled undergrowth to form free-standing archways or mihrabs; an eerie determination seems to have prevented these relics from crumbling away beneath the thick scrub which has reclaimed most of the ancient Kitoka Jamia mosque. The implicated boughs and creepers typify Africa. They jeer silently at civilization and are a natural warning to hopeful conquerors of the land.

Only the centuries-old baobab trees emerge unscathed by time and remain as indomitable evidence of the natural progress of the fallen seed. Noble and stripped of leaves for the best part of the year, the gigantic trunks are pitted and scarred, gleaming silver in the morning then purple as the day ages in the westering sun. Swahili legends claim that the devil himself upturned the trees in a rage, daring them to survive the indignity of his leaving their roots, which God would have protected within the dark womb of the soil, exposed in contrast to the punishing sun. There is a sarcasm in the shape of a baobab which produces a grotesque yet fascinating beauty. Their leaflessness defies their Luciferous penalty. It is not surprising that this site appealed enormously to Tania and Denys with its spectral Arab ruins. The house is perched on a steep slope. Denys cut steps in the rock edge where

. . . when the tide was out you could walk miles away Seawards [sic] from the house, as on a tremendous somewhat unevenly paved piazza, picking up strange long peaked shells and starfish. The Swaheli [sic] fishermen came wandering along there in a loincloth and red or blue turbans, like Sinbad the sailor come to life, to offer for sale, multicoloured spiked fish which were very good to eat. The coast below the house had a row of scooped out caves and grottoes, where you sat in shade and watched the distant, glittering blue water. When the tide came in it filled up the caves to the level of the ground on which the house was built and in the porous coral rock the sea sang and sighed in the strangest way, as if the ground below your feet was alive; the long waves came running up Takaunga [sic] Creek like a storming army.[2]

From the verandah Tania and Denys watched the margin of the reef. As the tide came in it ran like a thick white chalk line, emphasizing the course of the old dhows as they passed before the house. In the North East monsoon, their lateen sails patched, they bowed like scimitars before the wind. This was simply too beautiful not to be woven into her tales when Tania began to concoct them to amuse Denys. Where else in the world could a Sambuk[3] scrape the heavens themselves while skimming the vault of marine blue in one breathtaking glimpse. 'Here were the ruins of an old Arab settlement', Tania wrote, 'with a very modest minaret and a well, a weathered growth of grey stone on the salted soil and in the midst of a few mango trees.'[4]

The 'weathered growth of grey stone' is highly enduring coral reef cut from the present offshore metamorphic terrace which Tania likens to a piazza. It weathers to a grey colour which is 'surprisingly strong, cellular and vesicular making it light to work with. It cannot easily be dressed to a smooth finish but it can be cut to a fine precision and improves with exposure.'[5] The ruin, which is called Kitoka, was one of the three parts forming the city state of Kilifi. Of interest architecturally because of 'its unmoulded recesses' which occur in 'some architraves of mihrabs of the Lamu group but previous to them the pilaster recess does not appear to have occurred in Kenya except in two cases. The only pre-seventeenth century mosques north of Tongoni to have it are the small mosque at Mnarani and the nearby Kitoka Jamia (they are also the only mosques of that period to have octagonal columns) . . . with brackets and niches to take lamps and incense burners which are identical to those of the early sixteenth century mosque at Mnarani six miles away. These mosques are the only ones to make provision for women worshippers.'[6]

Historically, Takaungu, though once a leading slave market during the Arab conquest, later became a convenient place for lake-bound caravans to halt and restock with provisions – little was done here but the supervision of the collection of customs. But there is a record of one small heroic battle at the tiny settlement which was brought about by a burning desire to avenge a family name. This skirmish was provoked by a man called Mbarak, a son of Rashid ibn Salim who was 'the most serious local challenger to Zanzibar authority'. His father was the last independent Mazrui ruler of Mombasa. 'After the deportation of the leading members of the Mazrui family from Mombasa in 1837, Sayyid Said had nevertheless permitted two members . . . to remain local Walis in Gazi and Takaungu. The longstanding feud between his family and that of the ruler of Zanzibar intensified the recollection of his father's fate and filled him with . . . a fierce desire to recover what his ancestors lost. In 1850 when he had only just reached man's estate, he raised a force of his own and proceeded to Takaungu where he attacked and expelled Rashid ibn Hamis . . . who had just been appointed Wali of that place.'[17]

There are several intriguing aspects of Tania's story 'The Dreamers'. The setting is the great hearth of the sea in front of Denys's house in 1863 as time is wiled away on a dhow by three travellers who are sailing from Lamu to Zanzibar. They exchange tales of life and only at the end of this story is the identity of the coastline revealed: 'Those,' said Said, 'are the great breakers of Takaunga

[sic] Creek. We shall be in Mombasa at dawn.'[8] More fascinating than this or the fact that she outlines Said's revenge is that she has given two of the voyagers names which in Swahili mean drugs and drink, almost implying in her choice the power of each intoxicant as it speaks for itself, from a parallel experience. One is Mira Jama who is disfigured by the loss of both ears and his nose and is famed for his story-telling. Another is a red-haired Englishman, Lincoln Forsner (embodying all the characteristics of Berkeley Cole) whose nickname is Tembu* (Swahili for beer, palm-wine or alcohol). Her choice of names in relation to the umbrella of her title implies pleasant hallucination. The tales within the story are prismatic, unpredictable and contain 'gestures so fantastic that they border on madness' commented Robert Langbaum one of her critics when he summed up *Seven Gothic Tales*. In a typical Isak Dinesen moment of irony and wit, Tania explains that Mira is 'chewing the dried leaves which the Swaheli [sic] call murungu [sic] which keep you awake and in a pleasant mood, and from time to time spitting at a long distance. This made him communicative.[9] Mira or 'miraa' as it is more often spelled is a drug peculiar to the eastern side of the African continent. It comes from the Khat† tree which grows from Ethiopia to South Africa and the twig has been used by the Arabs and Somalis for many years to achieve a euphoric 'high'. The earliest recorded direct reference to miraa was in 1237 by an Arab physician, Naguib ad-Din, who used it to treat mental depression. It is known to cause hallucination and contains a substance closely related to amphetamine. The twig or young shoot is

---

* Tembu also means elephant in Swahili.
† Catha Edulis. It contains a substance d-norpseudoephedrine closely related to amphetamine.

chewed quite vigorously then, after rumination, spat out. The Kikuyu know it as 'muirungu'. Readily available, it may be used to induce wakefulness or to kill pangs of hunger; it is not looked upon as illegal any more than 'bhangi' which is smoked by the African as casually as a European might light up a cigarette. Tania is hinting at the effects of these stimulants by imposing them on the characters themselves. She describes the expansive contentment wrought by both, adding, 'The world drank in the young storyteller Mira. He went to its head, he ran in its veins, he made it glow with warmth and colour. Now I am on my way down a little; the effect has worn off. The world will soon be equally pleased to piss me out again, and I do not know but that I am pressing on a little myself. But the tales which I made – they shall last.'[10]

There is little doubt that Tania is describing from personal experience the after effects of what is commonly known in the world of drugs as 'a high'. Friends believe that she could have started taking drugs as early as the first years of anxiety over the divorce and noticed that there was a marked increase of evidence to this effect directly after Denys's death. Opium was suspected but it is far likelier to have been the harmless, cheap and easily acquired 'miraa'. Even the 'tombacco' which she and Farah used to mete out 'to the old women' when inhaled like snuff, or rubbed on to the flesh between lip and gum, produces a similar effect. Throughout her works Tania makes references to bhang, hashish or opium and the feeling portrayed is always seductive, producing adventures from which the subject is reluctant to return to reality. Perhaps this peccadillo gives a clue to the source of her capacity for highly bizarre fantasies which spin off at tangents from an already brilliantly creative mind. Her multiple flashes of ideas may produce two diametrically opposite effects on her readers. Some are carried along with all the magic of carpet rides into microscopic vignettes full of colour. Others are left groping for logical reasons and are baffled. Her preoccupation is with mortality, fire, bones, wings and possessiveness, rattling like skeletons in the aristocratic cupboards of her characters' lives. These dark realms are inhabited by noble twins, prioresses administering aphrodisiacs, opera singers whose heavenly voices echo an insatiable desire for the total adoration of young men; there are cardinals, crones, heroes, virgins and invincible slave-owners and their minions. Playing their appointed role to the full they are capable of a shocking and almost perverse deviousness that points the human moral: 'Things are not what they seem, they hardly ever are'. Liberty, in the tales, transports the reader back to a time of feudalism and peerage. Often dissatisfied, he is left standing on the pedestrian path of today, irritated even, by the author's inability to give a rational answer in exchange for his attention. It is as if she herself is unable to keep pace with the ambiguous twists and turns of her tales which, if farfetched, are a wonderful combination of romance and frosty inescapable truth.

An example of her witchery can be found in a story which was not published until 1942 in her collection entitled *Winter Tales*. In this instance Denys's house at Takaungu is employed as the background to a fragment of 'The Sailor Boy's Tale' and becomes the home of a fantastical old crone. She is a yellow-eyed woman, who changes into a peregrine falcon from time to time, which, within the labyrinthine coils of Tania's imagination, seems a perfectly natural metamorphosis as the woman explains: 'We Lapps often fly in such a manner to see the world. When I first met you I was on my way to Africa, to see my younger sister and her children, she is a falcon too when she chooses. By that time she was living in Takaunga within an old ruined tower which down there they call a minaret.'[11]

Orville Prescott who reviewed *Winter Tales* in 1942 commented 'Many of her stories have a suggestive quality of parables as if they had an oblique, sad, wise comment to make on life and all sub-lunary activities. But the point is never made quite clear . . . you must guess at what they mean, without any helpful hints to keep you from guessing wrong. Many of them have an elusive inconclusiveness, a way of dropping and fading away. . . . Since they are written with such abnormal sensitivity with such luminous craftsmanship, it is doubly unfortunate that their total effect is so disturbing, so disappointing. . . . If there is a hidden secret in these gold and ivory pages the reader has a right to share it and should not be repulsed.[12]

Whilst the foregoing is true to an extent and the question of enjoyability lies only within the reader's own personal taste and capacity to grasp what Tania offers, she probably intended her tales to be heard rather than read. She is ever present in them – not an intruder – but as the narrator.

These grown-up fairy stories abounding with erotic nuance, ambivalence and hedonism might have won a wider audience if they could have been introduced at bed-time, and read aloud, so that little by little the listener's literary digestion had time to take in the richness of her epicurean feast. 'The gold and ivory pages' of her first collection of stories were not created for silent, quick or private reading; no more than a delicate sauce is prepared patiently to be gobbled down furtively or alone without time to enjoy the subtle combination of herbs contributing to the end result. The original Gothic Tales were meant to be shared and were concocted for a very

good listener indeed; Tania intended to amuse and divert
him, provoke thought and argument and was cryptic by
intention for anything less enigmatic or elegantly contrived might have bored Denys. She wove her first adult
narratives for him. This information is slipped into the
pages of *Out of Africa* as unobtrusively as a butterfly
might skim a brilliant flower scarcely pausing in its flight,
but it is there, for all to see. 'I had been telling some
of the stories to a friend when he came to stay on the
farm.' Only the inquisitive reader, interested in the quality
of her writing, might then go back to the previous
passage and take in, 'I was young and by instinct of self-
preservation I had to collect my energy on something, if I
were not to be whirled away with the dust on the farm
roads, or the smoke on the plain. I began in the evenings
to write stories, fairy tales and romances, that would take
my mind off a long way off, to other countries and
times.[13] Her aim was to stimulate the mind, eliciting
ideas and comparisons with the 'ancien régime' of literature which would lead to 'the divine art' of conversation
and ensure that the discussions arising from her fables
would run deep into the night.

In Tania's 'Mottoes of my Life' speech to the Academy
of Arts & Letters she announced that she had written
two of the *Seven Gothic Tales* in Africa, admitting that
she wrote them to stave off loneliness. She apparently
showed three of them to her brother and read them aloud
to him when he met her at Marseilles after her final
departure from Kenya. Gustav Mohr's wife claimed that
Tania showed her five or six stories before she left the
country and she identified these when they eventually
appeared in *Seven Gothic Tales*.

Tania had been compared to Scheherazade by many of
her critics and this is very true in her relationship with
Denys. The seed of this suggestion was planted by her

own pen. There are numerous references to the Arabian Nights in her works and in *Out of Africa* she wrote:

Denys, who lived much by the ear, preferred hearing a tale told, to reading it; when he came to the farm he would ask: 'Have you got a story?' I had been making up many while he had been away. In the evenings he made himself comfortable, spreading the cushions like a couch in front of the fire, and with me sitting on the floor, cross-legged like Scheherazade herself, he would listen, clear eyed, to a long tale from when it began until it ended. He kept a better account of it than I did myself, and at the dramatic appearance of one of the characters, would stop me to say, 'That man died in the beginning of the story, but never mind.'[14]

Tania would not have chosen the words 'some' or 'many' in relation to the tales if she had only written two and probably the particles of her original stories are now scattered in her subsequent work. In the 'Mottoes' speech she refers to their relationship in terms of the Arabian Nights:

In the Gypsy Moth plane in which I flew with Denys over Africa there was room for two only, the passenger sitting in front of the pilot with nothing but air in front of him. You could not there help feeling that, you were like one of the characters of the Arabian Nights carried through the heavens upon the palms of a djinn. In the morning or afternoon when I need not fear the sun, I used to take off my flying helmet and the current of the African air would seize me by the hair and drag back my head, so that I felt it difficult to keep it in place.[15]

Tania's description of Denys and herself on the farm in the evenings bears a marked resemblance to Oliver Wendell Holmes's modern day Scheherazade in his nineteenth-century classic *The Poet at the Breakfast Table* and perhaps her own comparison springs from this source rather than the original cruel legend. Wendell Holmes makes a similar comment on the shortcomings of forgetfulness:

Our Scheherazade kept on writing her stories according to agreement . . . but some of her readers started to complain that they could not always follow her quite as well as her earlier efforts. . . . At last it happened that a prominent character who had been killed on an early page, not equivocally, but mortally definitely killed, done for, disposed of, reappeared as if nothing had happened towards the close of the narrative.[16]

In 'A Consolatory Tale' from *Winter Tales* two friends sit at a café table sipping wine; one is the narrator and the other the listener. Inescapably the originals are Tania and Denys – at the end of the tale the way in which Denys used his critical faculty after Tania had devised a story can clearly be felt, not to mention numerous small clues of identity which run through it.

Here Æneas finished his story. He leaned back in his chair, took out cigarette paper and tobacco and rolled himself a cigarette. Charlie had listened to the tale observantly, without a word, his eyes on the table. At the silence of his friend he looked up, like a child waking from its sleep. He remembered that there was tobacco in the world, and after Æneas' example he slowly rolled and lighted a cigarette. . . . 'Yes, a good tale,' said Charlie, and after a little while added, 'I shall go home now. I believe that I shall sleep tonight.' But when he had come to the end of his cigarette he, too, leaned back in his chair thoughtfully. 'No,' he said, 'not a very good tale really, you know. But it has its moments in that it might be worked up, and from which one might construct a fine tale.'[17]

Denys could not for one moment be compared with Sultan Schariah who, on discovering his first wife's infidelity, resolved to have a new one every night and strangle her each morning until Scheherazade begged to become his wife and by amusing him with her tales for a thousand

and one nights escaped his cruel decree, so 'he bestowed his affection on her and called her a liberator of her sex'. But Denys could be compared to The Astrologist, another character at Wendell Holmes's breakfast table, who was a mathematician given to 'too much lonely study, to self-companionship, to all sorts of questionings, to look at life as a solemn show where he is only a spectator . . . the daily home of his thought, illimitable space, hovering between two eternities.' Denys had those same qualities of melancholy, the wanderlust of mind and soul, a physical inability to remain for any length of time in one place.

Wendell Holmes remarks compassionately of Scheherazade the writer, 'We must pity the doomed lady who must amuse her lord and master from day to day or have her head cut off.' And indeed while Tania could entertain Denys she could claim in all honesty 'He was happy on the farm; he came there only when he wanted to come. . . . He never did but what he wanted to do', and so long as this state of perfection flourished, she was safe. Providing she could amuse him wittily while allowing him the freedom of a wild bird, the choice to come and go as he pleased, she could stay the moment of metaphorical execution. This condition depended entirely on her own ability to maintain a freedom of relationship which was a burden of untold private weight; for only then could she be assured of her great wanderer's return. The ineffable conditions which Denys imposed on their involvement are somewhat bluntly revealed in a poem he quoted to her by way of a reminder when, with the feeling of hopeless defeat, she was packing up the farm in 1931:

> You must turn your mournful ditty
> To a merry measure.
> I will not come for pity,
> I will come for pleasure.[18]

The original Scheherazade's thousand and one nights make up two years and sixty-five days. If Denys's absences on safari, business or leave in England are accounted for the time that he and Tania spent together might just about have equalled the same total. As it was, Tania's thousand and one nights were stretched like strands of joy over a difficult, often solitary framework of thirteen years. She was well aware that she could not contemplate a future with him that offered the same conditions as a conventional marriage but that did not prevent her from hoping or dreaming. She drifted along as all those tend to do who find themselves in uncertain circumstances but who love. She explained this herself, in *Out of Africa:*

But most of the time when we were together, we talked and acted as if the future did not exist; it had never been his way to worry about it, for it was as if he could draw upon forces unknown to us if he wanted to. He fell in naturally with my scheme of things leaving things to themselves, and other people to think and say what they liked.[19]

Thomas was the one person to whom she found it easy to explain her uncertainties and self doubts about the farm and her personal life. The conditions under which she lived and Denys's own meteor-like ethos were hardly qualities by which to restore a depleted reserve of feminine confidence. Yet she repressed her instinctive fears and convinced herself, for the greater part of the time, that she could cope. In October 1923 she wrote to Thomas on the subject of her future:

I could marry very well, as things stand at the moment, but I am fairly convinced that I don't want to marry without love, or just to achieve that position that I am suited to. To marry just to be supported I cannot even consider. On the other hand, I could go away with someone for a few years, which would do me some good and help me to manage on my own. . . . One thing I'm pretty definite about: I do not want to live among the middle classes. But I really do believe I could be very happy, once I had got it going, running, for instance, a little hotel for coloured people in Djibouti or in Marseilles. (This isn't anything I have thought of doing, but just the first example that came into my head.) . . . Denys Finch-Hatton [sic] has been staying here for a while and will be here for another week, I expect. I have been completely happy, yes, so happy that it's worth having lived and died, being ill, having all those shauries, because of having lived this week.[20]

Fifteen days later she wrote again to Thomas, who sees in her letter 'an overriding feeling for Denys' despite the farm problems and her fear of inadequacy as manager:

That a person like Denys exists, which I have suspected before, I suppose, but never dared believe, and that I have been so happy to meet him during my life and live so close to him, even if there have been long periods of missing him in between, that compensates for everything else on earth, and other things mean nothing in themselves. Incidentally, if I should die and you meet him afterwards, you mustn't ever tell him that I wrote such things to you.[21]

Clearly the days they shared were rapturous times, despite the almost demoniacal possessiveness that crouched within Tania's caverns of insecurity, waiting for the opportunity to ambush their relationship. Yet, like Scheherazade, she was utterly happy with Denys for at least one thousand and one nights. She did not regret the limitations, the terms Denys had imposed. All the unfulfilments and problems are swept away in the answer she gave to a woman friend who quizzed her during her fifties about her feelings for Denys. 'I worshipped the ground he walked on,' she replied.

One hopes that Tania's overpowering need to possess will be looked upon with compassion in retrospect. Because of her undreamed of success as an author, the myth has gathered momentum. It hardly pauses to allow her human vulnerability. Her weaknesses were not extraordinary but her warmth and the spontaneity of her fecund imagination were. Her entirely fascinating character – to which all those who knew her closely repeatedly testify – has left a disparity too. The life she now drifted into was no bed of roses. Thomas recalls that the first few months of 1924, as the divorce proceedings advanced towards the final stage, were probably the most difficult for Tania in her entire stay in Africa. When she speaks of marriage without love in 1923 she could be referring to Erik von Otter who, according to Parmenia Migel, proposed to Tania when 'The emptiness in her heart was such that she might easily have made a compromise and married Erik without love.'[22] But the person she 'could go away with for a few years' was Denys. In that phrase she seems to be testing Thomas's reaction to the situation: not asking advice for the future. In 1924 her letters were unhappy communications, filled with complaints for the lack of sympathy she receives from everyone with whom she has dealings; and Thomas comments that her swift rise of spirits at the end of a letter in January must surely be because 'Denys had unexpectedly appeared at the door.'

It is not difficult to imagine the tension of waiting and the longing Tania felt to hear the sounds which signalled Denys's return. 'He would set the gramophone going and as I came riding back at sunset, the melody streaming towards me in the clear cool air of the evening would announce his presence to me, as if he had been laughing at me, as he often did.'[23]

Paradoxically when Denys had 'no other home in Africa' the deprivation became infinitely greater during his absences. Naturally her pangs of misery, the solitude at the thought of his next departure, were felt even more.

The year before he had been in Kenya from Easter until September, when he returned to England to 'raise money' for some unknown reason. When he returned in the following January Tania wrote to Thomas: 'I am, as you know, one of the happiest people on the earth. Despite everything, I think life is wonderful, wonderful, and that the earth is a marvellous place to be in.'[24] At this point Denys planned to remain with her on the farm until July, when he intended to go elephant hunting in Tanganyika and afterwards to England in August. However, his mother fell desperately ill and this curtailed his arrangements. Among Tania's notes for *Out of Africa* is an entry: 'April 24. Went home. Lady W. died.' which refers to Denys's absence and her own abject misery and hopelessness at being alone again for eight long months. But before that year took a cloudy turn they spent January, February and most of March together at Mbogani farm.

Tania's grey stone bungalow was set in the centre of lawned grounds which gave her home a gracious atmosphere, and from this broad patch of emerald green 'mugumu', wild fig trees towered above the red-tiled roof. Slender Cape chestnuts with ruffles of dusty pink blossom housed pigeons which called to one another across the garden. The trunks of the trees in this area are distinguished by grey, scaly growth – not unattractive, but in reality a fungus to which they are susceptible. From two sides of her house there is an unsurpassed view of the Ngong Hills. They seem to roll back and away from it rather than tower above, creating the impression that the house and the hills are taking eternal stock of one another. Denys used Bror's old bedroom, which formed the corner of the house nearest the hills. Though not large, this was light and airy with spacious built-in cupboards. His outside door led to the verandah where Farah brought their early morning tea and corresponded exactly at right angles to Tania's door from her bedroom. Here the best view of the Ngong hills could be seen as the heavy mist cleared. Their five distinct peaks resembled knuckles on a tightly clenched fist; the Maasai have given each hump a name – Kasmis, Oljoro, Onyore, Olorien and Lamwia. Tania and Denys's favourite picnic spot on Lamwia was also the site on which they wanted to be buried. Sometimes when they drove out to the hills Denys would say to her 'Let us drive as far as our graves.' From this place on a clear day Kilimanjaro and Mount Kenya could be seen at the same time, under their caps of snow.

Within Tania's house their rooms were close enough for them to converse through an open door. A small bathroom, common to them both, was joined by a tiny passage to a large panelled drawing-room. A French door led to the garden at the back of the house: on either side of this stood Tania's famous millstone tables. From these she conducted farm business or sat at one with Denys late at night, watching the stars and enjoying a cigarette before retiring. Denys seemed drawn to the night sky, its clarity peculiar to Africa. Tania had enjoyed a rudimentary knowledge of astronomy in childhood, now Denys widened her interest, picking out Sirius the dog-star after which he named his Ridgeback dog. (He imported two pedigree lion-dogs with the intention of breeding them, eventually giving the pair to Rose Cartwright.) In Tania's work there are frequent references to the Pleiades and Aldebaran. It may be a coincidence but Denys's zodiac sign was Taurus – a star which Manilius calls 'dives puellis' (rich in maidens) for contained within its demibody are The Seven Sisters. Aldebaran, if not part of the Hyades, is in the same line of vision as that star cluster. Thomas recalls a conversation one evening which seems to reflect her private longing for Denys in his absence, but which her brother puts down to her being 'constantly borne up by her inner faith in the dictates of destiny, that she would achieve her goal':

'That's Sirius, the Dog Star . . . and there's Aldebaran. It's called *al debaran* in Arabic, the one who follows after, perhaps really pursues; debar, to follow.'
  'What is it then that Aldebaran is constantly trying to reach?'
  'Oh, that's the Pleiades, that stands a bit out on its own.'
  'And it'll probably never reach the goal it has tried to reach for so many millions of years – poor Aldebaran!'
  We sat for a long time talking about how to solve the problems of the farm – were they really so insoluble? When we got up to go inside, Tanne looked up at the starry sky once again, brilliant as it can only be in Africa's highlands, and her voice was firm: 'I expect Aldebaran will reach his stars.'[25]

Denys believed it possible to share a star. A friend asked him about this: 'But how do you share a star?' 'Why', replied Denys, 'we [presumably referring to Tania] settled on our star long ago.' He explained how, by watching the same one at night, the distance between them when they were apart meant nothing. With that same inner faith which defiantly buoyed up her hopes against destiny, Tania grew small rockery plants in the centre holes of each millstone table. They flourished like belated tributes to the spirits of the two Indians who had been brutally murdered at the mill whence the stones came. The rusting marks on the granite were vehemently claimed by her staff to be bloodstains. Tania quite often includes millstones in her stories. In *Out of Africa* she gives a factual account of how she acquired them supported by a tender allusion to the evening she and Denys shared before setting out to waylay the hunting party bound for Narok. She touches on the slaying of the lion and its mate, imbuing the shooting with the trappings of an almost sacred ritual – a strange benediction. Typically, the time and personal significance of the event have been extracted as delicately as marrow is taken from the bone. What she omits from her narrative is that the moment is not only a precious landmark in her mind but a painful one too. For from this moment a watershed in their relationship was formed, which gradually widened and flowed outwards. She gives the passage a feeling of regret for an omen which perhaps she failed in her happiness to recognize for all its rarity. 'From the stone seat behind the mill-stone, I and Denys Finch-Hatton [sic] had one New Year seen the new moon and the planets of Venus and Jupiter all close together, in a group on the sky; it was such a radiant sight that you could hardly believe it to be real and I have never seen it again.'[26]

Denys's influence can be felt when Tania refers to her 'fictitious' millstones in the idiom of the Bible – 'the nether millstone' which originates from The Book of Job: 'His heart is as firm as a stone, yea, as hard as a piece of nether millstone.'[27] She uses the quotation almost verbatim for the story 'Echoes' in *Last Tales*. 'Sorrow is turned to joy before her. Her heart is as firm as stone, aye, like the nether millstone.'[28] Later in the same story of maniacal possessiveness Tania gives her heroine, the diva Pellagrina Leoni, a few moments of faltering self-scrutiny and doubt in her avid quest for adoration from her pupil Emmanuele: 'She wondered how she had . . . overworked or scared him. He was not as hard as she: his heart was a long way from being like the nether millstone. She must be careful now; she must lure the bird back.'[29]

This relationship in 'Echoes' between the old singer and her young pupil has been attributed to her own with a young Danish poet, Thorkild Bjørnvig, whom she took under her wing and sought to encourage in the early 1950s. Indeed she has admitted that the sudden violence with which he suddenly turned away from her when he felt her overpowering influence, forms the basis of the rift behind this tale. But if Thorkild Bjørnvig served as the choirboy Emmanuele in 'Echoes' Tania's experience with Denys was similar too in that her possessiveness intruded on their relationship eventually. Even the title 'Echoes' implies an insistent feeling of repetition, a vibrancy which declares that Pellegrina Leoni has been there before. The turning away of the male as the diva's heart cries out in triumph: 'I have got my talons in him. He will not escape me' echoes more than Tania's first experience of this nature with the fleeing Thorkild Bjørnvig.

Her millstone appears again in her very first story 'The Roads Around Pisa' in *Seven Gothic Tales*. This could just as easily have been set outside her house at Ngong. 'A young Danish nobleman of a melancholy disposition . . . was writing a letter on a table made out of a millstone in the garden of an osteria . . . on a fine May evening . . . He could not get it finished, so he got up and went for a stroll while the people of the inn were getting his supper ready inside.'[30]

The room which could be called the heart of the house was the one which housed all Denys's books. He built the shelves himself. Before Tania left the farm in 1931 she mounted two tiny brass plaques on the fixed shelves upon which she had had engraved D. F. H. They are no larger than postage stamps; almost secretive in their unostentatiousness they evoke a small caress stretching out timelessly to reach the keen-eyed tourist who goes in search of the author's home. The shelves are simple – even a little crude in their finish. There are no embellishments other than a primitive fluting such as might be found on an old English pie-crust but they held his favourite books for eight years many of which were, after his death, packed up and sent to Rungstedlund with Tania's household effects.

This book-lined room was their after-dinner retreat when Farah had kindled the fire. Even today, stripped as it is of all Tania's Danish satinwood furniture, her antiques, it has retained the air of intimacy which they created as they sat by the fire listening to music, reading poetry to one another or the Bible, exchanging ideas at random. He taught her Latin and Greek, played the guitar or sang to her in this room – Tania's favourite aria – one he sang often – was Handel's 'Where 'ere you walk'. Or they wound up the Columbia 'grafonolo' which Denys has brought as a gift for her from England, perhaps to play *Petrouchka*, Mozart's *Don Giovanni*, or wile away the evening with Schubert's 'trout' quartet or the softly romantic music of Debussy. Here they read Shakespeare's plays together or Tania fabricated tales for Denys's amusement. The cold air was shut out, the atmosphere cosy from the books and silver knick-knacks shimmering now and then in the firelight. It housed Tania's old folding screen shielding the entrance to her bedroom door on the left of the mantelpiece. The Frenchman who painted its panels with eastern satraps, figures of Chinamen, squatting camels or negroes striding past exotic palms with leashed dogs would be flattered had he lived to know that his handicraft inspired fragments for her *Gothic Tales*. It is intriguing to see how she used these tiny, hand-painted tableaux to flesh out an aspect of one of her stories. And it gives her readers an insight into her creative faculty.

Clara Svendsen divulges in her excellent book *The Life and Destiny of Isak Dinesen* the personal importance of this screen to Tania. She explains how Tania did not unpack her cases which she brought back to Denmark from Kenya for thirteen years, with the exception of her books and Denys's, her manuscripts and this one piece of furniture which 'used to stand by the fire and in the evening the fire had made the pictures stand out and serve as illustrations to the tales she told Denys. She had looked at the screen a long time before packing it and probably it was one of the few objects that emerged from the boxes before she set to work at her father's desk.'[31] A passage from 'The Monkey' in *Seven Gothic Tales* supports this:

The supper table was laid for him in his aunt's private dining-room, which she had just lately re-decorated . . . with a wall whose pattern, upon a buff background, presented various scenes of oriental life. A girl danced under a palm tree, beating a tambourine, while old men in red and blue turbans and long beards looked on. A sultan held his court of justice under a golden canopy, and a hunting party on horseback, preceded by its greyhounds and Negro dog-boys, passed a ruin. The Prioress had also done away with the old-fashioned candlesticks, and had the table lighted by tall, brightly modern, Carcel lamps of blue china painted with pink roses. In the warm and cosy room he supped by himself. Like, he thought, Don Giovanni in the last act of the opera. 'Until the Commandante [sic] comes' his thoughts added on their own. . . . The wind was still singing outside, but the disquieting night had been shut out by the heavy drawn curtains.[32]

Not only the screen but the atmosphere Denys and Tania created themselves has seeped into the little room of her story-book guest. In *Out of Africa* Denys's influence – his attitude towards the reading of the Bible – is transformed into literature as her pen comes surging through. In the following example the reader is hardly aware that she has sandwiched her interpretation within a phrase from the Book of Job: 'The Kings of Tarshish shall bring gifts,' she declares and explains the gifts are the ability to dream well with the next best things in the waking world 'night in a big town where nobody knows one or the African night. There too is infinite freedom; it is there that things are going on, destinies are made round you, there is activity on all sides and it is none of your concern. Here now as soon as the sun was down the air was full of bats . . . the night hawk swept past too: . . . The little spring hares were out on the roads moving in their own way, like miniature Kangaroos. The Cicada sing an endless song . . . smells run along the earth and falling stars run over the sky, like tears over a cheek. You are a privileged person to whom everything is taken. The Kings of Tarshish shall bring gifts.'[33]

After Tania left Africa she sometimes dreamed that she heard Lulu's bell tinkling – reminding her of her happiest years, of nostalgia for Denys and his ability to quote freely from the Old Testament as in these lines from the *Song of Solomon*: 'Make haste, my beloved, and be thou like to a roe or to a young hart upon the mountain of spices.' When the timorous Lulu brought back her faun Tania found the visit 'a rare and honourable thing', yet the lure was Tania herself – she had the frail ability to enchant.

In 1965 Eugene Walter wrote in *Harper's Magazine* 'the Baroness Blixen, known also as Tania, as Karen, was quite simply the most fascinating human being that I have ever met'. Tania was seventy-seven when she died and weighed a pitiful ninety pounds, yet she remained an enigmatic sorceress to the end. Denys was fascinated by her no less than the men who came after him but who never replaced him in her heart. For him she was a woodland deity, able to capture the world of Pan and bring it to her own hearth.

12

1924–1927 – Exits and Entrances

In March 1924 Denys found himself unexpectedly aboard the s.s. *Llanstephan Castle* sailing to Marseilles. On the 21st he wrote to Kermit:

A line to give you my news in case you find yourself in England while I am there. I didn't intend going home this year until August as I had arranged to shoot in Tanganyika May, June and July. But last week I got bad news of my mother and came down to Mombasa on the chance of getting on to this ship although I was told I was a fool as she was bung full. However, as you see I am on her and am in a good berth; only as far as port Sudan so far but now I think they will find it difficult to push me off now that I have established a footing. I do not expect to be long at home if I find my mother allright as I have rather set my heart on this Tanganyika trip. I have a special *Governor's* licence for 25 elephant and I mean to get some good photos as well besides some good ivory and then go for a general shoot. There are good sable and greater kudu to be got there and they tell me that the lions need thinning out. [He goes on to describe his adventures on a recent safari to southern Masai, the bagging of a leopard early one morning, and asks:] When are you going to pay us a visit again in Kenya? . . . I was damned sorry I could not meet you in India to do that shoot. Fact is, I've had my hands pretty full in Kenya these last two years. I think we are all right now but we have had a struggle. Drop me a line Conservative Club. . . . I would like to get a sight of you again. Give my kindest regards to your charming wife.[1]

During the safari he speaks of an earthquake which Tania writes of in *Out of Africa*. 'Denys Finch Hatton who was at that time camped in the Masai Reserve . . . and told me when he came back that as he was woken up by the shock he thought "A rhino has got beneath the lorry." [2]

It was in this letter that he also told Kermit he was thinking of taking up white hunting to 'earn an honest penny'. Before embarking at Mombasa Denys had hastily scribbled a note to Tania to let her know he had been successful in getting himself a passage. Four lines are scrawled on cheapest yellow writing tissue: 'Dear Tania, Goodbye. I settled after all I ought to go home and I have managed to squeeze into the Llanstephan Castle. Goodbye and thank you for so many pleasant days when I was bad tempered. – Denys.' He arrived in England on 7 April surprising Toby by phoning him after arriving from Paris by air. He stayed at the Conservative Club, did a couple of days' shopping and drove down to Haverholme with Toby (in a new Rolls Royce) to see their mother. She had been suffering from a lung condition during recent years which had now imposed a strain upon her heart. There seemed no immediate cause for alarm; the brothers spent the weekend pike fishing, Denys went on to Norfolk and stayed with the Buxtons and then shortly after his thirty-seventh birthday was rushed into St George's Hospital himself with an emergency appendicitis (possibly his feeling out of sorts, the mention of his bad temper to Tania, was caused by a grumbling appendix condition.) Toby took the singular opportunity during this fortnight of visiting his nomadic brother every day. By 21 May Denys was allowed to go home to Haverholme to convalesce. Three weeks later his mother suffered a double thrombosis. Denys wrote to Kermit on 17 June: 'I was glad to get your letter of June 6th but I am sorry that you are not coming over for a while. My poor mother is desperately ill and I shall be staying in England for a bit. I will drop you a line about my plans later on when they settle down themselves. My best address in East Africa is c/o W. C. Hunter & Co . . . they are my agents and always know my whereabouts – their telegraphic address is Venator, Nairobi . . . yes, I have read Doughty's *Arabia* and wonderfully good it was. Glorious weather here at last. It is sad to think how much my mother would have enjoyed it.'[3]

The following day Toby summoned Topsy to Haver-holme as their mother's life faded visibly. She died three days later with her family at her side at 1.30 A.M. on 20 June; though they were all griefstricken they found 'her face looked quite lovely and v. peaceful – such a change in her face from what it has looked these last few years.' Their commemorative plaques for Nan and Henry set in Ewerby church wall reflect the difference of each parent's relationship with their children. Henry's epitomizes the distance which he kept between himself and them all his life. A strict code of loyalty pervades the perfunctory wording, composed by Toby: 'Erected by his children in ever loving memory of Henry Stormont Finch Hatton – November 3rd, 1852–14th August 1927.' In contrast, Nan's inscription discloses an all embracing warmth. As if through her death the sun which 'seemed to come out' as Ellen Terry put it, when she entered a room, had now been clouded over, leaving a chill. Denys wrote the inscription for her plaque at Toby's request. 'No effigy would do justice to the beauties of her person nor any epitaph express the beauties of her mind, therefore neither is attempted here. But those to whom she left the world a void, live in the humble hope that through the mercy of God it may be given to them when their time of departure comes, to be with her where she is. Anne, Countess of Winchilsea and Nottingham, June 20th 1924.'

Her funeral was held at Ewerby on Midsummer Day. After the weekend Denys accompanied Topsy back to London. Weeks of visiting friends followed, he met up with Brigadier Hoskins again, called on his grandmother Fanny Winchilsea at Daneheld; stayed with the Buxtons, went to Wimbledon, dined often at Claridges and went to the theatre, ballet and opera. Toby's diaries take on the same involvement with his younger brother as they had during their Oxford days. He seems from many of the comments in his journal to be entirely dependent on Denys in their bereavement, his life during these months revolving round Denys and all his activities.

On 15 October he wrote: 'City 11.00 after seeing Denys off to BEA. I am so sorry that he has gone again as I am afraid that he will not be back for some time though he says he may return in spring. M m returned with Denys to Paris on the same train.' Their mother's death had come at a time when Margaretta and Toby were experiencing tensions within their marriage; 'm m', as Toby always called his wife in his diary, was away a good deal. In this instance she was joining her father, who had also been unwell, at Cap Ferrat.

Tania had been alone, struggling with farm problems and her vacillating moods, for eight months by the time Denys returned. In his absence she had sent some of her oil paintings to Denmark for assessment and 'a few poems to *The Spectator* but I don't know whether they'll take them so don't mention them' Tania pleaded in a letter to Thomas, adding 'I have a few short stories I thought of sending them if they take the poems.' Missing Denys, she was fearful of slipping into a blank limbo overwhelmed by day-to-day shauries, without either the stimulus of conversation or the hopeful sound of Denys's return. She wrote to Thomas 'Write and tell me a bit about intellectual life today in England; I am so afraid of becoming an absolute idiot out here.' Thomas, their mother and Denys arrived together on the s.s. *Chambord* at Mombasa on 3 November. During this voyage Thomas got closer to

Denys than ever he did during his visits to Kenya. They played chess but when Thomas beat Denys on a number of occasions 'he was surprised and not entirely pleased!' Tania's brother admired Denys as 'perhaps the most noble British gentleman I have ever met but my knowledge on the whole was mostly confined to my sister Tanne's description of him. . . . Tanne took it for granted that he was her guest solely.' He found Denys 'Charming and witty with a wide variety of conversation who made a perfect companion for Tanne.'

Tania has marked against her list of dates in 1924 'Maclean – 1' which seems to indicate that this was Denys's first professional safari at the end of the year. Her mother and Thomas were with her until January 1925 so that it must have taken place between 21 November, when he attended a Committee meeting at Muthaiga, and 4 January when he and Berkeley were present and were voted on to the Wine Committee. Denys's contributions to Tania's household maintenance were the luxuries of life: wines, books, records and cigars. Toby made Denys presents of these each time he left for BEA from a permanent supply he maintained at Benson & Hedges. He kept a strict account of them in his diary – for example: 'Gave Denys 100 cigars (300 left)! When Denys returned from safari he brought Tania special gifts acquired during their course. Sometimes leopard or cheetah pelts which could be fashioned into fur coats or hats by her couturier in Paris, snake and lizard skins for shoes, belts or handbags and pretty marabou feathers for trimmings. On one visit to Abyssinia he found a ring of soft gold which could be screwed on 'to fit any size of finger' which he gave to her. She wore it on her wedding ring finger until three weeks before he left on his final flight to Mombasa, when he transferred it to his own hand.

'The visits of my friends,' wrote Tania with a joyous backward glance 'to the farm were happy events and the farm knew it,' elaborating:

'A visitor is a friend, he brings news, good or bad, which are bread to hungry minds in lonely places. A real friend who comes to the house is a heavenly messenger, who brings the *panis angelorum*.' When Denys Finch Hatton came back after one of his long expeditions, he was starved for talk, and found me on the farm starved for talk, so that we sat over the dinner-table into the small hours of the morning, talking of all the things we could think of, and mastering them all, and laughing at them. White people, who for a long time live alone with Natives, get into the habit of saying what they mean, because they have no reason or opportunity for dissimulation, and when they meet again their conversation keeps the Native tone. We then kept up the theory that the wild Masai tribe, in their Manyatta under the hills, would see the house all afire, like a star in the night, as the peasants of Umbria saw the house wherein Saint Francis and Saint Clare were entertaining one another upon theology.[4]

Denys used to tease Tania, comparing her with Madame du Deffand, whose 'salon' in the eighteenth century was renowned for its distinguished and witty coterie. And he compared himself to his ancestor, the wistful Anne, Countess of Winchilsea whom 'he had always insisted that he had inherited his character from ... the seventeenth century poetess Anne Finch'.[5] It is true that they shared some traits: a love of literature and the fact that she 'cared nothing for the idea of marriage', with a conviction that it was purely convention which thrust monogamous existence upon women. Virginia Woolf tried to find out more about this woman born out of her time but 'the more one seeks to find the facts about Lady Winchilsea ... one finds that almost nothing is known about her. She suffered terribly from melancholy ... and in her burned a passion for poetry ... she could have been taught to look at the stars and reason scientifically. Her wits were turned with solitude and freedom.'[6]

Anne's husband's 'constant passion found the art, To win a stubborn and ungrateful heart,'* and although Tania never goes so far as to protest that Denys has a 'stubborn and ungrateful heart' she seems to be dwelling on the difference between the sexes when she compares their interplay with that between the black and white races. Denys's attitude to love was like that of Byron's Don Juan: 'Man's love is of man's life a thing apart, 'Tis woman's whole existence.' Certainly one person generally loves, sacrifices more deeply, than the other. Shaw's maxim – that there is one who kisses while the other allows himself to be kissed – defines this in a physical sense, but the difference remains one which the female sex often finds difficult to accept. This is echoed in Denys's remark to Kitty Lucas when he commented on 'a hereditary weakness of her sex, namely that of expecting a little more than it is possible to give'. Tania contemplates this through the wisdom of hindsight in *Out of Africa*: 'If the lover or the husband were told that he did not play any greater part in the life of his wife or his mistress, than she played in his own existence, he would be puzzled and indignant. If a wife or mistress were told that she did not play any greater part in the life of her husband or lover, than he played in her life, she would be exasperated.'[7] Here is a gesture of justification, made in a calmer moment, for the way in which she overstepped the invisible limit in her demands of Denys. It is profoundly sad when considered in this light. And it is her possessive Pellegrina Leoni of 'The Dreamers' in *Seven Gothic Tales* who takes up the bitter reverberations of

* Written by Pope in *The Rape of the Lock*.

regret: 'I will not be one person again Marcus, I will always be many persons from now. Never again will I have my heart and my whole life bound up with one woman, to suffer so much. It is terrible to me to think of it even. That you see I have done long enough. I cannot be asked to do it any more. It is all over.'[8]

For Denys was Tania's whole life in Africa. Kamante remembers those days, when Memsahib Blixen's watchfulness ensured that everything should be 'mzuri sani, safi kabisa' (in Swahili: very good and completely correct) when Bedâr returned. Denys was a perfectionist in all things; this was not confined to choosing the best possible equipment for whatever he was doing, but also the best tailor, shoemaker and wine merchant. He was acutely observant, aware of the smallest details. All the silver had to be polished, the flowers specially beautifully arranged. Tania went about her tasks when he was coming home with pleasure and with the subjectivity of any woman enslaved by a man. The word Bedâr is a Somali word meaning 'the balding one', which is what Tania and Denys's servants called him, and she used it when referring to him in conversation with them. Outside Tania's household, however, Denys's nickname in Swahili was 'Makanyaga'. This 'seemed an opprobrious epithet but it wasn't. . . . Bwana Finch Hatton, the argument ran, can tread upon inferior men with his tongue. He can punish with a word which was a wonderful skill. It was indeed since Denys rarely used it on any but those whose pretensions, at least, marked him as their equals. And then he used it with profligate generosity.' Beryl Markham wrote this in her autobiography entitled *West with the Night* about growing up and taking wing in Africa.

As a newly fledged pilot herself she flew with Denys during the few months he had his Gypsy Moth in Kenya (later she flew from England to America solo). That

Beryl fell under Denys's spell is evident from the following eulogy, extracted from her book: 'He was a scholar of . . . classic profundity but less pedantic than an untutored boy. There were occasions when Denys . . . could despair of men but find poetry in a field of rock. As for charm, I suspect Denys invented it . . . a charm of intellect . . . of quick Voltarian humour . . . he would have greeted Doomsday with a wink – and I think he did . . . what came from him was a force that bore inspiration, spread confidence in the dignity of life and even gave, sometimes, a presence to silence.'[9]

Beryl was the only daughter of Lord Delamere's race-horse trainer Captain Charles B. Clutterbuck who came out to Kenya in 1904. In 1910 when his marriage foundered, he brought his six-year-old child from England to live with him in the wilds of Njoro. Her brother remained with their mother. Her unorthodox upbringing imparted a certain unfettered charm and she met Denys shortly after her first marriage. Then she had been unpolished but her tempestuous quality had gained through experience and confidence the poise, the coolness of an early Garbo. Her fearlessness, now banked down, gave her the aura of a destroying angel. In her brief glance men were inclined to drown quite willingly. She visited the farm at Ngong infrequently and claimed 'never to know Tania well'. She felt that 'Tania overlooked me, perhaps I was too young – perhaps she thought me foolish; she was rather remote and set herself apart – quite unlike Denys who was at home with everyone in all walks of life.' Tania's attitude, tantamount to dismissal, is interesting. Obviously there was a magnetic common denominator tugging at the lives of this small knot of people for in the mid-thirties Beryl became entangled emotionally with Bror for a while. Tania's visitors to the farm were predominantly masculine. In fact she admits in *Shadows*

on the Grass 'personally I have always had a predeliction
for boys believing a community of one sex, would be a
blind world.' In *Out of Africa* her comment is that
the 'love of a woman and womanliness is a masculine
characteristic and the love of a man and manliness a
feminine characteristic', comparing this to the fondness
of northerners for the people of the south from the
warmer climes. This attraction of opposites is as natural
as night following day. There is sometimes a blessed relief
in the transition from one to another. Tania's preference
is not unusual. She is displaying a crystalline honesty
seeing no reason to hide behind veils of coyness. She
elaborates in this vein: 'As it is almost impossible for a
woman to irritate a real man, and as to the woman, a man
is never quite contemptible, never altogether rejectable as
long as he remains a man.'[10]

These may be the reasons for the steady flow of male
friends who came to sup or dine with her at the farm. But
there was probably an unconscious fear of competition
from beautiful women too. She had had plenty of reason
to distrust them through Bror's gallivanting. Ingrid Lindstrom was always slightly puzzled over Tania's friendship
with herself because 'Tanne did not really like women
that much'. She had a surfeit of her own sex in childhood
and never established the rapport with her mother or
sisters that she had with her father and brother. Possibly
in Ingrid's tranquil and courageous nature Tania found
peace of mind and no need to defend her own territory.
Ingrid, says Tania, 'had all the broad insinuating joviality
of an Old Swedish peasant woman and in her weatherbeaten face the strong white teeth of a laughing Valkyrie.'[11]
In her she found a strength and impartiality which she
could draw from with confidence in times of need. But it
is doubtful if she fully recognized the depth of Ingrid's

shining loyalty even though her gratitude has been re-corded for the way she helped her when she finally left the farm. She leaned on Ingrid's translucent beauty of personality without realizing why her friend had so often sacrificed time on Sergoita – her own farm – to come and stay at Ngong. Nor did Ingrid ever allow her to know that her unexpected visits, which strangely occurred whenever Denys was about to leave for particularly long safaris, were anything but coincidental. They were arranged very carefully and thoughtfully for Tania's benefit. As soon as he had a definite departure date he cabled Ingrid arranging to meet her in Nairobi. He then drove in to meet her at the appointed time and place, bringing her back and explaining to Tania how he had by chance bumped into her – again – and how he had naturally insisted she must come home with him and stay with them at the farm at once. Tania never knew of Denys's elaborate attempts to break down her depression, the void he knew she underwent at the thought of his leaving again. It was a touching, responsible act, if rather hopeless. Nothing could stave off her misery, the abyss into which she sank every time he left. It was at the very end that Tania finally recorded with appreciation 'A friendly act of Ingrid's for it was difficult to get away from the farm.'

When Berkeley came to visit Tania in her 'sylvan retreat', as he called her home, he brought provisions from his own farmstead which had been raised on the rich laterite soil on the lower slopes of Mount Kenya. He 'arrived with his car loaded up with turkeys, eggs and oranges' (the latter hand-picked for Denys). Elspeth Huxley, like Tania, captures his same quixotic spirit which adding another dimension 'Berkeley Cole was one of the old, colonial Kenya's legends, impossible now to pin down; a man whose brilliant colours faded, when he died, like those of a tropical fish or a blue-and-orange lizard.

He had fine looks, supple conversation, grey eyes and a gay Irish wit. He never made money, entered politics, took life seriously or married.'[12]

Neither did he miss a chance to enliven a boring occasion. Once when dining at Government House during the reign of Sir Henry and Lady Belfield he amused himself by solemnly peeling a banana towards the end of dinner. Lady Belfield was deeply engrossed in conversation with a fellow guest who Berkeley considered was being a bore. Instead of eating the fruit he inserted it into Lady Belfield's rather large ear trumpet upon which she almost entirely relied as she became more deaf. Naturally all conversation came to a halt. Luckily Lady Belfield possessed a broad sense of humour.

When Berkeley stayed with Tania every morning at 11 o'clock he drank a bottle of champagne out in the forest. One day he confessed to Tania that the only shadow which marred this perfect ritual was that she did not use her best glasses. When she protested that she had so few good ones left, he took her hand gravely and said, 'But my dear, it has been so sad.' When the three dined together Tania writes 'they took the greatest pleasure in my Danish table glass and china, and used to build up on the dinner table a tall shining pyramid of all my glass, the one piece on top of the other; they so enjoyed the sight of it.'[13] 'They both had the ambition to make me a judge of wine, as they were, and spent much time and thought in the task.' Wine played an important part in their life. Probably the following scribble, attributed to Denys, was the result of a hefty consumption of 'fizz':

> And you really must complain,
> About Muthaiga Club Champagne.
> The most expensive kind of wine
> In England is a matter

Of pride and habit, when we dine,
Presumably the latter.
Beneath an Equatorial sky
You must consume it or just die;
And stern indomitable men,
Have told me time and time again,
The nuisance of the tropics is,
The sheer necessity of fizz.

Emile Jardine, a French wine merchant in Nairobi, acted as Denys's clearing agent in Kenya (Denys ordered his wines directly through his London wine merchant), and his store in Government Road was a favourite meeting place for many of Tania and Denys's friends any morning at 11 o'clock. Every day at this hour 'Emily Jarrdeen', as Tania's Scots' grocer Mr Duncan called him, dispensed Champagne to his customers. On an occasion when Denys received a bad case he wrote to his London supplier announcing his intention to ship it back, asking for a replacement. But the dealer waived the charge, issued a credit note, and Tania was delighted to use it for cooking. At that time she was earning only £40 per month as a manager and, if not as meagre as it sounds by today's standards, certainly it did not cover this type of luxury in her kitchen.

Denys and Tania christened friends with the names of wines as an identification code. It worked well when others were present. No loyalty was broken if they mentioned 'a rather bad port', 'a full bodied burgundy' or 'obviously going through its second fermentation' if someone was getting angry and, if the subject was a poor traveller, 'a typical Orvieto'! As co-members of the Food and Wine Committee Denys and Berkeley shared responsibility for the Muthaiga Club kitchen and cellar. Denys kept a discerning eye on the cuisine, hired or fired the chefs and arranged for Kamante to have cookery lessons in the club kitchen from an expert when Tania detected his aptitude for an art at which she excelled herself. There are thousands of references in Tania's work covering all facets of the universe of wine – from the growing and pressing of grapes by naked virgins to the connoisseur savouring the thought of a vintage port as he crosses his cellar by candlelight.

In one of Denys's letters to Kermit in 1924 he writes of Château Yquem.

Well, that is nice of you to be keeping up that Château Yquem against my projected visit. I shall simply have to come some time now. Meanwhile it is nice to think of them lying there improving shoulder to shoulder calmly awaiting their destiny. My brother and I have taken to investing in Pipes of port between us in vintage years and I have often found it a pleasant thought out in Africa to remember those silent rows of black virgins steadfastly awaiting me in England, ready or getting ready, preparing in fact to pour out their life's blood for me and my friends anytime after about 1938. I hope that you will crack one or two with me.[14]

Tania claimed that 'Eroticism runs through the entire existence of the great wanderers', and certainly Denys reveals a sensuality in that letter which he rarely disclosed. His pleasurable anticipation is on a par with that of Tania's Prince Nino 'who quoted the exquisite Redi in his *Bacco in Tuscany* saying only the barrels of wine of Tuscany should come to groan under his caresses.'

All Denys's friends knew of his fondness for this white wine, so often mentioned in Tania's writing. Topsy's son recalls how on one occasion his mother had gone to great pains to buy a bottle when Denys spent the night with them in London. After his uncle had gone to bed, Michael Williams saw his mother peering through the glass-panelled door of the room Denys occupied. 'He was lying motionless with a book on his chest and with ash on his cigarette seemingly inches long.' Worried lest he should fall asleep with a lighted cigarette in his mouth she tapped on the glass.

'Tiny, are you asleep?'

'Topsy, you don't go to sleep reading Proust,' Denys replied.

Michael Williams felt that this small incident encouraged him to read *Swann's Way* when those same two volumes were returned to Topsy after her brother's death.

In the following passage Tania not only includes the favourite wine, the setting appears to be her own house at Ngong:

> There were a great many white lilies so that the air was heavy with their scent. Upon a table were glasses and a bottle of the best wine I have ever tasted, a dry Château Yquem. This made my third bottle of the day.[15]

Rose Cartwright verifies that Tania had a passion for Candidum or Madonna lilies and remembers her talent for combining the most unusual flowers in her arrangements. With these elegant blooms she mixed little red roses.

'With Tania's touch' they looked perfect. The tall-stemmed lilies which Tania propped up in great sheaves or held occasionally when photos were taken were the same that Ellen Terry had favoured, reminding Denys of her visits in childhood. Rose enjoyed Tania's hospitality with a certain reverence and never forgot their real life mythos. 'Denys and Tania,' she explained, 'were people of great intellect, their conversation was way over my head yet they never made me feel stupid, ignorant or ridiculous. In fact I have been terribly shy all my life and as a result have never enjoyed staying with people but on the few occasions I came to Nairobi from Naivasha I always stayed with Tania and I felt completely and utterly at home with them both.' She remembers that Tania's method of dressing was 'highly individual'. 'She wore simple cotton frocks. They were quite plain. I recall our wearing great sashes round our hips with large bows but she wore hers with the waist where it should be and the skirt at calf-length rather than the 'dernier cri' which was shorter. She was a wonderful person without pretence. She was courteous, loyal and always most considerate of her servants and other people. She was a down to earth person and very very straight.' Rose's impression of Tania being down to earth contrasts sharply with other friends who felt that 'when you were with Tania you had the feeling anything could happen. There was an air of unreality about her, a witchery which enticed wild things to come out of the forest to her like Lulu and her baby who could be seen picking their way around the house quite unafraid, as the car drew up', or Minerva the owlet who adopted Tania's shoulder as a perch for a while, but whose passion for eating thread caused its death.

This sibylline aura impressed most people who went to the house. Ingrid Lindstrom remembers 'a wonderful evening when the three of us dined together. Tania was a wonderful cook – it was a gift – Denys was at home and on this occasion she looked very very beautiful. She used belladonna in her eyes which gave them a luminous sparkle, they appeared enormous.' Denys and Tania generally dressed for dinner. He wore a dinner jacket and black tie or sometimes a velvet smoking jacket. On this occasion Tania was wearing a white crepe dinner gown which displayed 'her beautiful shoulders' to perfection. Ingrid, Tania and Denys sat about the table long after dinner, eventually drifting into the drawing-room. 'We were all lying on the floor, chatting and listening to records; it was a remarkable night, with a full moon, well after midnight. Suddenly Denys said "Come on, let's go for a drive." Without hesitation we collected up our Somali shawls while he fetched the car. He drove us up to the Ngong Hills in the moonlight to find the herd of buffalo feeding.' Tania's magic quality was not confined to midnight or adults. Ingrid's children were fascinated, almost spellbound by the way, with her 'terrific imagination', she could turn a potato into a 'Troll' and weave a story to amuse them there and then. Other friends remember taking their three-year-old daughter with them to meet Tania who, on seeing the child, called Farah's 'toto' to come and greet her. She had golden curly hair and a rosy skin. The slim almond coloured boy in his best Somali clothes resembled a little Prince from the Arabian Nights as the two faced each other. With a sudden, brilliant smile he made his most ceremonial salaam, right down to the ground. Then he started patting her feet very swiftly and from them to her shoulders and down again. The fair child stood immobile at this 'unexpected but quite exquisite salutation, looking very pink and blue and astonished'. Tania herself was delighted by the success of the introduction and its hint of fantasy. But when Tania and Denys were together, the spell cast was of double strength and complementary, as the following comment affirms 'I never knew two people who were so completely on the same wavelength as those two were'.

Ingrid Lindstrom did not consider Tania to be vain but 'very ambitious'. She was often concerned about her weight, which fluctuated alarmingly at times, and took Marienbad pills in the hope of stabilizing it and in the belief that they would keep her slim. When Tania gained a lot of weight and some of her dresses no longer fitted, she gave them to Ingrid who was of the same height – only to ask for them back later when she had fined down! Tania loved pretty clothes and took pleasure in ordering them from her *couturier*. When she visited Europe she frequented beauty parlours (a luxury denied in Africa) for the professional care of her hands and skin and even at the end of her life was proud of her well-shaped legs and slender ankles. During the Prince of Wales's visit it was important for her to look her best and she looked outstanding. One of the other guests remembers her dancing with him at Muthaiga Club after a dinner party there. She wore a very full skirted dress with panniers that had sprays of flowers on them (so different from the brief hip-waisted dresses that were worn just then). On her head was a little white astrakhan fez (someone described it as a Cossack hat). No one but Tania could have carried that off but the effect was enchanting and she gave the whole evening the effect of a ballet. The note of fantasy they introduced was quite outside one's normal experience. They looked as though they might vanish at any moment.

Friends who understood the solitary vigils, her loneliness, came out while Denys was away to help to break the monotony. Kamante never forgot how, after a few months by herself, she sometimes put her head down on her arms, crying helplessly. Asking of him without wanting an answer why the Bwana Bedâr had stayed away so long. Mainly, however, her despair was private though sometimes she admitted to Thomas these moods of depression. Even Farah became intolerable at times:

It's good that I still have Farah. He's had a period of being quite insufferable, which as you probably know, Somalis can have, but now he's become an angel and that makes all the difference to my life . . . the roads have been impossible to drive on . . . coming back, nine Indian carts were standing in the water-hole in Forest Reserve. We had to help them unload and then load again, and then there was an oziko, so that we got stuck on the way home at Charlie's house, and I was so tired, with all the constant gear-changing, fear for the car and everything, that I just put my head down on the car and wept as if I were beaten, much to Farah's dismay. . . .'[16]

Her African staff were loyal and good. She made the best of the situation, enjoying the quaint intricacies of their minds, learning their strange beliefs, legends and resigned acceptance of harsh turns of fate; she took pride in the clinic she had established and in curing their ailments and an equal satisfaction in seeing the small 'totos' regularly attending her school on the farm. She learned a deep communication and humane sympathy but, like all those with whom one has close, daily relationships – they infuriated her too. On some days it was easier to be rational than others; she also had her own moods, the ebbing of joy, to contend with.

Thomas says that Tania 'could become furiously despairing at disappointments and annoyances, often over small matters' but his prevailing feeling is that of pride because 'first and foremost her courage shines forth – the persevering courage which she had shown since childhood.' As a brother he speaks with authority of many years when he comments 'but all through Tanne's life, sorrows and joys alternated with lightning speed. The reason why this letter ends in quite a different mood must have been that Denys had unexpectedly appeared at the door. "I am, as you know, one of the happiest people on earth. Despite everything, I think life is wonderful, wonderful, and that the earth is a marvellous place to be in. Always your faithful sister, Tania."'[17]

So when Denys was at home all her problems vanished into thin air. The farm never looked more beautiful or ran so smoothly. If the berries had emerged on the coffee, the branches were bowed down with the weight of their promise. Life was a dream: for a few short weeks or days. Thomas and Tania had had long discussions on the importance of a basis for man's philosophy which Thomas believed was a sort of trinity. Religion intermingled with Love and Art – 'approximately corresponding to the Christian Church's teaching in the Trinity'. He thought they themselves probably qualified as 'Unitarians' in their attitude towards this trinity, and told Tania:

'For you it is faith in and enthusiasm for its third line "the Holy spirit", Art, which carries your life along. I affiliate myself to "the Son", Love, as the force in my life. The first part, "the Father", Religion, doesn't really play much part in either of our lives, or is it just our abilities and faith that fail? Well, for you perhaps Destiny who is the Father; perhaps you can explain it to me better?' Perhaps [Thomas continues] I was too narrow in the judgement of Tanne's faith; it is likely that she learnt to know 'the Son' through Denys.[18]

Denys used to laugh at Tania's vacillations, calling her 'The Great Emperor Otto' who 'could never decide on a motto'. Like most mimics, he was inclined to observe people's mannerisms and accents instinctively. Some-times, after returning from Somalia, he let his hands hang down limply from the wrists – a typical Somali habit – almost as if his hands had withered as he watched her. Tania retaliated by saying 'Stop that' but found at the same time an elegance in this weird Somali stance.

They rode often; usually up to the first ridge of the Game Reserve in the Ngong Hills which they had decided would be a good spot to be buried one day. Thomas recalls that Tania was not a very good rider. 'Rouge was high spirited, unruly and sometimes very difficult to mount. Tanne tried six or seven times before giving way to a bout of impatience, swearing to give up horses and never to ride again, with exasperation.' But she kept Rouge till the end and was heartbroken at having to part with him when she sent him up to Gil-Gil by train. Denys usually rode Poor-Box, Tania's Irish horse, except when Rouge was being specially 'kali'.* He became very angry with Tania's syce,† remonstrating with him for hotting Rouge up with oats for his own pleasure and making the animal almost impossible for the Memsahib to ride. Kamau, a Kikuyu, bowed his head and agreed but it happened time and again and Rouge, sensing Tania's apprehension, played up according to her fears. So Denys rode Rouge when he first came home and when his behaviour was better he handed the horse back to Tania and the whole process started all over again. Pania or Dusk or Sirius, Denys's dog, trotted after them. Sometimes they took a syce along to bring the picnic basket and look after the horses, while they sat under their favourite tree. On Uncle Charles Bulpett's seventy-seventh birthday they drove him up for a small celebration. Uncle Charles Bulpett lived permanently at Lady McMillan's house and for Denys and Tania personified their ideal of the Victorian gentleman who fitted with equal comfort into their own age. He had achieved some dashing feats in his youth; he had swum the Hellespont like Leander and Lord Byron; explored the unknown waters of the Upper Nile about which he had written a book in 1907: *A Picnic Party in Wildest Africa;* swum the Thames for a bet in full evening dress including his top hat and had at one time been La Belle Otero's lover. One evening during Denys's absence he came out for a tête-à-tête dinner with Tania. She asked him if he appeared in La Belle Otero's *Memoirs* which had then just been published. He affirmed that he did though disguised by a pseudonym. Tania pursued the matter by

---

* kali – fierce, or peppery – in Swahili.
† syce – Anglo-Indian, meaning groom.

asking what Otero's opinion had been of the man she had ruined financially and then dropped. Uncle Charles Bulpett explained, 'She writes . . . that I was a young man who went through a hundred thousand for her sake within six months, but that she thought I had full value for my money.' When Tania cross-questioned him if he believed this to be true, he agreed, after thinking it over, that her claim was correct. During the birthday picnic the conversation turned on the question of 'whether if we were offered a pair of real wings, which could never be laid off, we would accept or decline the offer.' Tania wrote in *Out of Africa*:

Old Mr Bulpett sat and looked out over the tremendous big country below us, the green land of Ngong, and the Rift Valley to the West, as if ready to fly off over it any moment.
'I would accept it,' he said, 'I would certainly accept. There is nothing I should like better . . . I suppose that I should think it over, though, if I were a lady . . . [19]

Through this small fragment of an afternoon spent happily with a dear friend we are able to enter briefly into the world of Denys and Tania's kaleidoscope of conversation and ideas. It was like a collage in a sense – each piece added to give a new dimension to the whole – and we can steal a glimpse into how their discussions developed when they were alone. It shows too how Tania took tiny particles from the crucible of her life with Denys, harvesting them and insinuating them with all the skill for which she is renowned into her work. To reveal art and conceal the artist is art's aim. In this she is different. She does not conceal herself. She is always the narrator sitting at the feet of the listener but she obliterates the origins and frees herself from personal implication by dressing her characters in clothes and surroundings of a different era. It is as if she has spun a web, carefully enhancing each spandrel from many distinct points with the shimmer of a dew as she weaves each tale. For instance, she used the 'wings theory' discussed on the birthday picnic in 'The Supper at Elsinore' in *Seven Gothic Tales*. When the main flesh of the story is pared away the extracts I have given below represent a type of syssarcosis of that original conversation on the Ngong Hills. It is a simple matter to retrace in them each facet of the discussion, which ranges from the most basic of human daily functions such as defecation to the more attractive pursuits of travel or making love. Naturally all these would be drastically affected if a human being found himself encumbered suddenly with a pair of wings which he was neither used to manipulating nor able to extricate himself from.

The setting for the 'fictitious' but re-enacted conversation takes place round a dinner table when: 'The theme under discussion was the question whether, if offered a pair of angel's wings, which could not be removed one would accept or refuse the gift.' The first response to the question is very basic, probably coming from Tania herself who was forty-four years of age at the time:

'. . . but how would you, in a pair of white angel's wings, get out of – ' What she really wanted to say was, 'get out of using a chamber pot?' Had she been forty years younger she would have said it . . . and she said instead very sweetly 'of eating a white roast turkey?' . . . Still, her imagination was so vividly at work that it was curious that the prelate, gazing, at close quarters . . . into her clear eyes, did not see there the picture of himself, in his canonicals, making use of a chamber-pot in a pair of angel's wings.

Uncle Charles Bulpett plays the role of the Bishop, and obviously they have agreed that the chamber pot is the solution to this predicament. It would be impossible to negotiate the confining walls of the lavatory with a pair of wings to contend with – an essential visit prior to travel, Denys firmly maintained, and habitually referred to as 'preparing for a journey'.

The old professor of painting said: 'When I was in Italy I was shown a small curiously shaped bone, which is found only in the shoulder of the lion, and is the remains of a wing bone from the time when lions had wings, such as we still see in the lion of St Mark. It is very interesting.'

That part of the discussion we may take for granted was contributed by Denys. He is referring to the stone Lion of St Mark in Venice. It is a winged lion 'sejant' holding an open book. The bone to which he refers is well known to hunters in Africa. It is the highly prized 'floating bone' and occurs only in the 'cat' family. Much sought after by sportsmen it is absolute proof of their having been in at the kill. After a lion is skinned the tiny bone can be found suspended in its pectoral muscles in the insert of fat between armpit and chest. They are often capped in gold to form a small pin or brooch.

'Oh, if I had the chance of those wings,' said Miss Fanny. 'I should not care about my . . . monumental figure. But . . . I should fly.'

'Allow me,' said the Bishop, 'to hope Miss Fanny that you would not.' We . . . mistrust a flying lady. You have heard . . . of Adam's first wife, Lilith? . . . What was the first thing she did? She seduced two angels and made them betray to her the secret word which opens heaven, and so she flew away from Adam. That goes to teach us that there is too much of the earthly element in a woman, neither husband nor angels can master her.'

Here there has been a contribution from all three. Lilith, in Rabbinical writings, was supposed to be the haunter of the wilderness, a female demon alleged to be specially dangerous to children. In the Vulgate she is Lamia, Goethe brought her into his *Faust* and Rossetti (with whose poetry Denys was familiar) used a serpent for Lilith's vengeance in *Eden Bower*. Denys soon brings Tania to earth by reminding her of her female contours, with a brief Biblical reference thrown in for good measure.

'. . . in woman, the particularly heavenly and angelic attributes, and those which we most look up to and worship, all go to weigh her down and keep her on the ground. The long tresses, and veils of pudicity, the trailing garments, even the adorable womanly forms in themselves, the swelling bosom and hip, are as little as possible in conformity with the idea of flying. We, all of us, willingly grant her the title of angel, and the white wings, and lift her up on our highest pedestal, on the one inevitable condition that she must not dream of, must even have been brought up in absolute ignorance of, the possibility of flight.'

Here the allusions are to female liberation – the flying in the metaphorical sense which it is so difficult for women to achieve with grace, and to the unreasonableness of placing woman on a pedestal, never allowing her to step off. The next response comes from Tania, who touches on witches who are allowed to fly.

Said Fanny: 'We are aware of that, Bishop, and so is ever the woman whom you gentlemen do not love or worship, who possess neither the long lock nor the swelling bosom, and who has to truss up her skirts to sweep the floor, who chuckles at the sight of the emblem of her very thraldom, and anoints her broomstick on the Eve of Walpurgis.'

Later there is a sentence almost identical to one used in *Out of Africa*, when the original question was posed on the picnic. As usual the sex of the character has been changed.

If at this time she had indeed unfolded a pair of large white wings, and had soared from the pier of Elsinore up into the summer air, it would have surprised no-one.

And Tania has the last word, with a sly reference to her failed marriage:

We both of us have husbands and lovers at each finger tip. I, I married the Bishop of Sealand – he lost his balance in our bridal bed because of his wings.[20]

Like this Tania and Denys's long talks spiralled from one idea to the next. Because they went mainly unwitnessed they have been lost, as the cries and sounds of birds are lost in flight as they pass. But they have been partially preserved by Tania, and only by painstaking study with the help of small clues from the people who knew them both as individuals and as a pair, will the world ever be able to untangle the filaments threaded through her work. The more obvious facets, such as the Latin phrases, excerpts from Shelley, boys trading kisses for oranges, preoccupation with wines, the Greek Classics, music, theology and ballet are easy enough to spot. But others are better concealed. Denys was essentially a private person and Tania may have thought that by removing her tales from the modern world she was also freeing herself from any possibility of disloyalty to him. Friendship was 'precious' to her. The Somalis have a proverb about women: 'Who is the best woman: She who can keep silence.' Their dealings with the Somalis were close, both Tania and Denys were fascinated by these fanatical Mohammedans. They admired their unyielding code of honour even though it did not always work for the benefit of themselves. Tania has mentioned in *Shadows on the Grass* how she feels a certain taboo, as if she is breaking a covenant with Farah, when people write or talk of her. To many it is a strange way of thinking but it does explain Tania's request to her brother Thomas too, when she asks that if she dies and he meets Denys he must never allow him to know what she has said about him to her brother. For her it was the breaking of a covenant and might be seen to be so by Denys; she strove only for his admiration and the thought that she might fall short in terms of personal loyalty in Denys's eyes was unbearable to her. She needed to confide her love in someone whom she knew she could trust; who better than Thomas who would never gossip behind her back? But the feeling of guilt at having discussed something sacrosanct is in that request all the same. She did not want to answer for the breach. She has written that she and Denys believed hunting was on a par with seduction, and has spoken of Uncle Charles Bulpett's saying that 'The person who can take delight in a sweet tune without wanting to learn it, in a beautiful woman without wanting to possess her, or in a magnificent head of a game without wanting to shoot it – has not got a human heart.' *Ehrengard*, a fairy tale with what Tania described as 'dark shadows', was published posthumously. Full of intrigue and turbulence it deals with the necessity for a small duchy to acquire the all important heir. One of the passages in it can be identified with the epigram above and also with Kierkegaard's *Diary of the Seducer*, whose influence is always present in her work:

You call an artist a seducer and are not aware that you are paying him the highest of compliments. The whole attitude of the artist towards the Universe is that of a seducer. For what does seduction mean but the ability to make, with infinite trouble, patience and perseverence, the object upon which you concentrate your mind give forth, voluntarily and enraptured, its very core and essence . . . To be seduced is the privilege of women, the which man may well envy her. Where would you

be my proud ladies, if you did not recognise the seducer in
every man within waft of your petticoats? . . . The woman who
does not awaken in man the instinct . . . is like the horse of the
Chevalier de Kerguelen, which had all the good qualities in the
world, but which was dead. And what would we men be, did
we not endeavour to draw forth, like the violinist . . . the full
abundance and virtue of the instrument within our hands. . . .
But do not imagine . . . that the seducer's art must in each
individual engagement fetch him the same trophy. . . . I may
drink off a bottle of Rhine wine to its last drop, but I sip only
one glass of a fine, and there be rare vintages from which I
covet nothing but the bouquet.[21]

Here are strong echoes of Tania's ideas of response – a
book that is not read does not exist: a woman who does
not rouse a man is not a woman and so forth. The circle
turns fully back upon the motto of her life, given to her
by Denys in the form of a seal: 'Je responderay'. In all
aspects of life it is essential for her characters, be they
puppets, heroes or servants, to answer. It seems superfluous to elaborate further on Tania's love for Denys or
upon the effect he had on her work. Yet since the Book
of Job, the Bible and his interpretation of them seem to
form the base of her philosophy time and again, I have
included in an appendix to this chapter an extract from
the introduction to *The Poem of the Book of Job*.[22] This
was a paraphrase by the 11th Earl of Winchilsea, Denys's
gambling, great-uncle, when he was Viscount Maidstone
and was published in 1860. From childhood Denys was
taught to consider this section of the Old Testament
through his predecessor's eyes and as studious readers of
Tania's writing are well aware, references to this part of
the Bible abound in her work. Tania and Denys recognized in their Somali servants an identical courage and
fatalism. '. . . the Prophet's followers see the happenings
of life predestined and therefore inescapable. They are
fearless because confident, that what happens is for the
best.'[23]

Tania's final attitude to life, tending to border on masochism, was an unswerving conviction that suffering was an inseparable part of final grace; that one's head should be bowed before pain. Denys's introduction to his 'wicked uncles' paraphrase stimulated his interest in the Bible and he tried often to persuade friends to see it through his eyes. Just as he had urged his nephew to 'Read the Bible; it's a good book', he urged Tania and Rose Cartwright to do the same. Rose admits openly that her enjoyment of it today is entirely due to Denys's persuasion and that she keeps the Bible at hand always 'to read like a very good novel at whim'.

Denys took up flying again towards the end of the 'twenties in order to requalify to pilot his own plane. As he needed some flying hours with a passenger, Rose was his victim on several occasions. 'Victim' as opposed to companion because she was 'diabolically airsick' when Denys had to practise landing and taking off over and over again. He used to go up at Hendon and land at Croydon. After one of these flying sprees Rose was overcome by nausea and the pressing need to vomit when travelling back to town by taxi. She demanded that Denys stop the taxi, threatening to be sick there and then otherwise. But he refused, being more concerned that they found a house with a garden first! Eventually a suitable garden was discovered and he turfed Rose out unceremoniously on to some unsuspecting house-owner's front lawn. Rose recollected fondly, 'He teased me about it for a long while afterwards.'

Denys bought his Gypsy Moth in 1929 and shipped it out to Kenya. It was bright yellow and the Africans christened it 'Ndege'* but Denys and Tania nicknamed it 'Nzige' meaning in Swahili, locust. Today in Karen, the

---

* 'Ndege' also means bird or aeroplane in Swahili.

area of Ngong named after Tania, the road which edges his old landing field is named Ndege Road. Kamante remembers how 'Bwana Pincha Hattern' divebombed the house or looped the loop over in fun and how sometimes Tania rushed into the bungalow with her hands over her face in alarm saying 'He'll kill himself, Kamante. He is going to kill himself. Na kufa . . .' But as a rule when he flew close to the house it was a signal for Tania to come and collect him from the airstrip which he made on the 'vlei' on her farm. Once, after she and Denys had been up a very old Kikuyu approached them:

'You were very high up today,' he said. 'We could not see you, only hear the aeroplane sing like a bee.'

I agreed that we had been up high.

'Did you see God?' he asked.

'No, Ndwetti,' I said, 'we did not see God.'

'Aha – then you were not high enough,' he said. 'But now tell me: do you think you will be able to get high enough to see him?'

'I do not know, Ndwetti,' I said.

'And you, Bedâr,' he said, turning to Denys, 'what do you think? Will you get up high enough in your aeroplane to see God?'

'Really I do not know', said Denys.

'Then,' said Ndwetti, 'I do not know at all why you two keep on flying.'[24]

If the Africans found the Europeans incomprehensible on occasions so the reverse was true. But Tania, like so many settlers, tolerated their sometimes baffling approach towards life, if necessary re-assessing her own values. If their views bore no relation to her own priorities, she, like others, tried to understand. The following incident, recounted by Tania to friends over tea shortly after it occurred, seems to exemplify this discrepancy in African versus European comprehension. The words are Tania's own, memorable in their crispness and irony, when spoken in her sonorous Danish voice:

'You know,' Tania explained, 'we tend to forget how differently Africans look at things. A friend of mine was coming to see me the other day and as she passed that big "vlei" (you know the one on the left hand side coming from Nairobi) she saw an overturned lorry with four Africans lying around it. My friend is not at all a strong woman, in fact, she had just been rather ill, but she felt she could not drive on without doing something to help so she got out of the car and went over to the lorry. The man she took to be the driver, seemed the least hurt so she asked him: "Where have you come from?" "From Arusha, memsahib."

'So she said, "How many of you were there when you left Arusha?"

'And he said "There were six of us when we left Arusha." So my friend thought of the two men pinned under the lorry and said they must get the lorry on its side and though she was not at all strong she pushed and struggled and pushed until at last they got the lorry on its side and there was NOBODY THERE! So my friend got very angry.

"But you *said* there were six of you when you left Arusha," she said. And the driver said "But there *were* six of us when we left Arusha and two got off at Kagaido."'

The Africans on the farm distrusted Denys's aeroplane but their 'totos' came to accept the Gypsy Moth as part of their existence. They included it in their childish drawings, copying its registration number G-ABAK with painstaking care on to the pencilled wings created on scraps of paper with a persistence which claimed it as part of their own life. Clara Svendsen has stated that 'Flying over the African highlands must have influenced Karen Blixen's intellectual and spiritual development to a degree that can hardly be exaggerated.[25]

Tania's rapture at the idea of 'defying the laws of gravity' is clear and can be found in much of her writing.

'To Denys Finch Hatton I owe what was I think, the greatest, the most transporting pleasure of my life on the farm: I flew with him over Africa . . . we were up nearly every day.'[26]

It is primarily in connection with taking his mother flying that Ivan Moffat (Iris Tree's son) remembers Denys. Though he met Denys only two or three times as a boy of six or seven he recollects that:

Denys was always spoken of with legendary excitement – I keenly remember one time when I was ill and it was announced that Finch Hatton was that day coming back from Africa and coming back to the house and that I would be seeing him and that he was bringing me a present from Africa – a sort of get well present. I remember being faintly surprised that I should be receiving such a present from a man of whom I had but the smallest recollection. At any rate I was half disappointed, half secretly amused at what I knew was a form of innocent deception when a Hamley's style 'African Village' attached to cardboard arrived. It was a box about three foot by two with painted leaden zulus attached to its bottom by tiny strings, holding spears and assegais – about ten of them – a thatched hut with spreading bases painted green. I knew that this was not the sort of thing that Finch Hatton or anybody else 'Brought back from Africa'! I vaguely wondered at the time what the inspiration had been – it did not seem in the character of my mother or what I had come to imagine about Finch Hatton. Nor did it seem likely that my father had thought it up. It turned out that Finch Hatton never arrived at all and to save me from what they imagined would be disappointment they got this from Hamley's.

Because of his age, Ivan Moffat had no way of knowing whether Denys and his mother were lovers but 'always supposed that they were because my mother was a romantic and from what I know of Denys Finch Hatton I can imagine how easily his personality would have fitted her concept of a hero of that epoch.' But this question will probably remain unanswered. A confidante of Iris's can only say that she knew him well and that it was assumed by their friends in London that Denys 'belonged to Baroness Blixen alone – but one never knows'.

Tania was in Denmark for the greater part of 1925. Denys was taking out safaris by the beginning of the year and in May arrived in London with a fearful cold and very depressed. Just before he left Kenya he had the harrowing experience of attending Berkeley's funeral – his death was not unexpected. Even before Tania departed he had become the shadow of the witty jester they had known, and she had offered to stay behind and look after him. The doctor ordered Berkeley to bed for a month because of his condition, but he refused and deliberately disobeyed these instructions – he was acutely worried over finances and his heart could not take the strain. Jama, his Somal, learned to give him his daily injections, which helped but only temporarily. He died at Naro Moru on his farm on 21 April at the age of forty-three, three days after Denys's thirty-eighth birthday. Through his death Tania and Denys lost a much loved friend and it was a great loss to the Colony too. His faith in the country had not wavered since his arrival in 1905. He had imported high-grade cattle, sheep, race-horses and thoroughbred stallions, upgrading the country-bred stock. A fluent speaker, his perseverence as the elected member for Legislative Council for Western Kenya, had pushed through the Bill ensuring the construction of the Thika to Nyeri railway line. As far as all races were concerned he had been a trusted member of the community. Berkeley's brother-in-law, Lord Delamere, was the chief mourner and Denys broke his safari, rushing up to Naro Moru for the funeral on the farm. The coffin was made in cedar wood, grown on the farm and constructed at his own sawmills; and at his last request Berkeley was buried beside the grave of a loyal servant on the edge of the Naro Moru river.

On Denys's visit to London in 1925 Kermit tried to persuade him to travel on over to America but he declined the invitation with 'It's too bad, but I must get back to some business in Kenya.' When Tania returned Denys was still away; she wrote to Thomas with an aching loneliness:

Now that Berkeley is dead and Denys is at home, I have practically no one to whom I can talk, and I long for you and our discussions so much that I think my longing must draw you here over land and sea like a magnet. . . . And now that I have taken stock of my position, my happiness and unhappiness here, I think I can stop saying that if I'd known it might work out like this, and that I could stay here, with success in this enterprise that I now know the strange and devious ways of destiny happened to concentrate my life on, and if Denys were to come here as now, and relations between us were as now . . . then I would be happy as anyone can be in this life, i.e. what is called 'happy'. . . . There is, however, generally something in one's circumstances that indicates that they do not last for ever. . . . If I only knew that it would last, then despite everything, I would overcome doubts and scruples of many different kinds, a number of which I send to you for illumination, aware that I am very near Paradise. Just as well that you are not in Paradise now, for as I said, I am a child of Lucifer, and an angel's song is not for me, but I am as close to happiness and equilibrium as my nature can get. . . . Perhaps I will really see it one day. I may be sitting here, rather stout, not so far from all of you and everything at home, because I can make a journey home to you when it suits me, with success here on the farm, with Denys as my safe old friend, with descendants of Pjuske and Heather, and Farah's son as my butler, with more wisdom, harmony and equilibrium in my life than ever before.[27]

When she wrote that letter Tania was forty-one. Her isolation, when Denys started hunting professionally, was emphasized. Her confidence was seeping away in her need to be with him more, her lack of security in not being able to plan a future was becoming more apparent. She found this less and less easy to suppress.* In 1926 Denys was in Europe from April until November. By 12 September it is evident from the following extract of a letter to Tania that he has had enough of England:

I came back here to see if I could be of any use to my father who is now moving out of his home. But I find that in spite of his being very unwell he insists upon doing everything as long as he can stagger around: so that all I can do is stand around like the French clown of a circus. So as I have plenty to do myself before leaving England, I am going off to London tomorrow. The atmosphere here is very depressing and I shall be glad to get away from it. I am going over to Paris for a few days to choose some wine for Muthaiga and if possible to get a cook. . . .[28]

When he returned to Kenya Denys embarked on his longest safari to date. He had written of this possible assignment to Kermit from Haverholme Priory on 14 August 1925: 'Do you know aught of one "Patterson" whose chief call to fame is that he has made a hideous amount of money out of some patent penny-in-the-slot machine for correctly registering the sale of buns and ginger pop? I have been asked to take him out shooting in Kenya next year.' Kermit's reply must have been reassuring and favourable. The safari was eminently successful apart from the fact that Tania was left alone again.

* Since the original publication of this book, Karen Blixen's *Letters from Africa – 1914–1931* have been published in which it is revealed in the spring of 1926 she believed herself to be pregnant by Denys Finch Hatton for the second time. As Judith Thurman, Karen Blixen's biographer, writes: 'Daniel was never born and Karen Blixen never conceived another child. Given her age (41) and medical history, it is likely she had a second miscarriage although she herself was not positive she had become pregnant.' *Isak Dinesen: The Life of a Storyteller* by Judith Thurman. (p. 208) St Martin's Press, New York 1982.

But the beginning of the year had gone well for her. Her mother made a second visit and to her happiness was a guest in the house at the same time as Denys; the visit, despite a certain apprehension of disapproval from her mother, went well. Thomas received a letter from her written on 27 March 1927 'full of the joys of life, probably affected by the fact that Denys was her guest at the same time as Mother.'[29] In May Denys left to meet Frederick B. Patterson his American client at Voi, where the safari was to commence, and but for a brief interval when he broke the safari to see her, he was to be away for five solid months.

APPENDIX TO CHAPTER 12

The Introduction to *The Poem of the Book of Job* by George James Finch Hatton, Viscount Maidstone

No one who ever gave it a thought has doubted that the Book of Job is an Eastern poem of unexampled magnificence; still less will anyone doubt it who has endeavoured to restore it to its original state. Grand in subject, simple and unembarrassed in action, replete with glowing pictures of Eastern life, it represents with authority that which all the greatest poems of antiquity have shadowed forth in doubt and obscurity, viz: the contest between Powers of Good and Evil for the possession of man. This argument lies at the root of the Prometheus Bound; the Nemesis of the House of Atreus; the evil star of Oedipus. The ancients did not fail to perceive that the best men were often victims of a train of calamities which, personally, they do not appear to have merited; but in endeavouring to solve this problem, they wandered into every phrase and fable of conjecture and ended in fact, by admitting that the matter was too hard for them.

There never was a nation of aetheists; or perhaps, an individual that in his heart believed what his tongue might utter, viz: 'that the world and all that within it are the result of chance.' The wonders of nature, the capacity of man for knowledge, the recurrence of day and night, the regularity of the seed and the harvest, the beautiful and apparent order of the universe, intimating, though it may be disturbing, the presence of a disturbing cause are too marvellous and complete in themselves to admit of such a solution. Yet, the wisest men have been puzzled to explain the sight of their eyes and to erect a satisfactory system which should supply at once the rule and the exception, accounting for the existence of sustaining and disturbing causes in nature and recognizing the divinity of men's souls with his infirmities and his crimes. How fruitless and grotesque in many instances these efforts have been, it is needless to relate; but it may be safely remarked that few of the wildest legends of the Red Indian or Central African are equal in absurdity to the theories of the refined Greek and imaginative Brahmin. At the first view of the Homeric poem, the want of a solid basis on which to rear the supernatural cannot fail to strike every observer. Homer (be he one or many) was far too great a master to ignore the continual interference of a Supreme Power in the concerns of the world and the daily life of men. . . . In *The Poem of the Book of Job,* however, we have no such difficulty.

The author speaks with authority and, marvellous as the tale is, it is intelligible to the meanest of understanding and betrays itself in no contradiction. It presents the Almighty in a new and astonishing relationship with man; but still just as inscrutable and omnipotent. Grant his machinery to Homer and the result is poor, uncertain and disappointing but grant his machinery to the Book of Job and the action of the poem is not only sublime but reasonable and consistent. The special difference between these two works is this: the one gains, the other loses wherever the supernatural is introduced. Job's three friends are beset with the same difficulties which bewilder the Greek poets and philosophers. They obstinately refuse to admit that man can reap otherwise than he sows and persist in declaring that Job must have committed some great and secret crime which had been brought down upon him as such signal punishment. The patriarch, on the contrary, strong in his own innocence takes a much higher view of man's condition and the ways of the Almighty. He can understand that it may even be good for him to be afflicted even without a cause and acknowledges that God is just in all his ways at the same time as he resolutely denies the truth of the charges brought against him. In this respect Job's views are much advanced of his age and he is rewarded accordingly. Even under the Jewish dispensation, temporal prosperity was held to be the last of virtue, and calamity the badge of vice. It was reserved for the Christian dispensation to explain how this rule could be true in many instances; but fail Universal application, and only that could be done by introducing man to another life hereafter which should restore the balance and make up for the inequalities and shortcomings of this. The plot of the poem is simple but majestic; and there is no situation in the whole range of poetry comparable to the introductory scene, where Satan is represented as tempting his maker and cunningly devising for a good man the severest trials to which a mere mortal was ever subjected. The manners and customs of the East are introduced in splendid profusion and allusions to natural objects are thrown in with a richness and propriety that embraces almost every phase of illustration and leaves little for any successor to accomplish. It is difficult to conceive keener or more cutting satire than that with which Job (for all his patience) accosts his friends. Narrow-minded bigots they are, they deserve it richly; and we do not hear that he was ever accused of handling them too roughly. In the meantime his caustic remarks add point to his moral reflections and relieve several passages from the charge of tediousness. Job was, as we all know, the pattern of well regulated tediousness; but it is clear from his example that more is required to forfeit the true spirit of man or to put up tamely with impertinent attacks which are neither desired nor deserved. The work is truly colossal and yet it scarcely seems to have reached the popularity which it merits. I attribute this chiefly to the absence of rhythm and cadence in the translation without which every poem must appear bald and unsatisfactory and it has been my object in the following pages to remedy this defect at the smallest possible sacrifice to fidelity in the original. . . . I do not apologize for employing many quaint old English words which have now unfortunately fallen into disuse. They belong naturally to that period at which the poem was translated and those who may complain of their simplicity will scarcely deny their force. They are to be found in all the best ballads of our language and they flourish in the sermons of Latimer which are as fine models of pithy, printed discourse as any with which I am acquainted. To conclude if it be thought by good judges that I have given a version of this incomparable poem after the manner of Clement Marot rather than Sternhold and that I have succeeded in somewhat catching the spirit without departing too widely from the text of the original, I shall have obtained the object of my wishes and done a service to the public.

13

1927–1930 – Safaris and Shadows on the Grass

Denys planned to meet Patterson at Voi Station – they had only met briefly in London so he probably had not realized that his client was an apprehensive man. He was torn between a distinct fear of 'the African jungle' and exhilaration at the unpredictable prospect of the coming months. On the train Patterson did his best to 'conceal my excitement from' three 'unemotional Anglo-Saxon "cousins"' (his English co-passengers). Convinced that the train was about to run headlong into an elephant and overturn, he was sure they would be 'knocked off the track' at any moment 'as had happened recently on the East Indian railway'. But his fears were unfounded, Patterson arrived at Voi at midnight and 'the next moment I was shaking hands with Finch Hatton'.

He loomed tall in the darkness. He is six feet three inches tall. In the dark he seemed eight feet. The grip of his muscular fist reassured me. A word of greeting; then he led me over to where our Dodge car and two Chevrolet trucks were slicing white blocks out of the night with their headlights. . . . I remembered this spot was just below Tsavo . . . at Tsavo during the building of this railroad . . . man-eating lions had horrified the whole civilized world by their attacks on natives and white men. Once one of the big cats . . . leapt into a railway carriage, seized a white man, and escaped with its victim by plunging through a plate-glass window. 'Shall we go?' suggested Finch Hatton. Our destination was the camp almost seventy miles away . . . we followed hoof paths, mere trails . . . made by the game or the natives. . . . I soon began to be reminded . . . that I was really in Africa. Our lights picked up the shining eyes of a leopard. Then popped into the gleam the full form of a startled antelope. A gazelle flitted away from us terrified of the brilliance . . . we were surrounded by animals. We reached camp at about 2 A.M.[1]

After five months on safari Patterson felt that every tale he had heard of Africa fell short of the real thing and that . . .

I shall never with all the words at my command be able to tell enough. . . . Yes, there are still dangers in Africa. But they are somehow clean and definite dangers. So it is not fair to hang the coat of one's pride upon them to say that they are either as great or as harrowing as one's imagination longs to have them be. . . . I always found picturing game far more interesting and difficult than shooting it. Buffalo is the most exciting to hunt; the elephant the most fascinating to watch; the lion the most difficult and dangerous to photograph and the rhino far and away the most annoying at all times. Our pictures still and moving turned out most successful. Yet, I had no great equipment. I took two Bell & Howell moving picture cameras, one with a two-inch lens and one with a six-inch lens and one Graflex 4″ × 5″ . . . only having a six-inch lens meant that I had to get much closer to my animal making the risk greater. But I think I got better results in the end.[2]

Their first base camp was pitched at Maktau (one of Denys's favourite areas) and consisted of a personal tent for each of them and a large mess tent which was used for dining and daily living. Denys employed one hundred porters over and above the personal staff. An extra driver was taken on; Kanuthia his motor driver – 'a slim young Kikuyu with the watchful eyes of a monkey', Malima and Sar Sita, his 'bold, shrewd and fearless gun bearers and trackers' responsible too for the skinning, two mess boys, and making up the regular employees, the infallible Billea, who was never far from Denys and was responsible to him for the running of the safari staff, in his role of Neapara.*

Patterson, caution itself to begin with, had been warned by his doctor not to drink anything but filtered water. When his filter broke he was faced with drinking the same water as Denys – it was always boiled – but he was rather astonished when he did not come down with fever as a result. Soon Frederick Patterson was caught up in the whole spirit of adventure down to the technique of camping in the African bush, so different and 'far more comfortable, than he believed was possible. Their first hunting adventures took place in that location during June; Maktau Hill, Mbuyuni, Kasigau and Lake Jipe, which today fall within the confines of Tsavo National Park. Next they moved towards Serengeti, crossing it to reach Njoro before coming to Nairobi. Making base camps in each area they relied on 'fly-camps' when they wandered too far to return at dusk. By August they had reached the Lorian Swamp. Reluctantly they moved back to the civilization of Nairobi before returning to the Serengeti to improve upon and experiment with the filming of lions.

Denys's meticulous organization contrasted strongly with his instinctive quest for the new, the unexpected. His safaris were regulated by a stringent orderliness. Familiarity – the gentle poison of routine – so often insidiously destructive poses no threat in the African bush where each day is unpredictable except that it will be predictably different. Routine in camp provides the secure background canvas which highlights the risks experienced during tracking. There is a simple joy of comfort in the knowledge that a hot bath, freshly laundered clothes and a good meal await one at the end of a fifteen-mile

* Swahili for Headman or Foreman.

march. They awakened early, setting out as the nocturnal creatures padded softly to their lairs. The liquid notes of the bush-cuckoo already rising, melancholy in the thorn trees as, like shadows, hyenas and jackals slunk away. Dawn sounds have a character all their own. Even the habitually late, overcoming the moment of resentment for leaving the comfortable form of their bed, will concede that the beauty of a new day more than compensates for the intrusive reluctance of waking. On the plains in the morning, the upward thrust of flocks of tiny multicoloured birds falls suddenly, like confetti tossed on the wind. There is hope in the rush of flight somehow taking up the hope in a hunter's heart as he sets out. At midday when the sun burnishes the plain at 100°F Denys and Patterson followed the example of the animals, resting wherever they could find shade. Patterson confessed that 'my water bottle was almost empty by noon and Hatton's not long before dark. As he was more used to the country and drank less than I did.' They lunched simply while discussing their on-going tactics for the day which by that time had generally been decided by the creatures themselves.

Patterson found that the afternoon was the busiest time for photographing animals – especially elephant and lion. Usually they returned to camp at about 6.30 P.M. and while their baths were prepared had a drink of rum or tea before the daily ritual of tick removal began. This sounds revolting to the uninitiated but the small red game ticks flourish wherever plains game is to be found and creep unseen on to the body of their host. After two or three days in the bush even the most squeamish will admit that their removal has become a natural habit as routine as cleaning one's teeth. Dinner was served at about 7.30 by lamplight and meals consisted of soup, game birds or meat, canned vegetables and fruit and coffee. Patterson was especially impressed with Hamisi's freshly-baked bread which appeared automatically each day, but found, with his American taste for tarts and pies, that Hamisi's pastry needed improvement. When they came across a clutch of ostrich eggs, Denys and he experimented and found them a useful supplement to their camp larder. The champagne, without ice, or the facility for chilling it, went untouched. After the evening meal 'conversation touched on everything from politics to raising a family. It was at these times that Finch Hatton used to tell me some of his great stories of hunting adventures.'[3] Pleasantly weary from their day's stalking they were generally ready to turn in by 10.30 P.M.

During the entire safari it was essential to have meat for their vast fleet of porters. This vital duty was put before all else. Denys used N'dorobo trackers from the Tsavo area for his elephant hunting – feeling they were born to the skill – as were Maasai in the pursuit of lion. Patterson was astonished at the fearlessness of the Maasai, and was impressed that neither of his personal servants flinched in the face of danger, even when a rhino charged them and stopped only twelve feet away.

One of the greatest pleasures for those who love Africa is teaching the newcomer her ways. The repayment is the first flutter of interest which intensifies, reaching a full and generous enthusiasm for the country's beauty and wayward quirks. With so much to learn this is a rewarding process and at the same time there is a personal rediscovery of things which have been taken for granted. Freshness is easily recaptured; a sight which signals the close of day, for instance. When camp is pitched near a swamp, at the same hour each evening, as punctual as clocks, the sacred ibis wing over the tents. Pure white, with ebony heads and extremities, they represent a perfect chiaroscuro drawn up by chance. Each bird might have been dipped into a huge pot of Indian ink – first the head, then the wing tips and tail, so that as they fly, their shape is outlined as if by charcoal, clearly defined against the smoky evening light. Sometimes long wavering lines of crested cranes, their fragile golden coronets invisible, flap their wings with the sound of rusting gate-hinges to form a finely executed study in grisaille. Infinitely wild in flight, they tame happily by the pair for they mate for life. But the majestic sound for which all hunters wait is the roar of the ventriloquist – the lion. It is somehow the climax of the African night in the plains. He sounds close but his voice only indicates his whereabouts to other lion. The stubborn grunt, half moan, strains across the velvety darkness and tells his mate that he is stalking; driving a herd towards her. The human ear may have to reach out to hear it, and the newcomer may not recognize it at all. Mixed with the doleful wail of hyena or the sharp foxy bark of the jackal, all the while is the drowsy tune of the little nightjar. The insect chorus perpetually multiplies itself in endless scurryings, screechings and pipings. Like a language heard for the first time each contribution of sound only gradually becomes separate and identifiable in the general sibilance. Then, imposed upon this drone is the startling snap of branches, almost always a threat, stretching the imagination to the limit.

Each evening, Denys issued orders for the following day to the staff; last minute changes of plan were communicated before departure. Tania comments in *Out of Africa* that Denys had many adventures with lions and had great experience with them. Now, eighty-five miles west of Voi they had their first encounter. Confrontation in the bush is vastly different from a visit to any zoological park. At dusk Denys and Patterson shot a zebra for bait with the intention of photographing lion on a 'kill'. They dragged the disembowelled corpse of the animal not far from a waterhole. Next they built a hide of thorn-bush fifteen feet away in which they settled down to catnap until the lions got wind of the freshly slaughtered meat. At about 2 o'clock in the morning Patterson felt Denys's hand on his shoulder. Straining to see through the dark he identified something tearing at the bait but the flash-light only revealed a hyena. The roar of lion could be heard near at hand which scared off the scavenger. Patterson, unaccustomed to such sights, was not disap-pointed even though the activity did not develop that night. The following evening was the same. But by daylight the vultures had spotted another bait and had begun their approach, wheeling in the sky not half a mile away. When the men investigated its whereabouts, three full-grown lions sprang out of a thicket giving Denys's client his first glimpse of lions unconfined by bars. They dragged the zebra bait over to the lions' natural kill, built another hide and squatted down at dusk for the third night in succession.

When the humped, ungainly figure of a hyena loped in this time Patterson felt a sense of anticlimax. Then, with a shiver down his spine, he realized that the shadowy form standing only twenty-five feet from him was a fully-grown lion. He circled the hide suspiciously, moving up to the bait on a tour of inspection. Patterson recalled this formidable predator 'four hundred and fifty pounds of muscle fused with the dynamite of hunger and defiance'. The lion could 'resist his free meal no longer and settled down to sample it.' Patterson, concentrating on the mighty animal, had failed in the meantime to notice four others which had slipped in silently to join him. He was mesmerized in fascinated horror as the sound reached him: 'the noise of tearing and rending . . . mixed with guttural purrs and deep-throated growls'. The crunching of flesh and bone as the lions tore at the bait was hideous and he could not move. Suddenly a nauseating waft of decayed flesh entered his nostrils, bringing him to his senses. Turning his head slowly, he found to his horror he was staring into the face of the first lion, who had circled them again and was, through their thorn boma's flimsy intertwined branches, not more than four feet away. 'His mouth was open, his teeth gleamed in the moonlight, his eyes shone dully as though obscured by smoke and his mane bristled like wire.' Stillness is imperative in such a delicate situation. But Patterson was so shocked he jerked his head back in alarm and succeeded in startling the whole troupe. Luckily the lions returned a few minutes later to their meal 'including the beast who had nearly taken my [Patterson's] head in its mouth!' Denys silently indicated that his client should shoot the largest lion but in his excitement and terror he found he could hardly get his gun up without scaring them all off. Denys flashed his torch on the lions. They sprang up, pausing for an instant, giving Patterson his chance. To his joy and in spite of his shaking nerve he felled a lion but had hardly time to register his luck when the others were back on the kill. Deliberately and more calmly he fired a second shot and bagged another. There was no sleep that night – at daybreak the lions were skinned, their pelts carried back to camp to be sun-dried and salted. Then came the ritual dance enacted by the Africans to celebrate the slaying of his first lion. Patterson was touched at the private 'ngoma'* which they performed enthusiastically on his behalf. His first experience had been filled with tension but it whetted his appetite for more lion adventures and, when they moved westward and slightly south below Kilimanjaro, which rose magnificent and sheer twenty-thousand feet out of the African plains,† he was

* Swahili for dance.
† Actually 19,340 ft.

determined to get flashlight pictures of them. They followed the same baiting procedure and settled themselves in the hide with an aperture for the camera. The flash was then worked with two small, dry-cell batteries and a percussion cap. After an hour or two

. . . We were rewarded with a bloodchilling concert which started with a chorus of guttural purrings and ended in deep staccato growls. Suddenly the lions moved onto the carcass.

'How many are there?' whispered Patterson to Denys.

'Three I think,' he whispered back. But after a moment he clutched Patterson's arm.

'No – by George – , there are five – six!'[4]

There were four half-grown youngsters and an old lion and lioness.

Settling themselves on the kill, they went about their grim business with a dispatch that was sickening. We let them feed for a few minutes; the sight fascinated us. Even in the quarter-light there was a suggestion of the serpentine in their movements as they tore and rended; again the noise was indescribable. As soon as we used the flash to photograph they sprang bewildered, glared at the boma, then slunk off quietly.

But as he reset the flash, the lions returned, unable to resist their meal. Although the next flash scared them off for good the pictures of the kill were outstanding. Patterson commented: 'Now that I have heard lions tearing at flesh and bone in the darkness the stories of man-eaters which have held their gruesome feasts within earshot of their victim's family or comrades have become terribly real to me.' That night the savagery of being mauled by lions dominated the conversation and Denys recounted a horrible story which occurred in North Africa. Two brothers had been condemned to death by the local authority. For convenience they were shackled together to prevent escape. Somehow they had managed to get away but had been unable to get rid of their fetters. Finally they succeeded in reaching open country, struggling along side by side; after a day of walking and hiding they wandered on until midnight and were suddenly confronted by a lion. They were powerless in tandem to drive him off. After a ghastly period of deliberation, the lion threw the two wretches down and quietly began to eat the elder of the brothers. When he came to the ankle bound by the ring he became impatient and bit the leg off below its knee. Meanwhile the younger brother counterfeited death. So when the lion had satisfied his appetite and gone to a nearby spring to drink, he managed to escape and hide in a cave, dragging the gory leg of his brother behind him. Eventually he was recaptured and brought before the Chief, and was pardoned because of his ordeal. But, as Denys pointed out, lions, despite the incredible stories told of them, are not necessarily vicious. The bush is a world that exists in its own right. Imagination and superstition have contributed to his fabulous image; he shares the Royal Coat of Arms with the mythical unicorn. The hundreds of lion monuments adorning the byways of Venice with their silent stone growls present the same arrogant face as the lion in the plain lifting his head from the bloody centre of his feast. Natural law is not based on a concept of right or wrong; it existed before man and to it man's laws are quite superfluous. Cruelty and joy link hands with life and death in the bush. Denys could not turn his back on this world. He loved to quote from Walt Whitman who, he felt, echoed the lessons of the Book of Job:

> I think I could turn and live with the animals, they are so placid and self-contain'd.
> I stand and look at them long and long

They do not sweat and whine about their condition,
They do not lie awake in the dark and weep for their sins,
They do not make me sick discussing their duty to God,
Not one is dissatisfied, not one is demented with the mania
    of owning things,
Not one kneels to another, nor to his kind that lived thousands
    of years ago,
Not one is respectable or unhappy over the whole earth,
So they show their relations to me, and I accept them,
They bring me tokens of myself, they evince them plainly in
    their possession.

Denys felt that the capriciousness of the lion was the key to his powerful reputation. They are known to strike men down in one blow with a paw, stand over the victim and walk haughtily away after a few minutes without attempting to kill. Poets and dreamers see actions like this as merciful but it is just one aspect of his unending temperament; above all he is a creature of mystery. Tania questions the lion's ability to slay the giraffe in *Shadows on the Grass*:

Lions kill by breaking the necks of their victims and in view of the height of a giraffe's shoulders and neck the thing seems unlikely. On the other hand the strength and energy of a lion are indeed incredible things, and hunters have solemnly assured me that they have seen giraffes being killed by lions.[5]

Tania says of giraffe, it is as if they were 'not a herd of animals but a family of rare, long-stemmed, speckled gigantic flowers', artistically supporting Denys's opinion that they are totally ill-equipped to cope with the savage rules of bush survival. Ungainly at water-holes with their legs spread wide, they are no more designed to drink than cry out in defence against their destiny, for they are mute. In this position they are ideal prey for lion and consequently will delay drinking before putting themselves at his mercy. The lion springs upon the back of the helpless animal, using fang and claw to bring him to his knees.

Denys and Patterson came upon one whose neck had been broken but had escaped with his life. The lion must have been disturbed at the crucial moment for the giraffe to have survived. But generally Denys found lions were pleased to mind their own business and let man mind his. It is only in the first taste of human flesh or cattle that they become dangerous and habitual marauders and this sets their fate. Through his own experience of direct confrontation with lions, Denys admired the Maasai immensely and considered them not simply courageous but heroic. Patterson and he were camping not far from a Maasai boma, when in the middle of the night, they heard an unholy din coming from the manyatta 'as if all the cattle in the world had gone crazy with hysteria'. In the morning, when they went there to collect their lion trackers, they found a large lion lying outside the boma. It had jumped into the compound in the night and killed a cow, whereupon the animal's owner came out and speared him through the heart. His hardihood can only have sprung from the fear and hatred that all natives have for the lion. Two days later they met another Maasai who had shot an arrow into a sheep-marauding lion, killing it at a distance of forty feet.

Denys's imperturbability in the face of danger was recognized throughout the colony – not only by friends but by other hunters, who always have their share of danger. On every safari they are responsible for other men's lives. They know their own limitations but it is sometimes difficult to remain calm in a tight corner when the wrong move from another can cause disaster. J. A. Hunter, famous in the annals of great hunters, was out in the Maasai Reserve with Denys in 1931 – it was the last time they hunted together. One morning a Maasai

herdsman came to them in a great state of agitation: two
lions had been killing his cows and all attempts to drive
them off with his long-bladed spear had failed. The
Maasai wear only a blanket or improvised shift of cotton*
tied about them, so they are highly vulnerable physically
and often proudly sport the scars of mauling by lions.

Denys and I jumped at the chance. Hurriedly we . . . made our
way across the Uasin Nyero stream at Narok. When we reached
the herdsmen's land we saw the cattle stampeding . . . The
sounds of their terror could be heard a long way off. Clouds of
dust choked us as the cows raced round . . . in panic their tails
slashing and their hooves making the ground tremble . . . as the
smell of the lions came to them on the wind and they bucked in
fear from the bloodied ground where the marauders made
their kill. Denys and I made for the scrub where the cattle had
been . . . attacked. The Masai sprinted ahead . . . he was trying
to hurry us on and shouted over his shoulder that the lions had
killed five head of cattle in the last two days. He had seen them
. . . jump on the backs of the victims, which panic stricken into
a gallop, had had their heads forced down by the attacker, thus
causing them to stumble and break their necks as they fell.
Then the lions ripped the bodies to pieces and dragged away
what they couldn't eat on the spot. It was the usual method
with lions who are masters of this cunning art of allowing the
victim to kill himself . . . I heard Denys cry, 'There they are!'
The two lions were only a few yards off . . . Denys loped
towards them on his long legs, raising the double-barrelled rifle
he carried. From where I was a few yards behind, I saw the two
lions rear up on their hind legs as if prepared to dash Denys to
the ground. If they had been a bit quicker I could have done
nothing to save him for he was in my line of fire. But Denys
was quicker than the lions. I saw him stop, shoulder the rifle;
two shots rang out with scarcely a fraction of time between
them. Both lions fell to the ground immediately one of them
performing a miniature death dance as he fell.
   'Good effort,' I said.

* A 'shuka'.

'I'd take any chance with you behind me, J. A.,' Denys replied.[6]

Hunter recalls Denys telling him about a tense moment that occurred when he took the then Prince of Wales out on safari. Again the story had impressed Hunter because of Denys's composure. It typifies his sang froid.

The Prince was a keen amateur photographer and most eager to get a picture of charging rhino. The camera was set up and the rhino induced to charge. Finch Hatton allowed the beast to get within a reasonably safe distance of the Prince and then killed the rhino with a well directed shot. The Prince turned on him furiously:

'How dare you shoot without an order,' he snapped. 'I wanted to get him right up to the camera.'

'Your Royal Highness,' returned Finch Hatton coolly, 'suppose you look at the matter from my point of view. If you, heir to the throne, are killed what is there left for me to do? I can only go behind a tree and blow my brains out!' Finch Hatton said the Prince considered the matter for a moment and then agreed that the was right. I have often wished that I had Finch Hatton's calm assurance. A white hunter is responsible for his clients' safety and if clients insist on taking unnecessary risks the hunter is blamed – a difficult position for any man.[7]

Denys had a similar experience with Patterson at Mespots camp. 'Here we got a good picture of charging rhino. Finch Hatton turned the animal with a shot not six yards from my lens!' Patterson wrote later.

Five months with Patterson, striving all the while to obtain good photographs, convinced Denys that there was far more joy in photographing animals than bagging them as trophies. An incident with Patterson in Serengeti prompted Denys to write to *The Times*. But first Patterson's account of a lioness running abreast of their Chevrolet truck, which inspired the eventual article:

We flushed a lioness which ran to some thick cover nearly half a mile away. We sped after her doing about thirty miles an hour. Finally we actually ran alongside her at a distance of less than twenty-five feet. The way she concentrated on the race was a beautiful sight to see. She put every ounce of strength into her stride and literally flew along. Her ears were laid back, her tail was straight and every hair along her back was rigid. With mouth wide open, she flashed along, every movement showing the rippling grace of her gigantic muscles and straining tendons . . . There was no doubt she had taken our car for a rhino.[8]

Denys's article, headed 'LIONS AT THEIR EASE – STALKING BY CAR – A PRIVILEGE TO GUARD' appeared in *The Times* on 21 January 1928. His grim warning towards the end shows how well he understood the need for conservation.

My two companions and I started from Nairobi on September 8th . . . The road, for an African bush road, proved excellent and we reached . . . the Serengeti Plains in three days . . . a distance of over two hundred miles. The principal object of our trip was to obtain moving pictures of lions; and this we believed could best be accomplished from a motor car . . . We knew from past experience the great difficulty of getting near enough lions in the open and on foot to get good pictures and our idea was that if we could happen upon lions which had not previously seen a motor car they would not connect this strange sort of animal with man and therefore might allow us to approach . . . With this end in view, we fixed a bracket with a universal joint fitting for the cinema camera upon the left hand side of the car, the operator being in the seat next to the driver; the man with the gun for repelling any boarding parties was to be in the left hand rear seat at the back of the camera-man. We subsequently found that this arrangement worked very well.

ON THE PLAINS

September is . . . the end of the dry season. We found the plains themselves very bare holding . . . little game in the surrounding country, however, there were immense herds of zebra, wildebeeste and congoni [sic] . . . the car did not disturb them . . . Zebra and wildebeeste form the staple food of lions; and . . . we felt fairly confident in finding some during the fortnight which we had allowed ourselves for getting good pictures . . . find them we certainly did . . . we saw no fewer than seventy lions, counting males and females and cubs in varying groups from singletons up to one magnificent troop of twenty, which were seen by my two companions upon a day . . . We were after a certain black-maned lion whose skin we coveted more than his picture and we thought we had run him to ground in a dense patch of bush, covering a waterhole where he had apparently drunk. We arranged a drive resulting in eleven lionesses being bolted past us one after the other at about forty yards distance; and it was but little consolation to us for not getting the black lion, to think what a wonderful picture we might have got had we brought the tripod camera with us. But fate held better things in store . . . on our very last day we obtained a lion picture as good as any of us had ever hoped for or ever dreamed of. We were cruising along the bank of a dry river at about 11 o'clock, the going was good, hard sandy soil with large mimosa thorns here and there and occasional patches of thick brush in the river bed. We had been out since dawn . . . and were beginning to think our luck was out when we came upon a small pool in the river with a good reed bed above it . . . The water proved very brackish, but we found recent signs of lions. Getting back into the car, we crawled upstream and after going three hundred yards we spotted two lions and two lionesses lying right in the open, tied up on a red anthill in a most photographable position, about sixty yards from the river course. We steamed slowly up to within thirty yards of them and came to a halt broadside on, with the camera and the 450 bearing upon the mildly interested group. The camera started with a slight whir of gears. One lioness got up and walked off to another hill thirty yards to the left, the other one raising her head for one sleepy look, lay back and closed her eyes. One lion sat upright . . . with some show of interest. While the other continued to look in the opposite direction . . . We had the matter here for a perfect lion picture and after taking two hundred feet we slowly moved out of earshot and out of sight to prepare more film and more cameras praying to the God of the midday sun to keep the drowsy victims under his spell. Our prayers were answered. We were photographing these lions for four hours . . . at all distances from fifty yards to seventy feet . . . We were lucky enough to get a picture of one lioness making an unsuccessful stalk of some gazelles . . . her companions watched every move of the game and paid not the faintest attention to us in the car about thirty yards away. On one occasion when we got near the wind and an eddying gust gave them a suspicion they were up in an instant, scanning the surrounding country with a concentrated gaze for enemy man, apprehensive and alert. So uneasy were they that they eventually decided to move out some four hundred yards further in the open, where they lay down on an ant-hill which commanded a complete view of their ground. After giving them ten minutes to settle down we moved right up to them again in the car and we were received with the same apathy as before. It was clear that they in no way connected the motor-car with man.

A DECOY

At 2 o'clock my gun-bearer remarked that the lions were behaving very well and that as they looked hungry we ought to shoot a congoni for them as 'baksheesh' when we had finished the pictures! This seemed an excellent suggestion and gave the idea of trying to get a picture of the lions coming on to the kill. So we went off in the car and shot a congoni. Tying the antelope to the rear spring . . . we dragged him down to where the lions were lying and loosed him as we passed in full sight at about thirty-five yards. We then drove forty yards from the kill and . . . had not waited more than a minute before a lioness left the group and cautiously crept up to the congoni, finally taking possession with a little rush from six yards off. The others came up one by one and the feast began. Every now and then a blood red face was lifted to take a look at the car as we crept up . . . to get closer pictures. Intent upon the business in hand they showed no apprehension even when we reached seventy feet for the closest photographic range which included the whole group in our six-inch lens. After about half an hour they seemed temporarily sated and evidently felt the sun to be too hot for full bellies. One by one the two lionesses and the youngest lion walked slowly away and lay down under the big umbrella thorn nearby leaving the largest lion to bring the remains of the congoni to them in the shade. After a few minutes he picked up the half-eaten carcass of the large antelope in his mouth and carried it to a tree as easily as a retriever carries a hare, but with a slightly straddling swagger due to the congoni's legs. We had been photographing busily but the camera now jammed. So . . . after taking several still pictures of them under the tree, we pulled out for camp leaving the lions as unconcerned with our movements as . . . upon our first appearance. I cannot remember having spent a more interesting four hours watching wild animals. The opportunities which this district has to offer for the observation, study and photography of all kinds of game but especially lion are in my experience unique. During this fortnight we saw roan antelope, buffalo, cheetah, leopard, waterbuck, klipspringers, impala, Grant's and Thompson's [sic] gazelles besides immense quantities of the commoner sorts of game. Unfortunately it is a melancholy fact that unless some effective form of legislation is brought in by the Government concerned, this unique state of plenty is doomed to disappear in the very near future.

AN ABUSE OF SPORT

Shooting visitors to East Africa who are anxious to fill their bag as quickly as possible, are becoming increasingly numerous. Most of them want to get a lion and many of them do not care just how it is 'got'. At present there are not many easier or quicker ways of getting lion with other game thrown in than by taking a motor car to the Serengeti Plains. Of the seventy lions which we saw we should have had no difficulty in bagging more than half. We actually took away five lion skins and were obliged to shoot two lionesses in the process of getting one of the lions. Other parties are not so easily contented. I have heard of one party which came away from a fortnight's trip with nearly thirty assorted lions, lionesses and cubs – an orgy of slaughter . . . My friends . . . fear I may make matters worse by advertising this district in this article. My reply is that the district is already known by too many to try and save it by keeping quiet and it is in the hope of enlisting the assistance of those who can bring influence to bear, that this is written. It is possible for sportsmen to get lions by ordinary hunting methods over the greater part of the Tanganyika Territory. In many districts they still abound. But I can only think of one possible reason for not closing this district for lion shooting: on the score of the toll taken by lions from the herds of the natives. But wherever there are . . . zebra and wildebeeste in large quantities, lions are not inclined to take the risk entailed in killing stock, especially when the herdsmen are able to give as good an account of themselves as the Masai in their encounters with wild beasts which attack their cattle. I . . . saw the carcasses of two lionesses . . . killed by Masai; one . . . at close range by a spear – the other by a poisoned arrow. The Masai of the

Serengeti Plains . . . would appear to be well able to look after their stock . . . without the assistance of indiscriminate sportsmen.

THE CASE FOR CONTROL

The argument that the revenue would be lost for shooting licences is unsound in my opinion. I believe that many more people would be willing to pay for the privilege of seeing . . . game under the conditions which I have described and for photographing rather than shooting them. It will be seen from my account that the key to the situation, is to be found in the motor car. It is only by proper use of the motor car . . . that the great pleasure and privilege of observing these animals can at present be enjoyed. And it is by abuse of the motor car for shooting purposes, training the animals sooner or later to connect it with man, . . . this privilege will be destroyed. If anything is to be done about it, it must be done quickly. Is it too much to hope that the appropriate influential bodies and individuals in England who have the interest in natural science and study and photography of wild animals in their natural surroundings at heart, will bestir themselves in time to get the necessary action before it is too late?[9]

Within a year of publishing that feature Denys wrote a series of letters strongly protesting against the type of slaughter he had envisaged, which drew him into a verbal skirmish with the Tanganyika Government authorities.

For a break in their five-month safari Denys now booked Patterson into Muthaiga Country Club as his guest for a few days at the end of September. Collecting his accumulated mail from W. C. Hunter, he learned that while he had been incommunicado, Toby had become the 14th Earl of Winchilsea, for their father had died.

When Denys arrived at the farm, Tania was out in the shamba* inspecting her coffee. A friend had come over for tea with his wife in order to give Tania advice on the coming crop. Tania was overjoyed that Denys was back, even if only for four days – at the outside. After tea,

---

* Shamba – Swahili for garden, farmland or estate.

when her guests rose to leave Tania said they must stay for supper, that Denys had come in from a fascinating safari. They hesitated knowing that he had just returned from months in the bush but 'she said *he* wished us to stay'. Though they felt inappropriately dressed (unable to change for dinner), they acquiesced as Tania swept their protestations aside. Tania, well mannered, considerate of their predicament, did not change into a long gown that evening but put on a short dress and wore a crimson Somali shawl about her shoulders. Denys eventually appeared 'deeply bronzed' from his safari, bathed and changed into 'a comfortable brown velvet smoking jacket' (this was not usual in those days, when people on farms often wore 'maridadi'* pyjamas and dressing-gowns after their baths before dinner). Tania was at her most fascinating.

Their friends recall that evening in great detail as 'like a dream . . . the dining-room was dark and the polished table seemed like a pool with only the glimmer of the candles reflected in it.' Tania sat still and silent – as if a sudden move would break the spell. In the dark shadows, her face looked small and white and her dark eyes huge 'like a little woodland witch or something out of a legend'. (Tania's eyes were alert, vividly alive and sometimes disconcertingly penetrating though not very big.) She hardly spoke that evening, all three sat listening to Denys but Tania's delicate detachment appeared to be imposed, an almost conscious control, unlike Denys whose ability to 'kiss the joy as it flies' was an integral part of his nature. Yet at the same time a deep, invisible harmony, existed between them.

* Malidadi/maridadi – the Swahili equivalent of elegant or sophisticated.

During dinner he talked of some of his adventures with Patterson. As an Honorary Game Warden at that time, Denys was assisting the Chief Game Warden, Archie Ritchie, in a census. (They were attempting to define the pattern of migration.) One of the guests was surprised that Denys remarked on the quantity of Thomson's gazelle and kongoni he had counted. Having been brought up in Kenya, she had taken them for granted as a child when the numbers were 'so great that one might as well have counted native goats'. At that, Denys suddenly turned and looked at her 'as if seeing me for the first time' and then he 'began to weave a spell' round them 'till we felt we were with him in the strange and beautiful places he had just come from.' In particular they remember him describing 'a great concourse of baboons in some remote rocky place. He said they were all trooping in carrying things that they were offering to an enormous baboon whom they obviously regarded as a sort of king. He had never seen such a big baboon — it was orange in colour, an incredible sight.' At long last when the friends drove home that night they agreed that Denys, like the fabled Pied Piper of Hamelin, could have made either of them 'go where he pleased at the crook of his little finger'.

The baboon which Denys described at dinner had been spotted at a waterhole in the Serengeti. He and Patterson later discovered that it was the first of a rare species ever to be spotted by a white man. Known as the 'Golden Baboon', its face is 'reddish instead of grey'. Patterson had believed monkeys to be dirty vermin-ridden creatures but changed his views when they subsequently tamed a young baboon in camp. 'He was easily trained. There was nothing he would not attempt in the way of impersonation. He kept us convulsed with laughter. The odd part was that in spite of the fact that he was surrounded by his wild brothers he never made the least attempt to escape.'

The photographs of this animal depict a calm confidence in his captors. In one where Denys inspects its foot for a thorn there is absolutely no sense of fear. Denys explained. 'Just supposing, Patterson, you were locked up with a lot of other people in a small cage. Your cage wasn't cleaned any too often and you never had a chance to bathe. You did not have proper exercise and you were in a continual state of depression owing to your confinement. Don't you think you would gradually degenerate?' Patterson, whose previous knowledge of monkeys and baboons had been confined to zoos, was forced to admit Denys was right.

Tania linked this particular safari with Patterson with the time when things started to fall apart. His influence on Denys and encouragement of game photography is very apparent, and to a great extent, she was excluded. For Tania 'a lion-hunt each single time is an affair of perfect harmony, of deep, burning, mutual desire and reverence between two truthful and undaunted creatures, on the same wave length.' In *Shadows on the Grass* she generalized, 'Denys as a white hunter took out millionaires from many countries and they brought back magnificent pictures.' But her dismissal of even the best photographs which resulted from stalking with a camera is outright; one remark evidently refers to the experiences of Denys and Patterson on that specific quest – the filming of lion in the Serengeti: 'provided you can make the lion join in the spirit of it you may here, at the end . . . blow one another a kiss and part like civilized human beings.' Her resentment of being excluded from those shared adventures is echoed further on in the same passage as she elaborates on her distaste for wanton killing, yet admits that lion hunting has always been irresistible. 'It became to me an unreasonable thing, indeed in itself ugly or vulgar, for the sake of a few hours' excitement to put out a life that belonged in that great landscape and had grown up in it for ten or twenty, or – as in the case of buffaloes and elephants – for fifty or a hundred years.'[10]

When Denys returned to the farm for a handful of days, he and Tania usually stayed up late, conversing until dawn. At these times it was Denys's prerogative to invite guests to join them for dinner – and after they left she had him to herself again for a few more hours. She always preferred to be alone with him. As she grew older this trait developed to the point of obsession, and became suffocating in the powerfulness of her personality. Her relationship with Thorkild Bjørnvig was a case in point. Parmenia Migel comments 'as for . . . Bjørnvig, a long chapter might well be written by some future literary analyst about the sway Tania had over him and its consequences for both of them. For more than four years he was a very rewarding as well as acutely disturbing element in her life . . . the captive audience for the theories she wished to expound (Bror had never listened at all and Denys had countered with his own opinions).'[11]

Denys was perhaps the one person in Tania's life whose determination was as invincible as her own. When she had his entire attention as they shared a bottle of wine, reading one of Shakespeare's plays or poetry; entertaining him with a story she had worked on in his absence, she was satisfied. But from the moment he came home, immediate regret at the thought of his departure tainted the visit. On arrival her first question was inevitable. It is the same in every hunter's home. 'How long for?' Even were it not voiced in complaint, for practical reasons alone she had to know when he was leaving. His clothes had to be laundered and ready, servants advised accordingly, meals prepared, stocks replenished, problems arising during his absence discussed and dealt with in the time allotted. The pattern of the lives revolving round a hunter is not often one to be envied. Even now that radio communication may be a nightly routine reducing distance and time, few marriages survive the waiting and constant separation. When they do, each partner has learned to live a life of their own. The exceptions are rare and the hazard is recognized as occupational. When Tania was alone 'the minutes dripped from the clock, life seemed to be dripping out of you with them, just for the want of white people to talk to'. When Denys was with her those same minutes sped. It is understandable if she could not refrain from mentioning her discontent to him at times. Conversations inevitably were qualified with 'if' and 'but' and 'when'. For Denys it became difficult to talk with ease of departure plans, future dates for safaris – journeys which only emphasized small stabs at her confidence.

A relationship if it is a living thing, fluctuates perpetually – sometimes growing, at others waning imperceptibly or secretly regaining a little lost ground. It seldom stands quite still. Marriage would have calmed her feeling of insecurity. One of the problems now looming on her horizon was the fact that Bror and Cockie would soon be arriving in Kenya as man and wife. There would be another 'Baroness Blixen' and she knew this could not but impinge on her life. Suddenly she would need to qualify herself – explanations would become necessary. Ignominy and Tania could not sit at the same table. Perhaps she tried to fight this despair every time Denys went away and was able to cope at first with her apprehension, but gradually her dread worsened. It is a melancholy fact to have to recognize that the very impulse of love, the aspiration which makes people long to be together day and night at the beginning of love, is generally corrosive and responsible for the very diffusion of intensity in the end. Unlike each season which slips away gently after offering a beauty of its own before humanity becomes bored by it people tend to be more strident in their need for change. And where possessiveness defies the rational qualities of a being and is goaded by a demoniacal need for recognition then the little that can be done to assuage this feeling is never quite enough.

Donald Hannah believes that it is Denys Tania is describing in her unpublished story 'Carnival':

Although this is an intrusion into an aspect that she herself treated with reticence, one cannot avoid thinking that there may be a similarity between her relationship with him and one that is described in . . . 'Carnival'. In this one of the characters says about her husband that she is really deeply in love with him, but she is desperately unhappy because, if he knew what she felt, he would dislike it intensely: 'He wants me to run parallel with him in life . . . I deceive him very well. I do run parallel with him . . . I am his ideal friend and comrade, and he believes that it is his car, his aeroplane, and his collections that I love. But it makes one sad always to deceive.'[12]

There is little doubt that Denys formed the template for that character. In 'The Supper at Elsinore' Tania seems to be dwelling upon an aspect of their relationship when she describes Morten de Coninck – whose physical attributes resemble those of Denys – who failed to turn up at his own wedding and subsequently disappeared from his noble family and obligations in exchange for the freedom of the life of a pirate. A real fear pervades this sentence: 'Or has she yielded, and found the magic ineffective? Or had she been watching him, daily slipping away from her, and still had not the strength to offer the sacrifice which might have held him?' Whenever her fictitious characters seem to be based on Denys that same feeling of immutability is present. In 'The Old Chevalier' Tania describes the past existence of an unforgettable man.

He had a confidence in life, independent of the successes which we envied him, as if he knew that he could draw upon greater forces unknown to us, if he wanted to. It gave me much to think about, on the fate of man, when many years later I was told how this young man had, towards the end of his tragic destiny, answered the friends who implored him in the name of God, in the words of Sophocles' Ajax: 'You worry me too much, woman. Do you know I am no longer a debtor of the Gods?' I see that I ought not to have started talking of him, even after all these years; but an ideal of one's youth will always be a landmark amongst happenings and feeling long ago. He himself has nothing to do with the story.[13]

Tania was allowing herself by her own admission the indulgence of digressing a little, recalling someone whom she cannot forget. The description could just as easily have been lifted from the pages of *Out of Africa* when she talks of Denys's attitude towards their shared future. It is almost identical. In the same book, when she recounts their adventure on New Year's Day when they each shoot a lion feeding on the giraffe, she imbues the episode with complicity and love, while at the same time the act is filled with nostalgia. She then describes another incident when they slay lions together. But this time it is in defence of her farm oxen after a couple of marauders have killed two. This actually took place at an earlier phase in their relationship. There is a feeling of strength in their unity, of confidence. She recognizes with irony that she had been 'on the roof of her own life' that New Year's Day without realizing it. For, it is from that date that their relationship began a faltering downward trend.

In the first episode there is love ever present in a spellbinding way, and it surges through each detail. It is as if she has taken it all in in slow motion, and when she wrote it down saw it as a time when no clouds or threatening shadows of birds of prey were present to mar that evening.

The farm manager, Mr Nichols, tries to persuade

Tania to bait the second ox which had been killed with strychnine, so that when the lions return to the scene of their crime they will be poisoned. He is flustered, frightened to risk his own life (being a married man with responsibilities), but Tania calmly tells him that 'Mr Finch Hatton is here, in the house' and that he and she will deal with the matter.

I then went in to find Denys. 'Come now!' I said to him, 'and let us go and risk our lives unnecessarily. For if they have got any value at all it is that they have got none.' *Frei lebt wer sterben kann.*

We went down and found the dead bullock . . . it had hardly been touched by the lions . . .

'What do you think, Denys?' I asked him. 'Will they come back tonight?'

Denys had great experience with lions. He said that they would come back early in the night to finish the meat, and that we ought to give them time to settle down on it, and go down to the field ourselves at nine o'clock. We would have to use an electric torch from his Safari outfit, to shoot by, and he gave me the choice of the rôles, but I would rather let him shoot and myself hold the torch for him.[14]

In order to negotiate their journey in the dark through the coffee trees without disturbing the lions, they tied strips of white paper to each coffee tree flanking the passage to the bullock bait in the manner of Hansel and Gretel. It was 23 April, the day before Denys's birthday, just as the long rains had started. Tania remembers that while they dined together Denys was melancholic.

. . . reflecting that he had not had enough out of life till now. But something, I consoled him, might still happen to him before his birthday morning. I told Juma to bring a bottle of wine ready for us when we should come back. I kept on thinking of the lions, where would they be, now at this moment? Were they crossing the river, slowly, silently, the one in front of the other, the gentle cold flow of the river turning round their chests and flanks? At nine o'clock we went out. It rained a little, but there was a moon, from time to time she put out her dim white face high up in the sky, beyond layers and layers of thin clouds, and was then dimly mirrored in the white flowering coffee-field. We passed the school at a distance. It was all lighted up. At this sight a great wave of triumph and of pride in my people swept through me. I thought of King Solomon, who says, 'The slothful man saith, There is a lion in the way: a lion is in the streets.' Here were two lions just outside the door, but my school-children were not slothful and had not let the lions keep them from school. We found our marked two rows of coffee trees, paused a moment, and proceeded up between them, one in front of the other. We had moccasins on, and walked silently. I began to shake and tremble with excitement, I dared not come too near to Denys for fear that he might feel it and send me back, and I dared not keep too far away from him either, for he might need my torchlight at any moment.[15]

The batteries of Denys's torch were rather flat so that they knew they would have very little light when the crucial moment to fire came. Savouring every aspect, Tania goes on to describe the night, the coffee flowers, every intake of breath can be felt as she captures their physical awareness of each other; their soft tread in unison; the shine of the last shower on the still-wet coffee leaves and her mounting excitement in danger, lend a theatrical touch which gives the play of the dim torch the power of footlights below an invisible proscenium arch. Within three minutes three shots ring out. The lions are slain. In triumph the two of them – the hero and heroine – are surrounded by the happy clamour of her school-children, the little bright-eyed Kikuyu totos, who, airing their newly acquired English in their inimitable way, make up a song in celebration. They chant in a primitive ballad 'three shots. Two lions. Three shots. Two lions,' elaborating on the theme as they sing 'Three good shots, two big strong bad kali lions', adding the alphabet song A-B-C-D-like alert little multi-coloured parrots. Denys, detecting Tania's tension, teased her later, as they recapped on the details of the incident. 'The torchwork on the second lion was a little shaky!' Kanuthia skinned the lions. Bearded Pooran Singh appeared through the darkness in his 'dhoti' to beg the fat from the sleekest carcass said 'to ward off rheumatism and impotence'. Eventually she and Denys left the endearing flock of school-children and returned to the house. They were sodden and mud-bespattered. The red soil which clings in sticky clods to the soles of shoes in the rainy season was now intermingled on their clothes with the red blood of lions. So vivid is this recollection that one can almost hear the feathery vibration of the wings of the millions of flying ants which inevitably appear as the rain stops, hurling themselves against the light as they are magnetized by it. Together with ineffable harmony they drank their 'singing wine' by the fireside with a completeness which makes talk superfluous: 'We did not speak one word. In our hunt we had been a unity and we had nothing to say to one another.'[16]

They had been the principal actors in a drama that embraced all the sensual fusing of a seduction. The other participants had merely had walk-on parts, enhancing their own strong centre-stage presence. So now, when Denys began to share adventures with lions outside her realm Tania felt resentful. She felt left out and a feeling began to establish a foothold within her, less than but tantamount to jealousy. In a confessional passage from 'The Roads Around Pisa' Tania gives her readers a glimpse of this personal anguish with an insight which is chilling: 'It is not, he thought, that she is jealous of other women. In fact she is that least of all, and the reason is, first, that she knows she can hold her own with most of them, being the most charming and accomplished of them all; secondly, that she feels how little they mean to me.'

A nobleman is seated at a millstone and is trying to 'explain to his friend the reasons that had driven him from his home. He had the misfortune to have a very jealous wife.' The nobleman muses: 'Karl himself will remember that the little adventures which I had at Ingolstadt meant less to me than the opera, when a company of singers came along and gave us *Alceste* or *Don Giovanni* – less even than my studies. But she is jealous of my friends, of my dogs, of the forests of Lindenburg, of my guns and books. She is jealous of the most absurd things.'[17]

Denys was going away again: as inevitably as he had returned; leaving her to join Patterson for the last lap of the safari. Tania's fear at each departure is very real and causes an almost exclusively feminine void. A passage in 'Peter and Rosa' from *Winter's Tales* epitomizes this terror; there is a sense of personal erosion that shows Tania is no stranger to this emotional panic, a rising fear of rejection and resentment. On the previous page she has included 'Thou shalt not let me go except I bless thee.'

Yes, he was running away, that was his thanks to her for letting him come into her bed, and for liking him, since last night, better than other people. She went through their night talk, sentence by sentence. She had meant to be sweet to him – before she went to sleep had she not, in her fancy, stroked his thick glossy hair which once she had pulled, smoothed it, twisted it round her fingers? But he was going away all the same, to far places, where she could not follow him. He did not mind what became of her, but left her here forlorn, as in her dream. In two or three days he would be gone . . . And he would not think of her; and she would have gone from his mind – gone, gone she thought, and bit her hair which was salt with tears.[18]

At the beginning of October, Denys and Patterson intended to photograph elephant in the Lorian swamp.

They stalked one old bull from dawn to midday only to discover that his tusks were too small to make him worth shooting. But one morning, though out after buffalo, they came across a magnificently ivoried elephant. Patterson wanted to photograph him before bagging his tusks so he sent the runners back two miles to camp to get his camera. In the meantime Denys and he stood by watching the vast creature browsing destructively on the surrounding trees, wantonly pulling down branches, trampling on them without sampling most of the foliage. Suddenly he started to move off; the servants had not yet returned with the camera. Patterson was impatient and fearful of losing him. He had no true knowledge of the nature of the animal as he once was – until he learned that man, in a need to embellish the backs of hairbrushes, must attack him for his immortal tusks and transform his courage into gold – the elephant never forgets; he bears a deep grudge against his attacker – and could wait no longer. He 'put two quick shots into him at a range of fifty yards'. At first he did not think he had even damaged the animal for it suddenly took off as though stung by a bee, covering the next hundred yards in his shambling gait, 'quicker than a horse at full gallop'. Then he toppled over 'like a derailed locomotive'. As Patterson ran up to the huge grey carcass he felt himself regretting deeply his murderous shots for the animal was magnificent 'as the sifting red canopy of dust settled over him'. Not only had he destroyed a life but an institution, he felt, and indeed was so busy contemplating his remorse that he was totally unprepared for what followed.

As if avenging all his brothers who had fallen to put bangles on mistresses, keys on pianos or monarchs with their entourage of knights and bishops on chess boards since time immemorial, absolutely without warning, a vast grey wall rose up in front of Patterson:

Then an earsplitting blast. I had no time to wonder if the old bull was stunned or playing possum. He was on his feet and started in my direction, reaching for me over the few yards that separated us. I could only turn and run faster than I had ever run in my life. Hatton saved my life by sending a shot whistling into the elephant, bringing him down for the last time. We held a post mortem. I found that one of my two original shots had gone through the lungs and that the other had cut the main artery leading from the heart. Yet that last desperate charge had been made in the direction of the enemy. Here was an elephant who had been literally dead on his feet, yet had carried on. I confess I felt ashamed of the deadly odds in the modern rifle's favour.[19]

The removal of the tusks from an elephant is an obscene process by any standard. The natives feast on the meat as well so that it is a gory process not enhanced by the bloodlust for its flesh. Shame follows hot on the heels of any triumph or relief of escape from personal danger. Hacking out the tusks is nauseous; it leaves an unsightly raw hole, the soft pink centre nerve within the ivory sheath lies flaccid on the ground beside the huge immobile head which will never turn to sense danger again, nor use its sensitive trunk to guide its children tenderly through danger; yet its eye is still open, almost seeing, above the place where the tusk once grew. The whole carcass resembles some three dimensional monstrous jig-saw puzzle and, but for one or two pieces, complete; the ears may be removed, and the inner flank, some meat for a native feast. But only the vultures can transform it into a clean noble thing again, ribbon by ribbon of decaying flesh picked in their curved beaks until it becomes first a prehistoric carcass, then a pile of outsize bones.

Patterson got far more pleasure from filming than from killing them. He and Denys were kept amused watching the vast mother elephants gently guiding their babies along in front of them with their trunks, and Patterson was astonished at the delicacy and concern of elephant family life: 'Once I saw a baby standing with its mother in the river near our camp, holding on to her tail for dear life to keep it from being washed downstream. There were about twelve other elephants wading about in the water having the time of their lives.' Trying to photograph them in or near water had its drawbacks and awkward moments. One day he and Denys started to cross a river in order to film an old lone bull, and were knee deep in water when a truculent rhino 'with a snort that could be heard a mile' started to charge them. Fortunately after a few nerve-wracking lunges in their direction he changed his mind and moved on with the current. Then when they were almost across, a huge crocodile slid menacingly into the water nearby and submerged. They could do nothing but keep moving quietly as possible in order not to scare the elephant. 'What a relief it was,' Patterson recalls, 'to see that ugly crocodile's snout come up about fifty yards downstream,'[20]

Another time when they were filming rhino, an 'elderly dame who had her calf with her' suddenly heard the noise of the camera and swung about and charged.

Finch Hatton made a beautiful brain shot and brought her down twenty feet from the camera. Then the fun began, the youngster snorted and pawed the ground like a grampus. She never came to the point of a sustained charge but she made a dangerous nuisance of herself for forty minutes before we persuaded her that this was the kind of thing that no tactful young lady should do. Our hints took the form of firing shots all round her and kicking up the dust right under her ugly nose. It was an immense relief to see her finally trot away with her little tail stuck up over her back to indicate how mightily she had been offended.[21]

The whir of their camera seemed to aggravate rhinos when minutes before they had been oblivious and quite peaceful. One did charge them from the river and when Denys fired shots into the water to ward him off it had no effect at all.

With prodigious splashings and showing astonishing speed, the rhino actually got within six feet of us before I [Patterson] realized the danger. I promptly jumped behind Hatton, who crashed a shot into the beast's ugly face at the very moment it placed its forefeet on the ledge. That stopped him and he reeled back into the water, but only for a moment. With an effort that was positively heroic, he gathered his forces and came at us again, getting almost up the bank before another shot caromed off his armoured skull and sat him down again. This time he called it quits and after lashing about in an effort to clear his childish brain, he went off snorting down the river with an almost jaunty air. But we agreed hereafter that it would be better to see less of our prehistoric friend at such close quarters.[22]

Their adventures with buffalo – a matter of course out in the bush – were almost always nasty; buffalo like elephant lie up in the scant pools of midday shade and it is surprising how often the cautious hunter is caught unawares. Nearly all hunters in Africa can tell a similar tale:

Early one morning Hatton and I came upon one lying down and, as it did not have a particularly good head, carefully avoided it. About half an hour later we were again in the vicinity of this animal and this time it surprised us by a sudden charge. It was so close that I had no chance to shoot. There was just time to jump to one side and, as the buffalo rushed by, the vicious side-sweep of its horns missed me by inches. Stopping up short, it turned like a polo pony and was just about to finish the job when there was a tremendous report and the buffalo fell at my feet. Finch Hatton's bullet had found the beast's brain with a timely aim that saved my life.[23]

Those who have not ventured into the realm of hunting will perhaps not understand how easy it is for the professional hunter in his rôle of mentor to become GOD. He does not necessarily seek the rôle, but the client, the porters, the skinners and the trackers place him above themselves and defer constantly to his superior knowledge of the bush and the quarry. They will scarcely make one step in or out of camp without his approval. All decisions are taken by him and are final.

Patterson felt the scenes of grandeur and romance seeping away as he drew nearer to the coast. By late October the memories of five months' unique experiences were relit in the last few campfires. Unexpectedly the American felt a sense of loss at the thought of bidding farewell to the servants:

We had all slept together in a limited circle and the same campfires had warded off the approach of wild beasts protecting both natives and white men. I had grown accustomed to their weird songs of victory, the patient bearing of their loads while on safari, their native habits, superstitions and courage, . . I had much to be thankful for . . . Everything that had brought me to British East Africa had been accomplished. Upon at least two occasions I had had close calls from death or serious injury at the hands of these very animals I had learned to admire, and only the courage and accurate shooting of Finch Hatton had stood between me and trouble.[24]

Patterson's last hunt was for a sable in the Shimba Hills – they were lucky, they sighted the elusive creature at 9 A.M. although it took the rest of the day to get within a hundred yards. Then, Patterson recalls: 'I got a good running shot at a good bull . . . As he fell it seemed to me that Africa had at last bestowed her supreme gift . . . something in its beauty and regal bearing even in death, made me for the time being forget all past experiences –

as one forgets a confused dream in which there are too many forms and sounds.'[25]

Patterson's awareness, his ultimate reaction to exposure to African servants, is interesting. In a short time he experienced feelings ingrained in those who have lived in Africa for many years. The attitude of the immigrant towards the domestic employee is often misconstrued. Those who have not lived in a style which dissolved with the Industrial Revolution find it difficult to comprehend the interdependency between servant and employee. It is easy enough to scoff at the fact that the way a man's shoes have been cleaned may well set his mood for the day. But a domestic servant becomes an essential component of the family unit. Close daily contact solicits extreme sensitivity to one another's moods. Like a child in times of stress the servant turns to the mistress of the house calling her 'mama' (Swahili for mother). Tears may be spilled on either side without loss of face. Sympathy flows between the protagonists. Tania herself has come in for a good deal of criticism – her attitude dismissed as that of 'noblesse oblige' towards her squatters, to Farah – her major-domo – and other servants in her house or derided as 'semi-feudal'. This leaves a feeling of pretentiousness. But such clear cut lines cannot be drawn round these relationships. Tania fulfilled her convictions with passion. Her sense of obligation to her servants was one of genuine love and concern for their progress and well-being – a creed ever present in her autobiographical work and in her fiction. Tania was entirely dependent on her staff for the smooth running of her home – always the psychological fortress against the world – and they leaned on her in every dilemma for advice. But they earned their wages. She respected their dignity, their fearlessness, their ability to bow to the hand of fate, in humane terms. Tania has been labelled snobbish and, paradoxically, as 'pro-native'. But when she states that the native 'in the hands of a pedant dies of grief' she obliterates these criticisms at once and defines brilliantly her own comprehension of their untutored vulnerability. Patterson also touches on the African's sensitivity, in this case an intuitive withdrawal – although apparently none of the safari staff had been advised of his imminent departure:

Our natives appeared to understand that within a short time the safari would come to an end. They sang less as they marched along. Some of the enthusiasm which they spread in earlier days of our association was passing or at least strangely missing. For after all, the native in such expeditions, however small his task may be, feels himself part of the whole, and his manner of march and conduct in the field is but another indication of the pride he has in achievement of success on the part of the safari leaders.[26]

Patterson could not help mentioning Denys's innate love for Africa:

Hatton was talking of a return trip to England, but his eyes kept sweeping the horizon. He loved every inch of this country, with its magnificent settings of field, forest and jungle land. Hatton was trusted by the natives who knew him as a dependable hunter and friend . . . My boat I learned would sail for Marseilles within twenty-four hours. Hatton and I shook hands. 'Till we meet again,' he said. 'You will come back.' Then he was gone and I knew I must say farewell to Africa.[27]

The fact that he was not employed on a safari did not now prevent Denys from wandering – his travels seemed to increase from this time. He wrote to Kermit describing a motor trip he made from Masara on the Red Sea to Asmara:

a wonderful road rising 6,500 feet in about two hundred miles. I also spent two days ashore at Magadiscio [sic] in Italian Somaliland. They have a madman of a Governor there which is a pity;

he is playing the devil with the Somalis: forced labour very badly organized – families split up and sent to work 150 miles from their houses. The inevitable insurrections are suppressed with every brutality: women and children butchered in cold blood after the men have been rounded up and flattened out with machine-guns. All decent thinking Italians are disgusted by his regime and are praying that this man will not return after his leave.[28]

Kermit again invited Denys to visit him in 1928, and Denys had fully intended to go to the United States but he was commissioned to take HRH Edward, the Prince of Wales, on safari for a few weeks after he and his brother Henry, Duke of Gloucester, had completed an official tour of BEA. In Tania's notes she has recorded that Denys also took out a client named Phipps that same year. Presumably these two engagements are what prompted Denys to write to Kermit: 'Just a line in haste to say that I am awfully afraid I shall have to call my American trip off. Have not given up all hope yet but things look as though I shall have to get back to BEA sooner than I anticipated. Shall write you soon. My love to your charming wife.'[29] Oddly the letter is signed in full, from the Conservative Club, London. It was on one of his trips to England that Denys is reputed, while going through customs, to have thrown a chain of currency rings down on the counter. These were the old ten cent pieces with holes through the centre. As they clattered to the bench under the eye of the customs officer Denys explained in one word 'Gold'. Joining in the spirit of the thing, the official threw the chain back to Denys with the comment 'Gold? I should think so – curtain rings!' Indicating that there was no duty to pay.

The next entry in Tania's list of Denys's movements is 'Nov 1928 Wales'. This safari and Denys's connection with the Prince of Wales started off happily enough as far as Tania was concerned, for she was very much part of the festivities for the future King of England. But when Denys returned that Christmas because the Prince's safari was foreshortened due to King George V's illness, and she learned that Denys had enlisted Bror's help in order to bag a lion for the Prince, she was intensely upset. She was even more angry when she learned that Cockie von Blixen-Finecke had joined the hunting party at the request of the Prince. This incident had repercussions during 1930, when Denys again used Bror as a second hunter during the Prince's next safari. On this occasion the Baroness Blixen invited to Government House in Nairobi was not Tania. Denys brought the Prince to the farm by way of compensation but nevertheless the situation was as embarrassing to Tania as she had always feared it would be.

Though Tania may not have been aware of it, Denys had tried to get hold of his old friend J. A. Hunter to assist him but he was out on safari with two Americans and their reaction, when Hunter received a message by runner that he was to join the royal hunting party, was one of outrage. 'Who's the Prince of Wales,' the young American exploded. 'My money's as good as his!' And on consideration Hunter agreed that he would be letting his client down and reluctantly declined the honour.

In the week of 4 November, while Denys was attending to detailed arrangements for the safari, Tania was invited by the Governor's wife, Joanie Grigg, a close friend, to join the houseparty at Government House, Nairobi. Tania tells about the occasion in *Shadows on the Grass*, explaining that

. . . this was an opportunity of bringing the cause of the Natives, in the matter of their taxation, before the Prince and I was happy about the chance of getting the car of the future King of

England. 'Only,' I said to myself, 'it will have to be done in a pleasant manner. For if it does not amuse him, he will do nothing about it.' As I sat beside the Prince at dinner I cautiously tried to turn his interest the way I wanted, and he did indeed on the next day come out to the farm and have tea with me. He walked with me into the huts of the squatters and made enquiries as to what they possessed in the way of cattle and goats, what they might earn by working on the farm and what they paid in taxes, writing down the figures. It was to me later on, when I was back in Denmark, a heartbreaking thing, that my Prince of Wales should be King of England for only six months.[30]

When on Tuesday, 6 November the Prince suddenly announced his intention to dine with her on Friday, saying he would like to watch an Ngoma, Tania was in a total dilemma. Having taken great delight in describing the tribal dances to him, she now had only two days to arrange the evening. The date could not be altered – the Prince was in Nanyuki for two days and was leaving for safari with Denys the following Wednesday. However, the biggest obstacle lay in the fact that 'these Ngomas were ritual dances connected with the harvest and . . . the natives would rather die, than break with a sacred law of a thousand years. Farah was as deeply shaken by the news as I myself.' Obviously they could not refuse the Prince his request either. Farah and Tania decided to involve the important Kikuyu, Chief Kinanjuie, in the matter. With great persuasiveness they reminded him of how they had helped him over the use of a salt lick on her farm when great herds of native cattle badly needed this nutrient. After due consideration Kinanjuie cooperated and Farah reappeared on the morning of the great day, jubilant if hoarse and weary. 'Memsahib . . . they are coming all of them and they are bringing with them their young men and their virgins.' The evening was a triumph – they had not failed Denys or the Prince;

'between two and three thousand dancers gathered about a huge log fire that night, and under the full moon the Ngoma took place.' The magnificent meal she had prepared in honour of her guest – lobster up from Mombasa, spur fowl brought in by the Maasai morani and Kamante's Cumberland sauce – contributed to the memorable evening. The Prince was delighted with his unusual entertainment. He held a dinner party and dance at Muthaiga Club on Tuesday 13th, the night before he was due to leave on safari with Denys. The Governor, Sir Edward Grigg, was invited and his wife, the McMillans, Mr A. F. 'Tommy' Lascelles, who was in the Prince's hunting party and was his secretary, his ADC, Lieutenant-Colonel the Hon Piers Legh, Tania, Denys and forty other guests. Tania was one of the few women who need not content herself with the consolatory tune of the late 'twenties 'I've danced with a man, who's danced with a girl, who's danced with the Prince of Wales.'

Denys had planned that the safari should depart promptly at 9 A.M. on the morning of 14 November but by 9.05 A.M. he abandoned all ideas of travelling by road to Kajiado in Maasailand. The rains had started with a vengeance and they would simply not get through to their first camp. Hurriedly alternative plans were made for a freight train to take the party instead. At 2 P.M. the lorries and other vehicles were loaded on to the train. In this highly unorthodox manner the hunters began their safari. They were planning to move southwards to Longido, on to Arusha, west to Babati to the lake of that name where the Prince hoped for good duckshooting – thence to Kondoa-Irangi, Dodoma and Iringi moving westward to Mwenzo and Abercorn to Lake Tanganyika. The rains continued to be phenomenally heavy, which made camping slightly precarious. Clarence Buxton, a cousin of Geoffrey's who was District Officer at Kajiado, met them with a certain amount of relief – he had been bogged down on the Athi plains all night himself. One lorry which Denys had rather optimistically sent out that morning like a sort of 'Noah's dove' had not yet reached its destination. 'In fact the lorry was never seen again. Later however the chauffeur materialized out of the swallowing mud and sought much for consolation and much baksheesh.'[31]

Because of the deplorable camping conditions it had now been arranged that the royal party should spend the night at Clarence Buxton's house, before proceeding the following morning, as scheduled, to Longido. Dinner had in any case been arranged at Clarence's house. Every detail had been covered with the household staff and instructions had been given as to their behaviour – the protocol they must follow while the Prince was under their employer's roof. Most important of all, everything must be taken first to this illustrious man, then others served in the usual manner. According to directions, the staff proffered each course to the most distinguished guest present – which the servants automatically assumed was Denys, much to everyone's acute embarrassment including his own, for once. By some oversight, the one important piece of information had been overlooked: nobody had pointed out who the Prince actually was.

On Thursday 15 November the sky was clear, the outlook dry enough to set out immediately after breakfast. The motorcade consisted of the equipment and staff in four Albion lorries in the charge of Sergeant Nicholl of the King's African Rifles; Lord Delamere's Buick which had been put at the prince's disposal was driven by him; Denys drove his own Hudson, with Tommy Lascelles; and the two Willys-Knight safari box-cars were driven by Joey Legh and Kanuthia. Denys felt that because of the haste due to the Prince's limited amount of time he should warn his party that: 'Africa does not wear her heart upon her sleeve . . . no man, no matter how faithfully he had served her, can make a new-comer, not even a King's son her freeman, by way of casual introduction.' He added, 'You must live with her first and learn of her by hard experience.' The Prince had borrowed the Governor's camera and when Denys spied a lone bull elephant beyond the Ol Mberesha Hills, HRH expressed the desire to photograph it. The cover was sufficiently good to allow this and 'This was successfully done by Lascelles at a range of fifty prudent yards and by Finch Hatton at point blank exposure.' Suddenly they caught sight of another elephant in the vicinity and decided they would take his picture as well at a range of about twenty-five yards. 'This being accomplished they withdrew, walking delicately. Presently they noticed the second elephant walking delicately after them! The men decided on as unobtrusive retreat as possible.' They proceeded in the manner laid down by The Ancient Mariner for him who walks 'in fear and dread' and

> Having once turned round walks on,
> And turns no more his head

This was presumably recited by Denys between clenched teeth before they bolted for their lives. Apparently the elephant had no taste for Coleridge, for he charged them, making straight for Tommy Lascelles. Chalmers writes 'They separated and ran like rabbits. It was a ridiculous sight . . . there were four men, one of them heir to the throne, running for their lives with an irritated elephant rapidly overtaking them . . . Lascelles pulled out a final futile sprint. Denys Finch Hatton whipped up his rifle and snapped off a shot at the pursuer. Round swung the elephant on his quarters as neatly as a polo pony on the space of a cheeseplate. And the next moment he was gone. . . . The four fugitives stopped and tried to look as if they had not been running and had not been badly scared. They walked with dignity to the cars which were less than 200 yards away and then sat down to lunch.'[32]

On 16 November the party arrived at Arusha. Denys had contacted Bror arranging to meet him there.

It was an unofficial visit but all the town was *en fête*. The hotel was giving a dance; the Masai had arranged an Ngoma. A battalion of the King's African Rifles was paraded for inspection; a football match had been fixed up, there was as complete a festival atmosphere as the little town at the foot of Mt Meru could achieve. My wife and I had driven our 115 miles into the town like the rest and pitched camp not far from the hotel. I was just shaking a cocktail when a little man came into the tent and said: 'I'm the Prince of Wales, and should like to make your acquaintance.'[33]

Cockie and Bror had been married just three months and had made alternative arrangements for dinner that night. But Denys cornered Cockie and told her under his breath 'You've got to get out of it, Cockie. I want Blix to help me find the Prince a lion.' Of course, they cancelled their arrangements, Bror joined the hunting party and during the evening between dancing and dinner the plans were made to get a lion. At about 2 A.M. Cockie took the vehicle they had come to Arusha in and drove back to their small homestead at Babati alone, through the night along a terribly rough road. She arrived at 7 A.M. exhausted and took herself straight to bed. Meanwhile the men were out after lion. Bror wrote later:

I had the opportunity of discussing and planning a lion hunt with my old friend Finch Hatton, who was already a member of the Prince's party. Unfortunately the Prince had no more than two days to spare . . . no one knew that he could not extend his

time . . . so we had to look . . . in the immediate neighbour-
hood: . . at the foot of Mount Ufiomi – not far from my
farm.'[34]

The usual baiting procedure was followed. The first,
near the village of Kwakuchinjas, drew the lion who
feasted very well then slunk off. 'We had to return to
Babati with long faces,' recalls Blix, 'though the most
crestfallen of the party was naturally myself. But I was
not merely crestfallen – I was angry, and swore that the
Prince should have his lion.' At about midday of the
morning Cockie had arrived home from Arusha her sleep
was disturbed by voices and the sound of footsteps outside
her bedroom door. She opened her eyes to see Blix
standing there announcing that he had brought the Prince
for lunch. She protested strongly saying she had nothing
suitable to eat in the house and that she was still weary
from her drive. 'Whereupon the Prince himself appeared
at the door, saying, "Surely, Cockie, you can get me
something for lunch – you must have some eggs in the
house!" Indeed she had to admit this was so and they
lunched very well on scrambled eggs in the little mud and
wattle dwelling which was the von Blixen's new home. It
was on this occasion that the Prince took Blix aside after
eating and said, "I say, Blixen, you really oughtn't to let
your wife live in a tumbledown place like this." "I shall
never forget the tone of his voice," Blix later wrote.
"Naturally I felt ashamed, though my wife hadn't complained – and inwardly promised to put things right." '[35]

There are interesting and intrinsic differences here,
both between Denys and Bror and between Cockie and
Tania. Bror is anxious not to fall short of his reputation
with lions before the prince whereas Denys, while wishing
to please his royal client, has forewarned him that he
may be unlucky. Cockie is also quite relaxed in the

company of the noble guest and not in the least perturbed either about her simple home or the fact that she has nothing up to epicurean standards to offer him for a meal, whereas Tania would have been mortified under similar circumstances.

The Prince found Cockie so charming, felt so concerned that she would be lonely and miserable by herself that he insisted she join the hunting party at once. Being a tender-hearted individual, whose sympathy lay entirely with the animals, she was a notoriously bad shot, but she accepted the invitation with alacrity. The Prince eventually got his lion after two more attempts but Denys and Blix were worried because they had to hunt it, partly obscured in long grass. Bror's performance was impressive in his determination to get the trophy: 'Blixen (whose attitude towards lions is that of the prophet Daniel) decided to be the sole beater. He had not gone far when a lion appeared at the edge of the covert. It turned rapidly and re-entered the bush. "Shoo," said Blixen, not to be denied "Shoo," and he clapped his hands. Out bounded the lion. He really looked rather fine. Broadside on, he galloped across the front. HRH was shooting with a ·350 double-barrel Express lent to him by Grigg.' In fact the Prince took four shots to bring the beast down but he was 140 yards away 'the grass was tallish and the great yellow beast went bounding through in great leaps'. He measured 104 inches and was an old warrior. The Prince was well pleased with his lion-hunt.

Next they went after buffalo while 'Baroness Blixen had taken Legh and Lascelles to shoot guinea-fowl. The guinea-fowl beat her every time.' Unlike Tania, Cockie was hopeless with a gun; she went after a blue starling one day and succeeded in bagging it with the sole intention of trimming a hat; but after half an hour its brilliant plumage turned black, which she found disappointing, having taken the bird's life for its iridescent feathers. On another occasion she summoned up enough courage to shoot a giraffe for its skin; after three shots she failed to kill it, and gave up. However she accidentally pulled the trigger as she lowered the gun; it wasn't until her gun-bearer said 'Na kwisha kufa memsahib,' telling her that she had hit it with the unintended shot, that she realized what she had done. Cockie recalls that no matter what they were stalking the Prince, who had 'a marvellous sort of picnic box' from which he could make tea with a primus, always stopped for tea at four o'clock. He also had a Crichton ice-making machine which she coveted and he offered to send her one as a gift when he returned to England. Cockie forgot all about his promise until, three months later the parcel containing the ice-machine arrived, a wonderful innovation for safari in those days when ice for drinks was an unheard of luxury. What had really impressed her was that the Prince, despite the worrying days which followed, had taken the trouble to keep his word. On 23 November came the first indication that his father was unwell. But there seemed no cause for alarm. He went off hunting rhino and buffalo and it wasn't until 27 November that they realized the news from Buckingham Palace was grave and made worse by the guarded wording of the communication. The Prince's safari was finished. At any moment he might receive a blue and white envelope and learn he was no longer Prince of Wales. Cockie drove the Prince at once to Dodoma. (Blix and Denys were still out looking for buffalo.) He was pensive in the car, saying to Cockie 'Imagine,' in disbelief, 'I could be King of England tomorrow.' Blix recalls that the last thing he heard that night in camp as he fell asleep exhausted 'were the melancholy minor tones of the Prince's accordion. I relate this episode only to show what immense endurance and sportsman-like spirit the man possessed. That same day he had driven nearly 180 miles by car over rough roads, had hunted for six hours, and then for a whole evening entertained and chatted with a dozen people he had never seen before nor probably would ever see again – when he was consumed with anxiety and fear on account of the illness of his beloved father the issue of which might have for himself consequences of the deepest significance.'[36]

The Prince left Dodoma at 4 A.M. on the Governor's train and Denys went with him, attending to anything, no matter how small, that could lift the load from the Prince, trying to dispel some of the oppressive clouds now hanging over him. On 4 December, while aboard HMS *Enterprise,* the Prince wrote thanking Denys for his support. The friendliness and warmth of the letter shows that, despite the damp conditions throughout the safari and the fact that it had been curtailed abruptly for unfortunate reasons, they had established a happy rapport with each other and that the afterglow lingered on sufficiently to make the prince determined to return when the opportunity arose:

My dear Denys,

What a mess up this all is and this ship is vibrating at twenty-four knots to beat any face massage machine. But thank God it is making this high speed or I'd become quite mad with the strain of it all; it's bad enough when one was ashore and could at least have some things to do to take one's mind off it all a little. But it's hell now, particularly as the news of the King aren't any too good and they seem very anxious as to whether his heart will stand the long strain that it has had to endure for nearly a fortnight now. Whatever I may happen to be doing, and there just isn't a thing to do on board but eat and sleep, really, but even at meals I expect any radio message that I receive is the one to say he is dead. Living on the edge of such a calamity as I have been this last week is very wearing and a curious contrast to the happy life of our safari the first ten days.

It was great fun and I was enjoying it all so much and have to thank you a great deal for coming along and helping us so much and in so many ways as you did. We miss you very much now when you could still be helping us, and were very sorry when you pushed off back to the shore Sunday morning. Besides knowing more about hunting in Africa than nearly everybody you kind of get the form of people so amazingly well and that is another reason why I hope so much that we can go on safari together again some day and properly next time. I'm surprised that I have enough optimism left even to say that; but somehow I feel I will make East Africa again whatever happens. I absolutely must. This really is being an amazingly quick speedy voyage, as we make Aden at noon tomorrow and Suez 9 P.M. Friday. If the news isn't any worse we intend spending Saturday in Cairo and sailing from Port Said in this ship that night, making Brindisi Monday afternoon to make the Continental Express by which we should reach London Wednesday twelvth, at night. All of that must sound very complicated but then you see I am entirely concentrated on getting back the quickest way possible as you can guess and no delaying, though a few hours in Cairo will help and Tommy has a sister there and he wants to see her. I personally hope for a game of squash though I get some exercise with the officers of an evening who are a good bunch and helpful. They seem to have had quite an amusing week's shooting too and have some trophies in the ward room and the gun room which reminds me that I have left my lionskin and the koodoo [sic] head behind though I guess you know all about that and are having them fixed and will send them to England when they are ready. The lionskin I want particularly as I really was very pleased with that shooting. I wish I had got the buffalo but our luck and the light and Fournie were against us. I wonder if you've done any good with the box cars? It was disappointing that none of those shenzi followers of the Aga Khan fancied them as we hoped they would though possibly the addition of the royal feathers will attract some of them in Mombasa. If none of them play up I should try sticking the Aga Khan himself with them himself. It was damned bad luck doing your Hudson in though I guess you'll be able to get the cost of fixing it out of the Kenya Government grant for the safari. If you can't I hope you'll not hesitate to send the bill to me. This is a very messy letter but typing is none too easy with the shaking of the ship which is worse aft here in the Captain's cabin than anywhere else. Thank you again Denys for all your trouble and help. Hope you'll have a pleasant safari with the Frenchman and we look forward to seeing you in England around May. The best of luck.[37]

> Yours very sincerely
> (signed) Edward P.

Joey Legh, the Prince's aide, also wrote to thank Denys and confirm certain arrangements to deliver a note to Toby on arrival in England; nostalgia is the predominating feeling.

My dear Denys,'
We are reaching Aden at noon today so I am writing you a line before arriving as we are going ashore for a 'sweat'. It was very sad saying goodbye to you, and we all miss you very much and wish you were here with us. It is just three weeks today since we began our safari and I do not think I have ever spent a more interesting fortnight certainly never one which contained so many varied incidents. In all the ten years I have been with HRH I have never known him enjoy a trip more, and I do congratulate you on putting up such a wonderful show in such a ridiculous short space of time. . . . HRH has been wonderful as the news is none too good. It looks as if chances of recovery are about even money. . . . I do hope you did not have a very uncomfortable journey back on the *Anzania*, and I am very sorry you have got the worry of the disposal of the cars. I will not forget the little commissions you gave me and will expedite them as soon as possible. If you find there are any outstanding accounts left unsettled will you please let me know. . . . We shall look forward to seeing you in the spring, when I hope we shall have another encounter on the golf links. I hope you will have an enjoyable safari with your frog. Thanking you a thousand times and with every good wish for Xmas and the New Year,[38]

> yours ever
> Joey Legh

The Prince arrived home on 12 December and the King, after an operation for appendicitis on 13 December, improved steadily. Denys refused the Prince's invitation to accompany him back to England for two reasons. He had promised Tania he would be back for Christmas and in January he had another safari in the Marsabit area with a French couple.

When he arrived on the farm and Tania realized that Cockie had been among the Prince's entourage she was furious. She considered Denys's enlistment of her ex-husband in this safari a defection of loyalty, and she told him so. Through many people's eyes she may have seemed justified. But there had never been any rift in their friendships despite the divorce so that her new attitude of disapproval must have been puzzling. Although she put the blame on Denys, it was probably Cockie's presence which had brought about a twinge of resentment. Denys was taking Baron and Baroness Gourgaud on safari at the beginning of the year. On 1 January, the day he was leaving, Tania could not resist making a further reference to the matter in a note to him; Bror however becomes the motive and object of her reasoning. She wrote that 'it is a law against nature' that Denys is friendly with Bror, adding 'so would it be with you I believe if Bror had been your sister's husband or if you thought he behaved badly to your friend Mrs Fergusson'* Tania ends the note somewhat coldly with good wishes for his safari and 'love to Gourgaud† and Robert.'

It seems that from this point Tania allowed free rein to an inaccessible and repressed part of her mind. She started relentlessly to compensate for her maelstrom of insecurity by becoming openly possessive of Denys. She

* Believed to be a reference to a close friend of the Winchilsea family who had known Denys from adolescence.
† Baron Napoleon Gourgaud.

seems driven to demand more and more of him, giving
no rational thought to what she might lose. Reasoning
with her only appeased her black moods temporarily.
Initially he was firm and calm, going about his plans as
usual, though it was becoming more and more difficult
not to row with her. And there were financial strains too
at this time. Denys's company Kipliget Ltd had loaned
her money earlier for the farm but there had not been
enough cash available to take over the mortgage entirely
– nor was Denys prepared to risk more than £2,000 for a
first mortgage. He had taken pains to explain the exact
position to Tania, who seemed confused about the extent
of his committal. Clarifying this for her, he explained
that 'I should not be *buying* the farm . . . if I wanted to
buy the house and grounds I should have to come in at
the sale – just as any other buyer.' The tone of the
lawyer's letters coming from the firm in England who
acted for Denys, denote an infringement of trust in the
latter half of 1929. As if, as a result of his aid their client
has reached the limit of sympathetic involvement in a
crumbling insolvent coffee farm. Earlier, Denys had given
his assurance to Tania that 'I will do everything I can to
prevent your house and grounds going to the enemy' and
the conciliatory phrase which follows 'You are having a
bad time poor thing I wish I could help more . . .' is
hardly of the stuff which builds confidence, particularly
as their relationship was beginning to show flaws. The
tone of Denys's solicitor's correspondence to Tania is
firm – not to say impertinent – and it seems that the
finger of accusation of mismanagement is being pointed
in her direction. In October that year, presumably on
Denys's instructions, Tania received a letter which
reminded her that 'the Karen Coffee Company' – not
their client – would be responsible for the legal fees in
the question of an extension of time for redeeming the

debentures. Another communication is written in a similar vein 'Mr Finch-Hatton [sic] would not thank me for having put him to expense which has turned out useless so far as he was concerned . . .' Yet another warns: 'I would mention that Mr Finch-Hatton [sic] himself would not be prepared to . . . lend money beyond the extended date, because he cannot keep his money idle for any definite period.'

In the first instance Denys had only agreed to implicate his business because 'I could not see that it would stand to lose anything when the sale comes.' However he had been unwilling to risk his shareholder's interests further by putting up an extra £500 then required to man the estate for another three months. During this period Denys's concern for Tania reveals pity but discipline. And his mood coincides in timing the latter half of 1929 – with an opinion of one of their closest friends, who commented 'By the end of 1929 it was just about all over.' It is Denys's compunction which is disclosed when he wrote to Tania that he was sorry. 'I am sorry I cannot do more to help' – 'I am sorry you are so seedy' wishing with regret that he could do more . . .

That January, before Denys left civilization and the facility of a post office at Marsabit, he wrote to Topsy's sixteen-year-old son Michael expressing his intention to visit England in the summer. He tells his nephew that 'the Prince got a good lion and a 54″ greater kudu and enjoyed himself very much: in fact he has fixed up to come for a proper shoot next winter: perhaps he will not be able to unless the King gets well again. I hope you are amusing yourself at Eton and doing a certain amount of work as well. Learn as much mathematics as you can; it is useful. And read general history it is amusing. I expect to be home in June – Denys.'[39] While Denys was away, Tania learned from Thomas that their mother was ill and she left for Denmark. Her mother recovered but she stayed for six months. During this period, Thomas found his sister: 'not really unhappy at this time, I think, nor even discontented. But she was weak, self-absorbed, futureless, emptier than I had ever seen her before. I couldn't imagine what was going to happen. Eight days in England at the beginning of October helped a little, but I don't think she met Denys; she never mentioned it.'[40] Figuratively speaking the next eighteen months were the gestation period for the creation of the first Pellegrina Leon as she appears in 'The Dreamers' – in *Seven Gothic Tales*. By the time she was born Tania would know her well; the obsessive jealousy, the devilment towards other 'women of the opera' who called her Lucifera behind her back and the merciless soul which gave out no compassion nor expected any in return. For Tania's one undoing was like Pellegrina's 'she had to be absolutely the star of all the heavens of music,' particularly so far as Denys was concerned.

Thomas was now married with two children and full of responsibilities. He was engrossed with the exacting task of translating his book of war experiences and felt he was not giving Tania the attention he had been able to lavish on her during previous visits but she seemed understanding – not at all resentful – and they found time to take in the odd art exhibition, or walk together, but he found Tania's viewpoints on many things less easy to understand than before. In fact Thomas was mistaken when he says that he believes Tania did not see Denys. She actually went to stay with him at Buckfield, now Toby and Margaretta's home in Hampshire.* But it cannot have been radiantly successful or most certainly Thomas would have heard about it.

* The property was known as both Buckfield House and Sherfield Manor.

Denys left Kenya early in June, sailed to Marseilles and cabled Toby that he was going to Tunis for a few weeks. Just before he left the country a letter published in the *East African Standard* caught his eye. As it was a subject dear to his heart, he took up the matter in *The Times*, writing in Mombasa a letter that appeared on his return to England at the beginning of July.

HUNTING FROM MOTOR CARS: THE DESTRUCTION OF AFRICAN GAME: LAWS NOT ENFORCED

Sir,

A few days ago, inspired by Mr Marcuswell Maxwell's lion pictures, I wrote an article for *The Times* upon photographing African Game and in it, I protested against the apathy displayed by the Tanganyika authorities towards the wholesale slaughter of game from motor cars which has been going on for over two years in flagrant infringement of the existing Game Laws of the territory. Since then my attention has been drawn to a letter from Mr Andries Pienaar . . . This distressing letter comes in apt confirmation of what I wrote and I may perhaps be permitted to quote from it in the more appropriate passages: . . . 'last year certain Americans entered on African territory with a film operator. The last named is an acquaintance and thoroughly reliable. The tales he told me of shooting by this gentleman are absolutely disgusting. Animals were raced down by car before being shot. The buffalo bag alone was thirty-seven head, bull cows and youngsters were killed indiscriminately. Besides having the word of a reliable man, who confesses to have got sick of the butchery, I also saw the photographs of the dead animals which might be considered fairly conclusive evidence. Two years ago I met yet another party of Americans in East Africa. They had already killed twenty-one lions from the car, as the natives assured me. One morning they left camp with the words "Let us shoot at every living thing we can find today and see what bag is possible in one day." These words were repeated by the party's professional hunter and he might be accused of not being over sentimental on the subject. And what shall we say of the two gentlemen who entered the Serengeti by motor car and killed between them eighty lions? Can one think of anything more nauseating? And this is considered sport. No, worse than that, these men find circles abroad where they are admired. They figure in magazines as 'Famous Big Game Hunters'. The party who had the thirty-seven buffaloes, filled the American magazines with their pictures and tales of prowess for weeks on end. They had never been in Africa before but a single safari sufficed to raise them to the first ranks as the greatest hunters. These are facts not fancies . . .' Many readers of *The Times* will, perhaps find it difficult to believe that some of Mr Pienaar's statements are not exaggerated. But knowing the country as I do, and some of the visitors, I have no hesitation in saying that the truly revolting picture which his letter gives of the methods and manners of these licensed butchers is not exaggerated in any way. And if I have fixed the identity of one of the parties to which he refers, I can state definitely that his ghastly figures are not, in that instance, above the mark. What, asks Mr Pienaar, are we to say to these gentlemen? What indeed. But I find it more difficult to assemble words suitable to express in a letter to you, Sir, my opinion of an Administration which has had full knowledge of this disgraceful state of affairs for over two years, and which, although provided with the necessary legal machinery to deal with the situation and with a certain number of officers whose express duties are the maintenance of Game Laws, persists in abstaining from the simple and inexpensive measures required to put an end to this hideous abuse. I have the honour, Sir, to be your obedient servant,

Denys Finch Hatton MOMBASA
May 23rd 1929

Denys's motive was explicitly to reach Douglas Jardine,* whom he knew to be in London presenting a report of the British Government on Tanganyika to the Permanent Mandates Commission of the League of

---

* Douglas Jardine, then chief Secretary to the Governor of Tanganyika. Later Sir Douglas Jardine, Governor of Sierra Leone 1937–41. He was one of the triumvirate with Sir Donald Cameron and Sir Philip Mitchell who developed the system of indirect rule in Tanganyika (now Tanzania).

Nations. He knew it would outrage and embarrass Jardine before the Permanent Mandates Commission but realized that at least something would be done about the situation if he could focus attention on the matter while Jardine was in the limelight in London. The reaction he got to his letter was perfect. Jardine played straight into his hands, giving him the opportunity to recount his experiences with the Tanganyika officials. Mr Douglas Jardine's letter appeared on 8 July 1929:

HUNTING FROM CARS – LAW AND PUBLIC OPINION
Sir,
  My attention has been invited to an article entitled 'Stalking with a camera' by the Hon Denys Finch Hatton which appeared in your issue of June 29th, at the close of which he registers a strong protest against the infringements of the Tanganyika game-laws which forbids the use of motor cars in shooting game. He asserts that scores of lions are 'being slaughtered from cars without any effort being made by the authorities to prevent it.' In your issue of July 3rd he supplements this protest with a letter in which he quotes various instances of infringements of the law, instances for which he is indebted to a Mr Andries Pienaar. Mr Finch Hatton finds it difficult to assemble suitable words to give expression to his detestation of such revolting butchering as Mr Pienaar describes and still more difficult, but to do him justice, only in a letter to you, to express his opinion of an Administration which has had full knowledge of this disgraceful state of affairs for over two years, and which although provided with the necessary legal machinery to deal with the situation and with a number of officers whose express duties are the maintenance of the Game Laws persists in abstaining from the simple and inexpensive measures required to put an end to this hideous abuse. As a sportsman, if I may so dub myself, I bow to no-one – not even to Mr Finch Hatton in my detestation of such butchery as Mr Pienaar describes. But I must register my strongest possible protest against Mr Finch Hatton's reckless statement that the local Government has made no effort to prevent such outrages of the sportsman's code. What are the facts? It pleases, or so it seems, certain tourists with more money than taste to cross the Kenya border into

Tanganyika in swift and sometimes armoured motor-cars and there to massacre lion and buffalo and other game by the score. Tanganyika is the largest of our Dependencies in tropical Africa, being some 375,000 square miles in extent, and the game area which includes the Serengeti plain, where the outrages are said to occur, is a little less than the size of Scotland. The local Government has made it an offence to shoot game from motor cars in any circumstances and it employs a staff of European game rangers with African sub-ordinates whose duty it is to see that this and other provisions of the Game Laws are respected. But the difficulty of ensuring that no game is shot from motor cars in so vast an area is obvious. However large the staff might be, some infringements must remain undetected and the offenders will be at liberty to boast of their prowess. On the other hand, a few cases are detected and the offenders taken by the Game Rangers before the local magistrate. One such ranger, Captain M. S. Moore VC who like myself is at present on leave in England, informs me that he has successfully prosecuted four such cases. In brief, any law is extremely difficult to enforce and when you can enforce it, no fine which is likely to be imposed as a penalty is such as to prove an effective deterrent to wealthy offenders. All the world over, the greatest and sometimes the only instrument for enforcing the sportsman's code is a healthy and virile public opinion. How deplorably deficient such public opinion is in this case may be gauged from Mr Pienaar's complaint that the offenders are admired in circles abroad and figure in magazines as 'famous big game hunters'. Mr Finch Hatton complains that the Tanganyika Government is inclined to adopt a policy of wholesale game destruction and that we will allow natives to kill as much as they like. This insinuation is definitely untrue.

I am Sir, your obedient servant,

Douglas Jardine

Chief Secretary to the Government of Tanganyika.

New University Club. SW1

Denys replied the following day. Jardine had given him an ideal platform for his final speech on the subject, after which the Chief Secretary retired with a slightly red face pending personal and further enquiry into the matter. In this correspondence it is easy to understand how Denys earned his epithet 'Makanyaga' for the manner in which he 'could tread on a man with his tongue'.

HUNTING FROM CARS: THE AFFECTED AREA
Sir,
   Mr Jardine's letter in *The Times* of yesterday calls for a reply. The centre of the country to which I have been referring, in which the wholesale destruction of game from motor-cars has been taking place during the past two years, lies about sixty miles due west from the southern end of Lake Natron. It is comprised roughly within a parallelogram, the sides of which measure fifty-two by thirty miles. It consists mainly of open plains with a certain amount of open bush. A car can be driven from one end to the other and from one side to the other, in the same morning. It would be impossible for a party of 'shootists' operating with motor cars to remain undetected in this area by the Game Ranger who is also provided with a motor car. Their tracks would show where they had been and where they had camped, carcasses and trophies would tell what they had killed. The effective method of discouraging these gentlemen is not to fine them, but to confiscate their trophies. Shorn of the proof of their prowess they would be robbed of the pleasure so dear to their hearts, in astonishing the natives of their home towns. An energetic Game Ranger with a Ford car and a light truck for his provisions and boys, would very soon put an end to the abuse of motor cars for shooting purposes. Alternatively this small area could be closed altogether for hunting parties. I pointed this out to the Game Warden of Tanganyika Territory in an interview I had with him in November 1927 and told him of the slaughter that was going on. He was altogether sympathetic but he considered that the Government would not agree to the closing of this area for hunting. He hoped however, that he would be able to send a ranger to deal with the situation. At his request I made a sketch map of the country, and gave him all the information which I could upon the district. A year later in November 1928 I saw the Game Warden again at Kondoa-Irangi. He told me that he found it impossible as yet to send a man, owing I think, to the pressure of work put upon the Game Department in other directions. There had been difficulties, so far as I remember, in arranging for transport. He said however, that he hoped to

send a ranger shortly and again I gave him various information about the district and the best way of getting there. It was subsequently arranged that I should provide a native who had been with me and would be able to assist the Game Ranger in learning the Serengeti country. He was to be picked up by this officer as he passed through Nairobi. This native was still waiting in Nairobi in the charge of the Kenya Game Department, when I left on June 22nd of this year and as I was then informed by the Acting Game Warden, that as far as he knew, no Ranger had yet visited the area in question. I must repeat therefore what I wrote before – namely that the Tanganyika Government for two years, has had full knowledge of the wanton destruction of lions and other game which has taken place in the Serengeti plains and that up to June of this year, to the best of my belief, the simple measure required to stop this abuse has not been taken. Moreover this quite exceptional orgy of slaughter which has been going on is in a small, definite area about the size of Greater London, the nature of which admits to it easily being controlled by one Game Ranger in a motor car. These are not, as Mr Jardine pretends, reckless statements; they are indisputable facts which are well known as an open scandal to most people interested in the Preservation of Game in East Africa. And I further state, without fear of contradiction, that such a condition of affairs could never have continued for a month in Kenya where the Game Department is properly supported by the Government and where the Game Laws are consequently properly enforced. Mr Jardine definitely states that it is deliberately misleading to say that the Tanganyika Government appears inclined to adopt a policy of game destruction and to allow natives to kill as much as they like. I am more than pleased to learn this from such authoritative source as the Chief Secretary to the Government. It would appear that the Government has changed its policy since the report to the Council of the League of Nations for the year 1927 in which the following passage occurs:

148. An Ordinance amending the Game Ordinance is in draft under which it is proposed that natives (who are not of course provided with arms of precision) shall be exempted from the Provisions of the Game Ordinance to the extent of satisfying their legitimate needs for food: *and instructions meanwhile have been issued that proceedings against natives for breach of the Game Laws should not be taken*

unless in flagrant and exceptional cases! (The Italics are mine DFH)'

It has been my experience and that of several of my friends that since the issue of the instructions mentioned in this quotation, in many districts there has been no sort of control of the killing of game by the natives, who are able in fact to kill as much as they like. Before I left Africa I was authoritatively informed that it was the intention of the Government to introduce amendments to the Game Ordinance in which the principle would definitely be laid down that game was to be considered as being the property of the natives. This would, in my opinion, be the beginning of the end and I very much hope that Mr Jardine will be able to refute this also on behalf of the Tanganyika Government.

I have the honour, sir, to remain your obedient servant'
Denys Finch Hatton

Within three days of being on English soil again, Denys went down to Haverholme to inspect his parents' graves and 'consider the tablet' erected in his father's memory at Ewerby. Haverholme had been sold in the year of the slump, much against Toby's will, but with the proceeds – or part of it – he was able to purchase Buckfield House, Sherfield. Their father had died within two months of the sale – as if all his will to live had been relinquished after the disposal of the old estate had been completed. On this holiday Denys planned to re-apply for his pilot's licence and if he was succesful buy his own plane. His first few weeks were filled with hectic social engagements. He attended the Russian Ballet every night of its brief season, went to the theatre with friends and dined late night after night, generally going on to clubs with floorshows – which was unlike him – but he seemed to be immersing himself in all that London had to offer. When he went down to Buckfield near Basingstoke, it was his first visit to the new family home and he spent most weekends there. Denys made contact with the Prince of

Wales – enjoying a special showing of the films they had
made on his safari and making plans for another in the
coming winter. The next day, 27 August, he and Toby
lunched alone together. During this meal his older brother
tried to dissuade him from returning to Kenya so soon.
From Toby's diary entries it is apparent that he is dreading
the thought of his going off again. As a result Toby
offered an alternative suggestion. 'Terribly hot day.
Denys to lunch. I am afraid his plans are such that we
don't look like seeing a great deal of him so I offered to
put up £100 to enable him (if the service is a good one) to
fly back to Nairobi. This would mean that instead of
October 8th he could stay on till October 18th.' In theory
Denys accepted Toby's offer and the family relaxed about
his comings and goings. He went with them all to watch
the Schneider Trophy run – an air race which England
won with a Waghorn Pilot flying at 332 MPH. On 15
September he phoned Toby to announce that he had
passed his flying test and got his air ticket; he rushed
around inspecting various flying machines and decided
that he would buy a Gypsy Moth. On 3 October, Toby
records 'Denys arrived to stay in the evening bringing
with him Baroness von Blixen. Glynn Philpot was also
staying. He is trying to do m m's picture.'

Tania writes of her first meeting with Denys's family,
though it is not specified as such, in *Shadows on the
Grass*. She simply says, 'When in the 'thirties I was
staying in the south of England with Denys's brother, the
Earl of Winchelsea [sic] the painter John [sic] Philpot*
came down to paint a portrait of my hostess, who was
very lovely. He had travelled much in North Africa and
on an afternoon when we were walking together in the
park he recounted to me an experience of his there.'[41]

---

* Glynn Philpot.

In a manner which has become inseparable from her style she conveys no inkling of the personal feeling she experienced when she met Denys's brother for the first time, but takes an impersonal character from the household and uses his story to indulge her own private memory of an enjoyable afternoon spent with Denys and the artist; she almost seems to be veiling, protecting everyone involved, from prying eyes. Parmenia Migel, Tania's biographer, brought up the question of her subject's feelings on this occasion. 'One may wonder what her impression was on first seeing the place where Denys grew up. She never wrote or spoke of it. Perhaps it was too sadly linked in her mind with the sad events that followed.'[42]

The obvious reason why Tania never spoke or wrote of Buckfield is that Denys had never been there before. He had grown up at Haverholme, which, with its elegiac atmosphere and history as an early religious house, has far more bearing on Tania's preoccupation with nuns and prioresses in retreats where 'a proud and kindly spirit of past feudal times seems to dwell in the stately presence of buildings, and to guide the existence of communities . . . of no religious nature. They are retreats for married ladies and widows of noble birth who pass here the autumn and winter of their days and live in a dignified and comfortable routine, according to the traditions of the houses.'

It must remain conjecture, but it is not unlikely that the roots of Tania's story 'The Deluge at Nordeney' are embedded in Denys's knowledge of the history of the early flooding of the Haverholme fenland estate in 1139. Certainly it is the sort of incident that would inspire a writer to develop the theme of the predicament surrounding the victims of a 'fen drown'. Anyone who has experienced the sinister power of the wind 'which calls up the waters' at these times, could never forget it. And the threat is as forceful when it dies away; it leaves poultry, animals and humans stranded. The menacing slap of the water as it touches the dyke walls, mingles with distressed lowing and cries for help. Flat-bottomed boats will eventually come to the rescue, but sometimes they are too late to bear the victims from the rooftops to the safety and warmth of the rectory or church.

On Tania's first visit to Buckfield, though Toby welcomed her, he has managed to insinuate in his diary jottings during those days a distrust. His reference after the first day when he calls her 'Baroness von Blixen', is curt – discourteous even. It is unlike him not to use her Christian name after the formalities are over, yet all subsequent entries refer to her as 'Blixen'. For the first time in the lives of the brothers, one is left with a feeling of resentment in Toby. Possibly he instinctively felt Tania was a rival for Denys's attention. Probably this was subconscious but it was intrusive. Later Toby welcomed Tania to Buckfield and his daughters recall her visits with pleasure, but by then Tania was a link with Denys after his death. Perhaps Toby felt excluded by Denys and Tania's intellectual rapport and possibly their unconventional attitude towards life was irksome, failing to meet entirely with his approval. He may, quite simply, have felt left out. Whatever the motive, though Toby was charming and polite superficially the antagonism was there. Another relative who watched Tania and Denys from the outer perimeter of the family circle declared after the visit. 'I don't like that woman. She is trying to take possession of Denys. It won't work.' It was no secret within the family that Denys was adored by his brother and sister. Like all his friends, they too wanted more time with him. Because Toby felt such deep affection for Denys, he was often hurt by him.

On one occasion Denys flew to London with the sole purpose of seeing *La Boutique Fantasque*. He stayed with Tuppy Headlam at Eton for the night and flew back the following day to Kenya without contacting anyone. But Denys's visit incognito did not escape notice after all. Someone spotted his unmistakable figure at the ballet and when the news eventually reached Toby he was baffled and justifiably hurt for Denys seemed almost to be avoiding him. The extent to which Toby still counted on Denys is felt in a remark Margaretta made in her own grief after her husband's death in 1939: 'Well at last he is with his beloved Denys – where he always wanted to be.'

Tania stayed with Denys for five days at Buckfield – he drove her to Haverholme during this visit. On 28 October Toby's diary entry indicates an insoluble moment of hurt as he realizes that Denys has changed his mind about staying on, despite his offer of financial assistance for the flight back to Kenya. 'Denys and Blixen to London. Denys phoned that he has settled to go to BEA by boat and he is leaving tomorrow. Great shock as I had thought he would be going by plane and would not leave till 20th.' Whereupon Toby dropped everything and got a lift up to London to spend the last evening with Denys. On 9 October Toby wrote: 'Saw Denys off at 10.50 to Paris – was very depressed. Don't know why.'

Tania returned to Denmark to her family to spend Christmas with them. Thomas recalls the apprehension they all felt as they waved her goodbye on Christmas day at Copenhagen Station. 'None of us had tried to stop her; we understood each other so well, even if Tanne still appeared to hope and perhaps was also able to work up her faith in her mind. We knew that she could not, unless it was absolutely necessary, and without a soul-shaking farewell, leave her beloved home, Farah and the other people who were so close to her, and perhaps for always, Denys.'[43]

Tania would need all the moral fibre which her brother believed to be embedded deeply in her character. It took an immense personal courage to return from Denmark on this occasion. For she knew in her heart that she was losing her grip on all the things dearest to her. But she hid her feeling from everyone; dreading the thought of open failure it was almost as if by ignoring the situation by some miracle the problems which now gained momentum against her like a landslide would go away. Thomas believes that his sister learned to know love, as the force in life, through Denys. Unquestionably this is true. But often, love cannot be learned or recognized in its immensity without pain – they go hand in hand. It is not surprising that she wrote little to her family during the next eighteen months for they were probably the most harrowing in her entire life.

Farah met her at Mombasa in January. She hardly dare ask the direct question she longed to know, which was the tonnage of the coffee crop he had harvested in her absence. They skirted round the matter, shying away from the truth. This is not difficult to do with an African. Their code of courtesy is such that it forbids the onslaught of bad news at the moment of greeting. Niceties, the shaking of hands, take place first – later comes the bad news generally prefaced with 'lakini'. Roughly translated this means 'but' though it carries all the weight of doom as it is spoken. When one returns from a holiday to the house one may ask 'habari?' 'what news?' – and the classic reply is 'mzuri tu' – everything is good. A few minutes pause followed by 'lakini' may mean the house has burned to the ground, the cat has died, you have been robbed or a certain servant has disappeared. There is no telling at that moment quite what will follow. But the sense of ill-fate has already been communicated by that one single word – 'lakini'. On the evening of her arrival before going to bed, she could bear to delay the question no longer, and she asked Farah

. . . how many tons of coffee they had picked on the farm in all. The Somalis are generally pleased to announce a disaster. But here, Farah was not happy, he was extremely grave himself . . . and he half closed his eyes and laid back his head, swallowing his sorrow, when he said: 'Forty tons, Memsahib.' At that I knew I could not carry on. All colour and life faded out of the world round me . . . I did not say anything to Farah, and he did not speak again, but went away, the last friendly object in the world.[44]

In Farah's pronouncement lay her whole destiny. That pitiful 'forty tons' of coffee meant the loss of her farm and the sole means of her livelihood, her home but perhaps more crucial than either, Denys: her love, her mentor, her friend.

Sailing back alone to Kenya that October, Denys had written to the Prince of Wales drafting his ideas for their safari planned for early 1930. He received confirmation that the venture was on from Joey Legh; then the Prince of Wales wrote personally to Denys on Midland Hotel, Bradford notepaper, where he had been performing some official duty.

13th November 1929

My dear Denys,
Thank you for your long letter from the boat. You will have had Joey's cable now telling you that the trip is on and that you can go ahead with arrangements and organization of the safaris. The only snag seems to be the rains in Northern Rhodesia in mid-February, as we've had somewhat alarmist cables from the Governor to the effect that the Broken Hill–Abercorn Road is a doubtful pleasure at that season. However as we wouldn't get

any pleasure out of just travelling by motor, even in dry weather, we are surmising that he only means it will be damned uncomfortable for which we will be prepared. If the mail trucks can make it, surely we can? But we want your advice on this point too, as if you advise against attempting this route, we'll have to go down to Beira and take the boat to Mombassa [sic] where you will have to meet us instead of Dodoma. We also want to know what you think of the plan to do the Kilimanjaro safari before going to Nairobi at all. That would mean starting straight in off the road at Meru or the railway at Voi whichever way we travel north from Rhodesia. Of course we don't want to have to sweat down to Beira or in a boat for five days if we can get up by land. But also we don't want to be stuck for days and waste a lot of time so we must leave it to you to decide the route we should take.

I am going into the matter of rifles very carefully and the Duke of York is very kindly lending me his Purdy ·465 (DB) and a Rigby ·350 (Magazine). I have also seen Lancaster's about the new ·280 (DB) which he will send out if it is not ready by the New Year and I am going to try one of his ·360's (DB) when I shoot at the target with the others which I am having properly fitted this time. I'll also bring my ·280 (Magazine) which you saw. And that's for armament. I'm going to bring out an 'Eyemo' model movie camera as you suggested and like it at once. They also have shown me a new model Bell Howell which is a vast improvement on the old one, and has a lot of new 'gadgets'. I talked to them about the new 6″ lens and the light filters or screens and these will be fitted and only that Panchromatic film supplied. They also seem optimistic over coloured pictures and are anxious for me to try half a dozen special films for this work. So I thought it might be amusing to see what one can do in that direction but of course, only rely on black and white for the important pictures. We are into the winter good and proper now and I hate it and am longing to get away to Africa and the sun more than ever especially as I haven't any horses and golf is a damned rotten substitute for hunting. I am not being put off by the enclosed crazy letter which being annonimous [sic] is not worth the paper it is written on. But I think it will make you laugh! Tania Blixen's brother came over for the 'VC' dinner and I was glad to meet him. He told me she is still in Denmark but returning to Kenya soon. The reason for this queer paper is that it is written on the train from Manchester where I've been opening the Chamber of Commerce for the Wool Industry today. Cable me or Joey if there are any points you have to suggest. If it would be easier to meet in Nairobi before we start any safari I'm willing to do that.[45]

Yours (signed) Edward P.

When Tania returned to Ngong, Denys was well entrenched in the preparations for the Prince's safari. They spent a short time together on the farm and chose a suitable area for a landing strip for the Gypsy Moth. It was prepared while Denys was away. The dark cloud which neither could discuss with the other was the fact that Bror was joining Denys again for the expedition – at least the first part of it – as one of the extra hunters. On 7 February Denys left to meet Bror in Mombasa. His Royal Highness was arriving on the s.s. *Modessa*. They expected to be on the move until the end of April, gradually making their way to Khartoum.

14

1930–1931 – Farewell to the Farm

Because the Prince of Wales was impatient to begin his safari with the minimum of delay, it was decided over breakfast at Government House, Mombasa, that they should leave by train at 7.30 that evening. Denys suggested that the best plan would be to start the venture by hunting elephant, which he knew the Prince particularly wanted, allowing ten days for this purpose in the West Kilimanjaro area before travelling to Nairobi. The Prince went off to play a round of golf with the Governor while his hunters attended to last minute details. Both Denys and Bror liked their client, not simply for his unquestionable courage as a man but for his tolerance of unconvention and rejection of the puritanical restrictions which still rigidly confined royalty. Bror records his feelings about the Heir Apparent. 'There was nothing to prevent the Prince from surrounding himself with all possible luxury and comfort but he is notoriously not that sort of man. Despising all effeminate softness in others, he makes the greatest demands on himself. I can assert without hesitation that he is one of the three or four toughest sportsmen I have been out with, perhaps the toughest of them all.'[1]

There is little doubt that Denys and Bror enjoyed immensely the company of this man though there was a certain amount of worry in the burden of responsibility attached to the honourable assignment. Much of the success of the trip, as usual, depended on the efficiency of the organization. Joey Legh was again in the party, and two newcomers, Brigadier-General G. F. Trotter and

Major J. R. Aird. During its course various friends came
and went, including the odd extra hunter when necessary.
Patrick Chalmers writes from the Prince's personal
diaries:

In our case Finch Hatton had the thankless role of bear-leader.
His was the responsibility for lions, elephants and rhinoceroses,
for quaker oats, cartridges and candles. All things were on the
head of Finch Hatton and all things went without a hitch. He
never made a mistake. He forgot nothing. He foresaw everything. At last, his charges took off their solar topees [sic] to him
and said that he was the most efficient man in the world.[2]

At Mangau the party divided and toured the area for
elephant. The half of the party with the Prince – i.e. Bror
and Denys – found the spoor of elephant at Kasigau, he
gave them a twenty-mile walk through almost impenetrable bush but they never saw the animal though they
wore out their boots. On St Valentine's day the trackers
Denys had sent out came back and announced that they
had located a huge animal with great ivory towards Jipe
in the region of the Pare mountains. They departed at
9.45 A.M., taking a small tent in case they should not get
back that night and adequate rations for two or three
meals. The Prince in his enthusiasm travelled rather faster
than either of his hunters would have done but he did not
seem to flag despite the fact that the elephant they were
following did not take his usual midday siesta in a scrap
of shade. He plodded on and on. Bror recalls:

Our forced march continued hour after hour. I could not
help looking at the Prince from time to time out of the
corner of my eye. Finch Hatton and I, of course, were
trained cross-country runners and I knew by experience that
HRH had remarkable powers of physical endurance but he
had no opportunity of training himself in this particular kind
of walking. Nothing in his expression showed that he was

tired, that the blisters on his feet burned like fire – he did not give a sign of feeling inclined to call a halt. It was the darkness that stopped us.[3]

That night, forced by circumstances and driven by their own determination, they camped out in the open plain. This was a new experience for the Prince which left a deep impression. Hitherto his camping sites had been selected for him with an eye to beauty as well as practicality. Now, in this hastily improvised stopping-place, he was keenly aware of the 'Teeming silence which is absolute' and found the African night overwhelming and mysterious. It is true that the stars appear to shine more brightly in an African sky giving the impression of great proximity. There is somehow a feeling of being able to touch the shimmering girdle of the milky way. The sky itself hangs overhead, not unlike a worn canopy of charcoal-coloured velvet which has sagged and frayed with age and worn into a thousand million pinholes, each releasing light to form a star. It almost seems feasible to stretch up a little and blot out one of them by placing a fingertip against a tiny beam. This clarity provides the double sensation of being close to heaven yet dwarfed by its very infinity.

The Prince slept under the shelter of the bivouac. Denys and Bror lay on the open ground – stony and hardly conducive to a good night's rest. They were up at dawn their optimism high as they set out. The spoor was fresher and they congratulated themselves on the gap lessened between them and their quarry since the day before. By midday the land they crossed had no shade. There was not even a light breeze, the incandescent heat burned into them without respite. By sunset they had followed the best of forty miles and 'Our feet,' recalls Bror, 'were in a deplorable state. But give up? Not we!

We should get our fellow the next day.'[4] By now Denys had christened the invisible elephant 'Pontius the Pilot' on account of his guiding spoor determining their path.

The third day was much like the second except their food and water supplies had dwindled and now had to be strictly rationed. There was a certain whimsicality too about the ritual of the 4 o'clock tea break which took place daily, their feet were so badly lacerated and swollen that it was almost impossible for them to get their boots on. Had they had spare motor tyres to hand, Denys could have improvised primitive sandals for them all, as he did for his own safari when they became footsore, but in this case they had nothing to utilize so the boots were forced on again with a certain amount of agony. The first few footsteps were apparently the most excruciating and after these they could cope.

By sunset the hunt was among the Pare foothills . . . they had followed their elephant forty-two miles. But by now the three were on their mettle, all as lame as ducks and light headed for the want of sleep. Not till then, they said, had they properly appreciated the feelings of the exciseman in Ingoldsby, when –

> he screamed with passion, 'I'd rather grill
> Than not come up with Smuggler Bill!'

All were determined to overtake the tusker.[5]

Mad tenacity got them on their feet on the fourth day – they knew they still had thirty miles to cover in any case to get back to the railway line, whether they found the elephant or not. At two o'clock 'suddenly Finch Hatton became aware of the elephant, crept forward noiselessly and was able to establish that it was the beast we were looking for, as big as a house with tusks that must weigh nearly 400 lbs.* As silently as a spirit he worked his way

* Denys reckoned the ivory weighed 125 lb a piece.

closer . . . Denys Finch Hatton faded into the shadows and whispered to the Prince to come and take a shot. The vegetation was thick and the Prince would have to part the branches to get his aim, suddenly he trod on a dry twig through inexperience and bad luck, which sent his quarry crashing through the thicket like a tank. Pontius the Pilot was gone at the gallop and the Prince had not even as much as set eyes on him!' The three hunters could hardly utter a word. Dazed, unbelieving, they sat down and held a sort of post mortem. Bror believed that they practically 'sleep-walked' their way back to camp.

By 22 February they had bagged two lions, one buffalo, one leopard which almost pounced on Joey Legh from the bait as he wandered beneath the tree without spotting it – three rhinoceros, one eland, two oryx, one Grant's gazelle and 'several smaller antelope'. Not a very impressive collection but they all agreed they had had a good deal of excitement. They now entrained for Nairobi and went to stay at Government House for about a week. Protocol made it difficult for Tania to be included among the house-party because Cockie was present as the wife of one of the hunters. If it was humiliating for Tania it was equally embarrassing for her friend Joanie Grigg. Denys took the Prince out to the farm to dine with them both but nevertheless she was excluded from the parties, dances and receptions which took place at Muthaiga, Government House and Torrs hotel during a week of fashionably gay events. The newspapers cannot have helped when they ambiguously referred to Baroness Blixen's elegant gowns in the social columns. With Tania's nature it must have been an unbearable situation, made even worse when she learned that the Prince had again invited Cockie to join the party later in the week to witness a Maasai lion hunt with the Griggs and the

Delameres. Lord Delamere had arranged this so that the Prince could capture it on film.

This leg of the safari – regarded with the frivolity of a picnic – was to last three weeks in Maasailand. As the prime intention was to get good photographs the guns were only taken as weapons of defence. Bror's employment was finished after this phase. The party planned to continue with Denys, dividing the rest of the time between the Congo and the Sudan. The Prince had to be in London by 25 April so to allow for hazards Denys intended to reach Khartoum not later than 13 April.

Once more Clarence Buxton welcomed the party at Kagiado and guided them over the best route to Selengei, their next camp. Archie Ritchie, Kenya's Chief Game Warden, joined the group here. He greeted them with the good news that he had already located rhino and elephant for the Prince to photograph in the immediate vicinity. (It was with Archie Ritchie that Denys brought down an angry rhino just before it flattened the future King of England and made 'matchwood' of the camera 'not six yards from his lens'.) But there were problems for Denys to deal with. Archie informed him that the lorries had not yet arrived. Knowing that they had to negotiate a bad patch of black cotton soil Denys set off on foot at once to pilot them back himself.

Missing them and with them the opportunity of a ride back to Selengei, he eventually decided to spend the night in a native village . . . white rain storms booming up followed one another through the forests in luke warm deluges. It was sensible then to accept a native 'angareeb' [bedstead]. And accept Finch Hatton did. He refused no hospitality that was offered, fire, eggs, chapattis and coffee were all taken and wanted by him. But the native blankets were another story. The creature known at home [England] as the Margate tortoise, here in the land of Ham draws no colour line. What it left of Finch Hatton returned to camp the following morning![6]

Three days later the Griggs, Cockie and Lady Delamere arrived to watch the 'bonne bouche' of the picnic at Selengei, the Maasai lion hunt. Sir Edward Grigg described this in his book *Kenya's Opportunity*:

The Prince entertained us in a princely fashion. It was very hot and my wife notes in her diary with particular pleasure that our sundowners were cooled with ice from a fixture new for Kenya safaris – an ice machine. The lion hunt showed the amazing personal bravery of the Masai warriors. Their method is to locate the lion, surround him only with their painted leather shields and broad hafted spears. As the ring closes and spears are cast at very short range, the lion invariably charges and the warrior who receives the charge is almost inevitably mauled. This particular lion hunt followed tradition though its tension was curiously enhanced by a flight of aeroplanes containing (I think) newspaper men which circled overhead. One magnificently black-maned lion was duly surrounded and speared then two unrehearsed incidents livened the day which was very hot and still. The Prince of Wales and my wife were watching the hunt unarmed when a second black-maned lion leapt out of a thicket and confronted them at very close range. The Masai, however, turned at once and surrounded him; another moran was mauled but the lion was killed in the same way. I was standing about a hundred yards behind with a double-barrelled rifle, having Lady Delamere, Baroness Blixen and some other ladies under my care. This duty I was discharging as a dignified sinecure, when a third black-maned lion leapt out of a thicket half way between the Prince and our group. He turned his back disrespectfully upon the Prince and faced me, looking beetle-browed and indignantly lashing his tail. I was afraid of wounding him without killing him if I fired so I decided to leave the initiative to him. The suspense seemed very long; but at last he tossed his head and loped away. The Masai, having the Prince between them and him, had to let him go. For my part, I took off my hat to his departing hind-quarters . . . The two dead lions were nothing but pitiful pincushions when we went to look at them.[7]

Sir Edward Grigg may have captured the strategy of that lion hunt but the thrill and frenzy of the rite has somehow eluded his pen. The setting itself was dramatic enough; a natural amphitheatre formed by a sandy river bed, about sixty yards across rising steeply on either side in banks up to forty feet high. 'Except for the central sandy streak the gully was carpeted in places with long dry grass and lined with dense thorn bush, with shrubs like tamarisk and laurel.' A lion hunt has all the ceremony and pomp of a military operation, minus the uniforms. Its warriors are clad only in long cotton togas of a reddish, ox-blood colour. About fifty moran are elaborately finger painted with red-ochre, which dries and contrasts strangely, like a bleached tattoo, on their shiny ebony skins in dulled earthen squiggles and stripes. There is a great dignity and power in their bearing though they look as natural as animated cave-paintings – their bodies loose-limbed and at liberty to lunge and quiver. Armed with rungus, shields and spears, the privileged in previous combat with lion are crowned with their victim's tawny mane, symbolizing prowess. The lithe young men tremble. The excitement mounts in frenzy as they close in on the cornered lion. They begin to shout 'Simba, Simba, Simba' until in a crescendo of noise and splintered yells the final thrusts are made into the recoiled body of the terrified cat. He dies from a menacing passion – of a type that is seldom witnessed or legally practised. But the filming on this occasion was rather disappointing and a pale replica of the average ceremony. The history of the Maasai is written in blood. Even their diet of milk is mixed with it, tapped as it is from the jugular vein of their humped N'gombes.* It spurts into a gourd and is next prepared for drinking by stirring it: 'when the filaments twine round the stick the blood is mixed with milk and consumed.' Milk appears in their ceremonies

---

* Swahili for cows.

too; those who qualify for the embolostat* are sprayed with it, so are the triumphant hunters of lions and cattle raiders. The N'gombe is the Maasai's currency. Their strange culture is tempered entirely to meet the demands of the tough life into which they have been born. The white man with his concept of civilization has eaten up the heroic Maasai, has almost digested him completely with his churches and book learning and taboos about clothes. Long ago the 'el moran' – a Maasai blood – had to kill a man to qualify for the title of warrior. Usually this was an enemy slain in single combat. But the custom was abused and lions became the proving ground instead. The great years of the Maasai tribe were the twenty between 1830–1850. During this period their name inspired terror and their records rang in battle, murder and sudden death. The Kikuyu feared them mightily and it is said that in those years their inherent courage was imbued into the bones.

If the Maasai hunt did not quite come up to expectation it was still an extraordinary ritual for the Prince to watch. The other highlight in those few days was when Tom Campbell Black of Wilson Airways took him flying over the peaks of Kibo and Kilimanjaro which glittered 'in a mail of snow and ice'. When the news of elephant at Voi reached them they made for Kiu intending to follow up the news by rail. But the Prince and Bror came down with malaria and they returned to Nairobi instead. Before leaving for Uganda on 9 March the Prince was well enough to go dancing at Muthaiga Club.

In the meantime, Tania was grappling alone and despondent with the farm problems; dreading the foreclosing of the bank on the farm account, still wracking

* The ceremony which officially opens the circumcision phase and occurs roughly every fifteen years.

her brain for some way out; basically this meant postponing the moment when she would have to confront Denys, force the issue of their future together. She tells in *Out of Africa* how 'In the night, I counted the hours till the time when the Kikuyus should turn up again by the house.'

Then the last, unpredicted and most diabolical plague of all took its toll. Locusts arrived, clouding the sky with their army yellow hue, laying their eggs in the earth as a legacy: using their powerful mandibles to munch away the green flesh of every leaf in sight. All over the country farmers had instructed their labourers to take different precautions against the invading locusts. In some places it was believed sound would prevent them from settling. Servants were sent out with sticks and tin cans like a strangely gathered percussion section of an orchestra which, with its hideous cacophony, was guaranteed to frighten the 'dudus' away.* Tania remembers the loathsome masses of locusts. She writes about their overwhelming numbers graphically enough for anyone to imagine: 'They had broken a couple of big trees . . . and when you looked at the trees and remembered that each of the grasshoppers could only weigh a tenth of an ounce, you begin to conceive the numbers of them.' At their time of approach they can darken the sun like a cloud; the sky suddenly resembles a vast pointillist canvas of Seurat or, as if one were peering through a huge magnifying glass, becomes freckled intensely like a newspaper picture upon which the dots cluster together to intensify shadows or dark patches of a print. But they are always moving a little bit nearer. When Denys's de Havilland Gypsy Moth arrived by boat in the latter half of the same year, it was painted bright yellow and the natives (or Tania and

* Dudu in Swahili for any insect be it a moth, a spider, caterpillar or praying mantis.

Denys) christened it Nzige (Swahili for locust). Whether this was because it marked the year of the plague or because like some huge tin insect it came zooming out of the sky unpredictably to settle on the plain on Tania's farm, is not known. She refers to it thus in her notes: 1930 Nov Denys, Nzige, I. Lamu.

And, while the locusts were threatening the land of the lowliest squatter and the wealthiest settler Tania was wrestling with decisions about her future. She did not know which way to turn. Once she agreed to sell the farm, she had to have somewhere to live – if she announced she was returning to Denmark, Denys, she feared, might let her go. She knew if she threatened him with tears of hysteria he would go anyway and she would have forced his hand, possibly bringing their relationship to an end while it still had a chance of survival. Denys had admired in her, from the beginning, the very opposite qualities; she had not been a dependent, fawning woman; she could hold her own in wit and conversation. Her personal magnetism had far outlived the transient heady skirmishes of love which stem from fleeting attraction. Tania was once told by a friend that she had never known anyone 'so sensual and so little sexual'. She told her brother that the comment was 'not a bad way of putting it' in a nine-page letter on love and marriage which she compiled in reply to two articles on the subject which her brother had published in 1927 in the newspaper *Politiken*. After considering them she wrote to her brother:

What has captivated or attracted me or whatever you like to call it, has been a person's personality, or a common interest of one kind or another – or the whole situation has also been, if I may say so, like a game or dance. I have no ability to take a sexual situation in itself deeply seriously. Much as I like going hunting, or to a ballet, or travelling with someone I am in love with, it seems intolerable to 'be an object.' I have never in my life sat and stared with infatuation into a person's eyes. I don't think I'm capable of that . . . This can lead to the most intimate, the most momentous relationship between two people who unfortunately don't know each other . . . and don't even suit each other. A casual, so to speak, person, a woman whom you have seen for two days and never spoken to confidentially, because she represents for you one of life's greatest and wildest forces, can inspire you, make you happy, miserable, destroy you, drive you to madness much more easily than a long proven friend, yes, in a way in which he could never begin to do so . . .'[8]

So in her dilemma she kept her invisible sword of Damocles within her heart, adjusting her attitude to that of day-to-day living.

I shall give in, I thought, from this time forward, in all minor matters, to save myself unnecessary trouble. I shall let my adversaries have their way from day to day in these affairs, in talk and writing. For in the end I shall still come out triumphant and shall keep my farm and the people on it. Lose them, I thought, I cannot.[9]

With all the stubbornness her family came to accept within her make-up, like a limpet she now clung on to the sinking ship of her hope, convinced somehow that things would rectify themselves; and for a few more months they did. But she was living on borrowed time and she, even if no-one else recognized it, knew it.

Denys's safari with the Prince continued up to Uganda by train, then by car to Butiaba on Lake Albert. The road was probably the most beautiful forty-five-mile stretch 'in Africa or the Universe'. It climbs and winds through forests of blue-gum trees until at a certain level it reaches wide, rolling country which 'would make a setting for any myth of the Golden Age, a stage for any Theocritan idyll'. The crest of the escarpment 'overlooks the great sheet, Lake Albert. Two thousand feet below, lay its waters and the limitless blue shield of them reached to a horizon of dim silver.' At Butiaba they boarded the s.s. *Samuel Baker,* sailed to Ndandumire and transhipped onto the s.s. *Lugard.* Under a brilliant moon they steamed to Packwach and anchored for the night. The party split up the following day. The Prince, Denys and Captain R. J. D. Salmon, the Chief Game Ranger for Uganda, walked east to Rhino Camp, so called after Kermit's father, who as President of the USA in 1909, had come out on safari and shot so many of the scarce and harmless white rhinoceroses – better known to hunters as Burchell's rhinoceros – that on the Prince's visit, there were thought to be only one-hundred-and-thirty specimens left.

They moved downstream to Liri 'where on the bank stood a black rhinoceros and his family. HRH landed and took some studies of them until one, becoming resentful, charged so determinedly that Finch Hatton had to choose and choose quickly, between shooting the rhinoceros or seeing him make pulp . . . of the Prince of Wales and his camera.'[10]

Chugging upstream to Rhino Camp again they were met by the driver in charge of the Wolseley cars which had survived the six-hundred-mile journey from Tororo. He had driven via Lira, Kitgum, Torit and Juba and was now ready to take them into the Belgian Congo. On 21 March they set out for Arua and counted themselves lucky to come across Burchell's rhinoceros. Sweeter natured than their smaller brothers, they live in herds of up to twenty and are second only in size to the elephant. 'Better photograph them,' Denys commented briefly as he explained the differences between them and the ordinary rhino.

In the Congo pygmies were encountered, old friends revisited and new territory explored. On 1 April it was time to head for the Sudd. Appropriately enough for April Fools' Day, a driver misunderstood his instructions and managed to lose their baggage. Meanwhile a heavy deluge heralded an exceptionally early start of the rains. Fearing they would be cut off by the rising of the Kit river, they struck camp immediately and rushed back to Juba, leaving by aeroplane for Mogalla where the s.s. *Omdurman* was waiting to take them through the Sudd. This mosquito-infested area stretches greenly out in every direction. 'Not for nothing did the fabled professional hunter Denys Finch Hatton' dub these malaria carriers 'the peril that flieth'. Among the swampy reed beds of papyrus they breed in thousands by the side of hippo and a remarkable collection of bird life. But the Sudd is an eerie place, as Beryl Markham makes clear. '. . . visualize twelve thousand miles of swamp that seeths and crawls like a prehistoric crucible . . . the slowly heaving mat of decomposed and living-growth that in many places is fifteen feet thick and under which flowed a sluice of black water.'[11]

Upon the oozing black mud of the White Nile's banks, the crocodiles bask their evil eyes, like unseeing marbles. The party was intrigued by the area and its sinister reputation. If it did not disappoint them with its 'dreary novelty' they were very soon bored by its 'dreary monotony'. As compensation, the waterfowl were abundant. Now, their days were spent behind field-glasses trying to identify among the countless flocks, the whistling teal, the lesser and greater Nile geese, the comb ducks, storks, golden crested cranes, egrets and marabou. Twice they found the rare giant shoebill,* half stork, half bittern. Human life was savage and sparse. The three main tribes, the Shilluk with their matted hair who hunt the hippo,

---

* Balaeniceps Rex.

the Dinka and Nuers, when encountered were all stark naked, except for their incongruous, hefty bracelets of ivory worn high up on each arm (some of them as wide as 5″). Between the green waves of papyrus a small antelope with amphibian qualities (the Sititunga) flitted like a curious shadow able to submerge itself swiftly 'nose in the friendly mud'. The Prince photographed an antelope exclusive to the Tonga region in Africa. The Nile Lechwe – the prize of the Sudan. Hunters will travel for days across this inhospitable terrain overriden with leeches and insects for this trophy. Denys likened its horns, which rise thirty-five inches high, to the lyre of Apollo. Its dark and glossy pelt is traversed by an astonishing white 'saddle' across its back. This was their last prize as the safari drew sluggishly to an end. They reached Malakal on 12 April, flying to Khartoum the following day as planned. Denys flew with the Prince and Joey Legh to England. He spent the summer there. On 11 May he wrote an eight-page letter to Tania from Philip Sassoon's country house Trent, at New Barnet where he was staying for a week 'with the idea of flying his (Philip's) Gypsy Moth' but conditions were not good enough. Denys told Tania 'This is a cursed country . . . it has been such pestilential weather that flying has been "off". I have flown a Blue Bird and do not like them nearly so much as Moths.' He seems to be savouring the opportunity of an afternoon to himself after being coerced into endless games of golf. 'Everyone sallies out in this rain and plays golf and apparently likes it. I was made to play this morning . . . the Prince's pictures turned out much better than I expected: there are 6 really good ones and he is much pleased with them. He is here today having a golf lesson – he is mad about it.' In this letter he scolds her for sending a chain letter but his remonstration is light and teasing. 'By the way "Napo"* was furious with you for having sent him some "round robin" communication with instructions to pass it on to someone else on pain of incurring dire misfortune. He sent it on to one of your cousins hoping to keep the bad luck in your family if the chain was broken.'

Next there is gossip of mutual friends, Tommy Lascelles sends his regards, Kitty Lucas's cousin, Vivian de Watteville is marrying again. Then with a cynical touch he airs his views on the economic plight in Europe. 'Everyone says they are more broke than ever but there seems to be just as much money being spent on inane amusements as ever . . . The trouble is that the land, which cannot escape, is being taxed to death and English agriculture is at its last gasp; Australia is bankrupt, Germany full of unemployed . . . France seems to be the one country which is doing well. She kept her head when we were giving away everything and took everything she could get.' Realizing the strain she is under in his absence he urges 'I hope you have paid a visit to my coast property. I feel it would do you a lot of good to get away from Ngong for a little. I have no news and wonder how the Dickens affair worked out.' (This refers to a shaurie involving her farm manager which had arisen as Denys left.) 'Send me a line . . . I went to Paris last week' commenting on the opera *Parsifal*† 'It certainly is lovely music but too long – I went out and had dinner in the second act. Also heard Meistersinger‡ which is very

* Napoleon Gourgaud.

† *Parsifal* – Wagner's opera whose hero is 'a simpleton without guile' who restores a sacred spear to the Knight of the Holy Grail. Lohengrin, Knight of the Holy Grail with personal swan-drawn transport is, incidentally, son of Parsifal.

‡ Wagner's comic opera – the full title is 'The Mastersingers of Nuremberg' which also served as a platform for some of this composer's views on art.

exhilarating. Shall be quite ready to start back for EA all the same and hear it with you at Ngong.' He signs himself 'Denys,' the tone of the letter is familiar yet perfunctory if courteous. There is a marked difference from the mood of another letter he wrote to her in the late summer of 1926 shortly after his mother died. He had sent her two bulb catalogues (she was trying to grow peonies) and a long letter which ended with a paragraph in which he dwells on the serenity of the ritual of their evenings together. 'Those sunsets at Ngong have an atmosphere of rest and content about them which I never realize anywhere else. I believe I could die happily enough at sunset at Ngong looking up at the hills, with all their lovely colours fading out above the darkening belt near the forest. Goodnight – Denys.' There is a feeling of recognition, a confession that for the first time his wanderlust is assuaged: a wonder that his restlessness is appeased by Tania herself and by the peacefulness, the muted harmony arising from his almost coming to a standstill. The feeling of sentiment changed in the course of time – becoming a little threadbare. Shortly it became outlived altogether.

Toby's daughters remember Denys flying down to Buckfield that summer and the excitement he caused by landing in a field beyond the main lawn. He looked immensely dashing as he stood beside his fragile Gypsy Moth, huge, relaxed yet in control, laughing and jesting with them all. Diana recollects that her uncle liked to be thought of as young. 'Once he asked me how old I thought he was,' (he was forty-three at the time) 'but I had no idea of his age. I looked at him for a minute and I said "Oh, I should think about thirty", which seemed very old to me. He was almost ridiculously pleased. He feared old age and shied away at the thought of becoming decrepit.' In front of the house at Buckfield he seemed immortal; clad in a great coat he used for flying, entirely

lined in musquash, and with his flying helmet and enormous goggles. By this stage Denys's looks had hardened,
broadened, giving a feeling of great strength of purpose.
Tania infuses the personality of Morten de Coninck with
the same qualities:

His face was somehow coarser than before, weatherbeaten . . .
it had, with the dark, always somewhat sunken eyes, that same
divine play of light and darkness which had long ago made
maidens mad. His large mouth also had its old frankness and
sweetness. But to his pure forehead a change had come. It was
not that it was crossed by a multitude of little horizontal lines
for the marble of it was too fine to be marred by such superficial
wear. But time had revealed its true character. It was not the
imperial tiara, that once had caught all eyes, above his dark
brows. It was the grave and noble likeness to a skull. The
radiance belonged to the possessor not of the world, but of the
grave and eternity. Now as his hair had withdrawn from it, it
gave out the truth, frankly and simply.[12]

While the family were gathered round Denys waiting
to wave him off, the Gypsy Moth started to move off
towards a tree with which it became entangled. By some
oversight he had not braked properly. Toby and Denys
managed to extricate it, but a minor part was damaged
and his departure was delayed. The family were always
apprehensive about his flying, Topsy in particular was
very nervous for him. But he always reassured her 'as
long as one is very careful it is quite safe'.

As soon as Denys took up flying again he made a will.
On 7 October 1929 he bequeathed his guns to Toby
and all his hunting equipment. Topsy was his residuary
legatee, and in the event of her dying before him, her
children, Anne and Michael, were to receive £4,000 each,
after which the residue was to go to Toby. It is strange
that Tania was not mentioned as a beneficiary but perhaps
the strain in their relationship was already strong enough

to preclude any thought of a shared future. Denys's melancholy is difficult to explain: those who remember him speak of him only with adoration. Few realized that he suffered from depression. If Denys was too successful in his youth, there is no evidence that the rest of his life was an anticlimax by comparison. Nothing in his make-up shows that he feared competition. He ignored all forms of proof of success. The effect he may have had on Tania is again embodied in Morten de Coninck's make-up:

'Yes,' she cried, 'yes you may talk. But you mean to go away again and leave me. You! You have been to these great warm seas of which you talk, to a hundred countries. You have been married to five people – Oh, I do not know of it all! It is easy for you to speak quietly, to sit still. You have never needed to beat your arms to keep warm. You do not need to now.'[13]

Denys did not need to 'beat his arms' to solicit love or admiration either. From birth it came flooding round him. Perhaps it was all too much – if he had had to reach out for others a little bit, make an effort at something, things might have been different with Tania. But he never had to reach out. Everything was always there waiting for him.

Tania's descriptions of her flights with Denys over Africa are euphoric. Her joyful references to flying are scattered throughout *Out of Africa* in such a way that her readers feel she and Denys flew frequently together over the span of several years. She may have given this impression quite unconsciously; it may be quite simply a backward glance at the happiest hours they spent together at that time, high up and away from the earthbound problems which dogged Tania's last eighteen months in Africa. In reality these flights were strewn briefly over six months. Briefly, because during three of these he was taking two separate couples, the Marshall Fields, and the Sofer-Whitburns, out on safari. This new found liberty which defied the ancient laws of gravitation, gave the vital fillip to their relationship at a moment when it was becoming weighed down with banalities. In the way that a new child, whose birth is neither planned nor hoped for, will sometimes postpone a rift in a foundering marriage, flying brought interest and a feeling of temporary peace, a curious sense of the future to an undermined household.

The small Gypsy Moth became a familiar sight to Nairobi inhabitants, cutting its passage across a canvas blue sky, seldom broken by clouds. With it Tania's hopes soared upward like a flier in a dream whisked high on an errand of the winds. It was a magical experience to have the notion to fly to Lake Natron and to be, within one hour, skimming over the metallic core edged by an unreal trimming of cinnabar pink. They flew to Suswa or Lamu, Longenot over the Rift Valley or down to Mombasa as impulsively as birds would take off. Denys was enthusiastic – like a child with a new toy. The spontaneity with which he could take wing, the satisfaction of mastering a new element, gave him the elusive power of liberty found in dreams. Tania describes those excursions with the inspiration of an artist creating an intricate, foliate arabesque. When flying with Denys, her imagination knew no bounds:

This path, in fact, was the same as was, in the opposite direction, every evening taken by the Roc, when with an Elephant for her young in each talon, she swished from Uganda home to Arabia. Where you are sitting in front of your pilot, with nothing but space before you, you feel that he is carrying you upon the outstretched palms of his hands, as the Djinn carried Prince Ali through the air, and the wings that bear you onward, are his. We landed at the farm of our friends at Naivasha; the mad diminutive houses, and the very small trees surrounding them, all threw themselves on their backs as they saw us descending.[14]

One afternoon as Lady Delamere was having tea with Tania, Denys swooped low over the house like the Roc itself. This was his signal for her to meet him at the airstrip and the two women drove off at once. Tania writes:

But he would not get out of his aeroplane.

'The buffalo are out feeding in the hills,' he said. 'Come out and have a look at them.'

'I cannot come,' I said. 'I have got a tea-party up at the house.'

'But we will go and see them and be back in a quarter of an hour,' said he.

This sounded to me like propositions which people make to you in a dream. Lady Delamere would not fly, so I went up with him. We flew in the sun, but the hillside lay in transparent brown shade which we soon got into . . . When I came back to my tea-party, the tea-pot on the stone table was still so hot that I burned my fingers on it. The Prophet had the same experience when he upset a jug of water, and the Archangel Gabriel took him and flew with him through the seven heavens and when he returned, the water had not yet run out of the jug.

In the Ngong Hills there also lived a pair of eagles. Denys in the afternoons used to say 'Let us go and visit the eagles.' I have once seen one of them sitting on a stone near the top of the mountain, and getting up from it, but otherwise they spent their life up in the air. Many times we have chased one of these eagles, careening and throwing themselves on to one wing and then to the other, and I believe that that sharp-sighted bird played with us. Once, when we were running side by side, Denys stopped his engine in mid-air, and as he did so I heard the eagle screech.[15]

In January 1931 Denys wrote to Topsy's son:

Dear Michael,

Thanks so much for your Christmas card, sorry Coney (an Eton master) has given up his house. We are all getting very old it seems to me. I am still mobile and had a good trip with the Marshall Fields. Got some nice lion pictures, saw a bit of interesting stuff and finally bagged a good elephant after a difficult piece of hunting. I am just off on another trip with the Sofer-Whitburns. Don't know whether I shall come home this year but if I do I shall fly. I use my machine a good deal out here and find it very pleasant. Don't get lazy about your rotten work; pull yourself together and get the best of it – Denys[16]

When Denys returned from the second safari mentioned in that letter he moved off the farm and went to stay with his old, understanding friend Hugh Martin, a civil servant attached to the Land Office. Martin's biting cynicism was sharpened by his failed marriage, and was directed now at humanity in general. Tania described him as having developed 'an innate talent for looking like an immensely fat Chinese idol'.

On 10 April Tania wrote to Thomas apologizing for her tardiness as a correspondent with the explanation: 'it is because I haven't been able to see in any direction. I have had a lot to do with . . . arranging for my squatters and my boys, and hope to make things all right for them, but I haven't been able to see any kind of way ahead for myself, and so one doesn't know what to write.' She does not mention that Denys has gone. He had moved off, not because of the discomfort or inconvenience of packing cases. Tania and he had had 'a most shattering row', and he had grabbed his immediate possessions and gone to stay with Hugh Martin in Nairobi as a temporary solution.

Tania continued in that letter:

Now that I am nevertheless writing to you today, it is because both Denys and Mohr, who have been such true friends to me, think that I should, and that must be to their credit. They say that because of long exhausting spells and one-sided occupation with the same shauries, I now look wrongly at the situation, and what I should do is to have another try and attempt a plan. And they think that I should put this to you, as I am so far from being able to carry out any kind of plan independently, to see whether you agree with them and would be willing to help me . . .

As far as I can see from your letter, everyone generally interested in this matter reckons with my coming home and staying there. From my own point of view I just can't do this . . . I know very well that during my visits home, especially the last two, I have created the wrong impression with Mother, and perhaps with everyone, as far as both my own nature and the situation are concerned. This is almost unavoidable when one is at home for several months and one doesn't know when we shall meet again . . . But it does not fit in now and if I were to be at home all the time, I could not keep it up . . .

To sum up – I am no more good-natured than I was before, on the contrary, I cannot come home with regret and contrition; whatever has happened to me since and whatever I have had before, it is still true of me that death is preferable to bourgeois life, and in death I shall declare my faith in freedom . . .

Die happy; I can do that, and if you doubt it, then let me do it. Let me take Ngong together with everything it has meant into my arms and sink with it, and it will be without complaint, indeed in great gratitude towards life. There is so endlessly much that I love, out here as well as at home. I love you all and thank you for so very much.

Will you answer this letter by cable? Your offer to meet me in Genoa I think I would accept with great pleasure, if it comes to that, of course.[17]

The personal anguish which Tania was undergoing as she wrote that letter to her brother cannot be overestimated, for it must have been profound. Sensing her desolation he cabled her that he would come out to Kenya on 22 May to bring her home. Ironically in a by now established pattern, it is the unknown aspect behind her letter which gives it force. The power in her words is caused by sheer desperation. What has been concealed from the world has been concealed also in her work. It was the bitterest sacrifice of all which she had to face. She had already lost Denys. With this chilling knowledge of his rejection of her, life was without purpose or meaning. That irreparable quarrel had placed her on the edge of a precipice. Reading between the lines she could have been contemplating suicide. For she makes peace with her family, thanking them in full recognition for their patience and loyalty, which she senses they might feel to have been spurned. She even protects Denys in their eyes, precluding any ill feelings they might harbour against him. They may well have resented the fact he had never made her his wife after her divorce, for they were conventional souls. Unlike Tania they were puzzled as much by her as by such easily remedied situations. It has been written that freedom is the release from whatever must have bored and irritated Denys increasingly so that this seems the most likely reason for the row. Probably no-one will ever know what brought about the final denouement and if there is someone still living who does know it is doubtful if they would be prepared to reveal the truth. The fact remains that he left her. However he continued to come out and dine with her intermittently. On one occasion he sent her a bottle of claret 'which I hope will be drinkable. Jardine recommends it as being "bottled at the château" of one of his friends.' As if reminding her that he is not returning to Ngong he asks her to see that Kanuthia is available when he wants him. 'I am seeing how high I can get my Moth this afternoon. Do not let Kanuthia remain too long in the bosom of his family. He is to take me back from here to Martin's house.' His books were left for her to keep until he found somewhere for them. His own future was as unsettled now as her own. He needed somewhere to live and contemplated buying a plot overlooking the Ngong Hills and Athi plains just below where Kenyatta Hospital stands today.

Tania writes:

He talked of packing up his books, that had been in my house for many years, but he never got any further with the job. 'You keep them,' he said, 'now I have no place to put them.' He could not make up his mind at all where to go when my house should be closed. Once, upon the persistent advice of a friend, he went so far as to drive into Nairobi, and to take a look at the bungalows to be let there, but he came back so repelled with what he had seen that he did not even like to talk about it, and at dinner, when he began to give me a description of the houses and the furniture, he stopped himself and sat silent over it, with a dislike and sadness in his face that was unusual to him. He had been in contact with the kind of existence the idea of which was unbearable to him. It was, however, a completely objective and impersonal disapprobation, he had forgotten that he himself had meant to be a party to this existence, and when I spoke of it, he interrupted me. 'Oh, as to me,' he said, 'I shall be perfectly happy in a tent in the Masai Reserve, or I shall take a house in the Somali village. But on this occasion, he, for once, spoke of my future in Europe. I might be happier there than on the farm, he thought, and well out of the sort of civilization we were going to get in Africa.[18]

Friends knew of the rift between them but there was little anyone could do except offer tacit understanding. Denys was his own man, he made his own decisions and stuck by them. Two small incidents might have sparked off further acrimony during those last heartbreaking weeks; on one occasion when Denys came out to dine he took back the 'Abyssinian ring of soft gold' from her hand and put it back on his own because, according to Tania, 'he now thought I was looking at it with the intention of giving it to Pooran Singh, for he used to complain that whenever he gave me anything, I would at once give it away to my coloured people. To prevent such a thing happening he took it from my hand and put it on his own and said that he would keep it until Pooran Singh had gone. It was a few days before he went to

Mombasa and in this way the ring was buried with him.'*[19]

The other incident reflects Denys's melancholic mood, which she writes of quite openly in *Out of Africa*. No doubt he was wrestling with his own personal decisions; his conscience – his possible feeling of disloyalty for having let Tania down by denying her marriage and his name.

Denys, who held himself to be an exceptionally rational person, was subject to a special kind of moods and forebodings, and under their influence at times he became silent for days or for a week, though he did not know of it himself and was surprised when I asked him what was the matter with him. The last days before he started on this journey to the coast, he was in this manner absent-minded, as if sunk in contemplation, but when I spoke of it, he laughed at me. I asked him to let me come with him, for I thought what a lovely thing it would be to see the Sea. First he said, yes, and then he changed his mind and said no. He could not take me; the journey round Voi, he told me, was going to be very rough, he might have to land and to sleep, in the bush, so that it would be necessary for him to take a Native boy with him. I reminded him that he had said that he had taken out the areoplane to fly me over Africa. Yes, he said, so he had; and if there were Elephants at Voi, he would fly me down there to have a look at them, when he knew the landing-places and camping-grounds. This is the only time that I have asked Denys to take me with him in his aeroplane that he would not do it.

He went off on Friday the eighth; 'Look out for me on Thursday,' he said when he went, 'I shall be back in time to

* During an interview for a BBC documentary being made to mark Karen Blixen's centenary for British and Danish television in September 1984, in which the author was involved as a consultant, Rose Cartwright revealed that Denys Finch Hatton had confided to her in 1930 that, such was his concern over Karen Blixen's possessiveness and jealousy, in order to preserve what the two of them had shared and enjoyed, he would have to move off the farm before everything was destroyed between them. It was clear that he had made his decision after much thought.

have luncheon with you.' When he had started in his car for the aerodrome, in Nairobi and had turned down the drive he came back for a volume of poems that he had given to me, and that he now wanted with him on his journey. He stood with one foot on the running board of the car, reading out to me a poem that we had been discussing.

'Here are your grey geese,' he said.[20]

Before driving out of her life for ever, he read to Tania the poem which Iris Tree had written for him:

I saw grey geese flying over the flatlands,
Wild geese vibrant in the high air,
Unswerving from horizon to horizon
With their soul stiffened out in their throats,
And the grey whiteness of them ribboning the enormous
    skies,
And the spokes of the sun over the crumpled hills.[21]

But Tania did not quite explain that it was not on the same day. The reading of the poem was on 6 May, two days before Denys flew off. On the night of the 7th Denys dined with his friends Jack Melhuish and Joan Waddington at their home in Nairobi. His host was a dental surgeon, like himself a photographer with a keen appreciation of the wild 'the perfect mountaineer, untiring, thoughtful, gay . . . whose visitors' book was often jokingly referred to as a hotel register.' Denys often used Jack's dark room to develop his photographic plates. On that particular evening, Joan had invited Denys for dinner. A petite woman (commonly known at Government House as 'the Cypher Queen' as she was responsible for all cyphers) she adored Jack and his response if people accused him of 'living in sin' reflected his feeling towards her as he turned the phrase back in their faces. 'Living in love don't you mean?' Joan recalls how Denys appeared that evening dressed in his dinner jacket and black tie with his camel hair dressing-gown flung about his shoulders – presumably for extra warmth. He felt the cold badly. Nairobi is often chilly after the onset of the long rains and it is quite customary to have a fire after sundown. During the meal Denys flippantly asked Joan whether she would like to fly with him down to Voi – though in fact he had already made arrangements to take someone else. He probably knew she would refuse. 'Good God, Denys! Do you want me to commit suicide?' she replied, laughing at the ridiculousness of the suggestion. After coffee, Jack and Denys retired to work in the dark room for a while. She was never to forget that reply.

That Denys was preoccupied is substantiated by his last letter to his nephew, written on 2 May 1931.

Dear Michael,

Thanks for your letter of 21st March. The running commentary on the wireless does not seem to have given you very accurate information upon the boat race since you appear to have been under the impression that Oxford won, whereas I gather from the papers they were beat!

Hope you are getting on all right in the Army Class. I did not know you were going to be a soldier, they tell me that there are not going to be any more wars but you never know. There will be a good deal of air activity in the next war and I should think it will be the most amusing branch of the fighting services to be in. I have been using my moth a good deal out here and like having her out here very much. I don't think I shall be home this summer. I have a good many odd things to do out here and I am thinking of going on safari by myself to get a few elephant pictures in June. This country is being catcn up with locusts this year. There is always something helpful turning up! Goodbye – Denys.'[22]

He had already discussed this photographic safari with another professional hunter. Donald Seth-Smith. They were planning to go together. His purpose in flying to Takaungu was to deal with repairs on the house, which might now have to serve as his home and he needed to make it habitable. He wanted also to find elephant by air in order to decide where to pitch camp; he was toying with the idea of locating game by plane and offering this as a service to hunters which he believed would be a remunerative sideline.

Beryl Markham, by now separated from her second husband, was living in Denys's old cottage at Muthaiga Club. In *West With the Night* she describes her view of the events leading up to his death. She claimed that both Arap Ruta, her personal servant, and Tom Campbell Black, her flying instructor, had strange premonitions about the next few days. They were

. . . sensitive and had an awareness of things whenever these things were to affect them closely. One instance of this comes to my mind still [1943] with disturbing frequency. Many people who lived in Kenya at that time and who live there now will remember Denys . . . people all over the world remember him because he was of the world and his culture of it, though I suppose Eton and Oxford might argue a more specific source. Denys has been written about before and he will be written about again. If someone has not already said it, someone will say that he was a great man who never achieved greatness and this will not only be trite but wrong; he was a great man who never achieved arrogance. . . . My story about his death is simple enough, but it proves for my satisfaction the truth of that line contained in remembrance of him which appeared in *The Times* – 'something more must come from one so strong and gifted,' and in a way it did. . . . I had flown with him often in the plane he had brought out by boat from England and which he had added to the little nucleus of wings and fins and fragile wheels on the Nairobi airfield. . . . He had taken up flying too recently to be an expert, but the competence which he applied so casually to everything was as evident in the air as it was on one of his safaris or in the recitations of Walt Whitman which he performed during his more sombre or perhaps even lighter moments. He asked me to fly down to Voi with him and of course I said I would.

Denys said he wanted to try something that had never been done before . . . he wanted to see if elephant could be scouted by plane; if they could be, he thought hunters would be willing to pay very well for the service. It seemed a good idea to me, even a thrilling idea and I brought it to Tom in some excitement. 'I am going to Voi with Denys. He wants to see how efficiently elephant can be spotted from the air, and if it would be possible to keep a hunting party more or less in touch with a moving herd' . . .

It was a flyer's day. The open hangar looked out on the airfield on the plains, and the sky was lonely for clouds. Tom stuffed the bit of paper in the leather jacket he always wore and nodded.

'Sounds practical enough – up to a point. You'd find a lot more elephant than places to land after you'd found them.'

'I suppose so. But it seems worth trying – Denys's ideas always are. Anyway, we're just going to fly out from Voi and back again, no rough landings. If it works out there should be a good living in it. When you think of all the people who come out here for elephant, and all the time that's spent . . .'

'I know,' said Tom, 'it's an excellent idea.' He moved away from the bench and went out of the hangar door and looked at the field. He stood there for a minute or so without moving, and then came back.

'Make it tomorrow, Beryl.'

'Weather?'

'No, the weather's all right. Just make it tomorrow – will you?'

'I suppose I will, if you ask me to, but I don't see why.'

'Neither do I,' said Tom. 'But there it is.'

There it was. I went back to my cottage at Muthaiga and worked at bringing my log-book up to date. Denys took off for Voi without me.[23]

Beryl was still a learner pilot at this stage. She was finally dissuaded from taking off with Denys because she had arranged – tentatively – to have a lesson with Tom that same afternoon. In a final effort to keep her on the ground Campbell Black reminded her of this. So she decided not to fly this time with Denys and he took

Kamau, his Kikuyu servant, instead and flew direct to
Mombasa to do some repairs on his cottage at Takaungu.
As he landed at Vipingo he somehow chipped the wooden
propeller on a coral fragment. Immediately he wired Tom
for a replacement from Wilson Airways. Though Denys
was adamant that he could fit the new propeller without
help, Tom sent a mechanic down with the spare. By 12
May the refitting was completed and on the 13th Denys
took off, heading for Voi with Kamau. His servant was
terrified of flying and after an hour of scouting for
elephant became so airsick that Denys landed twelve
miles south of Maktau to give him two hours' respite in
the hope he would recover. When he felt Kamau was
well enough to continue they flew straight to Voi and had
the luck to spot a large herd of elephant browsing along
the Voi River. He had accomplished his mission and
arrived in very good spirits. He stayed that night with
friends – the DC and his wife. They had arranged an
informal sundowner party in Denys's honour. Mr and
Mrs Layzell, owners of a large sisal plantation flanking
the airstrip, were guests and so was J. A. Hunter who
was preparing to leave for safari the following morning
with an American client, Lee Hudson. It was a happy
evening. The Layzells were old friends whose daughters
Anne and Katharine 'worshipped' Denys. He had brought
the Prince of Wales to tea on his last safari. Anne can
remember clearly, though she was only ten years old,
'loving Denys passionately' as girls of that age are
inclined. Their mother arranged to drive Denys to the
airfield in the morning so that her daughters could see
their hero. J. A. Hunter remembers bidding Denys goodnight: the DC's wife, knowing of Denys's relish for
oranges, had filled his arms with them from her own
citrus trees, 'as he stood there in the doorway of the
bungalow the light was reflected brightly on the fruit'.

They must have cast a greenish light for Kenya oranges are seldom bright gold. Though ripe and ready for eating when they are plump, they are the colour of spring grass. On 14 May at 7 A.M. Margaret Layzell arrived with Anne and Katharine to collect Denys. The girls were bubbling with excitement not only because they would see their hero but for the chance to see 'Nzige'. The airfield then, as now, was situated just below Mbololo Hill. The car bumped along the rough track known as Caravan Road. Margaret Layzell took the vehicle over the uneven surface with care. Everyone was chattering and laughing. When they reached the aeroplane, several friends were gathered about it who had wandered down to see Denys take off. The Gypsy Moth was the lure; it looked amazingly bright, like a greatly magnified version of a weird yellow dragonfly standing against its dramatic and hilly background of granite and sombre blue sky. The early morning sun shone brightly. Denys refuelled the machine then turned to the children's mother.

'Come on,' he said persuasively, knowing she was longing to fly, 'let me take you up for a quick flip round Voi before I leave.' As she was on the point of accepting, Katharine the younger child unaccountably grabbed her mother's hand, imploring her not to go. When she sensed she was losing the battle she became hysterical.

'Don't go, Mummy, please. Please don't go, you'll crash, you'll die, I know you will. . . . No, No, No. . . . I don't want you to go, I don't.' Margaret Layzell loathed scenes and Katharine could not be placated – she seemed to be throwing the tantrum out of sheer naughtiness. It was obvious the experience of flying for the first time would have to be postponed.

'Another time,' said Denys briefly. And, bidding the small party of people goodbye, he clambered into the cockpit. Kamau got into the front seat. Denys adjusted his goggles and started the engine; with a casual wave he taxied gently down the runway. His friends stayed chatting, waiting to watch the yellow flying machine soar into the air. Within minutes the revving noise of 'Nzige' droned reassuringly. As the power increased up came the Gypsy Moth, rising steadily above the scrub blotting their view. It circled twice and turned heading for Nairobi. While gaining height it faltered for an instant. The engine seemed to stutter as it plummeted swiftly out of their horrified range of vision. Denys's friends and the two little girls stood fused to the spot. Stunned and appalled they were unable to do anything; even if they could have moved they were helpless.

At exactly that moment J. A. Hunter and his client were getting into their safari truck to leave. Lee Hudson suddenly grabbed J. A.'s arm and pointed to

. . . clouds of black smoke arising from the nearby aerodrome. Fearing the worst, we hurried to the scene. Denys had crashed . . . the plane was a blazing inferno, we were held off by the intense heat, a few blackened oranges rolled out of the wreckage. Denys opened up the Masai with me, he was fearless and fair and it was fitting that his remains should be buried in the land in which he had taken such delight. He lies there on the edge of the Ngong Hills. A stone marks the spot . . . he was an undaunted hunter whose memory I cherish in my heart.[24]

J. A. Hunter delayed his safari and took the charred remains back to Tania in Nairobi. She was accorded all the sympathy and tender respect which would have been given had she been Denys's widow, by her friends and all those who had known them together. Though they knew of it not one of them referred to the row.

Perhaps Beryl Markham describes Denys's passing more realistically, more aptly than anyone else:

Denys was a keystone in an arch whose other stones were other lives. If a keystone trembles, the arch will carry the warning

along its entire curve, then, if the keystone is crushed the arch
will fall, leaving its lesser stones heaped close together, though
for a while without design. Denys's death left some lives without
design, but they were rebuilt again, as lives and stones are, into
other patterns.'[25]

Epilogue

Though Tom Campbell Black flew down to investigate the crash, no conclusive solution was reached. Denys had complained during the last fortnight of his life that he had been suffering from cramp. Possibly this had affected him at a crucial moment when he needed all his faculties as a pilot to right an aircraft suddenly affected by a down draught, for which Voi has since become notorious. Several light planes have met disaster there. Now, aviation experience and increased knowledge of thermal conditions have made it possible to identify this as the reason for the other crashes in each case.

The tragedy was swiftly relayed to Nairobi, from station to station along the railway line from Voi. When Tania went in to shop that Thursday to deal with certain chores in the small town, its tradesmen already knew Denys was dead. As in any village, Nairobi was still little more, bad news travels fast, burning quickly when fanned by the wind of gossip. Because they were aware of Denys's recent defection they were made mute and dumbfounded by dread. They could not speak of the accident. And they could not utter a sympathetic word. She was so obviously ignorant of the tidings, how could they, any one of them, be the first to blurt out their ghastly newly acquired information. But Tania's sensitivity was such that she felt their shrinking horror though she did not immediately connect it with Denys even though he had not returned before she had left Ngong. With crystalline pain she writes of the sensations she encountered just before luncheon that day:

It seemed to me then that all my surroundings were in danger or distress, and that in the midst of this disaster I myself was somehow on the wrong side and therefore was regarded with distrust and fear by everybody. This nightmare was in reality a reminiscence of the time of the war. For then a couple of years people in the Colony had believed me to be pro-German at heart, and had looked at me with mistrust . . . But it must have gone deeper with me than I knew of, and for many years after, when I was feeling very tired or when I had a high temperature, the feeling of it would come back. During my last months in Africa when everything was going wrong with me, it sometimes suddenly fell upon me like a darkness and in a way I was frightened of it, as a sort of derangement.[1]

Within two hours she entered a haunting, nightmare world, a realm which Kierkegaard calls 'the absolute self-despair' as a fully awakened conscience is impelled by self-knowledge to give up all hope in itself. But when she arrived at Lady McMillan's for luncheon nothing was said. At least ten of Denys's and her friends were there, including Uncle Charles Bulpett. How any of them managed to swallow the meal and play-act their way through the next two hours with the knowledge that one of them must break the heart-rending news to Tania, is almost incomprehensible. They must have been governed by an iron loyalty. They too, better than the merchants, knew Denys was no longer hers. But they knew that what had to be done was as much for Tania's dignity as their own consciences and that it must be done in private. On some flimsy pretext Lady McMillan coaxed Tania into her small drawing-room and gently confronted her.

Tania's friends feared she would die of grief or kill herself. They rallied round her and would not let her stay alone. Farah was remarkable in his understanding. He appeared (for the rest of her life) to be an infallible sentinel – the only person she had left who knew everything. Inconsolable, her face like a death mask, Tania went through the motions required of her. She organized the digging of the grave in the Ngong Hills -- they could not get higher than the first ridge of the Game Reserve. The climatic conditions of the rainy season prevented it. The following day at about three o'clock 'over the same road came thirty or forty of his friends and comrades who had known and loved him'.[2] They climbed up in the mist which gathered round them like a respectful shroud, as if nature herself sympathized and allowed them to mourn with dignity. They lowered into the earth the long narrow coffin draped in the Union Jack. The priest read out a psalm: 'I will lift up mine eyes unto the hills.'

In England Denys's family were heartbroken but not entirely surprised at the way he had died. They had thought it an inevitable disaster. Someone cabled Toby from Kenya. He relayed the news to Topsy who was holidaying at Territet, Switzerland. She had been out for a walk with a friend who went back to the Mount Fleuri Hotel a little in advance of her for some reason. As Topsy approached the hotel steps her friend came out with a telegram in her hand. Topsy fatalistic and strangely calm did not need to be told its contents: 'It's Denys isn't it,' she said. A little while later she wrote to her son. He had just had his seventeenth birthday:

15th May 1931

My darling Michael,

I expect Nish or Anne will have written to you the terribly sad news about dear Uncle Denys. I had a cable from Uncle Toby this morning saying 'very sorry to tell you Denys killed flying East Africa'. I was always afraid this might happen, I *hated* his flying so much. I do not know how it happened. I don't know if Uncle Toby has heard more than just the bare fact . . . if so he will write I am sure. I think that Uncle Denys was always a careful flyer and he said to me 'it's quite safe if people are careful' but I expect something must have gone wrong. I only hope and pray that he was killed at once and he did not have to suffer. I am so miserable. You know how much I loved him – I shall miss him terribly. It will be lovely for him and Grandma to be together again – but I wish he could have stayed with us longer. Did you get the £1 he sent you? . . .[3]

The gift was for Michael's birthday, two days before Denys's own. He could have been forgiven that year for overlooking his nephew's anniversary but he had not forgotten. Topsy, so used to sadness and bracing herself for the worst, gained comfort from her implicit religious convictions and this is apparent in her next letter to Michael, written on 21 May:

You will have seen that *The Times* said that the skulls of dear Uncle Denys and his servant were fractured so that means they must have been unconscious so that they would not feel the agony of being burnt. I am so *very* thankful that was so. Dear Denys had what he always hoped for, a quick death. Though it is *dreadfully* sad it should have come so soon because he was such a wonderful person in every way and so loved by us all and will be so terribly missed. I thought too that Ascension Day was such a nice day to go and what a lovely welcome he would have from Grandma, Grandpa and Daddy and many others he loved when here. We must never think of him or they as dead – they are alive for evermore and I am sure Denys will be nearer to us really than when he was in Africa and can see us though we cannot see him until we too go where he is. So we must just think of him always as alive and look forward to seeing him at our journey's end as we looked forward to seeing him each time he came back from Africa . . .[4]

The Memorial Services in England were held at St Mark's, North Audley Street and at Ewerby Church, Haverholme. Toby took his brother's death very badly. He seemed diminished and there were times for the remainder of his life when he appeared to be divested of all gaiety. Daphne, his eldest daugher, was a debutante that season but Toby could hardly bear to fulfil his paternal role at the 'coming out' functions which he was expected to attend. He absolutely forbade his children to play the record of *Petrouchka* in his house again. Later he erected an obelisk on Denys's grave at Ngong, with a simple brass plaque inscribed with his name, the dates of birth and death and the extract from *The Ancient Mariner*:

> He prayeth well, who loveth well
> Both man and bird and beast.

A replica is set into the wall of Ewerby church. The one on the obelisk was stolen and never replaced.

Strange scenes have occurred on Denys's grave. When Mervyn Cowie,* who became Kenya's Director of the National Parks, as a young man went up to check that the grass was being cut near the memorial he found 'two lions lying on the concrete base, one at each corner, gazing out to the eastern hills with the stillness of monuments more impressive than Trafalgar Square'. The boundary to the Southern Game Reserve was far from straight and, with the approval of the Game Warden Archie Ritchie, young Mervyn Cowie moved all the cairns into a dead straight line. He created this 'line of beacons from the Mbagathi River to Lamwia, the highest point of the Ngong Hills' with some pride, because he felt he had helped the animals by establishing a line for everyone to see. This resulted in Denys's Memorial being just inside the game reserve instead of just outside. Archie Ritchie was perturbed by the change and asked Mervyn Cowie to bend the line back again. But before this was done it was established that the grave always was intended to be inside the game reserve anyway and the error had now

---

* Mervyn Cowie CBE. Founder and First Director of Kenya's National Parks. He was awarded the Order of the Golden Ark, for Conservation, in 1975.

been put right. In the 'sixties, when Topsy's daughter went up to the memorial out of curiosity while on holiday in Kenya, she found another visitor at the grave. They were astonished when it transpired that the Dane was Tania's nephew, while she was Denys's niece. The other memorial which was erected to Denys was the bridge at Eton, hewn in Grantham stone from Sir Edwin Lutyens's design. It straddles a nettlebanked stream, overlooking the playing fields and acknowledges his athletic prowess with the inscription 'Famous in these fields and by his friends greatly loved.' Many people from Kenya contributed towards the bridge.

Tania, so solitary and locked up with her wretched mortification though surrounded by a handful of loyal friends, slowly, painfully dismantled the last remnants of Denys's and her existence together. Peeling off fragments as clinically as possible with Ingrid Lindstrom at her side. She could not keep away from the grave. She and Farah fashioned a simple banner from 'Amerikani'. They strung this bleached calico pennant between two sticks so she could identify it from the farm. Like a brooding night bird, she clambered on to the roof with the aid of a ladder and gazed in its direction. Before she left, fearing that the weeds and Africa would reclaim the exact spot, she carried the white stones from her driveway and marked the grave. They are still there today.* At Muthaiga she could sometimes be seen, sitting immobile in the chair which Denys had habitually used when he went in there to read the London newspapers. Her face was heavily powdered, a chalkwhite, Thespian mask which would crack if she smiled. But there was no fear of

* At the time of writing the grave and obelisk are in danger of demolition while suggestions that the monument should be protected by the Ancient Monuments Act have been rejected on grounds of inadequate funds.

that. Finally she settled her squatters' problems and completed the task of packing all Denys's books. A small library of them went to fill the shelves of her now famous study known as 'Ewald's room' at Rungstedlund. These volumes included the book of Elizabethan madrigals and his Dictionary of Music awarded to him at Eton as a singing prize, the little Bible – given to him by his mother – and served as reassuring mementoes of their life on the farm together. Hugh Martin sent back the few possessions Denys had brought with him when he came to stay, to the Winchilsea family: his collection of hats and his strange specially designed shoes and his jewellery consisting of cufflinks, studs, watches and his very fine signet ring. He had taken it off in order to place the Abyssinian ring which he had once given to Tania, on his own hand. There was also a French grey, black and silver cigarette case which the Prince of Wales had given to him. A few books: the Works of Proust, Anatole France, Dmitry Merejkowsky – all in French. Di Pittura de Scultura – 15 volumes in Italian, Swinburne, Synge's works, Shakespeare, *China under the Empress Dowager* and a few others. Iris Tree's poetry book *The Traveller* perished with him in the crash. Later, when Tania was writing *Out of Africa* she wrote to Iris Tree and asked for a copy of the poem she had written for Denys – the last he had recited to her. In her own copy of *The Traveller* Iris wrote on the appropriate page in pencil 'A poem Denys Finch Hatton loved . . . Baroness Blixen quoted the poem in her book about Denys . . . he was buried in the hill where the lions played on his grave.'

A fragment from a letter written by a friend captures the bleakness of Tania's departure from Nairobi Station in July 1931:

. . . poor Baroness Blixen at Ngong, who is having to leave that lovely place and go home to Denmark. Her health is fearfully undermined by low fever and Denys Finch Hatton's death has been the last straw. It is so like Africa to just go smashing down one thing after another like that or perhaps in Africa one sees things more starkly. . . . On Sunday we went and saw the poor little broken Baroness away for good and so pathetic. Only Lady McMillan, the Delameres, the Munroes and three others were there and we were very glad we went. Lady Delamere was crying afterwards. . . .

Tania looked broken, her desolation underlined by the cardigan she wore: she seemed oblivious to a huge jagged hole in one of its elbows. The 'other three' were Gustav Mohr, Charles Bulpett and Hugh Martin. In less than three months Delamere and Hugh Martin were to die on the same day in November and Gustav Mohr was killed five years later while crossing a river in Tanganyika. As Denys once remarked to Tania, 'This Continent of Africa has a terrible sense of sarcasm.'

Hugh Martin, Tania says, 'had taken Denys's death much to heart. If any human being at all held a place in his queer, seclusive existence, it would have been Denys. . . . He had aged and changed much, his face was blotched and drawn.' Martin was said to 'idolize Denys'.* There is a feeling of worship in those words. After Denys was buried Hugh Martin often went up to visit the grave. He befriended a sixteen-year-old girl, whom he scarcely knew, and asked her to accompany him. At his request she picked flowers from his garden for these pilgrimages of mourning into the Ngong Hills. Then she would place them on the earth above Denys's coffin, Hugh Martin felt that 'only a pure young girl' was good enough to touch these tributes to Denys. When she was much older the

* Tania wrote about a Greek quotation that he translated for her because in the night it had seemed to him the perfect epitaph for his friend. 'Though in death fire be mixed with my dust yet care I not. For with me now all is well.'

bearer of these flowers reflected that the ritual was 'a touching act and hardly possible to believe in this day and age'.

It is doubtful if Tania ever lived through moments of such bitterness. A suicide note was found among her papers years later. Indeed she embraced the broken face of her world. But with great courage she harnessed her grief and made it work for her in a remarkable way. On returning to Denmark, thanks to the devotion, encouragement and conviction Thomas had in her literary talent, she steeped herself in the business of becoming an author. First in the writing and rewriting of *Seven Gothic Tales* which she originally planned to call 'The Poet and Other Tales'. Again one is reminded of Wendell Holmes's *Poet at the Breakfast-Table*, but for some reason she changed her mind. She also removed two stories from the intended collection: 'Carnival' which has now been published separately and 'The Caryatids – An Unfinished Tale' which was put into *Last Tales* instead.

There is much that can be attributed to Denys and his relationship with her in 'The Caryatids' – even a lovers' quarrel – but a passage which focuses sharply only his character is particularly worth mentioning:

Homo non sum, humanum omne a me alienum puto. He wondered what it was that these human people named human. It seemed to him that there was a curse upon him – of human beings loving him, and claiming love from him in return, when he could not, would not love! He thought of his mother, who from his early childhood had ever been hoping for some richness of life, through him and his love of her; of his friends at school, who had liked him and wanted him to like them. He was sorry for them all. But all this love – it was like the cravings of vampires with their large wings, asking for your blood, and offering you with deep sighs, their own thick hot blood in return.[5]

But who will ever be able to say for sure. The heart of the matter is concealed. There is little doubt that she did this intentionally; she was wise enough to know that she and Denys could still be immortalized, inextricably linked one to the other. For in that horrific swoop out of the sky at Voi, metaphorically Denys became hers once and for all. Paradoxically, through the very force, the annihilating possessiveness which had driven him away, he now became her own. She left a few scattered clues – enough for someone inquisitive to pick up one day. She has shown her readers she is right in her belief, put into the mouth of one of her storytellers: 'It is not a bad thing that you only know half of the story.' She understands completely a soul's rending: nearly all her stories are fleshed out with painful recollections of jealous pursuit and death. In one of them there is even a Dionysius – a twin child who burns to death. Pellegrina alias Ollala of 'The Dreamers' symbolizes her own frightening self discovery of the darkest side of her nature. She has admitted that the diva represents herself and that the loss of the singer's voice by fire, symbolizes the loss of her farm. But it was much more than that. Denys died by this element; yet, to be unswervingly loyal, she lost her voice, through self-imposed silence.

She became true to 'the old women who tell stories, we know the story of the blank page. But we are somewhat averse to telling it, for it might well, among the unin-itiated, weaken our own credit.' If she had to survive, the only way she could truly ensure their renown beyond the grave was to leave a flew blank pages to titillate man's endless curiosity. Much of her work evokes memories of Denys and his influence. Those boys chewing oranges and birds struggling to free themselves in panic from entangling rigging, mirror his nature and his final flight from her. Some of her work is concessional.

Out of Africa, with all the joy of anticipation captured in the lines from Shelley's Hymn of Pan 'From the forests and highlands we come, we come', sets out in a spirit of adventure. Then cynicism leads the last part to its sad ending 'Gods and men we are all deluded thus'. The beauty of *Out of Africa* is all the stronger for knowing it was written with the essence of love and happiness, the autobiographical account of their shared life.

It was a 'Book of the Month' choice. So were *Seven Gothic Tales* and *Winter's Tales'* and when Ernest Hemingway won the Nobel Prize for Literature in 1954, he gallantly stated that it should have gone to Tania. She became a literary lioness, a legend in her own lifetime. In 1959, when she addressed the Academy of Arts and Letters in America, her entire speech 'Mottoes of My Life' was woven round Denys's existence from start to finish. Yet, she contrived this with such subtlety that her audience remained unaware. Like the character she spoke of that day, 'Who, even after his final exit, does still form part of a play' Denys continued to form part of her life. After working for Tania for fourteen years, Clara Svendsen could no longer resist asking what a certain nightly ritual meant: 'She explained that she opened the door each night to look towards Africa and she went into Ewald's room to look at the map of her farm on the Ngong Hills. She did not mention the photograph that was standing on the window-sill by her desk, but there in fact, was a portrait of Denys Finch Hatton, her English friend, who was killed on the eve of her leaving Africa.'[6] She ended her speech before the Academy of Arts and Letters thus:

Upon the lips of a great poet, the passing, taken from the mighty harmonious beauty:

Nothing of him that doth fade,
But doth suffer a sea-change,
Into something rich and strange.

We make use of the words even when we are speaking about ourselves – without vainglory. Each among us will be feeling the inherent richness and the strangeness of this one thing – my life.

On 5 September 1962, Karen Blixen signed her last contract. She also wrote a birthday letter in her own handwriting to her sister-in-law, Jonna Dinesen, although it was not her birthday until the eighth, and said to her secretary 'It's important to get this off.' In the evening . . . Karen Blixen listened to music on a new record player, a present from American friends. It was installed in the chest Farah had given her and which in Africa had served as a record cabinet. One of the records she listened to that evening was Handel's aria 'Where e'er you walk' which Denys had sung to her. With difficulty and in great pain as so often through the years and almost constantly during the last twelve months, she managed to climb the stairs to her bedroom in the east wing. She did not walk downstairs again. She died on 7 September at 5 o'clock in the afternoon.[8]

Bibliographical Notes

Notes to Prologue

1. *Out of Africa* by Karen Blixen (p. 221). Published by Putnam, London, 1937. Reissued Cape Paperback 1964
2. *Shadows on the Grass* by Isak Dinesen (p. 41). Published by Michael Joseph, London 1960.
3. *Seven Gothic Tales* – 'The Dreamers' by Isak Dinesen (p. 335). Published by Putnam, London 1934.
4. *Last Tales* – 'The Blank Page' by Isak Dinesen (p. 100). Published by Random House, New York 1957.

Notes to Chapter 1

1. Sir Christopher Hatton: (1540-91) English courtier and Lord Chancellor. Born at Holdenby, he became the favourite of Queen Elizabeth I through whose influence he was made Lord Chancellor in 1587. He was educated at St Mary's Hall, Oxford and kept terms at the Inner Temple. Hatton is said to have first attracted the Queen's attention by his dancing at a masque and appears to have been extremely handsome and well versed in social accomplishments. He seems, however, to have had sufficient natural capacity to acquit himself without disaster on the Woolsack; he acted throughout as the Queen's mouthpiece, though his sympathies seem to have been with the extremer Protestant faction at court. His death was the result, according to tradition, of

'a broken heart' through the Queen's demanding payment of a debt which he was unable to meet.

His bushy beard, and shoestrings of green,
His high-crowned hat and satin doublet,
Moved the stout heart of England's queen,
Though Pope and Spaniard could not trouble it.

Gray: 'A LONG STORY'

2. *Dictionary of National Biography*
3. *Dictionary of National Biography*
4. In person Nottingham was tall, thin, and dark-complexioned. His manner was so solemn and the expression of his countenance was, generally speaking, so lugubrious, that he acquired the nicknames of Don Diego and Don Dismal, he and his brother, Heneage, first Earl of Aylesford, being known as the 'Dismals'. He figures as Don Diego in the *History of John Bull* and in the *Tatler* (1709), and Swift in his correspondence is always making fun of him. He is the subject of a famous ballad, 'An Orator Dismal of Nottinghamshire,' by the same eminent hand. When he joined the Whigs in 1711 the 'Post Boy' (6 December) offered a reward of ten shillings to anyone who should restore him to his friends, promising that all should be forgiven. Reference is made there to his 'long pockets'. He died at Burley-on-the-Hill, 1 January 1729–30.
5. *Ellen Terry's Memoirs* by Edith Craig and Christopher St John (p. 127). Published by Gollancz, 1933.

Notes to Chapter 2

1. *Victorian County History – Lincolnshire* – Religious Houses: Haverholme Priory.

2. *History of the County of Lincoln* – Haverholme estate is situated 'four miles east by north of Sleaford on an island of three hundred acres formed by two branches of the Sleaford river, which dividing itself at about two miles and a half from that place, unites again three miles lower'.

3. Aubrey Harcourt, Edith Finch Hatton's brother, was a frequent visitor to Haverholme and a close friend of Denys Finch Hatton's mother. 'A roué and an eccentric, his parties at the Gaiety for which he booked the whole front row of the stalls, were notorious. He wore a fez at Nuneham, never opened a letter from his mother and could not eat unless he was "piped" in to dinner. After the death of his fiancée (one of the Liddell daughters and a sister of Alice in Wonderland) he gave a series of macabre dinner parties. At one the gold and silver plate on the sideboard was replaced by carrots and turnips and the meal terminated in the release among the guests of a sackful of rats; at another, to which all the fattest women in Lincolnshire were invited, the male guests held a sweepstake on which weighed the most.' *Lady Muriel* by Wilfrid Blunt (p. 20). Published by Methuen 1962.

4. *Portrait of a Marriage* by Nigel Nicolson (p. 64). Published by Weidenfeld and Nicolson, London 1973.

5. *Victorian County History – Lincolnshire* – Religious Houses: Haverholme Priory.

6. *Lady Muriel* (p. 20).

7. *Seven Gothic Tales* – 'The Dreamers' – by Isak Dinesen (p. 416). Published by Putnam, London 1934.

8. *Anecdotes of Destiny* – 'Babette's Feast' – by Isak Dinesen (p. 30). Published by The Curtis Publishing Company, New York 1953.

9. This epithet was probably earned by the 2nd Earl of Winchilsea, Heneage Finch. He married four times and his wives bore him collectively twenty-seven children although only sixteen lived to 'some maturity'.

Notes to Chapter 3

1. Extract from the *Eton College Chronicle*, 6 April 1905.
2. Daniel Macmillan 1886–1964 whose younger brother Harold Macmillan became Prime Minister. He became a Scholar of Balliol College and later Chairman and Managing Director of the publishing house, Macmillan & Co Ltd.
3. *Lady Muriel* by Wilfrid Blunt (p. 35). Published by Methuen, London 1962.
4. The *Eton College Chronicle* – 'In Memorium' – 21 May 1931.
5. Sir Philip Sassoon, 1888–1939, Trustee of the National Gallery, Tate Gallery and Wallace Collection. His various houses Port Lympe, Trent Park and New Barnet were renowned centres of art and entertainment and always filled with politicians, painters, writers, professional golfers and airmen. Private Secretary to Lord Haig 1915–18, Under Secretary for Air 1924–9 and again 1931–7 and First Commissioner of Works 1937–9.
6. *Forks and Hope: An African Notebook* by Elspeth Huxley (p. 87). Published by Chatto & Windus, London 1964.
7. *Kenya Chronicles* by Lord Cranworth (p. 190). Published by Macmillan, London 1939.
8. *Ronald Knox* by Evelyn Waugh (p. 56). Published by Chapman & Hall, London 1959.

9. The Buxton family were descendants of the great anti-slave-trader Sir Thomas Fowell Buxton (1786–1845) the English philanthropist who married the sister of Elizabeth Fry. In 1818 he published his 'Inquiry into Prison Discipline'. He was elected MP for Weymouth. Buxton worked for the abolition of slavery in the House of Commons and devoted himself to a plan for ameliorating the condition of African natives. When the Niger expedition failed in 1841 he was deeply shocked and was said never to have recovered from the blow.

10. Sir Alfred Munnings, KCVO, President of the Royal Academy 1944–9.

11. *Memories* Vol 1 by Julian Huxley (p. 52). Published by George Allen & Unwin, London.

12. *Out of Africa* by Karen Blixen (pp. 346–7). Published by Putnam, London 1937. Reissued Cape Paperback 1964.

Notes to Chapter 4

1. *Out of Africa* by Karen Blixen (pp. 205–6). Published by Putnam, London 1937. Reissued Cape Paperback 1964.

2. By kind permission of Sir Osmond Williams, Bart, MC, JP.

3. *Ellen Terry's Memoirs* by Edith Craig and Christopher St John (p. 156). Published by Gollancz, London 1933.

4. As a young man Murray Finch Hatton had visited South Africa and brought back a female lion cub as a pet. On the homeward-bound journey it escaped and Murray dived overboard to rescue it. The lioness lived at Haverholme for a couple of years until it terrified the staff and inmates and became quite

unmanageable. In 1873 Murray arranged for the Royal Zoological Society to keep it at Regent's Park Zoo but he made frequent visits to the creature and all the Finch Hatton children went there on account of it and its progeny.

5. *Evening Standard,* 15 May 1931.
6. *Julian Grenfell: His life and the times of his death 1888–1915* by Nicholas Moseley (p. 139). Weidenfeld & Nicolson, London 1976. J. G. writing to his mother in 1908.
7. *Ronald Knox* by Evelyn Waugh (p. 83). Published by Chapman & Hall, London 1959.
8. *Lytton Strachey: A Biography* by Michael Holroyd, Penguin (p. 359). Published by Heinemann and Penguin Books, London 1967, 1968 & 1971.
9. *The New Elizabethans* by E. B. Osborne (p. 27). Published by The Bodley Head, London 1919.
10. *Ronald Knox* (p. 83).
11. *Julian Grenfell* (p. 225).
12. *Kenya Chronicles* by Lord Cranworth (pp. 190–1). Published by Macmillan, London 1939.
13. Obituary from *The Times,* London 1931.
14. *The Sassoons* by Stanley Jackson (p. 133). Published by Heinemann, London 1968.

Notes to Chapter 5

1. *Lady Muriel* by Wilfrid Blunt (p. 47). Published by Methuen, London 1962.
2. *Lady Muriel* (p. 48).
3. *East African Standard,* 17 May 1931.
4. *Lady Muriel* (p. 48).
5. A foolhardy attempt by Dr L. S. Jameson to overthrow the Transvaal Government of Paul Kruger. On 29 December 1895 Jameson crossed the border with

470 men in the expectation of a simultaneous Uit-
lander rising in the Transvaal. He was surrounded at
Doornkop on 2 January 1896 and subsequently
handed over to the British authorities. Rhodes, the
Cape Prime Minister, was involved and the Colonial
Secretary, Joseph Chamberlain, almost certainly
implicated. The Kruger telegram, a direct result of
the defeat of the Jameson Raid, was a famous congratulatory message sent by Kaiser William II to
President Kruger, which embittered Anglo-German
relations and encouraged Kruger in his policies. Jan
Smuts was so aghast at this breach of faith he wrote
'how shall I ever describe the sensation with which I
received the news of New Year's Day of 1896 of that
fatal and perfideous adventure'.

6. *Holy Bible* I Kings, X, 22.
7. *The Leader,* Local Notes: 11 March 1911.
8. *Forks and Hope: An African Notebook* by Elspeth Huxley (pp. 87–8). Published by Chatto and Windus, London 1964.
9. *East Africa and Rhodesia* compiled and edited by Allister Macmillan, FRCS (p. 216). Published by W. H. & L. Collingridge, London 1930.
10. *Kenya Chronicles* by Lord Cranworth (p. 48). Published by Macmillan, London 1939.
11. *Black Laughter* by Llewelyn Powys (p. 162). Published by Grant Richards, London 1925.
12. *Kenya Chronicles* (p. 192).
13. Letter to the author from Sir Osmond Williams.
14. *Isak Dinesen and Karen Blixen: the Mask and the Reality* by Donald Hannah (pp. 35–6). Published by Putnam, London 1971.
15. *White Man's Country* by Elspeth Huxley Vol 1 (pp. 256–7). Published by Chatto and Windus, London 1935.

16. *Lady Muriel* (p. 49).
17. *Out of Africa* by Karen Blixen (p. 218). Published by Putnam, London 1937. Reissued Cape Paperback 1964.
18. *African Adventures* by Frederick B. Patterson (p. 19). Published by G. P. Putnam's Sons, New York 1928.

Notes to Chapter 6

1. *Julian Grenfell: his life and the times of his death 1888–1915* by Nicholas Mosley (p. 202). Weidenfeld and Nicolson, London 1976.
2. *African Adventures* by Frederick B. Patterson (p. 8). Published by G. P. Putnam's Sons, New York 1928.
3. *African Adventures* (p. 8).
4. *Julian Grenfell* (p. 226).
5. *Under the Sun* written and published by Dr J. R. Gregory, Nairobi.
6. *Kenya Chronicles* by Lord Cranworth (p. 191). Published by Macmillan, London 1939.
7. *African Hunter* by Bror von Blixen-Finecke (p. 17). Published by Cassell, London 1937.
8. *West With the Night* by Beryl Markham (pp. 179–80). Published by Harrap, London 1943.
9. *African Hunter* (pp. 9–12).
10. *African Hunter* (pp. 15–16).
11. *Isak Dinesen and Karen Blixen: the Mask and the Reality* by Donald Hannah (pp. 25–6). Published by Putnam, London 1971.
12. *Mottoes of My Life* – A speech before the Academy of Arts and Letters in America in 1959, by Karen Blixen. Published in December 1962 by the Press and Information Department of the Royal Danish

Ministry of Foreign Affairs, Christianborg. Arranged by Bent Rying and Askel Danielson.

13. *The Gayety of Vision: a study of Isak Dinesen's art* by Robert Langbaum (p. 39). Published by Chatto and Windus, London 1964.

14. *Last Tales* by Isak Dinesen (p. 261). Published by Random House, New York 1957.

15. *Isak Dinesen/Karen Blixen: a very personal memoire* by Judith Thurman. Published by *MS*, 11 September 1973 (pp. 72–6). Interview with an unnamed Danish Countess.

16. *Mottoes of My Life.*

17. *The Mask and the Reality* (p. 23).

18. *Seven Gothic Tales* – 'The Roads Around Pisa' – by Isak Dinesen (p. 4). Published by Putnam, London 1934.

19. *Seven Gothic Tales* (pp. 4–5).

20. *Shadows on the Grass* by Isak Dinesen (p. 9). Published by Michael Joseph, London 1960.

21. Baobab also known as Monkey Bread tree, Cream of Tartar tree, Lemonade tree, Sour Gourd tree. *Adansonie digitata*. Maasai: *oi-imisera*, Swahili: Baobab, or Mbuyu.

This is one of the longest lived trees known and the largest in girth. It ranks with the Sequoia which is thought to live up to 2000 years.

Named after the Frenchman who discovered it in Senegal, Michel Adanson, who wrote, 'I perceived a tree of prodigious thickness. I do not believe the like was seen ever in any part of the world.' Livingstone referred to it as 'a carrot up-side-down'. It has been worshipped by the African since time immemorial probably because of the legend associated with it and for its many uses. In South Africa the tree is a protected species. It may be utilized as food, soap, necklaces, glue, rubber, fibre, medicine and cloth and has even been known to house a water closet in the hollowed out trunk while still growing! A beverage can be made from the seed pulp which tastes of creme of tartar and the seeds are edible.

22. *African Hunter* (p. 15).
23. *Out of Africa* by Karen Blixen (p. 208). Published by Putnam, London 1937. Reissued Cape Paperback 1964.
24. *Politiken*, 1 May 1934.
25. *The Leader,* 10 January 1914.
26. *The Leader,* 11 July 1914.
27. *Out of Africa* (p. 21).
28. *Out of Africa* (p. 29).

Notes to Chapter 7

1. *African Hunter* by Bror von Blixen-Finecke (p. 231). Published by Cassell, London 1937.
2. *Chronicles of Kenya* by A. Davies and H. G. Robinson (pp. 100–1). Published by Cecil Palmer, London 1928.
3. *Chronicles of Kenya* (p. 101).
4. *Kenya Chronicles* by Lord Cranworth (p. 198). Published by Macmillan, London 1939.
5. *White Man's Country* by Elspeth Huxley, Vol II (p. 16). Published by Chatto and Windus, London 1935.
6. *African Hunter* (p. 232).
7. *African Hunter* (p. 85).
8. *White Man's Country* (p. 17).
9. *Out of Africa* by Karen Blixen (p. 344). Published by Putnam, London 1937. Reissued Cape Paperback 1964.
10. *Out of Africa* (p. 344).

11. *Jim Redlake* by Francis Brett Young. Published by Heinemann, London 1930.
12. Galbraith Cole's imminent return from Zanzibar was announced in *The Leader* on 26 September 1914 as the deportation order had been rescinded.
13. *Kenya Chronicles* by Lord Cranworth (p. 191). Published by Macmillan, London 1939.
14. The Honourable Edward Finch, fifth son of Daniel Finch, seventh Earl of Winchilsea and second Earl of Nottingham, assumed the additional surname of Hatton pursuant to the Will of his aunt Anne, who died on 5 October 1764, and was the youngest daughter of Christopher, Viscount Hatton, by Elizabeth his third wife. There is no record available that he obtained either an Act of Parliament or a Royal Licence to make this change of surname, as was sometimes done, so that it appears to be a case of 'proprio motu' – without legal formality, as was possible if no change of arms was involved, and there was no condition of the Will which made an Act of Parliament or Royal Licence mandatory. It appears that Edward Finch Hatton, who was Envoy Extraordinary to the King of Sweden, and later to the King of Poland and the Empress of Russia, and who died in 1771, did not, in his lifetime hyphenate the name, as his names appear un-hyphenated in a pedigree officially recorded at the College of Arms shortly after his death, in which however the name of his eldest son George Finch-Hatton is entered with the names hyphenated. If the original assumption of the additional name in 1764 was a voluntary act, he was presumably within his rights in not hyphenating the names, but so equally would his son George be in the right of hyphenating them after his father's death, and in his descendants' continuing to do the same.

To sum up: from the data available, the combination of names was not effected by other legal process than the decision of the family (which would be legally valid) in which case it would be within the power of the family to vary the hyphenation from time to time. The great preponderance of the records indicate that for the greater part of the period since 1800 the name has customarily been hyphenated in official records. In concurrence with the wishes of Christopher Denys Stormont, 16th Earl of Winchilsea, his family and the author, the hyphen has been omitted in this book.

15. Letter from Denys Finch Hatton to Kitty Lucas, by kind permission of Father Denys Lucas.
16. *Kenya Chronicles* (p. 200).
17. *Black Laughter* by Llewelyn Powys (p. 168). Published by Grant Richards, London 1925.
18. *Seven Gothic Tales* – 'The Supper at Elsinore' – (pp. 276–7). Published by Putnam, London 1934.
19. *Mottoes of My Life*. A speech before the Academy of Arts and Letters in America in 1959, by Karen Blixen. Published in December 1962 by the Press and Information Department of Foreign Affairs, Christianborg. Arranged by Bent Rying and Askel Danielson.
20. *Black Laughter* (p. 167).
21. *Battle for the Bundu* by Charles Miller (p. 81). Published by MacDonald, London 1974.
22. Letter from Denys Finch Hatton to Kermit Roosevelt. Roosevelt family papers, Library of Congress, Washington DC.
23. Letter from Denys Finch Hatton to Kitty Lucas, by kind permission of Father Denys Lucas.
24. *War in the Garden of Eden* by Kermit Roosevelt (pp. 8–9). Published by John Murray, USA 1920.
25. *War in the Garden of Eden* (p. 20).

Notes to Chapter 8

1. *Kenya Days* by M. Aline Buxton (pp. 36–7). Published by Edward Arnold, London 1927.
2. *The Life and Destiny of Isak Dinesen* collected and edited by Frans Lasson. Text by Clara Svendsen (p. 73). Published by Random House, New York, 1970.
3. *My Sister Isak Dinesen* by Thomas Dinesen VC (p. 57). Published by Michael Joseph, London 1975.
4. *My Sister Isak Dinesen* (p. 58).
5. *Last Tales* – 'Tales of Two Gentlemen' – by Isak Dinesen (pp. 71–2). Published by Random House, New York 1957.
6. *Out of Africa* by Karen Blixen (p. 265). Published by Putnam, London 1937. Reissued Cape Paperback 1964.
7. Genesis, XXXII, 26.
8. *Out of Aftica* (p. 266).
9. *My Sister Isak Dinesen* (pp. 61–2).
10. *White Man's Country* by Elspeth Huxley, Vol II (p. 43). Published by Chatto and Windus, London 1935.
11. *The Leader,* October 1918.

Notes to Chapter 9

1. Letter to Kermit Roosevelt from Denys Finch Hatton. Roosevelt family papers: Library of Congress, Washington DC.
2. *The Leader,* 18 June 1918.
3. *The Leader,* 25 May 1918.
4. *Out of Africa* by Karen Blixen (p. 16). Published by Putnam, London 1937. Reissued Cape Paperback 1964.
5. *The Leader,* May 1918.
6. *My Sister, Isak Dinesen* by Thomas Dinesen, VC (p. 62). Published by Michael Joseph, London 1975.

7. *The Leader*, 21 December 1918.
8. *Shadows on the Grass* by Isak Dinesen (p. 85). Published by Michael Joseph, London 1960.
9. *Out of Africa* (p. 40).
10. *Sport and Travel in East Africa 1928–1930.* Compiled by Patrick Chalmers from the private diaries of HRH The Prince of Wales (pp. 173–4). Published by E. P. Dutton & Co, New York.
11. *Sport and Travel in East Africa* (p. 171).
12. *My Sister Isak Dinesen* (p. 56).
13. *Out of Africa* (p. 351).
14. *Seven Gothic Tales* by Isak Dinesen (p. 8). Published by Putnam, London 1934.
15. *Seven Gothic Tales* (pp. 368–9).
16. *Mottoes of My Life,* a speech before the Academy of Arts and Letters in America in 1959 by Karen Blixen. Published in December 1962 by the Press and Information Department of the Royal Danish Ministry of Foreign Affairs, Christianborg. Arranged by Bent Rying and Askel Danielson.
17. *Out of Africa* (p. 23).
18. *Out of Africa* (p. 217).
19. *My Sister Isak Dinesen* (pp. 99–100).
20. *Out of Africa* (p. 216).
21. *Out of Africa* (p. 25).
22. *Hunter's Tracks* by J. A. Hunter assisted by Alan Wykes (pp. 67–8). Published by Hamish Hamilton, London.
23. *Shadows on the Grass* (p. 45).

Notes to Chapter 10

1. *Out of Africa* by Karen Blixen (p. 352). Published by Putnam, London 1937. Reissued Cape Paperback 1964.

2. *Out of Africa* by Karen Blixen (p. 354).
3. *Out of Africa* (pp. 21–2).
4. *Shadows on the Grass* by Isak Dinesen (p. 101). Published by Michael Joseph, London 1960.
5. *White Man's Country* by Elspeth Huxley, Vol II (p. 61). Published by Chatto & Windus, London 1935.
6. *Titania: the biography of Isak Dinesen* by Parmenia Migel (p. 72). Published by Random House, New York 1967.
7. She was the sister of Sir Ulick Alexander: Keeper of the Queen's privy purse with King Edward VIII from succession to abdication, then to King George VI until his death and to Queen Elizabeth II for two years until his retirement.
8. *The Rainbow Picnic: A Portrait of Iris Tree* by Daphne Fielding (p. 35). Published by Eyre Methuen, London 1974.
9. *The Alan Parsons Book* compiled by Viola Parsons (p. 53). Published by Heinemann, London 1937.
10. *The Alan Parsons Book* (p. 52).
11. *The Rainbow Picnic* (p. 66).
12. Dora Carrington, gifted painter and close friend of Lytton Strachey, who married Ralph Partridge but was always known by her maiden surname. She eventually committed suicide after Strachey's death in 1932 unable to bear the loneliness of life without him.
13. *The Alan Parsons Book* (p. 89).
14. *Carrington: Letters & Extracts from her diaries,* chosen and edited with an introduction by David Garnet (p. 439). Published by Jonathan Cape, London 1970.
15. *Carrington* (p. 145).

16. *The Traveller and other Poems* by Iris Tree (p. 88).
    Published by Boni & Liveright, New York 1927.
17. *The Alan Parsons Book* (p. 149).
18. *Lady Muriel* by Wilfrid Blunt (p. 84). Published by
    Methuen, London 1962.
19. A lode of auriferous quartz.
20. *My Sister Isak Dinesen* by Thomas Dinesen, VC (p.
    68). Published by Michael Joseph, London 1975.
21. *Out of Africa* (pp. 82–3).
22. *Titania* (p. 78). (Extract from a letter to Parmenia
    Migel from Thomas Dinesen 3 July 1963.)
23. *My Sister Isak Dinesen* (pp. 70 & 72–3).
25. *Isak Dinesen and Karen Blixen: the Mask and the
    Reality* by Donald Hannah (pp. 28–9).
26. *My Sister Isak Dinesen* (pp. 81 & 83).
27. *Out of Africa* (p. 219).

Currency in East Africa

For many years the currency of Kenya and Uganda
had consisted of the Indian rupee as the standard coin.
. . . The British Sovereign was also legal tender at the
rate of 15 rupees to one sovereign. . . . The exchange rate
between the Indian rupee and sterling was maintained by
the Government of India at 15 rupees to £1 until towards
the end of 1917 when the increase in the sterling value of
silver gave the Indian rupee coin an intrinsic value greater
than 1s. 4d. sterling. . . . The sterling value of the rupee
continued to rise throughout 1918 and 1919 and reached
2s. 9d. early in 1920. . . . For some time during 1919 the
exchange flickered about 2s. 4d. At that rate the new
settler received only 850 rupees instead of the old rate of
1,500 rupees for every £100 which he brought with him.
. . . The farmer who sold his products to the United
Kingdom market received far fewer rupees than before

this distortion and so had to sell almost as much to meet his liabilities. . . . The Colonial Office decided to stabilize the East African rupee at 2s. and the decision was announced in the House of Commons on 25 February 1920. A settler who had borrowed say £2,000 *ipso facto* owed £3,000 and his interest burden was increased from £160 to £240 a year. The decision brought the Colony to the verge of financial collapse and the slump which followed made matters far worse. Many of the early settlers were ruined; others laboured on beneath a burden of debt for the rest of their lives; but many great hearts survived and recovered from a blow which shook the economic structure of a young colony to foundations, which in any case, were still far from secure.

Extracts from pages 51, 52 and 53 of *Planters' Progress – The Story of Coffee in Kenya* by M. F. Hill, published by the Nakuru Press, Kenya.

Notes to Chapter 11

1. *Out of Africa* by Karen Blixen (p. 231). Published by Putnam, London 1937. Reissued Cape Paperback 1964.
2. *Out of Africa* (p. 341).
3. Sambuk: a type of dhow. However Lincoln Forsner and his friends would have been sailing on a Mtepe, a sewn craft built almost exclusively at Lamu. Its bird-like prow was reputed to represent the head and neck of the Prophet Mohamed's favourite camel; no nail was used in its construction. Arab seamen never use the word 'dhow'; they name their ships according to the fashion of their prow or stern not the rigging, and the lateen sail is common to most types. They fall into two main categories which are double ended like the Boom, Dhangi or Bedani or have a flat, stern

transom such as the Sambuk, Ghanjah, Baghlas or Kotia. The Mtepe and Dau la Metepe are double ended and have passed into the limbo of history. The timbers were pegged with coir rope and sewn together but this has not been seen for about sixty years. The Sambuk hails from the Red Sea ports of Aden and South Arabia. Its name is derived from the Arabic 'Sabak' meaning fast. Its average length is 80 feet, beam 20 feet and depth 10 feet. Displacement varies from 75 to 140 tons. 'Her bow curves upwards from the waterline in a graceful sweep to end just above the hull. It ends in a typical manner and the whole shape of the bow can be likened to a bared scimitar, with the handle below the waterline and the business end above.' *Dhows at Mombasa* by John H. Jewel (p. 42). Published by the East African Publishing House, Nairobi 1969.

4. *Out of Africa* (p. 340).

5. *The Early Islamic Architecture of the East African Coast* by P. S. Garlake (p. 8). Memoir Number 1 of the British Institute of History and Archaeology in East Africa. Published by Oxford University Press, Nairobi and London 1966.

6. *The Early Islamic Architecture of the East African Coast* (p. 45).

7. *History of East Africa* edited by Roland Oliver and Gervase Mathew, Vol 1 (p. 246). Published by Oxford University Press 1963.

8. *Seven Gothic Tales* – 'The Dreamers' – by Isak Dinesen (p. 442). Published by Putnam, London 1934.

9. *Seven Gothic Tales* (p. 341).

10. *Seven Gothic Tales* (pp. 344–5).

11. *Winter Tales* by Isak Dinesen (p. 18). Published by Putnam, London 1942.

12. *New York Times,* 13 October 1958.
13. *Out of Africa* (p. 51).
14. *Out of Africa* (p. 217).
15. *Mottoes of My Life,* a speech before the Academy of Arts & Letters in America in 1959 by Karen Blixen. Published in December 1962 by the Press and Information Department of the Royal Danish Ministry of Foreign Affairs, Christianborg. Arranged by Bent Rying and Askel Danielson.
16. *The Poet at the Breakfast Table* by Oliver Wendell Holmes (p. 274). Published by Walter Scott, London 1857.
17. *Winter Tales* (p. 290).
18. *Out of Africa* (p. 339).
19. *Out of Africa* (p. 339).
20. *My Sister Isak Dinesen* by Thomas Dinesen, VC (pp. 84–5). Published by Michael Joseph, London 1975.
21. *My Sister Isak Dinesen* (p. 85).
22. *Titania: the biography of Isak Dinesen* by Parmenia Migel (p. 61). Published by Random House, New York 1967.
23. *Out of Africa* (p. 217).
24. *My Sister Isak Dinesen* (p. 86).
25. *My Sister Isak Dinesen* (p. 72).
26. *Out of Africa* (p. 145).
27. *Last Tales* by Isak Dinesen – 'Echoes' – (p. 174). Published by Random House, New York 1957.
28. Job, XLI, 24.
29. *Last Tales* (p. 184).
30. *Seven Gothic Tales* – 'The Roads Arounds Pisa' – (p. 3).
31. *The Life and Destiny of Isak Dinesen,* Collected and Edited by Frans Lasson. Text by Clara Svendsen

(p. 139). Published by Random House, New York 1970.

32. *Seven Gothic Tales* – 'The Monkey' – (pp. 135–6).
33. *Out of Africa* (pp. 91–2).

Notes to Chapter 12

1. Letter to Kermit Roosevelt from Denys Finch Hatton. Roosevelt family papers: Library of Congress, Washington DC.
2. *Out of Africa* by Karen Blixen (p. 288). Published by Putnam, London 1937. Reissued Cape Paperback 1964.
3. Letter from Denys Finch Hatton to Kermit Roosevelt. Roosevelt family papers, Library of Congress, Washington DC.
4. *Out of Africa* (p. 157).
5. *Titania: the biography of Isak Dinesen* by Parmenia Migel (p.80). Published by Random House, New York 1967. Anne, Countess of Winchilsea, 1661–1720, belonged to the great Hampshire family of Kingsmill and was Sir William Kingsmill of Sidmarton's daughter. She married Heneage, second son of Heneage, Earl of Winchilsea, who upon the death of his nephew Charles succeeded him in the title of Earl. 'This lady was of excellent genius'. One of the most considerable of her poems is the Ode on the Spleen. She called herself 'Ardelia' and by this name is referred to by Pope in *The Rape of the Lock*. Anne Finch left the service of Mary of Modena in the year of her marriage, while her husband retained his post in the Duke of York's household. When James went into exile the Finches were in disgrace and left poverty stricken. Her husband refused allegiance to William

of Orange 'thus debarring himself for the sake of honour from all personal gain under the crown'.

6. *A Room of One's Own* by Virginia Woolf (p.61). Published by Penguin Books, London 1973.
7. *Out of Africa* (p. 255).
8. *Seven Gothic Tales* – 'The Dreamers' – by Isak Dinesen (p. 430). Published by Putnam, London 1934.
9. *West With the Night* by Beryl Markham (p. 164). Published by George Harrap, London 1943.
10. *Out of Africa* (p. 25).
11. *Out of Africa* (p. 202).
12. *Forks and Hope* by Elspeth Huxley (p. 87). Published by Chatto & Windus, London 1964.
13. *Out of Africa* (p. 205).
14. Letter from Denys Finch Hatton to Kermit Roosevelt. Roosevelt family papers, Library of Congress, Washington DC.
15. *Seven Gothic Tales* (p. 21).
16. *My Sister Isak Dinesen* by Thomas Dinesen, VC. (p. 82). Published by Michael Joseph, London 1975.
17. *My Sister Isak Dinesen* (p. 86).
18. *My Sister Isak Dinesen* (p. 74).
19. *Out of Africa* (p. 204).
20. *Seven Gothic Tales* – 'The Supper at Elsinore' – (pp. 298–300, 303 and 320).
21. *Ehrengard* by Isak Dinesen (p. 10). Published by Michael Joseph, London 1963.
22. *The Poem of the Book of Job* by George James Finch Hatton, Viscount Maidstone. Published London 1860. See also the Appendix to this chapter, p. 231.
23. *Shadows on the Grass* by Isak Dinesen (p. 32). Published by Michael Joseph, London 1960.
24. *Out of Africa* (p. 234).
25. *The Life and Destiny of Isak Dinesen*, collected and

edited by Frans Lasson. Text by Clara Svendsen
(p. 134). Published by Random House, New York
1970.

26. *Out of Africa* (p. 227).
27. *My Sister Isak Dinesen* (pp. 106–8).
28. Letter from Denys Finch Hatton to Karen von Blixen,
by kind permission of Clara Svendsen.
29. *My Sister Isak Dinesen* (p. 110).

Notes to Chapter 13

1. *African Adventures* by Frederick B. Patterson (p. 19).
Published by G. P. Putnam's Sons, New York 1928.
2. *African Adventures* (p. 7).
3. *African Adventures* (p. 23).
4. *African Adventures* (p. 49).
5. *Shadows on the Grass* by Isak Dinesen (p. 42).
Published by Michael Joseph, London 1960.
6. *Hunter's Tracks: Great Men – Great Hunters* by J. A.
Hunter assisted by Alan Wykes (p. 68). Published by
Hamish Hamilton, London.
7. *Hunter's Tracks* (p. 69).
8. *African Adventures* (p. 47).
9. 'Lions at their Ease – Stalking by Car' by Denys
Finch Hatton. Published in *The Times*, 21 January
1928, London.
10. *Shadows on the Grass* (p. 44).
11. *Titania: the biography of Isak Dinesen* by Parmenia
Migel (p. 152). Published by Random House, New
York 1967.
12. *Isak Dinesen and Karen Blixen: the Mask and the
Reality* by Donald Hannah (p. 39). Published by
Putnam, London 1971.
13. *Seven Gothic Tales* – 'The Old Chevalier' – by Isak
Dinesen (p. 75). Published by Putnam, London 1934.

14. *Out of Africa* by Karen Blixen (p. 223). Published by Putnam, London 1937. Reissued Cape Paperback 1964.
15. *Out of Africa* (p. 225).
16. *Out of Africa* (p. 227).
17. *Seven Gothic Tales* – 'The Roads Around Pisa' – (p. 5).
18. *Winter Tales* – 'Peter and Rosa' – by Isak Dinesen (p. 212). Published by Putnam, London 1942.
19. *African Adventures* (p. 65).
20. *African Adventures* (p. 66).
21. *African Adventures* (p. 71).
22. *African Adventures* (pp. 73–4).
23. *African Adventures* (p. 76).
24. *African Adventures* (p. 81).
25. *African Adventures* (pp. 78–9).
26. *African Adventures* (p. 82).
27. *African Adventures* (p. 82).
28. Letter from Denys Finch Hatton to Kermit Roosevelt, Roosevelt family papers, Library of Congress, Washington DC.
29. Letter to Kermit Roosevelt.
30. *Shadows on the Grass* (p. 33).
31. *Sport and Travel in East Africa* – Compiled from the private diaries of HRH The Prince of Wales by Patrick R. Chalmers (p. 103). Published by E. P. Dutton, New York (undated).
32. *Sport and Travel in East Africa* (pp. 113–14).
33. *African Hunter* by Bror von Blixen-Finecke – (p. 153). Published by Cassell, London 1937.
34. *African Hunter* (p. 154).
35. *African Hunter* (p. 160).
36. *African Hunter* (p. 160).
37. Letter to Denys Finch Hatton from His Royal Highness, Edward, Prince of Wales, by kind permission of Sir Osmond Williams.

38. Letter to Denys Finch Hatton, from Lieutenant-Colonel, the Hon Piers Legh, ADC to HRH Edward, Prince of Wales, by kind permission of Sir Osmond Williams.
39. Letter to Sir Osmond Williams from Denys Finch Hatton, by kind permission of Sir Osmond Williams.
40. *My Sister Isak Dinesen* by Thomas Dinesen VC (p. 117). Published by Michael Joseph, London 1975.
41. *Shadows on the Grass* (p. 30).
42. *Titania* (p. 82).
43. *My Sister Isak Dinesen* (p. 120).
44. *Out of Africa* (p. 321).
45. Letter to Denys Finch Hatton from HRH, Edward, Prince of Wales, by kind permission of Sir Osmond Williams.

Notes to Chapter 14

1. *African Hunter* by Bror von Blixen-Finecke (p. 165). Published by Cassell, London 1937.
2. *Sport and Travel in East Africa* – Compiled from the private diaries of HRH, The Prince of Wales by Patrick R. Chalmers (p. 170). Published by E. P. Dutton, New York (undated).
3. *African Hunter* (p. 165).
4. *African Hunter* (p. 166).
5. *African Hunter* (p. 188).
6. *Sport and Travel in East Africa* (p. 200).
7. *Kenya's Opportunity: Hopes, Memories and Ideas* by Lord Altrincham (pp. 235–6). Published by Faber and Faber, London 1955.
8. *My Sister Isak Dinesen* by Thomas Dinesen, VC (pp. 113–14). Published by Michael Joseph, London 1975.
9. *Out of Africa* by Karen Blixen (p. 326). Published by

Putnam, London 1937. Reissued Cape Paperback 1964.

10. *Sport and Travel in East Africa* (p. 216).
11. *West With the Night* by Beryl Markham (p. 215). Published by George Harrap, London 1943.
12. *Seven Gothic Tales* – 'The Supper at Elsinore' – by Isak Dinesen (p. 316). Published by Putnam, London 1934.
13. *Seven Gothic Tales* – 'The Supper at Elsinore' – (p. 334).
14. *Out of Africa* (p. 230).
15. *Out of Africa* (pp. 231–2).
16. Letter from Denys Finch Hatton to Sir Osmond Williams, by kind permission of Sir Osmond Williams, Bart, MC, JP.
17. *My Sister Isak Dinesen* (pp. 121–2).
18. *Out of Africa* (p. 341).
19. *Out of Africa* (p. 360).
20. *Out of Africa* (p. 343).
21. From *The Traveller and Other Poems* by Iris Tree. Published by Boni & Liveright, New York 1925.
22. Letter from Denys Finch Hatton to Sir Osmond Williams, by kind permission of Sir Osmond Williams, Bart. MC, JP.
23. *West With the Night* (pp. 165–6).
24. *Hunter's Tracks: Great Men – Great Hunters* by J. A. Hunter assisted by Alan Wykes (p. 69). Published by Hamish Hamilton, London.
25. *West With the Night* (p. 168).

Notes to the Epilogue

1. *Out of Africa* by Karen Blixen (p. 345). Published by Putnam, London 1937. Reissued Cape Paperback 1964.

2. *East African Standard,* 16 May 1931, Nairobi.
3. Letter from Gladys Margaret Williams (Topsy) to Sir Osmond Williams, by kind permission of Sir Osmond Williams, Bart, MC, JP.
4. Letter from Gladys Margaret Williams (Topsy) to Sir Osmond Williams, by kind permission of Sir Osmond Williams, Bart, MC, JP.
5. *Last Tales* by Isak Dinesen – 'The Caryatids' – (p. 136). Published by Random House, New York 1957.
6. *The Life and Destiny of Isak Dinesen* collected and edited by Frans Lasson. Text by Clara Svendsen (p. 15). Published by Random House, New York 1970.
7. *Mottoes of My Life.* A speech before the Academy of Arts and Letters in America in 1959 by Karen Blixen. Published in December 1962 by the Press and Information Department of the Royal Danish Ministry of Foreign Affairs, Christianborg. Arranged by Bent Rying and Askel Danielson. Tania was quoting from *The Tempest.*
8. *The Life and Destiny of Isak Dinesen* (p. 221).

Index